AF560273

UNDERSTANDING TERRORISM IN SOUTH ASIA

Beyond Statist Discourses

The Regional Centre for Strategic Studies (RCSS) is an independent, non-profit and non-governmental organization for collaborative research, networking and interaction on strategic and international issues pertaining to South Asia. Set up in 1992, the RCSS is based in Colombo, Sri Lanka.

The RCSS is a South Asian forum for studies, training and multi-track dialogue and deliberation on issues of regional interest. All activities of RCSS are designed with a South Asia focus and are usually participated by experts from all South Asian countries. The Centre is envisaged as a forum for advancing the cause of co-operation, security, conflict resolution, confidence building, peace and development in the countries of the South Asian region.

The RCSS serves its South Asian and international constituency by: (a) networking programmes that promote interaction, communication and exchange between institutions and individuals within and outside the region engaged in South Asian strategic studies; (b) organizing regional workshops and seminars and sponsoring and coordinating collaborative research-, and (c) disseminating output of the research through publications which include books, monographs and a quarterly newsletter. The RCSS facilitates scholars and other professionals of South Asia to address, mutually and collectively, problems and, issues of topical interest for all countries of the region.

Queries may be addressed to:

Regional Centre for Strategic Studies
2 Elibank Road
Colombo 5
SRI LANKA
Tel: (94-11) 2599734, 599735
Fax: 2599993; e-mail: edrcss@sri.lanka.net
RCSS website: http://www.rcss.org

UNDERSTANDING TERRORISM IN SOUTH ASIA

Beyond Statist Discourses

Edited by

IMTIAZ AHMED

REGIONAL CENTRE FOR STRATEGIC STUDIES
COLOMBO

MANOHAR
2006

First published 2006

ISBN 81-7304-659-X

Published by
Ajay Kumar Jain for
Manohar Publishers & Distributors
4753/23 Ansari Road, Daryaganj
New Delhi 110 002

Printed at
Lordson Publishers Pvt Ltd
Delhi 110 007

Distributed in South Asia by
FOUNDATION BOOKS
4381/4, Ansari Road
Daryaganj, New Delhi 110 002
and its branches at Mumbai, Hyderabad,
Bangalore, Chennai, Kolkata

To

SHELTON KODIKARA

for his pioneering work in bringing

South Asian scholars together

RCSS is grateful to the Ford Foundation
for its generous support for the project on
Understanding and Combating Terrorism in South Asia
under Regional Collaborative Research Initiatives
on Non-Traditional Security in South Asia.

Contents

Acknowledgements

My first thanks are due to Professor Sridhar Khatri and the Regional Centre for Strategic Studies for providing me the opportunity to work with an excellent pool of scholars and on a topic whose importance and contemporaneousness can hardly be challenged. In the process of compiling this volume several people have come forward to help me with ideas, materials, even managing basic logistics during authors' meetings and workshops. Let me particularly thank Professor Amena Mohsin, Professor Jayadeva Uyangoda, Mr Shahab Enam Khan, and Ms Dilkie Perera for supporting me in various stages of this book. Special thanks are due to all the team members who have patiently borne the pain of receiving 'mild reminders', from time to time, while making sure that the paper reached me within a reasonable understanding of the word 'deadline'! I also take this opportunity to thank Ford Foundation for providing financial support to the project.

IMTIAZ AHMED

Introduction

IMTIAZ AHMED

Meanings tied to concepts are bound to change over time. At times the change is swift and dramatic, informing and impacting upon a wider section of the people. In recent times, the concept of 'terrorism' seems to have suffered from what can best be referred to as extravagant exaggeration or hyperbole. This is not to deny the qualitative leap of 'terror' in terrorism, whether state or non-state, but to point out its newly acquired blackhole status, sucking in and even redefining concepts, events and experiences that have consistently challenged the power of the state. 'Insurgency', 'civil war', even 'freedom struggle' are now being defined as 'terrorism', making the latter in many of the cases what it is not and therefore limiting resolutions of issues responsible for the actual birth and growth of *contemporary* terrorism.

9/11 is responsible for this, but I would say, only partially. This is because the state has always viewed dissent as an anti-state element or something bordering on terrorism. In this respect, 9/11 has surprisingly come to benefit the state, of both developed and developing countries, for it could now easily brand its own dissenters or anti-state elements as 'terrorist' and join the global or, more precisely, the US-led 'war on terrorism'. But interestingly the success of the state in depicting its dissenters as 'terrorist' has remained limited, failing mainly to impress upon the subaltern or dominated people, at times, even the liberals. This has been the case particularly with the colonial state, which seldom shied away from depicting the more militant anti-colonial forces as 'terrorist', although this hardly had any impact on the colonized population. Indeed, for the latter, such colonially defined 'terrorists' were nothing but national heroes.

In South Asia, Khudiram, Bhagat Singh, Surya Sen, Pritilata are good examples.

The opposing trend in the self-serving identification continued even after the colonial power left South Asia and the arrival of the post-colonial state. India's experience with the Naxalites, Nagas and Kashmiris (the latter two more sub-nationalized than the former) are of a similar nature, while Pakistan's labelling of the Bengali militants in the pre-Bangladesh period and the more recent targeting of the Tamils by the Sinhala-dominated Sri Lankan state are no different. In each of these cases, popular support for the 'terrorists' (particularly within their *own* community or people) outnumbered the support for the state in the campaign to contain and eliminate terrorism. Incidentally, this trend has continued at some level even with regard to Osama bin Laden and Saddam Hussain, and that again, not only nationally but also regionally and globally. The complexity in understanding terrorism cannot be denied, but attempts can also be made to go beyond the largely polemical statement or what Walter Laqueur called 'sophism' that one person's terrorist is another person's freedom fighter.[1]

Definitionally, terrorism is now an over-defined concept, with the state, organic intellectuals, and the dissenters constantly battling out the meaning of terrorism. In the midst of their contestations, a plethora of terrorism, or what could also be referred to as 'versions of terrorism', has flooded the vocabulary of scholarly languages. Schmid and Jongman have identified 109 different definitions of terrorism, with many having violence, fear, threats, psychological effects, discrepancy between the target and the victim, planned action, and strategy or tactics as key features.[2] But when such a collection of definitions is made one cannot help but remember the remarks of R.G. Collingwood, the English historian and philosopher, who had implored his readers 'to resist the vice of collecting "definitions" of this, that, and the other, as if anyone but a fool imagined that he could compress a thing like art, or religion, or science into an epigram which could be lifted from its context, and, so lifted, continue to make sense.'[3] He then went on to say, 'Giving and collecting definitions is not philosophy, but a parlour game.'[4] Indeed, if we were to extend Collingwood's contention then the overflow of definitions of terrorism is nothing but a reflection of the modernist quest to constantly and in some measure precisely understand the 'reason' of terror, albeit in an epigram form.

The search for reason has been a key quest in modernity and the modernist discourse. Ever since Rene Descartes came up with his ingenuous formulation: '*cogito ergo sum*, I think, therefore I am' (1637),[5] there has been no turning back for humans' quest to reason each and every phenomenon on earth and when possible in matters related to heaven as well. But Cartesianism attracted many minds craving for unrestrained freedom, some even challenging the divine and all the paraphernalia related to the latter, including the Church. In fact, Benedict de Spinoza, again basing on reason and bordering on something akin to rational pantheism, went on to claim that 'Nature is self-moving, and creates itself.'[6] It did not take long for the critics, particularly the Church, to denounce Spinoza as 'the prince of atheists, Christendom's chief foe, the new Mahomet'.[7] His Jewish background also unleashed a wave of anti-Semitic attacks on him, particularly with the publication of *Tractatus Theologico-Politicus* in 1670, which was quickly dubbed as an instrument 'forged in hell by a renegade Jew and the devil'.[8] The roots of modern or post-Enlightenment anti-Semitism could otherwise be found in the very unfolding of reason during the early period of Enlightenment or what is now commonly referred to as the period of 'radical Enlightenment'.

But the radicalism brought forth by Spinoza and a host of Spinozists needed to be tamed. Faith in the divine, if not in the Church, needed to be restored for the sake of societal stability and the power of the state. The person who could applaud 'human reason' without displacing the place of 'belief' was none other than the German philosopher and Lutheran, Immanuel Kant. In 1784 he made the following submission:

> Enlightenment is man's release from his self-incurred tutelage. Tutelage is man's inability to make use of his understanding without direction from another. Self-incurred is this tutelage when its cause lies not in lack of reason but in lack of resolution and courage to use it without direction from another. *Sapare aude*! 'Have courage to use your own reason!'—that is the motto of enlightenment.[9]

That is, it is not enough just to have 'reason', as the Cartesian dictum suggested, but one must also have the 'courage' to use one's reason. His submission otherwise reaffirmed his earlier contention outlined in the *Critique of Pure Reason* (1781) that 'knowledge' alone is not enough, there ought to be 'room for belief' in order to nurture and reproduce a moral dimension of freedom, immortality and religious fulfilment for man. Belief in the 'existence of God and a future life,' to which Kant remained firmly committed throughout his life, was brought back to the modernist discourse through the power of human reason itself. This was indeed a marked departure from the advocacy of 'reason' espoused by the scholars of the radical Enlightenment.

Let me at this stage make a slight but relevant digression to further clarify the place of reason in the modernist discourse. Ibn Arabi (1165-1240), the Islamic 'Sufi' scholar who earned the honorific *al-Shaykh al-Akhbar*, 'The Greatest Master', pondered exactly on the issue that brought Kant the much-acclaimed fame in the eighteenth century. According to Ibn Arabi, 'reason is innately constituted to set up distinctions and differentiations' and therefore the rational thinkers end up 'dissecting reality such that they lose sight of the underlying unity of all things'.[10] This, however, could be overcome, to follow Ibn Arabi further on this, by perceiving God's presence in all things through a process of 'unveiling', the latter 'rooted primarily in imagination'. That is, 'true knowledge depends upon seeing all things with both the eye of imagination and the eye of reason'.[11] Kant too saw the limits of reason and went on to point out that the belief in 'God, freedom and immortality' cannot be rationalized: 'I therefore had to annul *knowledge* in order to make room for *faith*.'[12] Reality for Kant then becomes inclusive of the world of both phenomenon and noumenon.

That the post-radical Enlightenment, particularly of the Kantian version, would base its understanding of reason on Islamic scholarship was too strong an idea for the post-theocratic 'enlightened' Europeans to digest. Two outcomes could easily be identified. Firstly, by the end of the eighteenth century a greater emphasis was given to the issue of '*Sapare aude*! Have courage to use your own reason!'—without of course referring to the obvious that the 'courage' be used to bring back 'faith', and for all practical matters the Christian ethos, into the Enlightenment and the modernist discourse. Modernity since the Kantian intervention no longer championed the cause of 'doubting' to the point of nurturing Spinozism or something bordering on atheism but had 'reason' and 'faith' conjointly informing and shaping the quest with the former itself making room for the latter. Kant is very explicit on this issue:

Solely by means of critique can we cut off, at the very root, *materialism, fatalism, atheism,* freethinking *lack of faith, fanaticism,* and *superstition,* which can become harmful universally; and finally, also *idealism* and *skepticism,* which are dangerous mainly to the schools and cannot easily cross over to the public. If governments do indeed think it proper to occupy themselves with the concerns of scholars, they should promote the freedom for such critique, by which alone the works of reason can be put on a firm footing.[13]

Interestingly, the Kantian intervention not only suggests a place for 'faith' but also an active role on the part of the government to 'promote' such a thing. This was not difficult to suggest in the light of the prevailing practices in Europe. In fact, in England, following Pope Clement VII's refusal to approve the annulment of King Henry VIII's marriage to Catherine of Aragon, the English Parliament, at Henry's insistence and through a series of acts not only separated the English Church from the Roman hierarchy but also made the English monarch the head of the English Church in 1534. The practice continues to this day.[14] In France too the debate was on during Kant's lifetime, and in 1790, following the French Revolution, the Catholic Church was nationalized and brought under the control of the government. Indeed, the modern separation of religion and state, no doubt a critical product of the Enlightenment, also saw the governmentalization of the Church, with the government incidentally carrying at times the burden of the latter!

Secondly, the search for 'reason' came to be understood as very specific to the Enlightenment and the modernist discourse, including the place of Europe itself, and therefore lacking in other religions and cultures, particularly Islam and the non-European world. When it comes to Islam the Orientalists needed to be credited in large measure. By the end of the eighteenth century the Orientalists had started dividing the Islamic scholarship into 'core Islamic thought' based on the practices of Muslim rulers predisposed to 'harsh legalism' and the 'abstract mystical philosophy' of Sufism 'indifferent to matters of religious law', with the latter suggestively having 'an external origin in India or elsewhere'.[15] A key Orientalist, Lt. James William

Graham, went to the extent of saying that the Indian subjects in fact regard the British as Sufis:

> We are, generally speaking, at least in this country, looked upon as a species or one kind of *Sufi*, from our non-observance here of any rites or forms, conceiving a worship of the Deity in mind and adherence to morality sufficient. In fine, the present free-thinker or modern philosopher of Europe would be esteemed as a sort of Sufi in the world, and not the one retired therefrom.[16]

The idea was mainly to isolate Sufism from Islam to the point of making the latter thoroughly apathetic if not opposed to reason and freethinking. This had profound implications for the people of both the Islamic and the non-Islamic world. Islam in the modern West came to be understood as devoid of reason, while the followers of Islam, often naively if not shamelessly agreeing to the western categorization of Islam, saw modernity as anti-Islamic. Only now, with post-structuralism advocating the limits of reason, do we find a renewed interest in the Islamic scholarship in the West. In fact, often a parallel is now made between Ibn Arabi's understanding of 'Real' and Jacques Derrida's understanding of 'différance', both trying to free their respective word/concept from the 'shackles of reason'.[17] I will have more to say about Derrida in the subsequent sections.

The understanding of contemporary terrorism could not help but be affected by such a modernist construction of things. In fact, as indicated earlier, the search for 'reason' has been central to the task of defining and subsequently typologizing terrorism. This could be brought under four major headings, the distinction largely based on the question of *who* is trying to do *what* to *whom*, and now, in the aftermath of 9/11, also *when* and *why*.

I

THE REASON OF THE STATE

There are several versions of terrorism identified with the reason of the state. In all of them, violence or threats of violence are carried out by the state either directly or indirectly, mainly for reproducing the power of the state. The coercive machineries of the state, including the power of the police and the military, are often directly involved in the execution of terror. The indirect contribution refers to a situation when violent groups or individuals are sponsored by the state or when such groups or individuals support voluntarily the existence and continuation of the state and are ready to carry out violent activities on their own. Let us now take a quick look at each of these versions:

1. *State Terrorism*

The use or threat of violence perpetrated by the state against its own population or against people of other countries either directly or through proxies for reproducing its own power. Countries that have resorted to state terrorism include Chile, Colombia, China, Germany, India, Indonesia, Iraq, Israel, Myanmar, Pakistan, Sri Lanka, the Soviet Union, United Kingdom and the United States, and, of course, a host of other countries as well. None of these states, however, particularly the incumbent governments, would accept the allegation that they have committed terrorism against their own population or elsewhere.

2. *Right-wing Terrorism*

The use or threat of violence to get rid of liberal democratic or socialist governments, mainly carried out against immigrants, minorities, and secular politicians and institutions. In the West, the right-wing terrorists have also been active in anti-abortion campaigns, including shooting doctors who perform abortions and bombing abortion clinics. This is also referred to as *neo-fascist terrorism.*

3. *White Terrorism*

The use of violence to challenge and obstruct the growth and development of the power of the revolutionaries. This meant limiting the violent activities and the power of the *red terrorists* who were active in the campaign to overthrow and change the monarchical state in the aftermath of the Bolshevik Revolution. It has been estimated that in Finland alone over 8,000 people became victims of white terrorism in 1918.

4. *Counter-terrorism*

When the state, including its coercive machineries like the police or the military, or groups favourable to the government resort to policies, tactics, and strategies to counter the violent activities of anti-state or anti-government elements. Counter-terrorism is different from *anti-terrorism* in that it is more 'offensive' in its approach. *Anti-terrorism*, on the other hand, would be more 'defensive' in its operation (concentrating more on special legislation, martial law, and the like). Counter-terrorism, however, would involve coercive measures including assassination and arbitrary reprisals at the hands of the state's own forces.

These four versions do not exhaust the possibilities of reproducing terrorism by the state or forces supporting it, but they are sufficient to reflect on terrorism related to the reason of the state. Modern terrorism, in fact, emerged from the womb of the modern state. The word incidentally came into use at the dawn of modernity, about 1375.[18] Four centuries later, the newly founded French Republic sought to reproduce its power through the Reign of Terror (1793-4), which also signalled the arrival of *terrorism* or government by intimidation as a valid instrument of statecraft. The 'reason' of post-Revolution France was no different from the reason that has followed since then. The state, or 'the fatherland', was in danger from internal and external enemies and only the age-old policy of terror brought down to the level of the public could now save the republic.

Interestingly, the philosophical foundation of limiting freedom and by implication providing the rationale for using force was laid down a century earlier by one of the earliest modern liberals, John Locke. As Andrew Wright, following his reading of Locke's *Thoughts Concerning Education* (1693), says:

> Locke identifies two necessary restrictions on our freedom to believe and act as we like. In the first place, though our beliefs will inevitably transcend the boundaries of knowledge they must not be allowed to come into direct conflict with reason. Secondly beliefs may be held only if they do not threaten the stability of society. The principle of freedom carries with it the responsibility of toleration, but there is no need to tolerate unreasonable beliefs that threaten the fabric of society.[19]

Incidentally, some two centuries and a half later, Karl Popper reiterated the Lockean contention in defence of 'open society' and the West: 'there are limits to the attitude of reasonableness. It is the same with tolerance. You must not, without qualification, accept the principle of tolerating all those who are intolerant; if you do, you will destroy not only yourself, but also the attitude of tolerance.'[20]

But what constitutes 'unreasonable beliefs' or 'attitude of reasonableness' remains an open question, although 'toleration' is no innocent or secular term either. Derrida and before him even critical theorists like Habermas have pointed out the 'religious roots' of tolerance. As Derrida points out in an interview, interestingly, immediately after 9/11:

> The word 'tolerance' is first of all marked by a religious war between Christians, or between Christians and non-Christians. Tolerance is a *Christian* virtue, or for that matter a *Catholic* virtue. The Christian must tolerate the non-Christian, but, even more so, the Catholic must let the Protestant be. . . .
>
> Indeed, tolerance is first of all a form of charity. A Christian charity, therefore, even if Jews and Muslims might seem to appropriate this language as well. Tolerance is always on the side of the 'reason of the strongest,' where 'might is right'; it is supplementary mark of sovereignty, the good face of sovereignty, which says to the other from its elevated position, I am letting you be, you are not insufferable, I am leaving you a place in my home, but do not forget that this is my home. . . .[21]

Indeed, when it comes to 'sovereignty' and 'my home', the secular layer combines with the religious layer to constitute the reason of the state effectively with the power to limit the practise of freedom should the latter prove destabilizing or threatening to the state and society.

And given the hegemonic nature of 'tolerance' and the 'reason of the state', it is not surprising that during the Reign of Terror some 10,000 people lost their lives, most of whom fell victim to the post-medieval yet 'tyrannical' secular state.[22] But this was only the beginning. By the twentieth century, assassination, incarceration, torture, mass murder, including the killing of 6 million Jews, 22 million Soviets and the no less horrifying number of people in Hamburg (some 40,000), Dresden (at least 70,000), Hiroshima (over 70,000), and Nagasaki (between 60,000 and 80,000)[23] were all carried out for the reason of the state, indeed for saving 'the fatherland' and the national state. In this context, Samuel Huntington's plea for the state's vigilance and rearmament in the face of an eventual 'clash of civilizations',[24] Walter Lacquer's tacit approval of states' coercive prerogatives because 'the state is based on its monopoly of power',[25] or George Bush's 'war on terrorism' remain identical for they all sanction violence and terror for the reason of the state.

It is from this perspective that elaborate definitions of 'terrorism' on the part of the state and its agencies become meaningful. The US Department of Defense and the FBI, for instance, define terrorism as 'the unlawful use of force or violence against persons or property to intimidate or coerce a government, the civilian population or any segment thereof, in furtherance of political or social objectives'.[26] The US State Department, on the other hand, uses the definition contained in Title 22 of the United States Code (Section 2656f [d]):

> The term 'terrorism' means premeditated, politically motivated violence perpetrated against noncombatant targets by subnational groups or clandestine agents, usually intended to influence an audience. The term 'international terrorism' means terrorism involving citizens or the territory of more than one country. The term 'terrorist group' means any group practicing, or that has significant subgroups that practice, international terrorism.[27]

It is not difficult to see from the above set of definitions that the state is responding to a precise version of terrorism. The inclusion and the corresponding exclusion of certain words in these definitions only reinforce the state's concern with the immediate, the purpose being to respond, even to retaliate violently, should such an event come to take place. The definitions only go to empower the state to be selective with a certain amount of manoeuvrability in dealing with the issue. It may be further noted that the US definition does not consider the possibility that terror may be a state activity and not something that is simply 'state-sponsored'.[28] This allows the US to formulate a definition of terrorism without itself being charged of engaging in it.

In this respect, the collective position of the South Asian states is an interesting one. When the SAARC Regional Convention on the Suppression of Terrorism was approved on 4 November 1987, it refrained from the task of defining terrorism. The Convention simply noted that 'the Heads of state or Government of SAARC agreed that cooperation among SAARC States was vital if terrorism was to be prevented and eliminated from the region'. Furthermore, to placate the extra-national but regional concerns of some of the key members, the Convention also noted that 'violence' that is regarded as a 'political offence' or 'an offence inspired by political motives' will not come within the purview of the Convention (Article II). But that was 1987. On 6 January 2004, that is, following the US-led 'war on terrorism' and the military intervention in Afghanistan and Iraq, the SAARC members signed an Additional Protocol on the Suppression of Terrorism which, while making an effort to curb money laundering and the financial support base of the terrorists, makes explicit the meaning of terrorism (Article 4):

> Any person commits an offence within the meaning of this additional protocol if that person by any means, directly or indirectly, unlawfully and willfully, provides or collect funds with the intention that they should be used or in the knowledge that they are to be used, in full or in part, in order to carry out:
>
> Any . . . act intended to cause death or serious bodily injury to a civilian, when the purpose of such act, by its nature or context, is to intimidate a population, or to compel a government or an international organization to do or to abstain from doing any act.

Once again 'terrorism' is defined keeping the state immune from the blemish of its own terror. Violence is otherwise 'legal' so long as it is carried out under the cover of the reason of the state. But if this is the voice of the state, the protagonist, then there is no reason to doubt the response of the subaltern, the antagonist. Interestingly such response at times comes in the form of violence and terror—indeed, the very means that have contributed to its subjugation.

II

THE REASON OF THE SUBALTERN

When it comes to the use of violence and terror there is a silent but sinister discourse haunting the reason of the state. This refers to the state's perennial battle with the subaltern forces, and this could include a whole range of dominated people, economically as well as racially, socially, and ethnically. In fact, with some groups like the peasantry, the subaltern element remains unique even when it chooses to join hands with forces intrinsically related to the state.

As Partha Chatterjee points out with reference to the early phase of the *Subaltern Studies* project in which a 'split' between 'the organized elite domain' and 'the unorganized subaltern domain' was deliberately constructed and pursued to make sense of the role of the latter in anti-colonial movements:

> The idea of the split . . . was intended to mark a fault line in the arena of nationalist politics in the three decades before independence during which the Indian masses, especially the peasantry, were drawn into organized political movements and yet remained distanced from the evolving forms of the postcolonial state. To say that there was a split in the domain of politics was to reject the notion, common to both liberal and Marxist historiographies, that the peasantry lived in some 'pre-political' stage of collective action. It was to say that peasants in their collective actions were also being political, except that they were political in a way different from that of the elite.[29]

But like any concept, the meaning of the subaltern, particularly the way it relates to the state, transformed over time. In fact, Chatterjee refers to the issue of post-colonial democracy in India and how it has influenced the lives of the subaltern classes, indeed, to the point of having newer forms of 'entanglement of elite and subaltern politics'.[30] In this context, Chatterjee further notes:

> Many of these (subaltern) groups, organized into associations, transgress the strict lines of legality in struggling to live and work. They may live in illegal squatter settlements, make illegal use of water or electricity, travel without tickets in public transport. In dealing with them, the authorities cannot treat them on the same footing as other civic associations following more legitimate social pursuits. Yet state agencies and nongovernmental organizations cannot ignore them either, since they are among thousands of similar associations representing groups of population whose very livelihood or habitation involve violation of the law.[31]

The sphere of illegality and the life and living of the subaltern have become even more complex with the advent of globalization. There is now a well-established relationship between and amongst 'dubious groups' and 'shadowy activities' ranging from smuggling of goods and people to illicit production and trading of small arms, money laundering, narco-production and trading, terrorism, and the like, and that again, across and beyond national, ethnic, racial, and even religious affiliations.[32] The subaltern classes, particularly the poverty-ridden and marginalized population, become easy targets of such groups and activities, but more importantly, their state of being itself becomes a factor for certain groups of (relatively well off) people to rally support and even clandestinely work, often violently, for their cause.

Indeed, in the context of colonization Frantz Fanon, the Martinique-born psychiatrist and Algerian freedom fighter, highlights the reason of the subaltern without a shred of remorse or anxiety. According to Fanon: 'The colonized man liberates himself in and through violence.'[33] He then intuitively points out the reality of things:

> The violence of the colonial regime and the counter-violence of the native balance each other and respond to each other in an extraordinary reciprocal homogeneity. This reign of violence will be the more terrible in proportion to the size of the implantation from the mother country. The development of violence among the colonised people will be proportionate to the violence exercised by the threatened colonial regime.[34]

Almost in line with Fanon and keeping the issue of 'wretchedness' in life in perspective, Ted Honderich makes an interesting comparison in the aftermath of 9/11: 'Is it yet more tasteless to make another remark about the day of September 11, when 3,000 were killed at the Twin Towers and the Pentagon? On that day, if deaths by starvation for 2001 were spread evenly throughout the year, 23,000 people died of hunger. . . . Each was as individual as each of the 3,000.'[35] He then ends by saying: 'it seems to me that at least some political violence has a moral justification'.[36] The reason of the subaltern is otherwise inversely at par with the reason of the state. Let me at this stage reflect briefly on some of the versions of terrorism directly related to the reason of the subaltern:

1. *Non-state Terrorism*

The use or threat of violence carried out by non-state organizations against the national state or foreign states and also against the population of either within the national state or outside. Historically, the non-state organizations lacked the power and the sophistication of the state in enforcing violence and therefore the threat from their violence remained limited, but lately, with the availability of modern weaponries the non-state organizations are becoming no less destructive than the state in the use of violence. Some of the violent operations of the Liberation Tigers of Tamil Eelam (LTTE) and Harakat al-Muqawamah al-Islamiyya (HAMAS) are good examples. There is also *non-state freelance terrorism*, which refers to violence carried out by organizations or individuals sympathizing with the cause of political groups or communities elsewhere in the world. The violent action of the Japanese Red Army in support of the Palestinian cause would fall into this category.

2. *Anarchist Terrorism*

Originally the violence, mainly in the form of assassination, which was unleashed in Europe and the United States from the 1870s to the 1920s. Although motivations may have come from the ideas propagated by Mikhail Bakunin (1814–76), particularly the latter's critique of governmental authority and the need for establishing a society based on voluntary cooperation and free association of individuals and groups, the anarchist terrorists mostly operated as small independent groups with little connection to the disempowered people in whose name they were supposedly carrying out all the violence. More recently, some of the members referring to themselves as anarchists are found participating in the violent protests against capitalism and globalization.

3. *Anti-state Terrorism*

Violence carried out by non-state organizations or individuals against the state or its machineries with the primary objective of ridding the state of its power. This could have both left- and right-wing versions. The Sarbahara Party of Siraj Sikder in Bangladesh and Timothy McVeigh's campaign against the FBI in Oklahoma would fall into such versions respectively.

4. *Nationalist Terrorism*

Violence carried out by a group or party for establishing a separate state for its own people, the latter often a minority and in a state of subalternity within the state. The failure of the state to resolve the grievances of a section of the people residing predominantly within a particular geopolitical location provides the immediate background for the birth of nationalist terrorism. The violent actions of the IRA in Northern Ireland, the Basque nationalists in Spain, or the LTTE in Sri Lanka are good examples.

5. *Revolutionary Terrorism*

The use or threat of terror for social transformation within existing national states or in colonial and semi-colonial situations. Revolutionaries, however, differed on its use. Lenin, for instance, branded the terrorist campaign as an 'infantile disorder' and thought of it as totally devoid of mass politics. The activities of the Nardoniks in Russia and those of the Bengal revolutionaries in colonial India fall within this category.

6. *Red Terrorism*

The use of violence by groups in the aftermath of the Bolshevik Revolution with the objective of annihilating people connected to the old order or persons obstructing political and social changes from taking place. At times red terrorism went beyond the territorial domain of Russia and the red terrorists were found active in northern and eastern Europe. According to one estimate, some 1,700 people became victims of red terrorism in Finland in 1918.

7. *Left-wing Terrorism*

Groups that seek to destroy capitalism and replace it with socialist or communist regimes. Many left-wing terrorists are also found advocating radical environmentalism or *eco-terrorism*, mainly to counter capitalist exploitation carried out by states and transnational corporations. The Naxalites of India and some of the violent activities of the Maoists in Nepal would be good examples of left-wing terrorism.

Save anarchist terrorism, the rest of the versions cited here are almost mirror images of the violence carried out in the name of the state. But, then, there are versions of terrorism which could go either way, and this invites the 'sophism' that Lacquer refers to, or for that matter the most commonly held misconceptions relating to the understanding of terrorism. It is this issue which I will now discuss in some detail.

III

BETWEEN THE REASON OF THE STATE AND THE SUBALTERN

Before taking up the critique let me briefly reflect on the versions of terrorism which could go either way, that is, it could end up rationalizing the use of violence as much for the reason of the state as for the reason of the subaltern classes:

1. *Good Terrorism*

When violent actions are justified by the oppressiveness of the system. This is also referred to as *licit terrorism* or even *democratic terrorism*. It is mainly on these grounds that governments, scholars, and groups across the globe differ as to who should be labelled a terrorist. There is popular support for violent actions carried out against 'occupation forces', as is the case with the Islamic countries when the violence is carried out by the Palestinians against the state of Israel. The same is true of the US intervention in Afghanistan and Iraq to overthrow the Taliban and Saddam regimes respectively.

2. *Religious Terrorism*

The use of violence for a religious cause or in the name of divinity. The Sicariis, Assassins, and the Knights Templars, of the Jewish, Muslim and Christian communities respectively, were the earliest religious terrorists. In modern times, the Zionists, mainly groups identified with the Irgun and the Haganah, were the first to resort to terrorism in the name of religion in British-occupied Palestine. Currently, there are over fifteen organizations which have carried out terrorist activities in the name of Islam, including the Hezbollas

(Lebanon), Abu Sayyaf (the Philippines), Al Qaida (on a global scale), and the Palestinian Islamic Jihad (West Bank and Gaza). The violent activities of these groups are also referred to as *Islamic terrorism*. Other religions also have their modern versions: the *Christian terrorism* of the anti-abortionists in the USA (the case of Eric Robert Rudolph, for instance) or the Christian militant groups in north-east India; the *Hindu terrorism* of Hindu militant groups in India; the *Buddhist terrorism* of Aum Shinrikyo in Japan or Sangha Ratna in Sri Lanka. In all its versions the public proclamation has been to overcome the grievances of the religious oppressed, although the complicity of the state in reproducing religious terrorism cannot be ruled out, for instance, the Taliban's support of the Al Qaida or Israel's support for extremist Jewish organizations in occupied West Bank and Gaza.

3. *Ethnic Terrorism*

The targeting of minority ethnic communities or foreign-born immigrants, also called *racial* or *xenophobic terrorism*. The Ku Klux Klan and the (protestant) Order in the USA, the Kosovo Liberation Army in former Yugoslavia, the neo-Nazi groups in Germany and the ULFA in Assam (India) are some of the organizations that have resorted to ethnic terrorism. Both the state and the subalterns are found, either directly or indirectly, supporting ethnic terrorism.

4. *Cultural Terrorism*

The wilful destruction of the cultural heritage of other religions or civilizations. This version of terrorism gained prominence when the Taliban government of Afghanistan decided to destroy the two enormous, fifteen hundred-year-old Buddhist statues in the valley of Bamiyan.[37] But cultural terrorism has been more pronounced in riots and civil conflicts between religious communities. The destruction of the sixteenth century mosque (Babri Masjid) by the Hindu fundamentalists in Ayodhya (India) in December 1992 the bombing of three mosques in Hugli district near Kolkata in April 2002; the attack and defiling of several Hindu temples in Bangladesh in the aftermath of the October 2001 elections; and the burning of a mosque in Kathmandu following the brutal killing of Nepali workers in Iraq are examples of cultural terrorism.

5. *Groupuscular Terrorism*

The violent activities carried out by the 'tiny, fissiparous radical activist groups' that had spread across western Europe in the 1970s.[38] According to one estimate, Italy alone had nearly 600 terrorist groups of this kind belonging to both left and right spectrums of political activism. Although the majority of the groupuscular terrorists campaigned for the disempowered and the have-nots, some were found attacking socialist or secular groups and tended to favour the power of the state. With regard to the birth and activities of the latter, the complicity of the state cannot be ruled out.

6. *Urban Terrorism*

The violence that is restricted to the urban locality, with the concentration of the population acting as the immediate reason for the target, and hoping that this would create the maximum impact in the minds of the public.[39] This version of terrorism has been used by the state, particularly through state-sponsored groups and agencies, as well as by the non-state. The West German Red Army Faction (the Baader-Meinhoff Gang), the Italian Red Brigades, United Kingdom's Angry Brigade, all have restricted their violent operations to urban centres.

7. *Domestic Terrorism*

When violence is carried out within the state with no external or foreign connections, also referred to as *local terrorism*. This is a common form of terrorism found almost in every country. In Bangladesh and some other parts of South Asia, this refers to the power of the non-state *mastans* or *mastanocracy*. With the rise of globalization, however, domestic terrorism has increasingly tied up with the international, particularly in the business of acquiring small arms and explosives, although politically, including in terms of its violent actions, it is largely tied up with the local. The state also resorts to domestic terrorism, often using its military, secret police, and intelligence services to quell state or governmental dissent.[40]

8. *International Terrorism*

When the perpetrator or the victim is from more than one state or when violent actions, like occupying territories, hijacking airlines, targeting foreign agencies or citizens, have direct international consequences. The US invasion of Iraq or Israel's occupation of the West Bank and Gaza and the violent activities of Palestinian militants against civilian Jews within Israel and outside are all current examples of international terrorism.

9. *Transnational Terrorism*

More recently, international terrorism has given way to transnational terrorism where several states jointly carry out violence against the civilian population of another country. The current Anglo-Australian-American joint incursion against the Iraqis is a good example of transnational terrorism. On the other hand, many non-state terrorist groups have turned transnational, that is, they are now more autonomous and decentralized in terms of recruitment and organizational set-up, often having members from more than one country. The transnational character of the Taliban force in Afghanistan is now a well-established fact. It even included the stateless Rohingyas from the Arakan region of Myanmar.

The two-pronged, seemingly contradictory affirmation of 'reason', or what is also referred to as the dialectics of rationalization makes the 'incomplete' quest of modernity central to its contention. Max Weber was one of the first to have identified this and he went on to hypothesize that the Enlightenment culture, far from being a fully exhausted force, 'held self-destructive seeds'.[41] His reasoning, though complex and controversial, remains intuitive and laid the foundation of what later came to be known as the critical theory. A brief exposition of Weber's thought will make this clear.

In *The Protestant Ethic and the Spirit of Capitalism* (1904–5), Weber tried to explain the success of capitalism in Germany. Basing his arguments very much within the 'cultural domain', he saw Calvin's formulation of the doctrine of predestination as creating the conditions for the rise of capitalism. The doctrine upheld the view that the 'sinful humans' suffer from a constant psychological insecurity because there is no way to know who would be bestowed with God's blessing and gain salvation. To overcome this insecurity, Calvin's followers took recourse to worldly affairs, seeking 'God's will in daily life' without enjoying the profit reaped from such labours.[42] This allowed for the rapid accumulation of capital in 'protestant' Germany, incidentally for the first time, as Weber would go on to claim, without the religiously sanctioned 'guilt' that is associated with such accumulation. But there was a flip side to this 'protestant ethic', something Weber was very much conscious about. The utilitarian goal of accumulation, although proving beneficial to capitalism, created disenchantment and alienation in the life and living of the mortals. And it is this disenchantment and alienation that created an instrumental understanding of rationality, where reason came to be applied in the task of 'controlling' the external, and this not only in the form of one individual controlling another but also the whole of mankind controlling the world.[43] The goal, however, was not to abandon the Enlightenment culture but to seize control and rectify it, even if it required taking recourse to violence. It may be worth pointing out here that Weber earlier in 1895 advocated the idea of 'liberal imperialism'![44]

Following the rise of fascism in Germany, it became quite evident how correct Weber's prognosis was with respect to the 'self-destructive seeds' of modernity. In 1947, Max Horkheimer and Theodor Adorno published their critique of modernity, *Dialectic of Enlightenment*, written largely during their exile years in the United States. The limits of modernity, which Weber highlighted at the beginning of the century, were once again reaffirmed, indeed without giving up hope on the culture reproducing it: 'Enlightenment itself, having mastered itself and assumed its own power, could break through the limits of enlightenment.'[45] Reason could still salvage the pitfalls of modernity.

But the person who popularized critical theory and had the greatest impact advocating the dialectics of rationalization, particularly the idea that the violence of one does not cancel the violence of the other, was Jürgen Habermas. In an interview immediately after 9/11, Habermas reiterates his position very frankly:

In one respect, Palestinian terrorism still possesses a certain outmoded characteristic in that it revolves around murder, around the indiscriminate annihilation of enemies, women, and children—life against life. This is what distinguishes it from the terror that appears in the paramilitary form of guerrilla warfare. This form of warfare has characterized many national liberation movements in the second half of the twentieth century—and has left its mark today on the Chechnyan struggle for independence, for example.[46]

Habermas, however, was arguing from the standpoint of his theory of communicative action. So long as there is 'a solid base of common background convictions, self-evident cultural truths and reciprocal expectations', as it is in the case of democratic societies, there is little chance of violence taking place. But the moment there is a 'distortion in communication' conflict is bound to erupt. Modern terrorism arises from this distortion in communication. Speaking about terrorism in the Arab world, Habermas points out that:

> To the Arab world, the USA is the driving force of capitalistic modernization. With its unapproachable lead in development and with its overwhelming technological, economic, political, and military superiority, the USA appears as an insult to their self-confidence while simultaneously providing the secretly admired model. The West in its entirety serves as a scapegoat for the Arab world's own, very real experiences of loss, suffered by populations torn out of their cultural traditions during processes of accelerated modernization. . . .
>
> This explains the fact that some of those drawn into the 'holy war' had been secular nationalists only a few years before. If one looks at the biographies of these people, remarkable continuities are revealed. Disappointment over nationalistic authoritarian regimes may have contributed to the fact that today religion offers a new and subjectively more convincing language for old political orientations.[47]

And since we now know 'what has gone wrong' this could be 'repaired', and indeed, by nurturing 'structures of a communicative situation free from distortion' can we overcome the current menace. Put differently, a return to 'radical democracy and enlightenment' is all that is required for modernity, although currently violent-prone, to have a renewed impact and a meaningful role.[48] But questions have been raised whether the 'meaninglessness' of 9/11 has brought disrepute to Habermas's dialectics of rationalization? We take up this issue in the next section.

IV

BEYOND THE REASON OF THE STATE AND THE SUBALTERN

There are versions of terrorism that defy rationality. In fact, violence and terror are carried out not only beyond the territorial domain of the state but also beyond the rationale usually put forward by the state or the subalterns. The following versions of terrorism, albeit in different shades and intensity, are in the business of threatening not only the state but also the life and living of the subaltern masses, and therefore remain generally unacceptable to both the state and the subalterns:

1. *Nuclear Terrorism*

The use of nuclear weapons or radioactive materials. Since the use of such weapons can never be limited to military targets and must include enormous civilian casualties, terrorism is intrinsically related to the use of nuclear weapons. This makes the USA for its use of atomic bombs in Hiroshima and Nagasaki in 1945 the only state in the world to have resorted to nuclear terrorism or terrorism beyond rationality. It may be pointed out that although an equal number of people died in Dresden, Hiroshima and Nagasaki, as indicated earlier, there was a marked difference between the aerial bombing of Dresden and the use of atomic bombs in Hiroshima and Nagasaki. In the latter two not only did 'a single bomb' in each of the two cities killed that many people but the consequences of the bombs—the radioactive fallouts—still remain a living thing. There is a growing concern now that the non-state terrorists are also trying to acquire radioactive materials, or what is more popularly known as the 'dirty bomb', but since there is no evidence of it till date nuclear terrorism remains the monopoly of the state.

2. *Bioterrorism*

The use of human-modified toxins or biological agents with the objective of harming or killing civilian populations. The concept of bioterrorism also comes within the understanding of germ warfare, and the most serious biological agents include anthrax, smallpox, botulism, tularemia, and viral haemorrhagic fever. One can trace its use as far back as 1346, when the Tartars took the bodies of people who had died of the plague and threw them over the walls of the city of Kaffa on the Black Sea, mainly to create an epidemic. Many believe that this resulted in the Great Black Death which wiped out 70 per cent of the city-dwellers of Europe.[49] Critics also refer to the distribution of cholera and smallpox infected blankets to native American population during the nineteenth century as a form of bioterrorism. A more recent case of bioterrorism was the anthrax-containing letter sent to Senater Majority Leader Tom Daschle, which actually led to the death of two postal workers.

3. *Narco-terrorism*

Violence carried out by drug traffickers for the production, trading, and consumption of illicit drugs. Such violence includes torture, assassination, extortion, hijacking, bombings and kidnappings of people (from judges and legislative members to government and security officials) engaged in the task of controlling or eliminating the flow of illicit drugs. The narco-terrorists, however, have a complex relationship with both the state and the non-state, particularly the militant groups, both benefiting directly from the proceeds of illicit drugs. The consequences of some of hallucinogens or psychedelic drugs (like cocaine, cannabis, PCP, LSD, or mescaline) have made narcoterrorism unacceptable to both the state and the subaltern classes.

4. *Cyber Terrorism*

According to the Federal Bureau of Investigation, cyber terrorism is 'the premeditated, politically motivated attack against information, computer systems, computer programs, and data which result[s] in violence against noncombatant targets by sub national groups or clandestine agents'.[50] Mainly the developed economies, particularly the West which is very much dependent on electronic transactions, are mainly vulnerable to cyberterrorism, although critics argue that such terrorism is 'overhyped' and the disruptions of communication networks would at the most cause annoyance rather than fear.[51]

5. *Catastrophic or Mass Terrorism*

Violence carried out mainly on the civilian masses on a large scale with vengeful or messianic goals. Mass terrorism is less political in that sense and could be carried out by states, groups or individuals with only 'fringe motivations'.[52] The carpet-bombing by the United States during the Vietnam War, the violent actions of Timothy McVeigh, the Tamil Tigers (particularly the notorious 'monthly' suicide-bombing in city centres), Al Qaida and the Aum cults, all fall into this category. The purpose of such violence could be more expressive than instrumental, and therefore is capable of being more destructive.

6. *Postmodern Terrorism*

A form of terrorism which has four critical features; firstly, the territorial domain of the terrorist is not limited within the boundaries of a national state. The whole world is now the field of operation. Secondly, there is genuine support for apocalyptic movements and millenarian goals.[53] Thirdly, it is less cohesive in terms of organizational structure. The bulk of the activities are carried out, to follow Lacqueur, by the 'lone terrorist'.[54] Finally, weapons that are far more lethal than before are now in the hands of the perpetrators. The violent activities of the Al Qaida and to a lesser extent the Hezbollas match the description of postmodern terrorism. One critic taking his cue from the 9/11 Commission Report, describes postmodern terrorism as 'sophisticated, patient, disciplined, and lethal', which has succeeded in making the apocalyptic phantasms of the Americans and the West real.[55]

7. *Suicide Terrorism*

When the perpetrator is willing to take his/her own life while committing violence. Although suicide terrorism is an ancient practice, used by the Jewish sects of Zealots and Sicarii in Roman-occupied Judea and later on by the hashish-addicted (Shi'ite as well as Ismaili) Assassins during the crusades, it became a tool of the state in modern times during the war. The action of the Kamikaze pilots during World War II is a good example in this context. Towards the end of the twentieth century, however, it became the ultimate weapon of the relatively disempowered subaltern elements, beginning with the Hezbollas in Lebanon in 1981 and later followed by the Tamil Tigers in Sri Lanka, the Kashmiri militants in India, the guerrilla insurgents in Iraq, and many more. With 9/11, however, it attained an international dimension, going beyond the territorial domain of the state and in terms of destruction also beyond state and subaltern rationality. With all the modern weaponries, particularly explosives, in hand, it is more likely that the latter element will continue to inform and define suicide terrorism.

Albert Camus, in fact, made a bold reflection on life and death in the middle of the twentieth century, which is very much relevant here. He said: 'There is but one truly philosophical problem and that is suicide. Judging whether life is or is not worth living amounts to answering the fundamental question of philosophy. All the rest—whether or not the world has three dimensions, whether the mind has nine or twelve categories—comes afterwards.'[56] Little did he realize that by the end of the twentieth century there would be numerous suicide terrorists, with some even having the courage to blow themselves to pieces while committing suicide. Traditionally, the aim of the terrorist was not to commit suicide. Even the Assassins and the Templars from the eleventh to thirteenth centuries AD committed suicide only when challenged. But to make the body itself a part of the weapon and that again with the knowledge that the body would be ripped apart while creating havoc in and around the target is something of an innovation, arising no doubt from the 'absurdity' of earthly life in the midst of all the violence and the kinds of modern weaponries, particularly explosives, that are now at one's disposal.

The arrival of the suicide-bomber is also the arrival of what I would refer to as *post-rational terrorism*. Edward Said, while referring to the terrorists of 9/11, provided some sense of this:

> I've never condoned or agreed with [Palestinian terrorism], but at least it is understandable as a result of a desperate human being who feels himself being crowded out of life and all of his surroundings, his fellow citizens, other Palestinians, his parents, sisters, and brothers, all of them dying or being hurt, wanting to do something, to strike back. . . . It's not something I agree with but at least you could understand it.

Now, here [illegible] talking about something different, because these people are obviously [illegible] desperate and poor refugee camp dwellers. The people who perpetrated the terror of the World Trade Center and Pentagon attacks were obviously middle-class, educated enough to be able to go to flight school in Florida, and could speak English. This is now transcending the political and moving into the metaphysical. And it's a leap that I think is very important to keep one's eye on, because it suggests the kind of cosmic quality—and, I would also say, the demagogical quality—of the minds at work here. They refuse to engage in or have no interest in dialogue or political organization or persuasion of the sort that makes political change and improves one's situation versus this kind of thing which is bloody-minded destruction for no other reason than to do it. Note that there was no claim for this terror bombing. There was no political message behind it. There were no demands. There were no statements. It was a silent piece of terror imposed on a population without discrimination or negotiation.[57]

So spectral has modern weapons technology become that even without actually having any of the sophisticated weaponries (only knives and mace, as officially disclosed by the US government), a dozen or so terrorists could hijack four aeroplanes full of passengers and transform them into deadly missiles.[58] Now a person, whatever that person's nationality may be, is barred from boarding a flight even with the technology for cutting nails, lest he or she be tempted to transform the technology into something demonic 'for no other reason than to do it'. This is not madness but a leap beyond rationality. The individual has at last become empowered with limitless freedom, albeit not to live but to die and destroy.

Interestingly, this is a process that Derrida sees as also informing and infecting the state, particularly the United States. He calls this, an *autoimmunitary process*, which 'is that strange behavior where a living being, in quasi-*suicidal* fashion, "itself" works to destroy its own protection, to immunize itself *against* its "own" immunity'.[59] Referring to 9/11 and the terrorists, Derrida explains how the United States has come to be infected by it:

Immigrated, trained, prepared for their act in the United States by the United States, these *hijackers* incorporate, so to speak, two suicides in one: their own (and one will remain forever defenseless in the face of a suicidal, autoimmunitary aggression—and that is what terrorizes most) but also the suicide of those who welcomed, armed, and trained them. For let us not forget that the United States had in effect paved the way for and consolidated the forces of the 'adversary' by training people like 'bin Laden', who would here be the most striking example, and by first of all creating the politico-military circumstances that would favor their emergence and their shifts in allegiance (for example, the alliance with Saudi Arabia and other Arab Muslims countries in its war against the Soviet Union or Russia in Afghanistan—though one could endlessly multiply examples of these suicidal paradoxes).[60]

Humans, largely on account of their relentless pursuit of reason, are finally at their wits' end and are now set to experience life and living beyond rationality. There is no guarantee that the worst would cease to visit them and renew afresh the terrifying images of terror.

The understanding of terrorism in South Asia cannot remain immune from the global discourse of violence and terror. The authors of this volume, albeit in the light of their own scholarly pursuits, have tried to make sense of the South Asian situation by going beyond the statist discourses of our time. Ranabir Samaddar (Chapter I) has sought to place the 'reason' of the (colonial) state in its propensity to both use and contain violence in terms of an 'exceptional' but 'permanent' relationship between state, law and terror. Three sets of arguments are critical here. Firstly, the state through its networks and machineries (intelligence, incarceration, torture, etc.) is constantly in the business of 'defining' terrorism, and in the process ends up providing the 'identity' of the terrorist. Secondly, laws are created not only to legalize violence but also to 'override rule of law' when required. The state has simultaneously carried out the task of 'law-making' and 'terrorising' the people. And thirdly, in the backdrop of 'an armed-to-the teeth colonial administration' the subalterns could not help but resort to terror. Put differently, if we go by the argument of Samaddar, the reason for the subaltern to resort to violence and terror rests not with the subaltern but with the state and its inescapable relationship with law and terror.

Rubina Saigol (Chapter II) and Shahedul Anam Khan (Chapter III) focus on the reason of the state and the limits of counter-terrorism with particular reference to two sets of countries. Saigol takes Pakistan and Sri Lanka, while Khan takes India and Bangladesh as their case studies. Saigol makes two general observations which are very pertinent to this volume. Firstly, there are times when the soldier and the terrorist merge together, particularly when 'the state's monopoly and right to violence is challenged and the state's own legitimacy, or that of its actions and motivations, is questioned'. Counter-terrorism of the state otherwise ends up reproducing terrorism which, for reasons of the state having a monopoly over coercive power, is often more violent than the violence of the non-state terrorists. Secondly, Saigol questions the religious identification of terrorism, blaming much of it to western prejudices and the current anti-Islamic bashing. In fact, she raises the issue of why the Nazi extermination of the Jews is not considered an acts of 'Christian fundamentalism' or 'Protestant terrorism'. When it comes to violence and terror, the reason of the state, as Saigol is very categorical on the issue, responds to a series of structural configurations—national, regional as well as international—and there is no reason to overlook one for the other. It is interesting to note that Saigol comes up with a 'working definition' of terrorism: 'any loss of civilian life, bodily injury or damage to property that occurs as a result of conflict between two states, two groups, a state and sub-national group, or a transnational movement and nation-states, constitutes an act of terrorism'. But given the post-rational nature of 'means' (modern arms and explosives) and 'ends' (suicidal mission or 9/11), can such a definition be operationalized and put to good use? There are very few optimists on this.

Khan contends that in so far as terrorism is concerned, 'the state was and continues to be a part of the problem'. Most often the state is the cause of the problem—the causal link of the issue—and in most cases it is either 'the unfortunate victim of terrorism or the perpetrator of terrorism', nationally or transnationally. The causal link between the sate and terrorism is 'universal and cannot be dispensed with'. Although the terrorism canvas of India and Bangladesh is vastly different from each other's, particularly from the standpoint of origin and scope, there is a remarkable similarity between them when it comes to combating terrorism, particularly in their reliance 'predominantly on the realist (statist) formula'. Many of the limits of combating terrorism are inbuilt in the system and in the attitude of the politicians and bureaucrats. While external factors exacerbate terrorism, taking refuge in this may not help to eliminate the phenomenon. State terror, a result of proactive or reactive measures, due to overreliance on the coercive tools at the disposal of the state results in a vicious cycle of violence where 'violence begets violence'.

Imtiaz Ahmed with Farid Ahmed Bhuiyan (Chapter IV) takes further the argument of the reason of the state, although not so much with acts of violence and terror but rather the means by which violence and terror are reproduced in modern times. Modern weapons technology has made a qualitative difference to violence and terror. Not only has the latter become awesome, particularly when it comes to automatic weaponries and explosives, but there is also now a conformity in the art and science of killing and terrorizing people. Added to this is the element of suicide bombing, which in some instances has taken terrorism beyond the domain of reason and made a spectre out of it. The complicity of the state, both in the development of weapons technology (from research to production) and in making them available to the non-state, remains a critical issue, almost making the state, as Derrida claims, succumb to a process of 'immunizing itself *against* its own immunity' or committing *hara kiri*. Ahmed then contends that 'innovations in political resistance' are required not only for restoring the spirit of the subaltern movements but also for replacing the reason of the state with newer formulations of life and living.

Jehan Perera (Chapter V), Dhruba Kumar (Chapter VI) and Sanjoy Hazarika (Chapter VII) refer to terrorism and subalternity within the geopolitical domain of Sri Lanka, Nepal and north-east India respectively. All the three authors have engaged in discourses beyond statism, referring to the struggle between the state and the subalterns, with the latter having ethnic, social, or even sub-national compositions, and historically specific transformations. As Gramsci once pointed out:

> The historical unity of the ruling classes is found in the state, and their history is essentially the history of states and of groups of states. This unity must be concrete, hence it is the outcome of the relations between the state and 'civil society'. For the subaltern classes, the unification does not occur; their history is intertwined with the history of 'civil society'; it is a disjointed segment of that history. . . . Among these (subaltern) classes, one will exercise a hegemony; this must be established by studying the developments of all the other parties as well, insofar as they include elements of the hegemonic class or of the other subaltern classes that are subject to its hegemony. . . . The study of the bourgeoisie as the development of a

subaltern class must therefore examine the phases through which it acquired autonomy from the future enemies it had to defeat and the phases through which it acquired the support of those forces that have actively or passively helped it; without this support it would not have been able to consolidate itself in the state.[61]

The subaltern, historically speaking, otherwise ends up taking refuge in the reason of the state, albeit by way of reproducing newer forms of hegemony. The displacement of the colonial power and the arrival of post-colonialism in both Sri Lanka and India are good examples. Nepal, even without being directly colonized, is no different. All three, and this time with the subalterns resorting to violence and terror with modern weaponries, virtually fall back on the reason of the state, bringing little hope to the promise of emancipation that the subaltern dissent otherwise carries.

Perera locates the birth of terrorism in the north and south of Sri Lanka on the 'lack of responsiveness of the political system' towards the minority Tamil community. In the post-colonial Sri Lankan state, Sinhala majoritarianism was built on the colonial structures, which were seen convenient by the new, albeit 'racial,' elite to reproduce its own power. But then Perera also finds the 'highly military nature' of the LTTE, although conditioned by the 'tyranny of a permanent majority, very limiting for resolving the issue. The way out would be a 'negotiated settlement', which would include not only 'political power' but also the 'discipline of democracy', as much for the LTTE as for the government in power.

Kumar explains the complexity in the relationship between marginalization and terrorism. In fact, he highlights a three-fold understanding of marginalization. Firstly, there is the social and economic marginalization of the 'impoverished people'. Both caste and class play critical roles in reproducing the power of the elite and the subaltern status of the rural poor. Secondly, there is the marginalization of the Maoists from the 'progressive', Left-oriented, political movements, which has pushed the former to violence and terror largely to lay claim on the state power. And thirdly, there is the marginalization of the marginalized (i.e. the rural poor), resulting from 'the spread of the Maoists' activities and terror throughout the country'. Kumar is of the opinion that the resolution of terrorism in Nepal requires addressing all the above three layers of marginalization, with the goal remaining 'democracy and deliverance of development' for the denied and the destitute of the Nepali society.

The subaltern status of India's north-east, particularly of Mizoram and Nagaland, cannot be denied, as Hazarika tries to explain, and this, following India's coercive diplomacy, has prompted the Mizos and Nagas to take up arms against the Indian state. Four sets of arguments have been put forward in this respect. Firstly, until very recently (and there are very good reasons for this, including the events of 9/11), the militancy in the north-east never came to be depicted as 'terrorism'. In fact, the militant groups were 'described variously as hostiles, undergrounds, insurgents or extremists'. Secondly, both Mizo and Naga fighters maintained a 'code of conduct' of 'not targeting civilian officials and their relatives'. Even reports of 'rape' by the militants were severely dealt with, even by execution. Militancy, therefore, as Hazarika contends, may not by itself subside into terrorism. Thirdly, if anybody is to be blamed for introducing terrorism in the north-east it is the Indian state: 'Terror was experienced by civil populations in the Naga and Mizo hills during the security operations.' And fourthly, the concept of 'non-state' is a limiting one in the north-east. This is because the militants, particularly in Nagaland, run a proto-state, with their own 'political administration', including a 'president', 'a prime minister', 'an assembly or parliament', 'a chain of command in the army', and the like, and because of this the militancy in the north-east, historically has evaded the 'broad definition of terrorism'. But this situation is changing fast, and by the beginning of the 1990s, with fragmentation in the composition of the proto-state, civilians were found to be 'deliberate targets'. In fact, in Assam some militant groups have used improvised explosive devices to target civilians. This is bringing disrepute to the militancy, which Hazarika finds is bound to undermine the genuine demands of the people of the north-east. What is required instead are 'people-to-people dialogues and political initiatives based on mutual respect and transparency', that is, a thorough if not radical democratization of the sub-nationalist movements and the state's equally democratic response to them.

Terrorization with increased civilian casualty is not the only thing that has lately infested the subaltern militancy. Nira Wickramasinghe (Chapter VIII) takes up the issue of globalization and the precise manner in which it has come to inform and influence such militancy. Basing her arguments mainly on the Tamil Tigers of Sri Lanka and the Maoists of Nepal, Wickramasinghe explains that globalization, far from changing the age-old nature of subaltern militancy, simply added to the 'efficiency' of what could be best referred to as the 'transnational mobilization of capital and people'. And this the militants used fully to their advantage. But then, this is more so with the Tamil Tigers, which has made creative use of transnational networking and the Tamil diaspora for its diverse range of activities, including arms procurement, fund-raising, even cyber terrorism, without however jeopardizing its geopolitical goals. The same cannot be said of the Maoists, which have remained mostly 'national' in the task of organizing and reproducing themselves. In this context, Wickramasinghe stresses the point that there is a greater need to be 'mindful' in our use of concepts, and the 'less sweeping and more precise' the concepts the better will be our understanding of what is surely a less-than-linear nexus between terrorism and globalization.

But then, as indicated earlier, there is no guarantee that in this age of violence and terror rationality will prevail. And it is precisely this spectre that is now haunting us all. The purpose of this volume, however, would be well served if the readers were to finally wake up to an understanding that violence and terror, both state and non-state, have created havoc on earth and the earlier an all-out effort—collectively as well as individually—is made to contain them the greater would be the chance for the coming generation of people to live a life with dignity and laughter.

NOTES

1. Walter Lacqueur, *No End to War: Terrorism in the Twenty-First Century* (New York: Continuum, 2003), p. 235.
2. Alex P. Schmid and Albert J. Jongman, *Political Terrorism: A guide to actors, authors, concepts, data basis, theories and literature* (Amsterdam: North Holland, 1988), p. 5.
3. R.G. Collingwood, *Speculum Mentis* (The Map of Knowledge) (Oxford: Clarendon Press, [1924] 1946), p. 111.
4. Ibid.
5. Rene Descartes, *Discourse on Method*, Part 4 (London: Essential Thinkers, 2004), pp. 52-60.

6. Jonathan I. Israel, *Radical Enlightenment: Philosophy and the Making of Modernity 1650-1750* (Oxford: Oxford University Press, 2001), p. 160.
7. Ibid., p. 161.
8. See, 'Influence of Descartes and the Geometrical Method', in *Encyclopaedia Britannica*, Millennium 4th Edition, cd-rom version.
9. Cited from Issac Kramnick, ed., *The Portable Enlightenment Reader* (New York: Penguin Books, 1995), p. 1.
10. William C. Chittick, 'Ibn Arabi', in Seyyed Hossein Nasr and Oliver Leaman (eds.), *History of Islamic Philosophy* (London: Routledge, 2003), pp. 501-2.
11. Ibid., p. 502.
12. Immanuel Kant, 'Preface to the Second Edition', *Critique of Pure Reason*, Unified Edition (with all variants from the 1781 and 1787 editions), Translated by Werner S. Pluhar (Indianapolis/Cambridge: Hackett Publishing Company, Inc., 1996), p. 31.
13. Ibid., p. 34.
14. With Prince Charles' marriage to the one-time divorcee, Camilla Parker Bowles, now becoming a reality the issue has cropped up again. Many are unwilling to accept Prince Charles as *both* Head of the State and Head of the English Church.
15. Carl W. Ernst, *The Shambhala Guide to Sufism* (Boston and London: Shambhala, 1997), pp. 16-19.
16. Ibid., pp. 14-15.
17. Ian Almond, *Sufism and Deconstructionism: A comparative study of Derrida and Ibn Arabi* (London: Routledge, 2004). See also, Godfrey Cheshire, 'Beasts of Burden: Why our official culture isn't sure it wants us to know about Ibn Arabi and Rumi', *Arts Feature*, 31 October 2001.
18. See, *Chambers Dictionary of Etymology* (New York: Chambers, 2003), pp. 1127-8.
19. Andrew Wright, *Religion, Education and Post-modernity* (London: Routledge, 2004), p. 134.
20. Karl Popper, *Conjectures and Refutations: The Growth of Scientific Knowledge* (London: Routledge, 1963), pp. 479-80.
21. Giovanna Borradori, *Philosophy in a Time of Terror: Dialogues with Jürgen Habermas and Jacques Derrida* (Chicago: The Chicago University Press, 2003), pp. 126-7.
22. Charles Townshend, *Terrorism: A Very Short Introduction* (Oxford: Oxford University Press, 2002), p. 37.
23. For the death figures of Hamburg and Dresden, see, Igor Primoratz (ed.), *Terrorism: The Philosophical Issues* (New York: Palgrave Macmillan, 2004), pp. 118 and 130. And for the death figures of Hiroshima and Nagasaki, see, *Encyclopaedia Britannica*, Millennium 4th Edition, cd-rom version, 2004.

24. Samuel Huntington, *The Clash of Civilizations and the Remaking of World Order* (New York: Simon and Schuster, 1996).
25. Lacquer, *No End to War*, p. 237.
26. U.S. Code of Federal Regulations, Number 28, Section 0.85, cited from http://carlisle-www.army.mil/ssi/pubs/2003/bounding.pdf
27. Cited from Michael A. Peters, 'Postmodern Terror in a Globalized World', *Globalization*, vol. 4, no. 1, 2004.
28. Ibid.
29. Partha Chatterjee, *The Politics of the Governed: Reflections on Popular Politics in Most of the World* (Delhi: Permanent Black, 2004), p. 39.
30. Ibid., pp. 39-40.
31. Ibid.
32. For a closer examination, see Imtiaz Ahmed, 'Contemporary Terrorism and the State, Non-State and the Interstate: Newer Drinks, Newer Bottles', in Sridhar K. Khatri and Gert W. Kueck (eds.), *Terrorism in South Asia: Impact on Development and Democratic Process* (Colombo: Regional Centre for Strategic Studies, 2003).
33. Frantz Fanon, *The Wretched of the Earth* (London: Macgibbon & Kee, 1965), p. 67.
34. Ibid., p. 69. One should not, however, take Fanon to be an advocater of violence. This is clear from his conclusion:

    Come, then, comrades, the European game has finally ended; we must find something different. We today can do everything, so long as we do not imitate Europe, so long as we are not obsessed by the desire to catch up with Europe. . . . Let us decide not to imitate Europe; let us combine our muscles and our brains in a new direction. Let us try to create the whole man, whom Europe has been incapable of bringing to triumphant birth. . . . For Europe, for ourselves and for humanity, comrades, we must turn over a new leaf, we must work out new concepts, and try to set afoot a new man (pp. 253-5).
35. Ted Honderich, *Terrorism for Humanity: Inquiries in Political Philosophy* (London: Pluto Press, 2003), pp. 23-4.
36. Ibid., p. 170.
37. Kristin M. Romey, 'Cultural Terrorism', *Newsbriefs*, vol. 54, no. 3, May/June 2001.
38. Townshend, *Terrorism*, p. 68.
39. For a closer exposition on the impact of terrorism on urban centers, see Edward L. Glaeser and Jesse M. Shapiro, 'Cities and Warfare: The Impact of Terrorism on Urban Form', *Harvard Institute of Economic Research (HIER)*, Discussion Paper Number 1942, December 2001.
40. Anneli Botha, 'Fear in the City, Urban Terrorism in South Africa', Monograph no. 63, July 2001, http://www.iss.co.za/Pubs/Monographs/No63/Content63.html.

41. Borradori, *Philosophy in a Time of Terror*, p. 69.
42. Arthur Mitzman, 'Max Weber', *Encyclopaedia Britannica*, Millennium 4th Edition, cd-rom version, 2004; see also, *The Iron Cage: An Historical Interpretation of Max Weber* (New York: Alfred A. Knopf, 1969), pp. 194-5.
43. Borradori, *Philosophy in a Time of Terror*, p. 70.
44. Mitzman 'Max Weber', op. cit.
45. Max Horkheimer and Theodor W. Adorno, *Dialectic of Enlightenment: Philosophical Fragments*, edited by Gunzelin Schmid Noerr (California: Stanford University Press, [1947], 2002), p. 172.
46. Borradori, *Philosophy in a Time of Terror*, pp. 33-4.
47. Ibid., pp. 32-3.
48. 'The Dialectics of Rationalization', an Interview with Habermas by Alex Honneth, Eberhard Knodler-Bunte and Arno Widmann, *Telos: A Quarterly Journal of Radical Thought*, no. 49, Fall 1981, p. 13.
49. Jonathan Shaw, 'Battling Bioterrorism,' *Harvard Magazine*, January-February 2002.
50. Ronald L. Dick, 'Cyber Terrorism and Critical Infrastructure Protection', 24 July 2002, www.fbi.gov/congress/congress02/nipc072402.htm2.Id.
51. Mark Ward, 'Cyber terrorism "overhyped"', BBC News, http://news.bbc.co.uk/go/pr/fr/-/2/hi/technology/2850541.stm.
52. Ashton B. Carter has popularized the term. See, Cover Article, 'Understanding Terrorism', *Harvard Magazine*, January-February 2002; see also, Ashton B. Carter, John Deutch, and Philip Zelikow, 'Catastrophic Terrorism: Tackling the New Danger', *Foreign Affairs*, November/December 1998.
53. Andrew T.H. Tan, 'The Emergence of Postmodern Terrorism and Its Implications for Southeast Asia', *Perspectives*, Institute of Defence and Strategic Studies, Nanyang Technological University, Singapore, http://www.ntu.edu.sg/idss/Perspective/research_050107.htm.
54. Walter Lacqueur, 'Postmodern Terrorism', *Foreign Affairs*, September/October 1996.
55. Per Serritslev Petersen, '9/11 and the Apocalyptic Enemy Within: Terrorist Scenarios in Postmodern American Fiction and Film', University of Aarhus, Denmark, http://www.hum.au.dk/engelsk/naes2004/download_paper.html?ID=148(Denmark).
56. See, Albert Camus, *The Myth of Sisyphus* (London: Penguin Books, 1975), p. 11.
57. David Barsamian and Edward W. Said, *Culture and Resistance: Conversations with Edward W. Said* (London: Pluto Press, 2003), pp. 112-13.
58. The 9/11 Commission Report mentions that that 'One of the callers from United 93 reported that the hijackers might possess a gun. But none of the other callers reported the presence of a firearm.' Furthermore, the Report mentions, 'We believe the bombs were probably fake.' The

spectre of modern weaponries is such that the passengers all believed that the hijackers possessed guns and bombs although there is no evidence of it. See, *The 9/11 Commission Report: Final Report of the National Commission on Terrorist Attacks upon the United States* (Authorized Edition) (New York: W.W. Norton & Company, 1st edn., undated), pp. 5-13.

59. Borradori, *Philosophy in a Time of Terror*, p. 94.
60. Ibid., p. 95.
61. Antonio Gramsci, *Prison Notebooks*, vol. 2 (New York: Colombia University Press, 1996), pp. 91-2.

CHAPTER I

Colonial State, Terror, and Law

RANABIR SAMADDAR

Pestilence, invasions, and mutiny—these are issues of concern, terrifying matters for the state, because, above all they bring unsanctioned and unwarranted deaths. In this sense, while the form of the state has undergone changes since the time it made its appearance in our world, the state in all forms has experienced terror at the prospect of uncertain deaths, that is to say, deaths that bring or symbolize uncertainty. Extraordinary measures are taken, juridical serenity breaks down, schizophrenia takes possession, and collectively they give a push to a reorganization of polity. Most of the time we know this prospect by the word 'terror'. Terror means uncertainty, the capacity to scare, 'terrorize', violence, symbolic violence, extra-ordinary methods, unaccountability, uncertain prospects, different rules (if you understand them) of engagement and murder, and different methods—but in whichever way you interpret and make sense of the word, this is a game with death. The act and the response, both are locked in death acts. Yet, because terror denotes uncertainty—terror is uncertainty—the state wants to make sure that the world of terror becomes law-bound, its grammar is subjected to cognition, so that terror is stripped of uncertainty, it is made certain in terms of definition, knowledge, action, and retribution, and thus the uncertain is legally defined, becomes subject to the state's reasons, to the world of knowledge, therefore to calculated decisions. Yet, and that is another surprise, another paradox: the process of attempting to subject the essential uncertain to the most extreme certainty, *law*, is coupled with a recognition of the limits of this enterprise, and therefore with a frenzied invocation of the great arbitrary method of governing from time immemorial, *intelligence*, that forms the bedrock of the trinity—state, terror, and law. This is clear today after the Patriot Act in the US or the numerous anti-terror legislations in India or elsewhere. Governing must be preceded by the collection and analysis of information; law must protect not only ways of governing, it must also decree ways of collecting information. Indeed on that will depend how law can help the state to face terror, employ terror, and counter terror. Yet in studying the trinity, it will serve us if we remember that the colonial strategies of governing have been the basis on which the unity of the three elements of politics stand today, namely, state, terror, and law; and it is this unity that has made a law-bound world amenable to what a French jurist working in Algeria, Olivier Le Cour Grandmaison, has called the 'permanent exceptions'.

The suggestion to study 'permanent exceptions' besides carrying historical and philosophical interest carries also a momentarily embarrassing irony, because it will inevitably raise the question, how can law be so close to terror, so close that terror can never be thought of without its legal definition, without the legal mechanisms to cope with it—indeed without terror becoming one of the most significant moments, or at least the next moment, in the development of law? The entwined or entangled story of law and terror presents to us the appearance and disappearance at will of what we can call the 'will of law' or 'the will to legislate'. Now going beyond law to combat or inflict terror, now shrinking back to the confines of law to take stock and legislate in order to forge an appropriate tool of terror and counter-terror, the *will to legislate* becomes contingent on elaborate phantom-building exercises. Drawing the widest canvas of a terror that has supposedly engulfed society becomes the occasion to legislate. The most hard measures enacted are found, therefore, suspended in a kind of mythological abyss of terror, horror, and calamity, which becomes quickly the caricature of constitutionalism, a caricature that law cannot tolerate for long. The normalization of terror in politics becomes a juridical task of high priority—normalization in the sense of bringing the phenomenon back to the 'normal' level, also 'normalizing' the level achieved. The story of the colonial state in relation to terror and law is significant for it shows in embarrassing clarity the material conduct of the state in an age when terror has once again appeared as one of the most essential ingredients of politics, and therefore physical control has become once again one of the chief instruments of ruling.

I

The colonial state in India was an extraordinarily war-like state. In some ways it had continued the record of the pre-colonial state in making war, conquest, and large-scale murders the basis of state foundation, expansion, and consolidation. But the colonial state raised the level of violence to an unprecedented level. Throughout the nineteenth century, the truly colonial century in India's history, wars, plunders, conquests, battles of attrition, destruction, mutinies, revolts, massacres, famines, pestilence, and widespread depopulation marked the country's life. While many new history writings tell us something of the cultural canvas, they tell us little of the way in which the physical lives were spent, destroyed, reshaped in this century of wars and extraordinary violence.[1] In this war-torn century, empire making meant terror at every level and every step. It meant employing warriors and guns, raising mercenary armies, anarchic modes and results of taxation, seizing land, planting or replanting it, forcibly colonizing tracts with huge loss of lives, imposing trade rules with devastating effect; the war-struck century meant, due to all these, a terror-struck century. It also meant that a huge land mass dotted with points of intense violence needed to be aggressively ruled by guns and regulation-making at a ferocious pace. What the liberal history of the nineteenth century India paints as one of increasing tranquillity and civility is actually what modern administrators and policy makers would call 'pacification', achieved through terror and rules, which required an entire century of will to legislate. Yet as we all know, the pacification that started with Regulation III of 1818 did not quite achieve the success that it claimed. With the onset of the new century violence struck the political horizon of the country again. The early terrorists had learnt the lesson—the violent colonial state understands only the language of terror, or at least mass non-violent movements must be laced with appropriate measures of terror and violence. The geography of the violence in the nineteenth century was an indicator as to why terror would remain a permanent feature of the political life of the country.[2] The size and the spread of violence and terror in all forms throughout the century—assassination, internment, deportation, exile, physical torture, random death penalty, increasing monopolization of means of violence and murder (by which individual murder became an occasion for the state to decide who is guilty and confer the death sentence), incarceration, artillery development, punitive taxation, collective punishment (as in the suppression of the Mutiny), race violence, forced labour employed by the army, and starving massive groups of people to death—meant that violence had a deep impact on the political forms of action in the society; that the political action was to be marked by an awareness that *sarkar* might be a *ma bap sarkar*, but this *sarkar* was of the *huzoor* who tolerated the scoundrel, at times showed affection, but would cane the beast regularly with a reserved and unchallenged right to rule. In this uniquely ubiquitous violent society, terror was the birthmark of politics.

Some of the last words of the early revolutionary, Khudiram Bose, recorded by the Special Branch before he was hanged to death were:

> I was naughty in my childhood . . . (But after I entered the Midnapore Collegiate School), a change overtook me. Physical culture absorbed all my attention instead of study, and one thought always was uppermost in my mind—how to be strongest amongst my classmates. But in the meantime an idea struck me, 'I must do something proven for my motherland'. We discussed the subject, I and two friends. . . . Just at this time we heard that famine was raging in the country. Subscriptions were being raised in the classes. But it would often happen that he who raised the subscription usurped half the amount instead of spending the whole for whom it was intended. My mind grew disturbed and I thought that the Government was indifferent to the matter. Since then I began to detest the Government. Not only this, there were other causes which substantiated my hatred towards the Government. Then when I gathered the real state of affairs from books and histories, the landing of the English in India and its subsequent conquest by them, there arose an uncommon hatred in my mind. We, myself and the said two friends pledged to put an end to our lives by some patriotic deeds. At that time the partition of Bengal was declared. Then we realised that we would not be able to redeem our pledge by remaining within the confines of our domestic life . . . I became restless . . . I realised nothing could be achieved in this way. At this time I met a

genuine patriot. He began advising me as to how my efforts would be of proper use. . . . At the instance of my Guru I went to Anandapur with a friend to learn the art of weaving. . . . At this time the *Jugantar* (the revolutionary publication—R.S.) came out in Calcutta. Reading it we realised that weaving would not lead to freedom. An article deeply impressed upon me. It is as follows. 'By (after?—R.S.) handing over the country to the foreigners, you are invoking Swadeshi; it is like guarding the streets after allowing thieves inside the house.'

Weaving lost its lure after I read these lines. . . .

During this time there was an exhibition in Midnapore. I became a volunteer. I got some pamphlets on the merits and demerits of the English. I began to carefully distribute them, but got arrested. By using physical strength I somehow got off . . . I was arrested (again), and then bailed off. I was committed to the Sessions and was again put to *hajat* (jail custody) for a day . . . and on the second day I heard that the Government had withdrawn the charges against me. I was then 15 years old.[3]

The sheer physical dimension of a possible political activity ensured that with terror politics would be born in the colonial land. For after all, the colonial wars, violence, and terror were a physical reality—bodies were being tormented, killed, forced into labour, starved to death, dumped, or confined and controlled in multiple ways, and the physicality of the milieu marked the articulation of politics. Indeed, as we shall see, terror had no other purpose than to make a political declaration; and, politics had no other purpose, at least at the outset, than to strike terror in the enemy camp. Gavrilo Princip, the nationalist assassin whose fateful shots not only killed Prince Ferdinand of Austrian in Sarajevo, but in a way heralded also the beginning of the first Great War, had similarly confessed his desire to become strong, courageous, and strike physically the enemy, the Austro-Hungarian Empire, and the dynasty.[4] Hatred was first of all a physical reality and called for a physical response. However, first a few words on what this unending century of conquests implied in terms of the ground that was being prepared for the explosion of explicit political violence.

The literature on the Great Game has made us familiar with the colonial wars of conquest, annexation, and suppression on the western side of India. What we immediately did not see was the connection between the Wahhabi threat to colonial rule and the imperial policy of guarding the frontier. It became clear much later when Lord Mayo, the Viceroy, was assassinated in the Andaman Islands by the Wahhabi prisoner Shere Ali in 1872. Indeed the punitive and pacification policy of the British created something new in Indian reality, the jail system; as one historian says, the colonial society became a penal society, where the social, political, and physical order was sought to conform with the normative order of colonialism.[5] Jails became the breeding grounds of the early terrorists. State surveillance only increased hatred. The colonized was not just a subject, but a convict–subject bound by rules of segregation, punishment, impressive spectacles of power and benevolence, and obedience to personalized authority. The colonial penal policy grew directly out of the needs of conquest and pacification, and thus from the beginning penalizing had little to do with reform and more with control. The procedural forms of punishment were elaborately laid out with the formalization of the Penal Code, Criminal Code, Evidence Act, and the jail system. The whole idea, which generated only hatred, was that while justice theoretically might be individuated, punishment was to be collective whenever required. And where guilt was collective, the punishment to the individual was to be severe and 'equal', thus denoting the collective reality behind the crime and punishment. As if colonial rule, law, justice, order, and magistracy, by the acts of hanging, lynching, caning, exiling, interning, torching, confiscating, and impounding, were addressing not the subject of law but the collective society behind him. Thus, no wonder, shame and hatred spread rapidly. Law born out of conquest and war ensured that only hatred could be the site of politics. Revenge, punishment, and pacification were uppermost in the colonial conduct in the wake of the south Indian wars of conquest as well. After the defeats elsewhere in the last period of the eighteenth century, British governing and military establishments went on the offensive, not just in terms of warfare but also in terms of rule and suppression, on a massive and successful scale. The fall of Tipu Sultan and Seringapatnam was in that sense more significant than or at least equal to the exile of Bahadur Shah II, the killing of his sons by Hodson, and the fall of Delhi, fifty-eight years later in the suppression of the Mutiny. Hereafter colonial rule was to be a race rule, law was to provide how this rule was to demonstrate terror when necessary, anti-colonial terror became the dominant form, the other side of the war; and as identities solidified and multiplied, terror, which is always linked to a politics of identity, became the universal form of politics. Again, we need not anticipate the factor of identity here. What is crucial here is to understand the role of war and the extraordinary violence in making terror a form of politics.

We can see what happened in the north-eastern part of India throughout that century. Though no Russian bear was breathing down the neck here, colonial rule was always in search of a safe line—a frontier, a boundary—a border, which would make the rule safe. Thus each community, each settlement, each area the colonial army came into contact with aroused in the colonial power the irrepressible urge to conquer and bring that community, settlement, and area under control—till another big power, or a sea, or a thousand-mile forest, or a snowbound mountain range of several hundred miles, or a river system, met the continuously forward pressing army and the administration—and fix the border for the colonial kingdom. The Burmese Wars, the Treaty of Yandabo in 1826 and the Commercial Treaty that accompanied the Yandabo Treaty did not stop the wars. The British moved into Burma with the commercial interests of the British merchants providing a *causas belli*, in 1851–2; 'King Pagan fell, the rich Delta came under the British flag, and Upper Burma waited uneasily for the final jump of the British Lion.'[6] The British pressed on.

By Article 2 of the Treaty of Yandabo the King of Burma had renounced all claims on Assam. Now if Assam was annexed to the empire, how was this to be done? The upper portion of the Brahmaputra Valley went under British administration, the frontier tract, inhabited by the Moamarias, Khamtis and the Singpos, was excluded from direct administrative control, the Assam Light Infantry was posted to protect the frontier and prevent both the Assamese and the hill tribes from eating each other; and to control both the sons of chiefs of the tribes were taken as hostages. And yet, by 1830 rebellions had broken out in the frontier tracts. In 1842 new areas were annexed—Sadiya and Matak. Civil rebellion in North Cachar had to be suppressed. However, there is no doubt that with the Treaty of Yandabo, a huge new tract had been prised open. Access to Burma meant that all the adjoining territories were to be annexed also. In the next seventy-five years, the Cachar Plains, Khasi Plains, Jaintia Plains, Assam Hills, North Cachar Hills, Garo Hills, NEFA, Lushai Hills, and the Naga Hills were subjugated in 1830, 1833, 1835, 1838, 1858, 1873, 1875, 1890, and 1904 respectively. Conquest was followed by rational rules of administration which necessitated measures one after another such as the Scheduled District Act of 1874, Backward Tracts Act of 1919, the Excluded and Partially Excluded Areas Act of 1935, and by the enactment of Special Powers such as the Armed Forces Special Powers Act, which conferred immunity on the conquerors and administrators. With terror the conquerors sealed their conquest; by conferring immunity they covered their foot soldiers; with the rules of exclusion they divided the subjects and pacified them; and with all these they guarded the frontier—but the necessity of defending the frontier meant that colonial law had indeed created permanent exceptions.

II

We must come to the issue of law, law that follows conquest. It is here where we shall find the story of permanent exceptions. With colonial history everywhere began the modern legal story of permanent exceptions. Consider, for instance, today's much talked about area—Guantanamo Bay, a site leased under duress from an unwilling and unrecognized state—an area legally held where all laws are indefinitely suspended, a *terra incognita*, a suitable site for experiments in pre-emptive justice (we can find a precursor in the form of the Andaman Islands and the Prison). Modern Cuba regularly demands the return of the land (120 sq. km.), leased by the US, the new great power in that hemisphere, from the departing colonial power, Spain, in another age with an annual amount of $4,000 in the Paris Conference in 1903, where no representative of Cuba was present. Now being used by the US to hold captive 'enemy combatants', another legal fiction, the place is what Jeremy Seabrook calls 'a legal black hole', where laws, conventions, and rules are in permanent suspension.[7] And all this is backed by a hoary US Supreme Court decision of 1950, to the effect that non-resident enemy aliens have 'no access to (US) courts in wartime', even if a particular war has never been legally declared, or will never be legally over.

Permanent exception, the administrative-legal strategy to tackle resistance, was invented by the colonial rule as a mix of terror and the principle of responsible government. Indeed, the two discourses of exceptions and responsibility came roughly at the same time. The invention of the wheels of responsible government did not come much later than 1818. We have already noted that terror, necessitated by conquest, was a physical fact. Yet, this was not enough. The task was to combine terror with law, suppression with responsibility, conquest with constitutionalism—a juxtaposition that I have called elsewhere 'colonial constitutionalism'.[8] Built on the physicality of the fact of rule was a discursive strategy of the colonial power to call the opposition to its rule, particularly subaltern opposition, as terror-driven, and to counterpose its norms of 'responsible governance' to the 'terrorist' methods of the opponents. These two techniques combined effectively in devising permanent exceptions, thereby making colonial rule a success. With colonialism thus began the paradox; we can in fact say that almost from the beginning of liberal jurisprudence, the world of juridical–political knowledge had taken a somersault. The distinctions between terror and terrorism, colonial rule and constitutionalism, control and freedom, security and democracy, individual guilt and collective punishment, and information and intelligence vanished as a result of this acrobatic feat. In this upturned world of juridical knowledge, the operation of law making had one important aim among several, namely, legally defining terror, that is to say, how to include some acts as acts of terror and omit others from that definition. This was the founding moment, self-foundation or otherwise, of law that has always held a fascination for philosophers who have chosen to comment on law. Primarily a legal task, but never completely legal because defining terror always depended on gathering of intelligence about militant opposition, the founding moment of law, as the nineteenth century history of India showed, was as much a mythological moment as a legal one, because each enactment depending on 'external sources' was marked with the fearful anticipation that this definition could soon prove inadequate calling for new necessities and new enactments in the wake of new attacks on the State.

Regulation III of 1818 was to be thus succeeded by many measures in the first part of the twentieth century including the Defence of India Rules. Law-making and terror-acts or terrorizing thus went hand in hand in colonial times.

It is not that the transition to post-colonial rule has not seen any discontinuity in this deployment of dual strategy. Indeed there has been one significant change in the form of the dual strategy. The legitimacy of the nation-state and nationalism now firmly established with the coming of the post-colonial state, the opposition to dominant power has become widespread, because the opposition can take everywhere a national form—the most particular yet the most universal—mass politics and democracy have similarly spread. In this situation, it is not enough for the dominant power to say that the opposition has resorted to terror; it is necessary for the State to construct a theory of terror, that is, 'terror-ism', to create a reality of an ideology as part of the warfare in which the state is engaged with its opposition. The development of the legal discourse in constructing a full-fledged theory of terrorism is evident in India. But then again, the beginnings go further back. Some can say that it has been always the same—in Roman times law led philosophy by the hand; in the long age of natural law this was again the case when despotic power accompanied the invocation of natural law; and now, in the age of positive law, defining terror and legally running a regime have become the twin tasks of a state. However, here too colonial history has substantive lessons to offer, as we shall soon see, by proving two tasks of statecraft important—making terror a subject of law and making intelligence operation (an exercise fundamentally beyond law) a crucial instrument in this exercise of legality. The second, I submit, was the more significant of the two. Intelligence gathering became critical because: (a) intelligence was a grey area in state operation, little controlled by law and norms of accountability; and (b) terror had become 'democratic', with the means of violence within reach of many, hate becoming widespread and opposition to rule deep—all these therefore requiring the state to gather greater and greater information about 'irresponsible opposition'. With each and every development of military technology of the superior powers, the terrorists were also learning new modes or using old modes in new ways—an equally potent revolution in military affairs, half-noticed and half-understood. Thus new techniques of gun-making, bomb-making, clandestine voyage, radio transmission, new organizational techniques, financial laundering, robbery, cryptography, and train-wrecking, combined with old forms like stabbing, beating, or strangling people to death using rope—fill the pages of intelligence files.[9] Terror became cost-effective and democratic. Therefore intelligence gathering became crucial. As a result, the spies of the government became the most hated objects of the militant nationalists or the early terrorists. Consequently, before law could pronounce certain truths, it was important for the colonial rule to find out who killed whom, when, where, and by what means—even now a key issue in military affairs relating to terrorism. The geography of fear and terror determined what Paul Virilio indicated much later as the 'open sky'—here, the ground and the waters are open to surprise attack, contestation for control, and capture. In attempting to understand the issue of terror in our political history in the background of perpetual war that marks it, we shall be also able to throw some light on how mass killing (by the rulers) and terrorism (selective killing by the nationalists) produced the same effect—hysteria—and spoke of the same pathology, same society, namely, a hysteric polity, which forgot kindness, which learnt to live only by the spirit of revenge, a polity which promised liberal institutions precisely at a time when massacres were a feature of the nights and days of this country for almost a year, 1947. As the future chroniclers of colonial rule, we can say that the 'age of terrorism' as defined by the colonial rule was also an age of hysteria because the pastoral form of power, which wanted to rest on a combination of care and punishment, could have never survived on a durable scale, and finally broke down. This was the permanent gift of the colonial past—the legal discourse on terror, and the techniques of terror and counter-terror were an indication that hysteria had become an integral part of democracy.

To understand the critical role that constitutional rule accorded to intelligence in the colonial period, we have to note the most important fact that this role had become strategic. Earlier, intelligence was for the king, for the benefit of his counsel, for selected things and targets, and its role was tactical. Now intelligence had become strategic, it called for analysis and recommendations on political goals.[10] Thus, the Intelligence Bureau published in colonial India two books which went beyond the simple goal of collecting information piecemeal on some individuals and activities, and presented strategic analyses on colonial security threatened by terrorist activities. The first, *Political Troubles in India: 1907-1917* by J.C. Kerr, Special Assistant to the Director of Criminal Intelligence from 1907 to 1913, was published in 1917, and the second compiled by H.W. Hale, specially deputed to the Intelligence Bureau for this purpose, in 1937 to cover the period between 1917 and 1937. With pride, Ewart, the then Director of the Intelligence Bureau stated on the latter, indicating at the same time the strategic role that intelligence was playing as a technology to buttress the colonial rule. 'The book in final form represents an immense amount of research among the scattered and defused contemporary records.'[11]

We can see the beginning of the very modern phenomenon whereby, in democratic countries, one after another, such as the US, the UK, or even India, intelligence people become the back-room boys of the administration.[12] The wisdom of the colonial administration enriched by the Irish, Indian, and similar experiences was a significant source of this development. Indeed Act XIV was enacted in India in 1908 on the advice of the intelligence officials. Likewise, in the promulgation of the Ordinance of 1924 and the Defence of India Rules intelligence advice was crucial. Again it was the intelligence community, something that took shape in India in the first quarter of the twentieth century, which began analysing the interface of the mass 'non-violent' movement and militant violence—a problem which exercises the CIA and the Israeli intelligence minds today. While the colonial political leadership was baffled at times by the strong mixing of the two currents, the intelligence report was busy in *analysing* the import of the inter-mingling of the two.[13] In 1932, R.E.A. Ray, Special Superintendent, IB, CID, prepared a 'Brief Note on the Alliance of Congress with Terrorism in Bengal', where he noted the progress made by the early terrorists in influencing mass non-violent movements with their ideas of militant nationalism. In 1921, he noted that terrorists had taken part in the Non-Cooperation Movement after coming out of prisons following the Royal Proclamation of December 1919. They then managed representation in the Bengal Provincial Congress

Committee in 1922. In 1923, they supported C.R. Das in the 'return for Mr. C.R. Das' connivance at the secret conspiracy'. The brief noted that the Swarajya Party led by C.R. Das was supporting the militant nationalist cause, and had begun opposing the 1924 Ordinance. And though Das died, with 'Mr. Subhas Chandra Bose succeed[ing] Mr. B.N. Sasmal, terrorists [had] regain[ed] representation in Congress Executive'. In this way, in 1928, the report noted that the Independence League was formed. And by 1929, the 'Complete Independence resolution [was] passed at Lahore.' With 1930, the report continued, both civil disobedience movements and terrorist campaigns began anew. The 'Jugantar Party' backed Subhas Bose. Ray's report cited many names in this connection, of persons who were denizens of the two worlds—the underground and the overground. The key part of Ray's report dealt with his analysis of 'Terrorists' views on their connection with the Congress'. It noted the popular nature of the issues related to civil liberty, ignored in the Gandhi–Irwin Pact of 1931. Prisoners were still in jail, hundreds were awaiting trial for years, many were not even 'charge-sheeted', there was large-scale detention without trial, several persons were being deported or interned, many were being executed, the situation was inflammable, and then the report tellingly cited a letter to Gandhi from an under trial accused in the Chittagong Armoury Raid to Gandhi in 1931:

> You cannot certainly deny the fact that in almost all the provinces the Congress programme has been worked out by the men most of whom have got violence as their policy in heart and especially in Bengal where the disobedience campaign has achieved the highest amount of success, ninety percent of the Congress workers are open revolutionaries to whom no doubt all the credit of the success goes.[14]

This letter could have been an intelligence ploy; but there is no doubt that the hawk's eyes were on strategic questions of politics.

In the same breath, intelligence officials, as we know, were *analysing* what political scientists today call the civil society organizations. Thus the Ramakrishna Mission,[15] Tagore's Santiniketan, Karmi Sangha, and many other institutions came under scrutiny. The author of the intelligence report on the Mission 'analysed' Vivekananda's teachings and his impact on the militant nationalist movement in a manner which anticipates in many ways that of the modern social scientists, and commented wryly in the report:

It will appear from the foregoing that there is evidence to show that the Ram Krishna Mission itself has been used in the past as a revolutionary agency, under the guise of religion and philanthropy, and that the greatest danger at the present time lies in the unaffiliated asrams which have grown up like mushrooms in the affected areas in Eastern Bengal without the knowledge or sanction of the headquarters mission at Belur. In fact Swami Vivekananda's command to go out and preach the gospel of Sri Ram Krishna and found branch asrams throughout India has been taken up by the revolutionaries in Bengal to such good effect that it is evident that even admitting the best intentions in the world, the authorities of the mission at Belur are unable to control them.[16]

Therefore all social forms that supported militant nationalism were to be put under the scanner. More significant is the way in which the analytic community was pointing out one of the chief indices of the popularity of a cause—the decentralized organizational set-up, the flexibility in the organization of war, and the myriad ways in which the party of war and contest permeated existing organizations and institutions. Historians of civil society would do well to take note of these when sketching out their ideas of the problematic of the civil/political in the anti-colonial political milieu where, contrary to their ideas of a neat division, everything was civil and at the same time everything was political. Seen in this light, and considering how counter-insurgency officials today concentrate on townships and settlements (destroying a town like Jenin or restructuring a rebellious city or university location as in Paris or Calcutta after the 1960s and 1970s which they consider as hotbeds of terrorism or militant protest, it should not seem strange that in colonial India intelligence officials besides investigating the Mission were also investigating the town structure of Benaras (Varanasi today) in order to understand how that town could patronise large-scale terrorist activities. The report began with wondering aloud that:

The position of Benaras as a centre of revolutionary activity is very similar to the position, which it holds in the religious life of the Hindu inhabitants of India. Whatever branch there be of Hinduism, there is practically none in which Benaras is not revered as a sacred city of great and mystic import. So also do we find that rarely has any conspiracy arisen in India, in which some connection with Benares [spelt thus in the original – author] has not been found out.

It is easy to explain how this is, for Benares is far more cosmopolitan than most Indian towns; and owing to continuous arrivals and departure of pilgrims, a stranger can visit and often stay quite long periods at Benares without arousing that curiosity with regard to himself and his private affairs, which though permissible according to Hindu manners and customs, seems so strange to the foreigner. Thus, it happens that during the last ten years or more during which special enquiries have been made into the revolutionary movement in India, we have found that Benares has often been used as a convenient meeting place and also as a harbour of refuge for absconders in political cause.

Enquiries at Benares have been fraught with difficulties, difficulties which in India are extra ordinarily hard to overcome. They lie principally in the difficulty of enquiry into the doings of persons of different nationalities by the local police. The various communities at Benares reside in particular *mahallas* and lead lives, which keep them peculiarly apart from the other citizens of Benares. Bengalitola, in and around which over ten thousand Bengalis reside, is completely self-contained and so, on a smaller scale, are the *mahallas* in which Mahrattas and Madrasis reside. Again there is the inevitable reluctance of the local police to probe among strangers, who apart from any source of profit they may be, have not caused them any trouble, and regarding whom strange officers in distant provinces are aggravatingly inquisitive and importunate for discussion.[17]

The report spoke of the visit of Tilak to Benaras in 1900, and noted the congenial atmosphere that the city offered to the 'Poona Party' 'so closely connected with the murders of 1897', and guessed that it was the 'Marhatta' connection that had led to the beginning of Bengali terrorist activities in the town. It mentioned various names and castes, and cited the instance of the founding of the Anusilan Samiti in Benaras by Sachaindra Nath Sanyal and Deo Narain Mukherji. The report dwelt at length on Basanta Kumar Biswas who had come to Benaras in 1910. Basanta was of course one of the illustrious names among the early terrorists of Bengal and the entire country. He was a member of Jugantar and was conspicuous for his organizational skills. He was also an important intermediary between the Calcutta office of the *Jugantar* and the 'co-conspirators' in Chandannagar. Basanta was very young when he started to work on his own in 1910, and was sent to Puri and eventually to Benaras where he was said to have taken shelter in Ramakrishna Mission. In 1911, he came into contact with Rash

Behari Bose, who was in Dehra Dun and who himself had been in close contact with Benaras. Basanta along with others had organized funds for the activities—something that came to light later in the Benaras Insurance Fraud case. Sachindra Sanyal and Rash Behari Bose, the two veterans, linked up the Bengali Diaspora in almost all major towns outside Bengal, principally Puri, Patna, Benaras, Dehra Dun, and Delhi, as the sustaining network for militant activities, and Basanta was one of the principal activists. Many other names occur in this strange story. Basanta's story comes to an end when he was finally apprehended and hanged subsequent to his conviction in the Delhi Conspiracy case in 1915.

Denham's report on Benaras is a part of the systematic gaze that the colonial rulers cast on the landscape of violence in the country, and read in detail tells us of the way in which the colonial state buttressed its law, order, and justice machinery by raising intelligence activity to the status of strategic necessity. Indeed, one can say, and things are possibly no different today, conspiracy cases, the main plank on which British counter-insurgency technology of justice was based, always depended on wholesale intelligence reports, true and fabricated, and only those that could build up the FIR in which conspiracy against the state acted like a framework of punitive verdict. We know, for instance, that Basanta was not given the death penalty in the lower court on the grounds of lack of sufficient evidence, but was hanged on appeal, on the strength of the case being presented as a 'conspiracy'. What is conspiracy? That, of course, the law does not define. Also, we have no select indices of it. In what precise way does it connect to sedition? Again we have no answer. Was the last emperor of a free country, Mughal India, guilty of conspiracy and sedition, and could he be deported under Regulation III of 1818?[18] Was he a subject of the British sovereign? To build up the factual–legal–mythological world of sovereignty, which could then form the basis for the entire law and justice machinery to work, the intelligence machinery provided the framework. In that sense intelligence has been to rule of law what epistemology has been to philosophy: the problems have to do with ways of knowing, making a meaning out of knowing, the meaning of knowledge. Rule must be backed by knowledge about its ways, means, consequences, and impediments. Intelligence must be built around a core of solid body of knowledge about the organizational style of the terrorists, the modus operandi of the activities such as political robbery, the decentralized functioning of the main groups, etc. Thus, a published government report titled 'Terrorist Conspiracy of Bengal, 1 April-31 December'[19] described in detail several organizational networks of the terrorists, and had significant implications for legislation to control and suppress terrorism, something we shall discuss shortly.

Thus, one of the crucial instruments of the colonial government in India, in this case the fortnightly summary of the situation based on reports of the zonal level police, intelligence officials, and the administrators and sent by the Chief Secretary of Bengal and Assam to the Government of India, was concerned with the crux of intelligence: *knowing, analysing, deploying—what has developed today as counter-intelligence, information and misinformation*[20]*—and finally strategizing.* Terrorists, at least the early terrorists, were the product of this discourse: they were conspirators, men (at times women) who walked the shadowy and the open worlds, gunrunners, dacoits, assassins, murderers, baboos, elites, Hindus (mostly), Bengalis and others duped by the Bengalis, infiltrators in Congress and other organizations of 'open society', men whose crimes had distinct relation with ordinary crimes. In this way, intelligence gathering had unknowingly contributed to one more significant aspect of the reality of political terror in society. A terrorist is one who has an 'identity' as a cause. This sets him apart from a democrat. A democrat fights for democracy, rights, and constitution. A terrorist fights for identity. In the build-up of the intelligence reports, we are repeatedly presented with the questions: Who is a terrorist? What are his marks?

III

We can see how the anticipated discussion on law is continuously deferred as we try to come to terms with its foundations. From its early days modern law had never freed itself from the identity trap, and always had to solve the question of identity in its framing, operation, and verdict, in terms of who are the breakers, who are the culprits, what are his/her intentions, who are the subjects, and given all these what is the gravity of any violation of law. No amount of objectivity has freed law from these questions, and so we find the colonial officials repeatedly asking, interrogating, and examining the biographical background of the terrorist. H.L. Salkeld, a magistrate on special duty and F.C. Daly, the DIG, Special Branch wrote on investigating and reporting procedure in exhaustive detail so that the government could break through the veil of secrecy and know who the deep dissenters were. Therefore, each year the colonial administration produced history sheets of persons and organizations, detailed their caste identities or caste basis, behavioural proclivity, and the dress, the look, the handwriting style, the manner of speaking. . . . So we have in government files the photograph of a baboo, of a coolie, of a terrorist-baboo, of a raider.[21] And then, as if the government wanted to resolve once and for all the enigma of who could be a terrorist, we find in the files pages and pages on a terrorist's love for death. Thus, for instance, the government wanted to know, why Charu Chandra Bose, who was hanged in 1909 and who had one useless hand, had joined the movement, why just a few days before he assassinated the public prosecutor in the Alipur Conspiracy case had he gone to a studio to photograph himself, why had he wanted to meet his relatives before his death, why he, a meek and silent person, had done 'this', and thus possibly solve the enigma of Charu's identity: 'About mid-day today (16 February 1909) Superintendent Ellis accompanied by Mr Percy visited the Alipore Jail, took three photos of the prisoner—one in his ordinary clothes, front—one in same, side and the third in his jail jangia (under-clothes) bare body exposing his arms'.[22] Even today the counter-insurgency experts who are engaged, for instance, in pacifying Palestine, have not solved the enigma of why a young woman, aged eighteen and a mother of two sons, photographs herself or allows herself to be photographed before she leaves on a mission? Who is a Palestinian terrorist, a Tamil terrorist, or a guerrilla of Peru?

Yet this search for a completely sure way of identifying a terrorist produced a continuously deferred result. I want to mention here the paradox latent in this search. The deeper the law-and-order machinery went into the politics and organizational existence of militant nationalism, and the more it sought to identify what it took to be the aberrations in the society it was ruling, the stronger was its need for special or extraordinary measures. And the more the measures went into operation with the certainty behind them that this time they would be successful, the greater would be the bafflement of the colonial officials at the continuous emergence of 'terrorists'. Hence the search would go on for an answer to the question: Who are these terrorists? As mentioned earlier, the Bengal Ordinance was important. The publication *Terrorist Conspiracy in Bengal* refers to the need for continuing Regulation III as a special measure, and the need for other special measures.[23] The Bengal Criminal Law Amendment Act of 1925 came close on the heels of the 1924 Ordinance. The government noted the appearance of what it termed as the 'New Violence Party'. It prepared yet another 'Memorandum on the History of Terrorism in Bengal'. It spoke of 'want of evidence' which justified the Revolutionary and Anarchist Crimes Act of 1919, preceded by the Indian Criminal Law Amendment Act XIV of 1908, because what was needed was a speedy, one-sided trial, 'where the accused shall not be present during an enquiry, unless the magistrate directs, nor shall be represented by a pleader during any such enquiry'. Section 15 of the Amendment Act said:

> If the Governor-General-in-Council is of opinion that any association interferes or has for its objects interference with the administration of the law or with the maintenance of the law and order, or that it constitutes a danger to the public peace, the Governor General-in-Council may, by notification in the official gazette, declare such association to be unlawful.

Several associations, the Samities in Bengal, were banned in January 1909 under this Section 15 (2 b), for instance the Suhrid Samiti in Mymensingh, Anushilan in Dhaka, Swadesh Sadhana Samaj (Mymensingh), Bandhab (Barisal), and Brati Samiti (Faridpur). And as the gloss of the Royal Proclamation of Amnesty in 1919 wore thin, Section 121 A of the IPC started to be invoked again to defeat 'waging war against the King' (Barisal Conspiracy Case); and two successive Bengal Criminal Law Amendment Acts came into effect in 1925 and 1930. In all these matters of understanding as to who were the terrorists and on the basis of that understanding recommending strong punitive measures, the most unambiguous was the decision of the Court of Commissioners constituted under the Defence of India Act, 1915, in the Lahore Conspiracy Case of 1916 (which included the bomb attack on the

Viceroy on 23 December 1912). The Commissioners spoke of terror as of '. . . dacoits, seduction of troops, villagers and students, manufacture and collection of arms and bombs, projected and accomplished attacks on railways, bridges, arsenals, and general communications, and finally projected as general uprising, which was to be the culminating act of war'; and then the Commissioners declared, 'We regard acts done up to July-August as acts of conspiracy to wage war; acts thereafter, when once the war had started as acts in furtherance of that war, and in abetment of such war.'[24] The Commissioners were severe—in the first case, of the eighty-two accused, seventy-eight faced trial, and of them twenty-four were sentenced to death and twenty-six were sentenced to transportation. Only five were acquitted. One was sentenced to death and promptly hanged in a separate case and had no opportunity to face the trial. In the second trial, seventeen were tried, of them one approver was pardoned, six were hanged, and five were transported for life. The colonial law identified terrorism and terrorists as the vital link between three phases of the militant anti-colonial upsurge in colonial India: (a) the attack on the Viceroy and the network of activities in Calcutta, Benaras, Dehra Dun, Delhi, and Lahore; and the Ghadar movement; (b) then the renewed phase of organization; and finally (c) the Hindusthan Socialist Republican Army (HSRA), and Bhagat Singh. By the third phase, the use of terror had become highly selective, the links with mass movements were stronger and the aim was to create a series of revolutionary movements to drive the British out of India, and the bombs were meant specifically 'to instil fear in the minds of the British official classes'. This was as the HSRA said, 'the philosophy of the bomb'.

The philosophy of the bomb had another import too—this time from the rulers' point of view. As William Vincent, Chairman of the Komagata Maru Committee Of Enquiry, raised and remarked on the 'question of firearms' being used in the Budge Budge incident; that Sikhs had used firearms, they had been armed and violent, and had refused to proceed to Punjab, that soldiers and police did not fire indiscriminately, and the evil influence of seditious literature was the root of the trouble. On the basis of all these, in the background of their Sikh identity, the report went into the details of each mutineer's identity, village, and the circumstances of his joining the revolt in Calcutta—Gurdit Singh, Daljit Singh, Narain Das, Jawahir Mull, Inder Singh, Sunder Singh, Kehar Singh, Suren Singh, Harnam Singh . . . the roll call goes on.[25] The issue was, and still is, access to arms. Clearly terrorists were those who challenged the colonial state's monopoly of the means of violence. Everything else could be ignored by the colonial state, tolerated, or postponed, but the fact that they were armed, they wanted access to arms, and were taking any step necessary to acquire arms, was singularly grave.

Hence, above all, the colonial discourse stressed the fact that the terrorist was an armed man, and all legal and penal provisions were directed at disarming him—beginning with finding out and choking the routes of the supply of arms to tracing the factors behind the widening of the skill in the manufacture of arms and drying it out, to stopping the intermingling of armed men with the unarmed population, to finally killing the armed man. It was nothing short of war. The attrition between the terrorists and the colonial state reflected at the most basic level in this war. The intelligence files, the will to legislate, and the litany of enactments, collectively this was the colonial state's unconscious. There we find evidences like deep fissures and fault lines of the exasperating situations over the decades, threatening the machinery of law and order and the project of colonial constitutionalism.

This was also a 'protracted war', marked by moments of tremendous violence, and though in the 1940s it seemed all a matter of mass movements only with isolated terrorist acts appearing, as in the days long past, the violence of 1942, 1945-6, and 1947-8 showed that the whole nation had become terrorist. Like the global war against terrorism today, then too the British administration switched and changed the personnel and tactics of rule in the colonies—primarily Ireland, India, and Sub-Saharan Africa, with Malay occasionally entering the picture. Exactly as in today's global war, then too communism, terrorism, and militant nationalism cast a long shadow over the empire. And exactly as now, law, violence, terror and the state formed a phalanx against angry populations. And exactly as now, the military factor did not count alone, much to the dismay of the early terrorists. It was law with its strategy of permanent exceptions that tilted the balance, so much so today, when people in independent India read the provisions of freedom's laws in the Indian Constitution and come across phrases like security, public order, public morality as the legitimate exceptions to the freedom's laws,[26] they rarely look back and think of the very particular military and juridical origins of these exceptions which lie deep in the provisions of the IPC, CRPC, and all other major enactments of security dating back to the early nineteenth century.

It is instructive then to understand how the identity question in hard politics is perched on an extremely contentious process. Defining a terrorist is a product of contentious politics. Also linked with this realization is another lesson, namely, beneath identification and definition lies a process of law, the act of legislating, and the dynamics of 'preparing the brief' which includes calculations of war, punishment, analysis, intelligence operation, knowledge of the enemy, capacity and the means to terrorize those who want to oppose the rule, and ways and means to disarm an entire population. It was as a part of the preparation of this brief that the Criminal Investigation Department (CID) came into existence in 1906. The provincial special branch was expanded and upgraded as the Special Branch in 1910. Armed constabulary was organized along Irish lines. Laws and other measures were enacted. This has therefore been always a game of roulette: the attributes have to be defined in order to define a person; the attributes can be defined only when the situation has been defined; the situation can be defined only when it has been summed up in an exact way, that is, in a juridical way; the juridical essence of a situation can be summed up only when the situation has been properly analysed by observing the person of the terrorist. Thus, rules of organization building, behaviour, the 'modus operandi', 'enticement of minors and young boys', spreading 'ideas' and increasing the capacity of their 'reception', all were under the scanner of J.E. Armstrong when he sat down to report on who were the likely terrorists and terrorist organizations. Everything was to be found out, if necessary by torture, so that everything could be put under the scanner. While in pre-colonial times torture meant either the divine necessity of securing a confession, or satisfying Nature, or an expression of the pure retribution of the throne (impalement, for instance), torture now became linked with securing information on a systematic scale. Added to this was the urge of the colonial rule to present the terrorist to the society of 'peace-loving' subjects as an inherently unruly, rogue element who needed to be exemplarily punished.[27] Torture was in this way the deep voice of law. At times even the law could not recognize its own voice, so deep it was. Torturing the terrorist then, as now, was essential for the law to operate. It was the signature of the sheer physicality of the colonial world.

Particular identity and particular acts made up the world of terrorism—a terrorist and the terrorist acts. The Intelligence Bureau of the Home Department of the Government of India summed up the rigmarole in 1937 thus:

> Terrorism as distinct from other revolutionary methods, such as Communism or the Ghadr movement may be said to denote the commission of the outrages of a comparatively individual in [*sic*] nature. That is to say the terrorist holds the belief that Indian Independence can best be brought about by a series of revolutionary outrages calculated to instil fear into the British official classes and to drive them out of India. He commits other outrages for the purpose of arms, for the making of bombs and for the maintenance of his party, hoping that the masses will be drawn to his support either by fear or admiration.[28]

Even though it may surprise us to learn how little of this physical world was reflected in the legal history of the colonial rule, yet these laws were like the hardened crust of earth and foam that enormous convulsions leave from time to time. It began with Regulation III of 1818 for the detention of suspects. Act I of 1900, known as the Press Act, was passed to regulate the publication of newspapers and other printed material, and to contain sedition and seditious literature. The Defence of India (Consolidation) Rules of 1915 conferred wide powers on the government to detain people on the grounds of anti-government activities. The infamous Rowlatt Act found its new form in the Indian Penal Code (Amendment) Act No. XVI of 1921; it amended Sections 121 and 122 of the Code. The Criminal Law Amendment Act of 1925 strengthened the ordinary criminal laws; close on its heels came the Bengal Suppression of Terrorist Outrage Act of 1932. Police circulars became more detailed. For instance, one such circular suggested that police evidence alone was enough at times for a *prima facie case*; reports were to be exact, meaning it was enough if they were streamlined in terms of the format. The Explosive Substances Act and Arms Act were pointed out as provisions under which culprits could be booked.

Can we say that this was just a pure process of repetition? At one level, there were more laws, more powers, more incidents—but repetition of the moves was essentially the name of the game. At another level, the process was also producing difference. Each incident was new, each new legalized power was to contain a new phenomenon, each new militant act was a variation, and each new action was producing a new effect—the difference was affirming the validity of terror in politics. The power of this affirmation at the heart of repetition and difference resembled a classic Deleuzean scene, where resistance was taking on a micro-character, and while law held sway, order remained intact, yet with myriad terrorist acts (at an individual level, micro level), mutiny had become a virtual reality.[29]

IV

The modern terrorist, more precisely of the early terrorists, appears at the junction of two broad stages of warfare. This is another major window which offers us glimpses of the political–legal world of terrorism, and I propose to mention this very briefly at this stage. The seventeenth century had already shown, in many cases, new signs of total war. Absolutism made war a part of politics, and wherever there was absolutism, militarism flourished with new military regulations, rules, new ways of requisitioning provisions, large-scale forced labour for the army, new and massive punishment methods, and new military formations such as the light infantry. These developments became clear with two new phenomena—revolutionary wars and the beginnings of industrial warfare. Colonial war organization bore some of these trademarks. Against colonial war organization was a population which had been systematically disarmed through several expeditions and conquests.

Between 1757 and 1914, the colonial powers took over the world by disarming the rest. State finances were mobilized to produce armies which beat the adversaries. The colonial conquest began with the systematic disarming of the kingdoms and empires in eastern Europe and Western Asia. Armed irregulars of the Ottoman Empire were soon defeated. By 1757, Western-style infantry, new techniques of siege and storm with attacking explosives, and unified command proved better than the military capabilities of the countries that were invaded. In India, the colonial army improved in the wars against the two kings of Mysore between 1767 and 1799 where it could finally win with superior resources and Marhatta assistance. The test was even more severe in the second Anglo–Marhatta war between 1803-5. The Maratha infantry was equally skilled. And in the punitive expeditions in the north-west, the limits of the Western-style military campaigns became apparent. As guerrilla campaigns erupted in many places, counter-insurgency measures became harsh and at times, even genocidal. Clan, village, religion, and other ties were crucial in sustaining the wandering resistance. In the Indian Mutiny, for instance, after the fall of Delhi scattered groups of mutineers fought on in an atmosphere of several minor revolts: insurgent armies withdrew in the face of the colonial army's assault (as in Lucknow) only to reappear as guerrilla bands. Yet, suppression of the guerrillas, at least temporarily, was possible because of the weaker means of political organization of the insurgents, scanty foreign help for them, repeated famines, and the destruction of kingdoms. The insurgents failed repeatedly, while the colonial army and administration wrecked the ability of the insurgents with superior organization, industrial technologies, superior formation of the armies, sustaining supply lines, and better legal ability to stabilize a volatile situation. This situation, we can note, changed only after 1945, when guerrilla movements were bolstered by massive popular support, improved firepower, and a compelling political vision of nationalism.[30]

The modern terrorist appears at this conjuncture of the old and new stages of war. He is anti-colonial, a national vision has inspired him, he is modern, he is educated, he knows the importance of firepower, he organizes in a new way, his notion of justice is deep, and he knows what modern law is and how the colonized are always at the receiving end of the law. He has emerged from the debris of destroyed institutions, ties, and histories. He knows that the least thing he can do in the beginning is to put terror in the hearts of these new rulers. His past has left him with no other weapon but terror. He has emerged wherever colonialism has made its appearance. In Algeria, Ireland, Serbia, Turkey, Egypt, India,

Palestine, Sudan, Peru, and in many other countries—in fact, across the globe terrorism marks the history of modern colonialism and modern nationalism. Early terrorists are the early nationalists, and the history of the emergence of the national movement in India has to be revised in that light.

The greatest contribution by the terrorist to the war between the colonizer and the colonized was that he did not allow the dust to settle. Each rule in the past, more so a colonial rule, was haunted by the fear that violence had slipped through its structure of lids, and that the carnage that had accompanied the rule had brutalized the society over which it was ruling so much that civility would be extremely difficult to restore. Therefore the grammar of rule has always included techniques of restoration, most desirably through an impartial agency like law. The apocalyptic post-carnage vision of each regime, in this case the colonial regime, has to legitimate past violence and de-legitimate present violence by creating myths of the peaceableness of the population, rulers, and even the army.[31] Like violence, this myth too usually has a long pedigree, unsullied and untouched by long memories of riots, violence, carnage, and large-scale deaths. Ethnic myths acquire power in this context. The terrorist upsets this scheme, therefore, he is barbaric. In contrast to the peaceable rule and peaceable society, the terrorist is violent and schizophrenic, bent upon intoxicating the public mind with sudden frenzy and madness. The terrorist is a menace to the normalizing mission of rule. Therefore, each landmark in the project of colonial constitutionalism bears two characteristics: first, a recognition that the rule has to be responsible to the people being ruled; and second, those who are being ruled must grow up, cease to be infantile, and behave and act responsibly, that is, with responsibility towards this peaceable society and the rule. Indeed this legal exercise plays an important role in recreating and sustaining the myth whose function is to suppress the fright and scare that mark the society and the rulers. What happens when the terrorist makes his mark? The John Bulls with vulgar swagger of course reappear, but more significant is the fact that the figure of the terrorist is used to terrorize the society, to teach them constitutionalism, to tell the population that peaceable as they are, their path is not violence but peace: the dream path Kant had taught the rulers long ago was the constitution.

It is difficult to say who wins in this tussle—the street or the constitution. It is equally difficult to predict if at all the constitution by reworking the myths of peace is able to help the population to overcome the fear of the violence of the state and the nation. We can only say this much that in this discourse of responsibility that is at the core of constitutionalism, historical continuities are present. All that which alarmed the colonial rulers, alarms the rulers of the independent nation too. Nehru was weary of the word 'satyagraha', C. Rajagopalachari was emphatic that government must demonstrate intolerance towards 'lawlessness', that one must not demand the same amount of evidence in judging terrorist crime as one demanded in the case of ordinary crime, and that there was and should remain a divide—between the patriots and the citizens, and the traitors and anti-nationals.[32]

The position that the terrorist therefore occupies in the history of warfare revolves around a set of issues which the myth of peaceable society and peaceful rulers hides: what is extreme violence and how are we to understand it? What makes singular acts of violence scarier than a process of genocide? What are the problems in the characterization of violence in politics? What is meant when it is said that terrorism is total violence? But it is beyond the scope of this paper to discuss these issues in detail. Perhaps there are no general answers. However, in so far as these issues throw light on the unique position that the anti-colonial terrorist occupies in the role of warriors and terrorism in the history of warfare, we can make some observations.

First, we can note that terrorism in the discourse on extreme violence is equated with torture, rape, genocide, ethnic cleansing, and other forms of mass killings. The notion of 'extreme violence' with which the terrorist is associated, and the knowledge of which has passed on from the files of administrators and other colonial officials to the work of social scientists today, has a lot to do with fatigue. For instance, Hannah Arendt, who was clearly suffering from fatigue from what she called 'total violence', thought that there was no juridical–political remedy to violence beyond a point. She never explained what she meant by extreme violence, except by alluding to the involvement of the entire society and its unhesitating commitment to violence. It is remarkable that she opposed the violence in the US university campuses against the Vietnam War on the grounds that it went against constitutionalism It is a kind of deep, beyond-history abyss in which the terrorist is dumped with other actors of violence. In this pit, Khudiram and Eichman stand together. 'Extreme violence', with which the terrorist is associated is one that is offensive to our sense of civility, humanity, and political existence. The terrorist does not carry the cultural and historical representations of violence, he is unique in every way; he is pure evil.[33]

Secondly, in this bottomless beyond-history pit where we find the terrorist there is no distinction between different kinds of killings—killings to subjugate, to destroy, to eradicate, to make a mark, to free, to enslave. Yet it is important to differentiate between the destruction processes in the act of killing—not to honour, which may be legitimate or not, but to see the way violence features in society—because behind the seemingly individual acts of destruction that the terrorist symbolizes are the collective processes of permission, organization, and commemoration, which show that the terrorist is the civilian–warrior crossing the liberal divide between the civilian population and the armed forces, a divide the ICRC never tires of emphasizing.

Third, the aporia that the established discourse of violence faces in understanding terrorism is because of the social preference for consensus, a sort of 'democratic weakness' that de-historicizes all that we dislike. Terrorist acts are looked upon as acts of 'total violence' because they violate social preferences. As Isabelle Sommier notes, 'Terrorism spontaneously evokes excess, radicality, and disproportion between the end and the means'.[34] The League of Nations defined 'terrorism' as 'all criminal acts directed against a State and intended or calculated to create a state of terror in the minds of particular persons or a group of persons or the general public'.[35] Thus, here too we find that the historical problems of legitimacy are erased. In lieu of those problems, we find three issues of 'concern' pervading the discourse: planned annihilation of people, using death as the instrument, and lack of moral outrage at acts of terrorism. These concerns produce the *Terrorist* who is a *fanatic*, whose fanaticism becomes the subject of behavioural studies in advanced conflict study and behavioural sciences projects and centres. Hatred, fanaticism, and infatuation with death become trans-historical subjects requiring investigation. Scared by the nationalist fury evident in so many uprisings, historians write of the history of (occasionally the reigns of) terror, violence, and of fanaticism. One of the densest historical subjects, the terrorist, becomes the mythic figure of fury. The myth consumes the actor also. Thus the Russian revolutionary, Sergei Nechaev, who perished in the Tsar's prison in 1882 wrote: 'We are guided by hatred of all those who are not of the people. . . . We have an utterly negative project that no one can alter: complete destruction.' And Bakunin admiring Nechaev wrote, 'They are magnificent, those young fanatics, believers without a God and heroes without flowering rhetoric.'[36]

A material study of war, warfare, and warriors will show that as financial, technological, managerial, and industrial factors become more crucial and violence is de-historicized, figures of war vanish, as if everything is now a matter of thinking, and force has disappeared from politics. In this scenario, the history of colonialism, which allows us to revisit the possibilities that this history showed—not of suppressing force, but turning it against itself—is the best way to bring our feet back on the ground.

A sense of history is important finally because it helps us to understand better the juridical project that any regime has. All historical forms of rules have inequality, but what is different and particular to the modern form of rule is that it proclaims equality as its objective and claims that it can achieve it. Thus equality of law, equality before law, equality in the marketplace, equal rights, etc., are the great principles on which constitutionalism stands. The freedom's laws that the constitutions include now as matter of habit are the high symbolic gesture of acknowledgement of the principle of equality. Yet, and for the first time, the legal definition of terrorism and its juridical invocation introduces the possibility of a constitutional sanction of inequality—on the basis of a person's or group's association with violence (other inequalities were matters of deficit) —thereby making some citizens, some half-citizens, and some outlaws on whom freedom's laws are not conferred. This becomes a new way to define citizenship—earlier gender, property, education, status, identity were the criteria, which constitutionalism long ago discarded. Now two tests become crucial—territorial location in the form of national identity and identification with violence. The refugee or the non-state person (association with location) and the terrorist (association with violence), become the two great outsiders to the promised world of citizenship, that is, equality. While the relation between the immigrant and equal citizenship is of a more recent origin,[37] the political fact of association with violence as one of the disqualifications for citizenship is older. The strategy of 'extraordinary exceptions' that colonial constitutionalism initiated has produced the legal sanction for turning people into half-citizens and non-citizens for whom the world of citizenship holds no promise. We can see how the organic quality of nation has depended from the beginning on inheriting one of the essential features of pre-national political formations—armed rulers and unarmed peasantry. In terms of liberal polity it has meant that those associated with violence will be disqualified from citizenship. The disqualification began with the colonial strategy of creating permanent exceptions.

We can thus suggest here a rereading of the history of citizenship. In the received history, citizenship is associated with achievement of rights. In the suggested rereading, a complicated scenario emerges. Some are not granted citizenship, or would soon be deprived of it because of their association with violence. The curve of militancy that went up via popular mobilization comes down with grant of citizenship. Armed people cannot have the right to vote. A permanent disqualification in the form of exceptions to freedom's laws appears. Constitution making in the independent country therefore has depended to a great extent on colonial laws and enactments which foresaw who were to be disqualified. This is admittedly a reading based on the reality of passive revolution that independence through the specific route of decolonization has been to the once colonial countries.

The terrorist is the first outlaw of a polity based on liberal legal principles.[38]

V

We must return to the issue of law once again. As indicated earlier, the colonial legal strategy, in order to exclude some from the rule of law, depended on making *responsibility* the cornerstone of the legislating exercise. To talk of law is thus to talk of responsible government. Responsibility was the principle that was being defined at different levels and purposes.

James Bovard has shown in detail how in the United States, after the events of 11 September 2001, the Patriot Act was hurried through Congress contravening all subcommittee and committee rules of drafting and hearing, and bamboozling the dissenters and sceptics into silence by invoking day in day out the need to be responsible for the lives of countless Americans. The state was responsible for the lives of its citizens, therefore it needed to be armed, and it had to be given powers that could override the rule of law.[39] In this strategy, as in many other respects, the colonial experience was the predecessor.

What makes the Indian colonial experience particular is that the principle of responsibility was laced with three elements of a constitutional design which worked as both inclusive and exclusive strategies: the parliamentary system, the federal structure, and the basic civil and criminal laws providing the backbone of the administrative system. All three elements proved durable and were left practically untouched by the new constitution of independent India. It all began with the exercise of 'regulating acts' by the Home Government on the basis of which local governments and subordinate governments were set up. That remained the essential design, which meant that while the basic structure was provided from above, local participation at the bottom was allowed gradually. Rule of law also demanded that de-linked from commercial interests as well as direct imperial interest, a form of government be found that would look like one of Indians, albeit with the help of some Englishmen ruling India or who were being trained to rule India. The passage from the Company's rule to rule by the British emperor, that is, rule of the constitutional government at 'Home', was the first step towards rule of law, and it came only with suppression of the Mutiny, which had been to the colonial rule the most terrorizing and horrific act by the Indians in that century. Already the Governor-General-in-Council by the Act of 1833 (Section 85) to take steps to mitigate the state of slavery, and to provide by laws and regulations for the protection of the 'natives' from insult and outrage to their persons, religions, and opinions. Macaulay furthered the vision of rule of law by saying:

. . . For all the evils . . . the Ministers of the Crown are as much to blame as the Company—nay, much more so. For the Board of Control could, without the consent of the Directors, have redressed those evils; and the Directors most certainly could not have redressed them without the consent of the Board of Control. . . . It may be the public mind of India may expand under our system till it has outgrown that system; that by good Government we may educate our subjects into a capacity for better Government; that having become instructed in European knowledge, they may in some future age demand European institutions. Whether such a day will ever come I know not. But never will I attempt to avert or to retard it. Whenever it comes, it will be the proudest day in English history. [40]

We can see how the multilayered politics of responsibility was building up: the Crown was responsible for good governance; the Company was responsible to the Home Government; the Government was responsible for initiating Indians into self-governance and good governance, and the Indians were responsible for their self-education. Terrorism and mutiny were the evils that aimed to destroy this scheme; hence they had to be suppressed without mercy. Rule of law demanded the suppression and the destruction of the evils of violence. Rule of law also demanded that the regulations be transformed into law. The Bengal Regulations had been extended with some variations to the North-Western Provinces. These Regulations were clumsy and intricate where administration was not detailed and was rickety. In the Non-Regulation provinces and districts, too, a mass of executive orders were turned into law. Executive legislation, the usual way in which extraordinary measures originate, has thus an ancient beginning.

The thrust was towards codification, which meant the consolidation of rule. The Regulation of 1781 (Impey's Civil Code) satisfied in anticipation the principle of the 'cognoscibility of law', that is, the law should be capable of being known by persons whose rights and duties it determined—a principle that Bentham was to stress later. A Code of Regulations needed the Courts of Justice who could provide redress against infringement of the Regulations. By the Act of 1797, Parliament sanctioned legislation and codification by the Governor-General-in-Council. *The Code of Gentoo Laws and Ordinations of the Pundits* (1775) was the beginning; *Judicial Regulations* (1772-1806) followed it. Then came John Herbert Harington's three volumes of *An Elementary Analysis of the Laws and Regulations* (1805-17). Princep's *Abstract of the Civil Judicial Regulations* was published in 1829. And thinkers like Bentham and Mills, who were powerless or unwilling to change the lot of their own country, concentrated their energy on constitutional experiments in the colony. Indeed Bentham wrote an essay, *On the Influence of Time and Place in Matters of Legislation* with the object of considering what modifications were required in transplanting his system of law codes to a colony.[41] No wonder all these thinkers honed their skill, in liberal reforms during their stint at the India House.

Section 53 of the Act of 1833 upheld, 'such laws as may be applicable in common to all classes of inhabitants . . . of the regard being had to the rights, feelings, and particular usages of the people, should be enacted; and . . . all laws and customs having the force of law . . . should be ascertained and consolidated, and, as occasion may require, amended'.[42] The power of making laws and amending was vested in the Governor-General-in-Council, and the task of ascertaining 'all laws and customs having the force of law' was entrusted to a Law Commission. Thus the First Law Commission came into existence. It was required by Section 53 of the Act of 1833 to streamline laws and provisions regarding administration of justice and police establishments, all forms of judicial procedure, the nature of operation of all laws—civil and criminal—and suggest necessary alterations in the interests of rule of law. As can be expected, Macaulay compared the work of the Indian Law Commission with that of the Code Napoleon. Law was to be concise and lucid—we can see the reason for the frenzied search in the next hundred years for a precise definition of terror, different crimes, and precise punishment. Even acts were divested of their names. The work on the Penal Code started around the same time, 1837. The Second Law Commission formed in 1853 assigned priority to a 'simple system of pleading and practice uniform as far as possible, throughout the whole jurisdiction . . . which is also capable of being applied to the administration of justice in the inferior courts of India'. The work of the Commission was transferred from Calcutta to London. On the basis of its recommendations, forwarded by the 'Home Government', the Legislative Council passed in 1859 the Code of Civil Procedure, in 1860 the Penal Code, and in 1861 the Code of Criminal Procedure. The High Courts Act came in 1861. The same year the Third Law Commission was appointed 'to prepare for India a body of substantive laws, in preparing which the law of England should be used as a basis'; and as if this was not enough, the Fourth Law Commission recommended in 1879 that, 'English law should be made the basis in a great measure of our future Codes, but', as a concession to the colonized, it said, 'its material should be recast rather than adopted without modifications . . . in recasting those materials due regard should be given to Native habits and modes of thoughts'.[43] And what was that English law? It was, to say the least, developing in response to factors such as the situation in the colonies and wars of annexation, which required repeated raising of money and men, recurrent famines in the Isles, internal religious quarrels and conflicts, the Irish situation, the challenge of the Chartists, in past encounters with republicans and present encounters with poverty, vagabondage, destitution, and industrial unrest, so much so 'the number of offences in Britain commanding death penalty by the end of the eighteenth century amounted to more than 200 (with) little wonder that the criminal statutes were known collectively as "The Bloody Code"'.[44]

When large-scale mutiny after 1857 became impossible for close to another three quarters of a century, and the populations had been completely disarmed, also with the relentless institution through legal means, as described earlier, of an armed-to-the teeth colonial administration, terror in the incipient nationalist politics became the signature of the milieu; indeed, terror was the only way to become national in politics in opposition to the responsible politics of graded constitutionalism that colonialism was ushering in. The structure of administration initiated by Lord Ellenborough was in place by 1843 with separate 'Home' and Military departments besides Foreign and Finance. District administration was strengthened. Regulations were issued to set up a body of commissioners to take up municipal and police functions, as in Calcutta. The judicial administration was bolstered at the bottom by the union of the magistrate and the collector. The colonial administration was embarrassed at this, but it served them well. As we know, the union of judicial and police functions continued long after India became free. Equally important was the creation of the Civil Service whose members, as Rivers

Thompson, the Lieutenant-Governor of Bengal, observed in 1883, 'have abandoned caste, [they] have surrendered religious feelings, [they] have broken family ties and set themselves against the devout sentiments and doctrines of their ancient creeds', [45] and selected on the basis of competition and produced through special training, they became, along with the judges, the police officers, intelligence officials, and the army generals, the main elements of the framework of rule that stabilized the empire shaken repeatedly by a thousand mutinies, revolts, and terrorist outbursts. Again we must note that the strength of the framework was that it was *legal*; a hundred years of law-making in this enterprise was as essential as other critical aspects of colonial rule. We have no reason to be surprised by this, because in classic liberal thinking reform had been one of the essential virtues. Reforming the society and punishing the culprits was one of the great tasks of the liberal enterprise in India—therefore setting up a police force, courts, and jails was more important than setting up schools and colleges.[46]

The impregnable administrative massif that the nationalist warrior would face was partly a result of the transfer of power from the Company to the Crown—in many ways as significant as the much better-known transfer of power about a century later. It meant direct control of the colonial power, a ruthless transplantation of modes of politics prevalent in the 'Home' country; for example, with a cabinet mode of governing which had little to do with parliament, and more to do with a centraliszd executive mode led by the Governor-General-in-Council. Thus Lytton kept secret his Afghan War and annexation of Upper Burma; similarly, under Kitchener, the most prodigious centralization of all armed forces took place in 1909; and Canning candidly admitted it should mean 'paramount authority of the head of the government'.[47] Princes became practically feudatories. The transfer of power further meant that the Anglo-Saxon legal system was founded here, resulting in, as mentioned earlier, Law Commissions, plus the Penal, Criminal, and other Codes and Acts. By the same token, with the Indian Councils Act of 1870, all regulations for 'peace and good government' became parts of basic laws.

The transfer of power brought centralization in the administrative and social sphere. The result could be seen when the first signs of organized terrorism against colonial rule became evident. Lord Minto, the co-author of the 'liberal' Morley–Minto proposals initiated repressive laws and quartered the military and the punitive police in an unprecedented manner in the service of what he termed as 'Law and Order'. The legislative councils, particularly the Imperial Legislative Council, in their composition were to be rid of the 'influence of the professional classes', the breeding ground of protest politics and terrorism. It was only in this way that in 1915 the Defence of India Act with its provision of Special Tribunals was rushed through the Council in a single sitting. This was in the footsteps of the Defence of the Realm Act passed in England. The Special Tribunals became notorious. Immediately, at Lahore twenty-four persons were sentenced to death, although only six had been found guilty of murder.

The other significant transfer of power came in the form of the shifting of the capital from Calcutta to Delhi. With the institution of Lieutenant-Governorships and Chief Commissionerships provinces were strengthened, and though the Bengal Partition was annulled, the country had been reorganized at one stroke. With the reorganized administrative structure of British India, the honing of an electoral policy along communal lines, the centralization of laws and codification, and the successful organization of a stable military force, colonial rule was now ready to face the militant nationalist threat. It could now take its time and say, as Curzon as a member of Lloyd George's coalition cabinet had indeed said, that its goal was 'to ensure progressive realization of responsible government in India as part of the British Empire' and the British Dominion.[48] The Rowlatt Committee's Report was only one evidence, though the best known, of this strategy.

The Defence of India Act of 1939 has to be seen in this light. By Article 2, it conferred on the government almost unlimited emergency powers to prevent, among others, 'any attempt to tamper with the loyalty of the persons in, or to dissuade from entering the services of His Majesty', 'acquisition or possession without lawful authority or excuse and publication of information likely to assist the enemy', and to prohibit besides meetings and rallies 'the possession, use or disposal of explosives, inflammable substances, arms and ammunitions of war . . . transmission of ciphers and other secret means of communicating information . . .', and prevent 'disclosure of official secrets', etc. The Indian Official Secrets Act was reinforced in this Act, by Article 6. The Indian Press (Emergency Powers) Act of 1931 and the Indian Aircraft Act and the Indian Navy Discipline Act, both of 1934 were similarly reinforced. Chapter 3 of the Defence of India Act reinforced the policy of setting up Special Tribunals for summary trial. In many ways it was the predecessor of the Defence and Internal Security of India Act, passed by independent India's government in 1971. Other subsequent legislations, such as the Terrorist Activities Detention Act (TADA) and the Prevention of Terrorism Act (POTA) also followed the same path. In a strategy to control what is now considered to be a particular variety of terrorism, that is, 'cross-border terrorism', many safeguards against flouting the provisions of rule of law were ignored. Thus, Under Section 18 of POTA, the central government can list any group as a terrorist organization not only for committing acts of terrorism but also for 'promoting' or 'encouraging' terrorism or terrorist groups. POTA also allows the police to file the charge sheet within one year, and once it is done, the accused can remain in judicial custody for years. The names of witnesses may not be disclosed to the accused. It allows confessions extracted through interrogation while the accused is in custody (thus torture) to be used against him/her as evidence. Since the accused remains in police custody, the provision of a magistrate deciding on the veracity of the confession becomes meaningless. In the same way the Armed Forces (Special Powers) Act followed the Armed Forces (Special Powers) Ordinance, 1942—an Act, as we know, the Supreme Court refused to strike down because it did not think that it was a violation of fundamental rights; it was only a reasonable restriction on due grounds, though the Court directed in 1997 that the armed forces had to follow a guidelines of a specific set of rules (for instance, they cannot interrogate suspects but must hand them over to the civilian police). One can see in this background of the history of the basic legal structure that while the earlier special laws were built on a fundamental reality of race inequality, by the time Indian gained independence, these legislations had become a deep a part of basic laws—so deep that it was now essential to retain them to prevent a volatile India from exploding. Many techniques of race rule had been thus internalized and naturalized.[49]

In a situation marked by mass discrimination and misery, an unarmed population, a revolutionary intelligentsia, a massively organized apparatus of coercion of people with elaborate legal arrangements of governing, destruction of earlier organizations of rule, and an atmosphere of conspiracy, we have, in brief, conditions that gave rise in the colonial days to the relevance of terror in politics; these conditions are also to be found in many parts of the world long after colonialism has departed. Also to be found are the marks of the continued legacy of the colonial technique of permanent exceptions, which meant in the main incarceration, summary trial, execution, certain specific forms of terrorization and torture, confiscation, and collective punishment. Thus, in the light of what has been discussed thus far, the following questions arise, often ignored in the massive literature on terrorism:

1. Who terrorises whom, yet who becomes a terrorist?
2. How does terror become relevant to politics?
3. Are all terrors same; do they belong to the same category?
4. What is then effaced when terror is substituted by the word 'terrorism'?
5. What then is the function of law?
6. How does law relate to terror?
7. What roles do intelligence and analysis play in this?
8. Why indeed does law need terror (as an occasion and as instrument) to develop itself?

These eight questions gain great significance in the light of the history that has been outlined here of 'permanent exceptions' as part of a rule of law. This is no doubt a colonial history. Also we have to admit that protest politics in independent India has forced the state to discontinue many of these, though it is equally true, that meanwhile, other new forms of extraordinary legislations and measures have appeared. Terrorism, as it was then, still remains a legal product.

Yet, is there nothing more to terror as part of politics? This is where I think that we need to reflect a little more and find out what remains unconsumed and un-exhausted even after the nearly two-century long will to legislate.

VI

Although terror has been seen mostly as individual, scattered, and demonstrative acts of hatred, revenge, sacrifice, redemption, and various millenarian ideas, yet in the light of the history of terror in colonial India we need to look at some of the less noticed dimensions of the issue we are discussing here. Briefly, these dimensions relate to the nature of collective action and collective violence; these dimensions also reflect on the way in which the colonial state and the law perceived collective actions. Until we look at the collective nature of the act and learn to differentiate one form of terror from another, our understanding will remain at the primitive level—like the way we view the early nationalist/early terrorist as a sort of primitive rebel—and we shall continue to see acts of terror as a singular mass, an enigma, given only to psycho-social knowledge and behavioural studies. The voluminous outpourings of such studies on terrorism have only reinforced the myth of the terrorist as an angry man (and today the woman as well). Indeed Martha Crenshaw has written:

> Terrorism per se is not usually a reflection of mass discontent or deep cleavages in society. More often it represents a disaffection of a fragment of the elite, who may take it upon themselves to act on behalf of a majority unaware of its plight, unwilling to take action to remedy grievances, or unable to express dissent. . . . This discontent, however subjective in origin or minor in scope, is blamed on the government and its supporters. . . .
>
> Given some sources of disaffection—and in the centralised modern state with its faceless bureaucracies, lack of responsiveness to demands is ubiquitous—terrorism is an attractive strategy for small organizations of diverse ideological persuasions who want to attract attention for their cause, provoke the government, intimidate opponents, appeal for sympathy, impress an audience, or promote the adherence of the faithful. Terrorists perceive an absence of choice. Whether unable or unwilling to perceive a choice between terrorist and non-terrorist action, whether unpopular or prohibited by the government, the terrorist group reasons that there is no alternative. The ease, simplicity, and rapidity with which terrorism can be implemented and the prominence of models of terrorism strengthen its appeal, especially since terrorist groups are impatient to act. Long standing social traditions

that sanction terrorism against the state, as in Ireland, enhance its attractiveness.

There are two fundamental questions about the psychological basis of terrorism. The first is why the individual takes the first step and chooses to engage in terrorism: why join? Does the terrorist possess specific psychological predispositions, identifiable in advance, that suit him/her for terrorism? [50]

The problem is squarely one of a failure to see the relation between collective action and an act of terror, and looking at it as purely an individual act. But the history that I have sketched above shows the following:

- What we consider loosely as 'terrorism' is not so much individual acts, as continuing acts of violence around persistent boundaries such as between the colonizers and the colonized, or any other persistent deep differences.
- Equally continuing is the mixture, or at least the striking conjunction, of large-scale public displays of force such as revolt, attack, mutiny, non-cooperation and insubordination, and small-scale sudden attacks on persons and property.
- Violent encounters recur in various and changing forms.
- Organized networks are supporting and building terror acts.
- There is repeated fragmentation of organized forces.
- A variety of weapons and forms of attack are employed.
- Finally, in lieu of an all-encompassing political identity to back up collective violence, the plurality of political identities, social settings, and forms of interaction provide compelling avenues to sustain violence.[51]

In all these, or through all these, two things stand out—both borne out by the colonial experience. One is the *illegality* of the entire process—the way an organization grows, persons are drawn, or the techniques that are employed to shield from surveillance. The second is the *irregularity* of the mode and rhythm in which terror is used as a form of political violence—depending on the success or failure of negotiations with the authority (again, think of colonial India), the fate of relatively peaceful collective actions, the state of the legal arrangement of the government of the day, or the scope to employ opportunism to launch an attack (thus, the attack on the imperial procession in Delhi in 1912). It is these two salient features—illegality and irregularity—that the state thinks it can tackle by legality and regularity, by which we mean more and more legislation and more and more deployment of the army, intelligence, police, and bureaucracy. With these two features, illegality and irregularity, becoming at one point parts of the daily tactics of the colonized, both government and the popular opposition turn to using each such attack as an occasion for negotiation—the ultimate recognition of the terrorist by the State as an honourable enemy, and terror being similarly acknowledged, albeit in a slightly backhanded way as a tool of political violence. Here too the history of negotiations in colonial India bears a strange similarity with the present history of negotiations between the state and the rebels—in India or in the troubled land of Israel–Palestine.

And that, to say the least, is the limit to legality which is illustrated by our history of last two hundred years, of the development of basic law/s. Colonial legality never came to terms with what can be called actions in the public space symbolizing opposition to law.[52] Similarly, the deployment of coercive means in wars and domestic control in the colony presented to the colonial rule two problems: (a) the requirement that to the extent the colonial ruler was successful in annexing territory and subduing population the ruler had to now provide *rule* in terms of administration of land, goods, services, and people, in other words, conquest had to be normalized into a form of rule, that is, energy had to be diverted from war to administration; and (b) there was no way, however, in which the colonial ruler could ensure that a normal administration would be looked at as such by the ruled, and coercion would become thereby the exception and not a matter of daily necessity of the ruler. The colonial strategy of rule in the process built a state which wanted to be both coercive and paternalistic, and that is where the precedence and the ongoing reality of violence and terror in politics posed a problematic to which the colonial rule had no answer. The strategy of conquest, coercion, domestication, and normalization faced one inveterate challenge—that posed by the early nationalists who were also early terrorists, and who were singularly insistent in their aim that this strategy of normalization must not succeed. That challenge we know invited more coercion which, in turn, developed the modern state in South Asia.[53] This development has been thus through 'securitising' its own existence, which has invited a thousand conspiracies: 'The administration of a great organized molar security has as its correlate a whole micro-management of petty fears (resulting in) . . . a macro-politics of society by and for a micro-politics of insecurity. . . .'[54]

In a sense, then, the problem that terror and violence pose for law is elemental. Briefly it can be formulated thus: How can law forget or come to terms with its own founding moment—the founding moment of violence? How can the countless murders that were originally perpetrated be normalized by law so that vengeance, which has now enveloped society, can be quarantined, its instruments brought back to the fold of state monopoly, and the order be satisfied with one or two sacrifices? Law's path, of course, as shown by the colonial experience of vengeance, is to develop a well-policed society where public vengeance is the property of the judicial system. Law cannot afford that acts of terror appear as individual acts. Even though it may begin responding by emergency legislation, it knows that such legislation can only give it a bad name. So, as the colonial history showed, the will to legislate arises from the fact that law has to discount individual particularities and the uniqueness of a given situation. 'To act under its aegis is to apply a norm, to subsume a particular case under a general rule.'[55] Yet law's own founding violence cannot but generate a mimetic desire, at times not just desire but, to take a phrase from Rene Girard, 'a monstrous double'.[56] It is in this sense that the entire colonized society immersed itself in terror in 1947, when it realized that the colonial judiciary's monopoly of committing murder was not to last any more.

Just as a guilt-ridden individual wants to forget the violence that s/he has committed, similarly, the law encourages everybody to treat the past founding violence as a sacrificial rite which is happily over and which we can all now forget. Modern nations, like India cannot go ahead if the sacrificial rite does not fulfil its goal, namely, forgetting past violence—the violence that founded the colonial rule, the violence that built the early nationalist articulation, and the violence with which law wanted to bring a final solution to the question of the terror that brings unwarranted and unsanctioned deaths.

NOTES

1. Refer to the series 'Subaltern Studies', New Delhi: Oxford University Press.
2. On an unconventional history of empire-making, see Linda Colley, *Captives: The Story of Britain's Pursuit of Empire and How Its Soldiers and Civilians Were Held Captive by the Dream of Global Supremacy, 1600-1850* (New York: Pantheon Books, 2002).
3. There have been several Bengali prints over the years of the short testament that Khudiram gave about himself in jail before intelligence officials. The original was in Bengali. Used here is the English translation prepared by the Special Branch, Bengal, 1908, now reproduced in Amiya Kumar Samanta (ed.), *Terrorism in Bengal—A Collection of Documents* (hereafter *TIB*, 6 vols., all published in the same year), vol. 4 (Calcutta: Government of West Bengal, 1995), pp. 1388-9.
4. Wars in the Balkans.
5. Satadru Sen, *Disciplining Punishment: Colonialism and Convict Society in the Andaman Islands* (New York: Oxford University Press, 2000).
6. A.C. Banerjee, *The Eastern Frontier of British India, 1784-1826* (Calcutta: A. Mukherjee, 1943), p. 529.
7. 'A Legal Black Hole', *The Statesman*, 29 February 2004, p. 9.
8. 'Colonial Constitutionalism', www.codesria.org/Links/Publications/icp/july_2002.htm; *Identity, Culture and Politics*, 3 (1), July 2002.
9. *TIB*, vol. 1, speaks of bomb making, train-wrecking, and the proliferation of small arms, pp. 32-3, 45; at places intelligence officials make the administrators aware of the organizational structures of the secret societies (p. 221), Home, GOI, 1937, Simla.
10. Michael Shapiro calls the politics of surveillance as the 'bio-politics' of our age when, following Michel Foucault, he argues that surveillance and control of bodies has become crucial for the state to manage security. I am grateful to Shapiro for providing me access to his essay, 'Bodies, Surveillance, and the State'.
11. *TIB*, vol. 5, Introduction, p. ii.
12. On the US experience, one of the most fascinating accounts is, Thomas Powers', *Intelligence Wars—American Secret History from Hitler to al-Qaeda* (New York: New York Review Books, 2002); see also Christopher Andrew, *The Sword and the Shield—The Mitrokhin Archive and the Secret History of the KGB* (New York: Basic Books, 1999).
13. *TIB*, vol. 1, pp. 20-1, 364.
14. All citations are from R.E.A. Ray, 'Alliance of Congress with Terrorism in Bengal', *TIB*, vol. 3, pp. 939-57.
15. This is the infamous report of Charles A. Tegart, then the Special Superintendent of Police, Intelligence Branch, 'A Note on the Ramakrishna Mission', 1914, *TIB*, vol. 4, pp. 1134-75.

16. Ibid., p. 1367.
17. G.C. Denham, Superintendent of Police on Special Duty in the Criminal Intelligence Department, 'Notes on Benares as a Centre of Revolutionary Activity', Criminal Intelligence Office, Circular 4 (Political), 19 July 1915, Simla, *TIB*, vol. 5, p. 137.
18. In this connection see 'Report of the Government of Eastern Bengal and Assam on Deportation', Political Branch, File no 706 of 1909, *TIB*, vol. 4, pp. 1281-331. The report deals with the deportations under Regulation III of 1818 of Aswini Kumar Datta, Satish Chandra Chatterji, Pulin Behari Das, and Bhupesh Chandra Nag. The report speaks of their activities, political profiles, and place in 'terrorist activities'. It must be noted that the report nowhere speaks of their direct involvement, but always points towards their leadership roles in the districts of Bengal.
19. Government of Bengal, *Terrorist Conspiracy in Bengal* (Calcutta: BG Press, 1926).
20. One of the early attempts was the story put out by the police during the trial of the Delhi Conspiracy Case that Rash Behari was a spy.
21. *TIB*, vol. 1, p. 353.
22. 'Papers Relating to Charu Chandra Bose and His Photograph', *TIB*, vol. 4, pp. 1391-7.
23. Government of Bengal, *Terrorist Conspiracy in Bengal*.
24. *TIB*, vol. 5, p. v.
25. Ibid., pp. 1055-1101.
26. Ujjwal Kumar Singh, 'Democratic Dilemmas—can Democracy Do without Extraordinary Laws?', *Economic and Political Weekly*, 38 (5), 1 February 2003, pp. 437-40.
27. For instance, one of the well-known cases is the torture in the Cellular Jail in The Andamans of Ullas kar Dutta who went mad. There are several accounts of British torture of the early nationalists in the nineteenth and early twentieth centuries.
28. *TIB*, vol. 1, Introduction, p. xv.
29. Gilles Deleuze, *Difference and Repetition* (tr.), Paul Patton (London: Continuum, 1997).
30. For an overview, Holger Herwig, Christon Archer, Timothy Travers, and John Ferris, *Cassell's World History of Warfare* (London: Cassell, 2002), Ch. 11.
31. On this, Jon Lawrence, 'Forging a Peaceable Kingdom: War, Violence, and Fear of Brutalization in Post-First World War Britain', *The Journal of Modern History*, 75 (3), September 2003, pp. 557-89.
32. Cited in 'Democratic Dilemmas—can Democracy Do without Extraordinary Laws?', p. 439.
33. Jacques Semelin, 'Extreme Violence: Can We Understand It?' *International Social Science Journal*, 174, December 2002.

34. Isabelle Sommier, '"Terrorism" as Total Violence?', *International Social Science Journal*, 174, December 2003, p. 473.
35. Cited in '"Terrorism" as Total Violence?', p. 473.
36. Ibid., p. 475.
37. Here too colonial history had much to teach modern state running worldwide—first, of course, it made race integral to the notion of citizenship; second it showed how the global communities of colonial labour (mostly in indentured form) were de-linked from the democratic universe of citizenship of the decolonized countries. Thus Indian labour abroad could not return to India after 1947. Various Acts were passed in the last decade of the colonial rule in India, such as the Registration of Foreigners Act of 1939, The Reciprocity Act of 1943, The Trading with the Enemy (Continuance of Emergency Provisions) Act of 1947, The Foreigners Act of 1946. See also in this context the deliberations on the Immigration into India Bill. For an insightful analysis of the relation between citizenship and decolonization, see Paula Banerjee, 'Aliens in the Colonial World', in Ranabir Samaddar, *Refugees and the State* (Delhi: Sage, 2002).
38. Here the present author is extending some of the arguments of Immanuel Wallerstein's essay, 'Citizens All? Citizens Some! The Making of the Citizen', *Comparative Study of Society and History*, 45 (4), October 2003, pp. 650-79.
39. James Bovard, *Terrorism and Tyranny: Trampling Freedom, Justice, and Peace to Rid the World of Evil* (New York: Palgrave Macmillan, 2003), Ch. 4.
40. Cited in Anil Chandra Banerjee, *The Constitutional History of India* (hereafter *CHI*), vol. 1, *1600-1858* (Calcutta: Macmillan, 1977), pp. 196-7.
41. See Eric Stokes, *The English Utilitarians and India* (Delhi: Oxford University Press, 1982), p. 51.
42. Cited in *CHI*, vol. 1, p. 303.
43. Ibid., pp. 302-16.
44. Karen Farringdon, *History of Punishment and Torture* (London: Chancellor Press, 1996), p. 6.
45. Ibid., p. 439.
46. On the influence of liberal thinking on the drafting of the Penal Code, see Eric Stokes, *The English Utilitarians and India*, Ch. 3, 'Law and Government', pp. 140-233.
47. Cited in *CHI*, vol. 2, p. 62.
48. The Simon Commission later admitted the fact of the limitless centralization that one century of legal reforms had brought about. See *Report of the Simon Commission*, vol. 1, paras. 138, 139.
49. Very few members objected to the unfettered emergency powers during the Constituent Assembly discussions. One exception was H.V. Kamath; see *Constituent Assembly Debates* (*CAD*), vol. 9, pp. 105-6. One jurist

admitted that maintenance of 'national integrity and protection of sovereign rights of India were thought as important as individual freedoms and state autonomy', Shivraj B. Nakade, *Emergency in Indian Constitution* (Delhi: Cosmo Publications, 1970), p. 222. Justice H.R. Khanna admitted as much when he reviewed the history of the idea of a Bill of Rights for India. See, B.R. Khanna, *Constitution and Civil Liberties* (Delhi: Institute of Constitutional and Parliamentary Studies, 1978).

50. Martha Crenshaw, 'The Causes of Terrorism', in Catherine Besteman, *Violence—A Reader* (New York: Macmillan Palgrave, 2002), pp. 113-14. She of course makes a distinction between different situations, yet fails to see the point that once one has adopted the term 'terrorism', there is no way but to standardise the experiences, causes, phenomena, explanations, and strategies—which indeed is the task of an ideology.
51. Charles Tilly shows through some focused case studies that acts of individual violence do give us an idea of the collective processes that may become the backbone of such acts. See Tilly, *The Politics of Collective Violence* (Cambridge: Cambridge University Press, 2003), particularly Ch. 5, 'Coordinated Destruction', pp. 102-29.
52. Pierre Bourdieu reminds us of the symbolic power of certain acts in *Language and Symbolic Power* (tr.), Gino Raymond and Matthew Adamson (Cambridge, MA: Harvard University Press, 1991), pp. 116-17.
53. See Charles Tilly, *Coercion, Capital, and European States, AD 990-1990* (Oxford: Basil Blackwell, 1990). Tilly, of course, misses the role played by colonial rule in developing means of coercive apparatuses.
54. Gilles Deleuze and Felix Guattari, *A Thousand Plateaus* (tr.), Brian Massumi (Minneapolis: University of Minnesota Press, 1887), pp. 215-16.
55. Emmanuel Terray, 'Law Versus Politics', *New Left Review*, 22, second series, July–August 2003, p. 71.
56. Rene Girard, *Violence and the Sacred* (tr.), Patrick Gregory (Baltimore: The Johns Hopkins University Press, 1977), p. 143.

CHAPTER II

The State and the Limits of Counter-Terrorism – I: The Experience of Pakistan and Sri Lanka

RUBINA SAIGOL

UNDERSTANDING TERRORISM

THE SOCIAL SCIENTIST'S DILEMMA

Any attempt to understand terrorism must necessarily examine its myriad manifestations, multiple dynamics and causes, and complex consequences. Analyses based on singular visions, either from the perspective of global hegemony or from the peripheries of subjugation and oppression, miss the deeply intertwined nature of the different forms of terrorism. Understandings which focus on a monolithic perspective of state terrorism, fail to make the vital connection of state terrorisms with transnational and sub-national forms of non-state terrorism. On the other hand, analyses focused entirely on the terrorism by non-state actors tend to be blind to the various ways in which states encourage, promote or incite terrorism within their own boundaries and across national borders. The dyadic pattern of state and non-state terror, and the mutually reinforcing relation between them, are central aspects of terror, which need to be understood if a holistic picture of the phenomenon is to be constructed.

In order to grasp the new, globally hegemonic discourse of terrorism, it is important to develop a working definition of the term 'terrorism', which seems to have a vast array of often conflicting and contradictory meanings. The term is so deeply enmeshed in geo-strategic and geo-economic global politics that it eludes the kind of definition that social science requires for understanding any object of inquiry. As a result of the widespread confusion, it has become commonplace to argue that 'one man's terrorist is another man's freedom fighter'. Whether one views an action as resistance, freedom struggle or terror, has come to depend on one's location and the position from which one examines the issue.

Since different actors are located and positioned differently in an unequal world, a multiplicity of interested perspectives are bound to arise. Social science, on the other hand, is expected to reflect a certain degree of objectivity and critical detachment from the object of inquiry. In other words, it is not expected to associate itself with any one position. It is difficult, if not sometimes impossible, for social science to either completely detach itself or become entirely objective without losing a measure of ethical consideration. Located as it is in the activities, interests, conflicts, and positions of human actors in complex interactions with one another, social science must yield to a degree of moral and ethical underpinning. In other words, responsible social science must be able to highlight right and wrong in a situation despite the calls upon it to provide independent, objective, rational and detached analyses. Combining moral judgement with critical detachment and objectivity may be a Herculean task, nevertheless the social scientist is located uncomfortably between the worlds of science and moral philosophy, and cannot completely shun one in favour of the other. A modest attempt is made in this chapter to critically understand state and non-state terrorism and their interlinkages in Pakistan and Sri Lanka, without losing a sense of moral judgment or objectivity.

THE CURRENT DISCOURSE ON TERROR AND ITS LIMITS

The most striking feature of the current discourse on terrorism is that despite a massive proliferation of articles and papers on the subject, a clear, comprehensive, inclusive, and fruitful definition fails to emerge. In seems curious to speak about a subject without knowing what one is talking about, yet this is what is being done almost daily in newspapers and articles. Eqbal Ahmad examined at least twenty US documents on terrorism and found that not once was terrorism defined. He came to the conclusion that this was deliberate as the policy was inconsistent and the application selective.[1] Definitions tend to be restrictive and confining when the political imperative is to have the flexibility of including or excluding any action within a term such as 'terrorism'. Additionally, definitions impose the moral necessity that they be applied evenly across the board to all actions that fit within their parameters. As the actions of the US have been highly selective in the response to terrorism (targeting certain countries and overlooking others for the same or worse actions), it suits the imperial purpose to intentionally keep the notion vague. The deliberately chosen vagueness, and the consequent inconsistent application of the term, has direct implications for countries like Pakistan where terrorism results from a combination of global and internal factors. This point will be made clearer in the section on Pakistan.

A second prominent feature of the current dominant discourse on terrorism is that it is remarkably ahistorical, even in its explanations of central causes. The overwhelming concern seems to be the terrorism that exists today, particularly since 11 September 2001, its effects and the measures to counter it. There is virtually no recognition in this discourse that the present is the product of the past. When stripped of history, any phenomenon, including terrorism, seems to look 'natural' or as arising from 'inherent evil', 'backwardness', 'barbarianism', lack of civilization, rationality or modernity. This kind of essentialism is clearly evident in the statements emanating from the White House since September 2001 in phrases such as 'Axis of Evil', 'barbaric attacks' and so on.

Like the reluctance to define, the inability to situate events in history is also not entirely accidental. The fear of the past reflects the 'skeletons in the closet' syndrome. There is a discernible fear that a journey down the lane of collective memory will make it impossible to argue that people commit terrorist acts because they are 'inherently evil, they hate freedom and love terror'. Digging out skeletons from the closet of repressed memories will mean confronting collective terror unleashed in the past upon those who were less powerful. This fear is clearly evident in the writing of Georg Witschel who argues that contemporary terrorism has very few leading principles, 'for example, the hate against America, against Israel, or against countries and governments supporting them'.[2] This remarkable example of ahistorical thinking essentializes hate, and uses it as a category of explanation without explaining the hate itself—its source, reasons, origin or basis. A psychological category (and that too a problematic one) is used as explanation for phenomena that have a history and a basis in the political economy of West Asia. A trip down the lane of collective memory would have forced Witschel to confront the reality of the occupation of Palestinian land and the incessant terror unleashed upon Palestine by Israel with America's help. Witschel continues to turn his eyes away from history in his criticism of the Organization of Islamic Countries' insistence that peoples' struggles against colonialism, imperialism, aggression, occupation, and hegemony should be exempted from a definition of terrorism, as, in his opinion, this would be too dangerous.[3] This kind of argument implies that acts of the occupation, imperialism, and aggression are not terrorist, a highly untenable position. Such arguments become the main justifications for conquest, occupation, and aggression by powerful states against weaker states.

Similar forms of justificatory arguments are evident in P.R. Chari's assertions that there exists a phobia against Israel, the US, and India in 'the Muslim world', and that there is, therefore, a legal basis for the pre-emptive strikes against Iraq.[4] The failure to find any significant sources of threat or WMDs in Iraq give the lie to Chari's claims, his invocation of the psychological concept of 'phobia' notwithstanding. Chari's fear of history and its propensity to bring up causes is evident in his contention that the *consequences* of international terrorism are more important and one should not 'indulge in fruitless semantics about its *causes*'.[5] By blocking a reference to causes, an exploration of prior terrorism, which may have led to the current one, can be avoided. Explanations of terrorism by resorting to notions of 'evil', 'wicked', or 'phobic', lead one into tautological thinking: 'they committed the act *because* they are evil; they are evil *because* they committed the act'. Explanations devoid of history, and based on psychological essentialisms, fail to serve as explanations at all.

A large part of the intellectual confusion in thinking about terrorism comes from the questionable assumption that only states can be victims of terrorism, while terrorists can only be non-state actors. Witschel argues that the UN Security Council has recognized 'the inherent right of individual or collective self-defense in accordance with the charter, *if a state is the victim of a terrorist attack*'.[6] This contention creates a serious contradiction in Witschel's argument since aggression, occupation and colonization are always constitutive of terrorist attacks without which they cannot be accomplished. For example, the shock and awe operation to which Iraq was subjected was clearly meant to terrorize and create fear. According to Witschel's own argument, Iraq should have the inherent right of collective self-defence. Yet, the actions of resistance fighters are continually described as terrorist acts by the occupying powers and the global media.

This brings us to the third significant feature of the current dominant discourse on terrorism, namely that the state is presented as the victim and non-state actors as perpetrators. In presenting the state as the victim of terrorism, values of good are attributed to states and the perpetrators represent all that is 'evil', 'wicked' or 'cowardly'. The latter descriptions are often used for non-state actors irrespective of whether they are resistance fighters or terrorists. The assumption that states represent good and terrorists evil is not only questionable but hopelessly naïve, as so often terror resides in the very structure of modern nation-states that seek to homogenize diverse identities into a monolithic one. A number of writers fall into the trap of attributing terrorism only to non-state actors. For example, Akmal Hussain considers it to be violence designed to induce fear by an individual or group against other groups within the same state or non-combatant citizens of other states.[7] The state is also absolved of responsibility by P.R. Chari, who believes the 'international system' to be a victim of terrorism by religious extremists who should be dealt with by force of arms.[8]

When the state and non-state actors are both found to be implicated in terrorism, the distinction between a soldier and a terrorist also seems to disappear. Soldiers, like terrorists, are trained to kill or die for some cause assumed to be greater than the self.[9] The distinction between the soldier and suicide bomber collapses, as the actions of the one are hardly distinguishable from the other. If terrorism can be defined as a wilful, premeditated attack which leads to the death of or injury to innocent civilians and damage to property, war and terrorism become indistinguishable. Civilians die as much during war as they do in a terrorist attack, even though in the former the death is explained away as mere 'collateral damage'. Damage to property and infrastructure can and does occur in both forms of violence. War can be as illegal, unprovoked or baseless as a senseless terrorist attack, and this was amply demonstrated by the invasion of Iraq in 2003, declared illegal even by UN Secretary General Kofi Annan in a BBC interview. Wars waged by states and violence carried out by non-state actors are both claimed to be for some higher ideal or justified cause. The only factor that seems to distinguish soldiers from terrorists is that the state has monopoly over legitimized violence. Once the state's monopoly of and right to violence are challenged, and the state's own legitimacy, or that of its actions and motivations, questioned, the soldier and terrorist seem to merge. Social scientists have so far failed to grapple with this issue as terrorism has not been defined in a manner that is acceptable to all. For an acceptable definition to evolve, the state needs to be problematized as a social category.

The fourth significant feature of the existing work on terrorism is the attribution of terrorism to 'religious extremists' and/or the singling out of religious belief as the prime motivation for terrorist attacks. This is discernible in the works of Georg Witschel and P.R. Chari. Witschel argues that 'more and more religiously motivated terrorism has superseded other forms—or rather motivations—of terrorism'.[10] Chari contends that 'religion has supplanted politics as the main principle animating terrorist groups'.[11] Chari then goes on to single out Muslims as the main source of terrorism.[12] Apart from the fact that this discourse is patently racist, it is also clearly untrue and more so in the context of modern South Asia.[13] The Liberation Tigers of Tamil Ealam (LTTE) in Sri Lanka and the Maoists in Nepal are motivated by various considerations which are secular in nature. Struggles against occupation and colonization, such as those of the Palestinians, come to be couched in religious terms by both sides but are essentially struggles against the violent occupation of lands through terrorist means. By attributing terrorism primarily to what is problematically called 'Islamic fundamentalism', we would be overlooking the state terrorism unleashed upon the Palestinians by Israel and against the Muslims in Gujarat and Kashmir by the

Indian state. The latest example of terrorism by the followers of a religion other than Islam is the violence committed on Iraq against all international norms and values.[14]

Four important points must be made here: one, that religion is not the only, or even the most vital, motivation for terrorism as there are struggles that are based on separatist and nationalist agendas or against occupation and class injustice; secondly, where religion is a dimension of the conflict, it is not any one particular religion that is implicated, rather followers of all religions are capable of violence; third, even in cases where religion may come to seem the main motive, the real struggle may be over land, occupation or resources, with religion purely a means of mobilization; and fourth, and this is where racism and prejudice play a major role, social scientists and thinkers attribute differing and opposing motivations as explanations in different situations reflecting similar phenomena. For example, the extermination of six million Jews in the Second World War is not attributed to 'Christian fundamentalism', or 'Protestant terrorism' or any such essentialist category. Historical, political, economic and secular motivations are used to explain the holocaust, even though the followers of one particular religion exterminated those belonging to another. On the other hand, when the followers of Islam commit a terrorist act, it is invariably attributed to religious motivation, and the explanations offered overlook historical, economic and political causes such as occupation of their lands. This failure of social science is similar to the manner in which Washington describes all violent actions against itself as terrorism, and all violent and genocidal actions committed by itself or its allies as self-defence.[15] Interestingly, this is where the discourse of George Bush mirrors that of Osama bin Laden—both claim to fight for freedom, against terrorism, for a just cause, and against evil! Their vocabularies are so similar that statements by the two are virtually interchangeable.[16] Social scientists need to detach themselves from both, that is, violence committed for sacred or secular reasons, if terror is to be understood in all its complexity and varying manifestations. Responsible social scientists need to explain rather than fall into the very categories being used to construct a particular view of terrorism.

A major failing of the discourse on terrorism is that attempts have been made to understand it without reference to the notion of conflict, so central to social science. Terrorism is an effect and a method by which conflict is addressed by any party. It is not *the* conflict itself. Modern societies are torn by a number of conflicts, which can occur singly or together with an overlap between them. For example, conflicts occur on the basis of class, caste, gender, sect, religion or linguistic identities. All societies, and particularly those in South Asia, are vertically and horizontally divided along these axes. Conflicts may cut across class and religion or gender and religion and at times one identity may supersede another. The state is expected to be neutral with regard to categories of social differentiation, however it is often difficult for the state to be impartial or neutral for various reasons which will become clearer in later sections of this chapter. The state is required to mediate social conflict but often fails because of its own lack of neutrality.

The conflict may be between the state and a sub-national group, the state or a religious sect or group, or between two social groups each representing a different religion, sect or ethnic origin. Such conflicts can take on transnational characteristics when the identity is shared with groups or states across national borders.[17] Terrorism is one among several means that the state or the sub- or transnational group uses to achieve its aims. It defies explanation without reference to conflict. It needs to be clarified that the notion of conflict is not being used here in a negative sense as conflict is necessary for social change. However, conflicts can, and often do, take violent forms which have come to be labelled as 'terrorism'. Any effort to grasp the motivations, causes or dynamics of terrorism is fruitless without understanding the underlying conflict over the distribution of resources, services and power among groups within and across states.

It is difficult, if not impossible, to understand terrorism without referring to the power differentials between peoples, governments, groups, and states. Apart from the vast differences in the capacity of states to kill and inflict material damage, there is unequal access to the means and methods of the production of 'truth'. The knowledge industry and the media play a pivotal role in the manufacture of 'truth' about who is a terrorist and who is not. The corporate global media toes the line of the rich and powerful states, which are also strongly dominated by corporate interests. The inconsistent and selective application of criteria for the labelling of terrorists and terrorist states is undertaken daily by the media. The power to define, redefine, not define, and shift the criteria for defining rests with the powerful states and their massive 'truth industry'. The power to make and unmake meaning, to remember and to forget, to tell and not to tell is the ultimate form of power deployed in the construction of the regime of truth. The monopoly over this kind of power by the powerful states and their media has obfuscated the issue of terrorism rather than contributing to its understanding. Intellectual discourse seems to have *followed* rather than *interrogated* the dominant notions of terrorism peddled by the media. The counter-discourse in the alternative media has not been able to effectively contest the mainstream notions of terrorism since the terms of the debate are set by the global knowledge regime.

The result has been a dichotomous understanding of terrorism wherein *either* states *or* non-state actors are terrorist, *either* the government *or* a sub-national group is terrorist, *either* the imperial powers *or* transnational movements challenging them are terrorist. Depending on one's location in the world and vantage point, terrorism is attributed to one side or the other. What gets obliterated in this binary setting of the debate is that terrorism forms a continuum from the global to state to sub-state levels. No state or sub-national group is permanently terrorist, while any state, group or transnational movement can resort to terrorist methods in a given situation and under certain conditions. In other words, when, how, and why a certain movement, state, group or imperial power commits terrorist attacks is contingent upon a number of historical factors. The latter may include resistance against prolonged occupation with no relief in sight, a prior terrorist attack, resentment against a subordinate social status, persistent maltreatment by state powers, perceived or real injustice, loss of privilege, threat perception or unequal access to state resources in comparison with another social group. The global, national, local, and transnational factors may interact to produce a particular terrorist act or movement. Terrorism, therefore, cannot be apprehended within the confining dichotomy of either/or.

It is against the backdrop of historical, global, national, sub-national, and transnational forces that the specific case of Pakistan can be understood. The complexity of the situation in Pakistan, and its various forms of terrorism, cannot be grasped without situating the issue in the context of historical, global geo-strategic and geo-economic power politics. From the foregoing discussion, a working definition of terrorism can be derived for the purposes of this paper: any loss of civilian life, bodily injury or damage to property that occurs as a result of conflict between two states, two groups, a state and sub-national group, or a transnational movement and nation-states constitutes an act of terrorism. It is assumed that all such acts are deliberate and premeditated, as there is no such thing as an accident whenever a planned attack takes place. This definition includes acts of colonization, conquest and occupation. However, it excludes the different forms of terrorism currently under discussion, for example, the economic terrorism of globalization, eco-terrorism against the environment or cyber terrorism. Although the latter forms do constitute terrorism, they do not fall within the scope of this paper. The definition provided here includes action by individual members of a group or state if the action is designed to further group goals, but it does not include individual acts of murder or damage to property, which are based on personal enmity or individual motives, as the latter actions would constitute a crime. The working definition devised for this chapter forms the conceptual framework within which the case of Pakistan and that of Sri Lanka are examined.

II

THE CASE OF PAKISTAN: TRAPPED IN HISTORY AND GEOGRAPHY

Pakistan as a state is both the victim and the perpetrator of terrorism. However, the victims and perpetrators differ by class, religion, region, and access to power. For example, the victims often include ordinary citizens, religious or sectarian minorities, peasants or workers. On the other hand, the perpetrators include members of the classes and of the groups that wield power—the military, police, political parties, militant organizations, secret agencies, bureaucrats, landlords and capitalists. At times, the perpetrators also become victims, for example, the killing of members of the police force by MQM militants in Karachi, the attacks on the life of President Pervez Musharraf, or the murder of leaders of militant outfits such as the murder of the Sipah-e-Sahaba leader, Maulana Haq Nawaz Jhangvi. Similarly, victims of political or state terrorism can become perpetrators, as in the case of the fighters in Baluchistan in the decade of the 1970s, or MQM activists in the 1990s. The interactive relationship between state and non-state actors sometimes dissolves the distinction between victim and perpetrator.

Terrorism in Pakistan is deeply linked to conflicts that reside at the core of its origin, structure, and geographical location. There appear to be four fundamental sources of terrorism in Pakistan: (1) Pakistan's origin in the foundational myth of the two-nation theory; (2) Pakistan's failure to evolve a viable federal structure, given the regional diversity at its origin; (3) communalization of the state, and (4) Pakistan's location at the nexus between South and Central Asia, that is, its proximity to Afghanistan, often considered the gateway to Central Asia. Pakistan is thus trapped in its own history, geography, and the resulting problems of the structure of the state. Although the four sources of conflict and terrorism in Pakistan are intertwined in a number of ways, they need to be discussed separately for purposes of conceptual clarity.

The Founding Myth of Pakistan

The foundational myth of Pakistan is the two-nation theory, which posits Muslims and Hindus as two mutually exclusive, separate, and irreconcilable nations. This ideology divided the freedom struggle against British rule as early as 1909 with the Morley–Minto Reforms in which the principle of a separate electorate was acknowledged by the British government. It subsequently remained the main slogan of the Muslim League and led to the division at independence by religion. Within the two-nation paradigm, two states emerged, a Hindu India and a Muslim Pakistan, although Indians generally see their country as secular.

The emergence of Pakistan within a struggle divided by religion meant that religious identity came to be the defining characteristic of Pakistani citizenship. This implied that other, sometimes older, sources of identity in language, region or culture had to be suppressed if not entirely erased. The construction of Pakistani identity as Muslim required the forgetting of the identities of Bengali, Sindhi, Punjabi, Pathan or Baluchi. In a speech on national integration in 1962, Ayub Khan declared:

> Pakistan came into being on the basis of an ideology which does not believe in differences of colour, race or language. It is immaterial whether you are a Bengali or a Sindhi, a Baluchi or a Pathan or a Punjabi—we are all knit together by the bond of Islam.[18]

The same sentiments were reiterated by him in 1963 when he said:

> I do hope that in a few decades, which is not a long time in the history and progress of nations, our people will forget to think in terms of Punjabi, Pathan, Sindhi, Baluchi and Bengali and think of themselves as Pakistanis only . . . our religion, our ideology, our common background, our aims and ambitions unite us more firmly than any geographical boundaries could have.[19]

The process of national integration, that is, the forced and artificial homogenization of diverse cultures and peoples, is an inherently violent process. It imposes a monolithic identity, which is expected to override the sentiments of other identities arising from multiple belonging. The latter may include regional, sectarian, caste, class, gender, linguistic or regional identities, which become difficult to accommodate in a state based on a centralized notion of identity. The excluded sources of the self do not just fade away or die out over time, as is hoped by authoritarian rulers like Ayub Khan. Instead, they are stirred and mobilized into action when the highly centralized state fails to distribute resources equitably or otherwise excludes certain sub-national groups from power.

Although the basic premise of the two-nation idea is essentially false because it posits two groups of people as polar opposites and overlooks all mixtures, overlaps, and commonalities, it has been a powerful notion in guiding (or rather misguiding) the Pakistani state's actions. The two-nation theory has led to serious conflicts and violence, which have plagued Pakistani society from its inception. The conflicts ensuing from, and related to, the foundational myth are primarily of two types: one, Pakistan's failure to develop a just and viable federal structure in order to accommodate ethnic minorities, and two, the theory has produced the ideology of Islamization that lies at the heart of the sectarian and Jehadi struggles.

CONFLICT AND THE STRUCTURE OF THE STATE

Owing to the vast cultural, linguistic, and ethnic diversity within what came to constitute Pakistan, the structure of the state was required to be a federal one, with a system for parity between the five provinces. A democratic, plural, and just framework required the state to be decentralized with adequate representation of different ethnic groups and regional minorities. However, the failure of the rulers in state formation led to serious disaffection with the centre, and feelings of alienation among minorities and those distant from the centre of power.

The alienation from the rulers was expressed as early as the 1950s when there were language riots resulting from attempts to make Urdu the national language. Since the East Pakistanis, who spoke Bengali, constituted the majority of Pakistani citizens, it was patently unjust to impose Urdu, a language spoken by a small minority, as the national language. However, this controversy was resolved by declaring both Urdu and Bengali as Pakistan's national languages. Another major source of conflict was the infamous One Unit, according to which Sindh, Baluchistan, NWFP, and the Punjab constituted a single political unit called West Pakistan. This move created resentment, particularly among the smaller provinces in West Pakistan where people felt the domination of the largest province, the Punjab. As a result of agitation and protest, One Unit was abolished by Yahya Khan.

However, the biggest crisis rooted in the inability to evolve a federal structure came with the elections of 1970. The Awami League of East Pakistan led by Sheikh Mujibur Rahman won the elections overwhelmingly. The West Pakistani rulers and politicians refused to hand over power to the legitimately elected party, which resulted in agitation and protest all over East Pakistan. The agitation and resistance to West Pakistan's domination was met with the most violent forms of state repression in the history of the state. The military was sent to East Pakistan in March 1971 where it murdered scores of people opposed to West Pakistani control. Twenty-four years of being treated as a colony and exploited by West Pakistan, led to demands for secession in East Pakistan. What followed was one of worst forms of mass genocide and terrorism by the state. Thousands of East Pakistanis were butchered, women were raped, and a reign of terror was unleashed upon the people. This massive state terrorism and violence ended only with the defeat of the West Pakistani army and East Pakistan's emergence as a separate state of Bangladesh in December 1971.

The events of 1971 did not end the conflicts between the state and its federating units. The next province to offer armed resistance to the centre in the decade of the 1970s was Baluchistan. According to Selig Harrison, Baluch insurgents waged a guerrilla struggle over an extended period,

> culminating in a brutal confrontation with 80,000 or more Pakistani troops from 1973 to 1977 in which some 55,000 Baluch were involved, 11,500 of them as organized combatants. Casualty estimates during this little-known war ran as high as 3,300 Pakistani soldiers and 5,300 Baluch guerrillas killed, not to mention hundreds of women and children caught in the crossfire. At the height of the fighting in late 1974, United States supplied Iranian combat helicopters, some manned by Iranian pilots, joined the Pakistan Air Force in raids on Baluch camps. The Baluch, for their part, did not receive substantial foreign help and were armed only with bolt-action rifles, home-made grenades, and captured weaponry.[20]

In 2004, violence once again erupted in Baluchistan as the military attempted to set up cantonments and the local Sardars opposed the army's actions. As the largest province in Pakistan but one with the smallest population, Baluchistan has historically received a smaller share of the national resources. As a result of the underdevelopment and inadequate remuneration for its resources, such as natural gas, resentment continues to simmer in the province. This situation is pregnant with the dangers of future conflict because of uneven development and inequitable sharing of national wealth.

The decade of the 1980s saw the province of Sindh up in arms against the government in Islamabad. This time it was the Movement for the Restoration of Democracy (MRD) against General Zia-ul-Haq's illegal military rule, and his justification of all repression in the name of Islamization. Sindh has a long history of sub-national stirrings expressed in the form of the *Jiye Sindh Mahaz* and other parties premised on Sindhi nationalism. August to December 1983 saw a massive civil disobedience movement in Sindh, during which several activists courted arrest and risked imprisonment and state violence. The MRD movement was supported by anti-military-rule activists in other provinces, but Sindh bore the brunt of the General's wrath. Helicopter gunships were used by the military to suppress the revolt in which hundreds were killed and wounded. Selig Harrison reports that in this uprising, 45,000 Punjabi troops faced makeshift Sindhi guerrilla outfits and the Sindhi death toll came to 300 people.[21] Although the rural-based militant movement against military rule was crushed due to lack of support primarily from the majoritarian province of Punjab, it highlighted the excesses of the military government and its use of the most violent methods to suppress the uprising. In 1986, another wave of violence and state repression arose in Sindh. According to Shahid Kardar, 'the alleged death of 50 students at the Thori Railway crossing, and the horror of the action taken to suppress the Sindhis in 1986 have left very deep wounds in Sindh'.[22]

The early to mid-1990s were dominated by armed militant conflict between the Urdu-speaking migrants from India—the Muhajirs—and the forces of the state. This conflict had its roots in the 1970s, when Zulfiqar Ali Bhutto instituted an urban–rural quota in government jobs and college admissions in Sindh. The measure was designed to give rural Sindhis a chance to compete against the urban Muhajirs concentrated in Karachi and Hyderabad. Historically, the better-educated urban Muhajirs had dominated the state bureaucracy. However, over time Punjabis came to be over-represented in the civil and military bureaucracy, leading to a threat perception among the Muhajirs. Since no other province in Pakistan had the urban–rural quota system, the Muhajirs resented this move. Additionally, a large number of jobs in Sindh were filled by migrants from the Punjab and Frontier Provinces. The result was a sense of economic threat from other ethnic groups. In the 1980s, the military regime of General Zia needed to counterbalance the influence of the Pakistan People's Party, whose leader had been deposed. The military, therefore, relied upon the Muhajir resentment and threat perception, and gave the movement further impetus. Together these factors led to the formation of the Muhajir Qaumi Movement, which later became the Muttahida Qaumi Mahaz as it integrated more people into its fold. Over time the organization of the party became increasingly fascist and its armed wing, the Black Tigers who had an oath to kill or die for the party, unleashed a reign of terror in Karachi.[23] While there were clashes with the Pathans and Sindhis, even the Muhajir community itself was terrorized into submission as the young men collected donations for the Muhajir cause. A large number of Muhajir men and members of the police and military were killed during the prolonged conflict. The fascist character of the movement was brought sharply into focus when MQM torture cells were discovered in Karachi. Farida Shaheed correctly points out that the role of the state exacerbated the conflict and led to more deaths than that inter-group ethnic conflict. The failure of the state to provide protection to its citizens led each community to seek shelter and protection within the immediate sub-national group.[24]

The fact that the state in Pakistan clashed with virtually all of its sub-national groups showed the failure of the rulers to evolve a federal structure with maximum provincial autonomy and a fair distribution of resources. The highly centralizing tendencies, evident from the repeated imposition of military rule, led to the alienation of smaller or distant ethnic groups. The domination of the state by one ethnic group, that is, the Punjabis who were over-represented in the civil and military bureaucracy, is another factor which contributed to the alienation of other groups from the centre. As Hamza Alavi points out:

> The moment that Pakistan was established, Muslim nationalism in India had fulfilled itself and outlived its purpose. Now there was a fresh equation of privilege and deprivation to be reckoned with in the new state. Virtually overnight there were ethnic redefinitions. Punjabis who were the most numerous could boast of a greater percentage of people with higher education and were most firmly entrenched in both the army (being 85 per cent of the armed forces) and the bureaucracy. They were the new bearers of privilege, the true 'Muslim' for whom Pakistan was created. The weaker 'salariats' of Bengal, Sindh, Sarhad and Baluchistan did not share this and accordingly they redefined their identities as Bengalis, Sindhis, Pathans and Baluch who now demanded fairer shares for themselves.[25]

The forced attempts to contain Pakistan within the religiously defined confines of the two-nation theory came into conflict with the linguistic, regional or economic definitions of identity. The near-total conflation of Pakistani with Punjabi identity led to other ethnic groups redefining themselves regionally. The ensuing conflicts led to armed guerrilla insurgencies in which terrorist methods come to be employed by all sides as a means of achieving aims which otherwise seemed to elude them. The seeds of violent conflict thus inhere in the structure of the state, which is in tension with the founding myth of oneness. The various attempts by the state to appear to decentralize have been seriously flawed. Whether it was Ayub Khan's scheme of Basic Democracies, General Zia's local bodies or General Pervez Musharraf's flagship devolution plan, the tendency to centralize has underpinned all such attempts. The latest Local Government Plan by the current government of General Musharraf has been widely criticized for its failure to devolve power to the provinces by the centre and for creating a direct federal hold over the districts. The rejection of the plan by the provincial governments, especially in the Frontier and Baluchistan, bears further testimony to the tension between the center and the federating units.[26] The widespread belief that the District system is designed to empower local elites and collect taxes at the local level lends credence to the view that this plan is a 'decentralization of repression' rather than of authority or service delivery.[27]

Although armed insurgency based on sub-national articulation of identity is currently not visible on the Pakistani landscape, struggles over resource distribution arise from time to time and contain the potential to break into a militant insurrection. For example, the Punjab and Sindh have been locked in a struggle over the sharing of the Indus waters and the building of the Kalabagh Dam. Similarly, the provinces have demanded an increase in their share in the National Finance Commission award. Uneven development remains a persistent problem with regard to the different regions of Pakistan. These problems, coupled with increasing poverty and the widening rich–poor divide, threaten to unleash terrorism in the future because of the conflict inherent in state structure, centralizing tendencies, immature political parties, and the widespread availability of small arms.

Communal State and Sectarian Conflict

The roots of Pakistan's sectarian and religious conflicts lie in the contradictions that characterized its birth as a separate country. Pakistan's origins within the communal two-nation paradigm meant that religious identity would override other bases of self-definition. On the other hand, the state was also conceptualized as a modern, liberal democracy with a parliamentary form of government. The main, and most serious, contradiction is that democracy by definition requires the state to be secular.[28] As equal citizenship is a fundamental requirement of democracy, the privileging of one religious group over others means that religiously different citizens are not equal. On the contrary, the country's origin within the two-nation theory meant that one religion would come to be prioritized over others as the very basis of the new country. In other words, it is not possible to be democratic without also necessarily being secular. This contradiction lies at the heart of Pakistan's troubles with national identity. Although there were a number of economic and class interests driving the Muslim League, the rallying slogan was religion. Since people had been mobilized on a religious basis, demands to define the state in religious terms were bound to arise. With the passage of time, the state failed to become either liberal, since liberal freedoms were frequently curtailed under the pressure of conservative clerics and military rule, or democratic, as military rule time and again replaced representative institutions.

Measures to define the state in religious terms came as early as 1949, when the Objectives Resolution was made a substantive part of the constitution. This resolution institutionalized religion within the state structure and became the basis for a number of subsequent demands and arguments for an Islamic state. Almost all of Pakistan's rulers resorted to religious arguments for the legitimization of their policies and actions. The year 1953 saw the Punjab chief minister, Daultana, playing a role in the anti-Ahmadiya agitation.[29] In the regime of Ayub Khan religious arguments were used in an attempt to deny Fatimah Jinnah's right to contest the elections for the country's top office.[30] Zulfiqar Ali Bhutto called his legitimizing ideology 'Islamic socialism', and General Zia-ul-Haq perfected the art of deploying religion in the service of justifying illegal rule. Nawaz Sharif's infamous Shariat Bill (proposed Fifteenth Amendment) and General Musharraf's proclivity for making deals only with the Muttahida Majlis-e-Amal (MMA) while excluding the mainstream non-religious parties from Pakistan's political landscape, are all examples of the way in which every ruler, whether civil or military, has used religion for her/his own continuation in power.

Although the roots of sectarian violence and terror lie deep in Pakistan's history, the Islamization of the era of General Zia intensified and multiplied sectarian divisions to the extent not witnessed before. Eqbal Ahmad succinctly explains the connection between the policies of Islamization and sectarianism:

> Religious sectarianism was an inevitable outcome of 'Islamization'. There is first of all the simple insight that appears to have escaped several generations of politicians and soldiers of Pakistan: When a state claims a theocratic mission, it is bound to provoke conflicts over whose model shall prevail. Secondly, when religion is pushed explicitly into politics it becomes a currency of power. Any one who can uses religion to garner support and undercut actual or potential rivals. To verify this, one may need count only the number of religion wielding newcomers in national and local politics since Zia's Islamization began. The most virulent hate-mongers of today also belong to his era.[31]

According to Abbas Rashid, the Islamization policies of General Zia fostered sectarianism in a number of ways.[32] The policies, which were deeply influenced by the Jamaat-e-Islami, seemed to be creating not just an Islamic but a Sunni Hanafi state. The levying of *zakat* and *ushr* in 1979, and a number of other ordinances, led to feelings of a threat perception among the minority Shia community that Pakistan was being redefined as a sectarian state. The provision of *zakat* funds to Sunni *deeni madaris* (religious seminaries) led to a proliferation of sectarian religious schools. The Tehreek-e-Nifaz-e-Fiqah Jaffria (TNFJ) was the Shia response to Zia's Sunni measures. In turn, the Anjuman-e-Sipah-e-Sahaba-e-Pakistan (ASSP) was formed to oppose the Shia landlords of Jhang by stoking the prevailing resentments against feudal power. Over time, such processes led to the formation of a large number of sectarian outfits representing Shia and Sunni sects and sub-sects. Various religico—political organizations representing the Deobandi and Barelvi versions of Islam sprang up all over the country and became locked in violent conflicts. Some of the militant religious outfits that gained prominence include the Shia Sipah-e-Muhammad Pakistan, an offshoot of the TNFJ, the Sunni Sipah-e-Sahaba (SSP), an offshoot of the Jamiat-e-Ulema-e-Islam (JUI), the latter a leading Sunni Deobandi political party.

Sectarian violence in Pakistan escalated dramatically with the murder of Maulana Haq Nawaz Jhangvi, founder of the SSP, in February 1990. This assassination led to large-scale arson in Jhang in which numerous houses and shops were destroyed. In December of the same year, the murder of the Iranian Consul-General in Lahore intensified the violence between Iran-supported Shias and Saudi Arabia-supported Sunnis. As a result of financial and material help from various countries promoting their own brand of sectarianism, the religious militants gained increased access to small arms of all kinds, available in the black market. Abbas Rashid reports that in the Punjab, 1994 was one of the worst years in terms of sectarian killings when seventy-three people were killed and three hundred were wounded.[33] In the latter half of 1996, sectarian violence in Parachinar and part of Kurram agency claimed hundreds of lives. Sectarian violence also led to the killing of the Commissioner of Sargodha and Deputy Commissioner of Khanewal in 1996. The murder of people in mosques during prayers, or while attending funerals became common in various parts of the country. In one of the worst incidents of this kind, in January 1998, twenty-two people were killed in Mominpura, Lahore, while they were praying. This incident was designed to coincide with the anniversary of the killing of Maulana Jhangvi.

Muhammad Amir Rana reports that the greatest increase in religious parties was recorded between 1979 and 1990, and a major chunk of it is accounted for by a staggering rise in the number of sectarian outfits.[34] While Jehad-related organizations increased by 100 per cent, the rise in sectarian parties was 90 per cent. Since there were ideological and other differences between them, the fighting, coupled with the easy availability of arms, led to an enormous increase in violence and terrorist activity. The state had, through its myopic policies, created a monster it could barely control. The extent of terror and violence unleashed upon society can be gauged from the number of people killed or injured in sectarian terrorism. Between 1987 and 2002, 1,016 people were killed in incidents of sectarian violence throughout Pakistan. In the same period, 2,450 people were injured in 1,342 incidents of terrorism. Between 1990 and 2002, 593 Shias and 388 Sunnis were murdered, while 44 people belonging to the police department and the administration were killed.[35] The violence intensified due to myriad factors including Pakistan's state policies, the Iranian Revolution of 1979, the Afghan Jehad beginning with the Soviet invasion of 1979, the interference of the United States, Iran, and Pakistan in Afghanistan, and the formation of the Sipah-e-Sahaba in Jhang in 1985 to counter the Iran-backed TNFJ.

Sectarian terrorism continues to plague Pakistan to the present day. In the most recent attack, a suicide bomber was killed when he tried to bomb a Shia Imambargah, Bargah-e-Hussaini in Rawalpindi, in February 2004. Although no one else was killed as the bomb went off prematurely, the attempt is yet more evidence of the continuing sectarian scourge in Pakistan. In March 2004, unidentified gunmen opened fire on the Yaum-e-Ashur in Liaqat Bazaar, Quetta, killing over forty people and injuring scores of others.[36] Sectarian violence greatly escalated in October of 2004. On 1 October 2004, twenty-nine people were killed in a Shia Imambargah in Sialkot. On 7 October 2004, a bomb blast in Multan killed around forty people in a mosque and on 10 October 2004, a bomb blast in a Shi'ite mosque in Lahore led to the death of four people. The state's policy of establishing one religion as the state religion, and further giving priority to one sect, the dominant Sunnis, is fraught with dangers as it can potentially lead to more violence in the future. State policy has become an instrument of dividing civil society along the axes of religion, sect, and ethnicity.

Although a number of parties joined the Milli Yakjehti Council designed to counter sectarian terror, the leaders are economically dependent upon sectarian disunity and discord in order to collect funds, and sectarian harmony does not suit them.[37] Additionally, members of the capitalist classes and traders have agents within the sectarian parties in Karachi, and they use them to have their competitors' goods declared un-Islamic on one pretext or another. The sectarian conflict ties in with business conflicts within the capitalist class, thus rendering sectarian violence lucrative. The state, foreign countries, secret agencies, members of the administration, business classes, and leaders of religious outfits, all have a vested interest in sectarian disharmony, and all contribute to its perpetuation. For the young men who are drawn to sectarian violence and Jehad, unemployment is a major reason for joining such parties. Pakistan has 10,000 *deeni madaris* where a million students receive religious instruction. About 7,000 students graduate annually from the seminaries and fail to find employment in Pakistan's weak economy. The political economy of sectarian violence thus runs deep and efforts to create sectarian harmony are scuttled by vested interests.

The state's origin within a communal split thus led to its definition in religious terms. When the state acquired for itself a religious identity, it was only natural for each sect to try to have its own interpretation imposed as the 'true' version of Islam. State policy is thus directly responsible for the proliferation of militant sectarian outfits which terrorize people, kill, murder, and destroy property. Countering sectarian terrorism is difficult for the state precisely for the reason that it means fighting against its own self and its own ideological contradictions. However, the state does not act alone. In a highly interdependent world, state policies are deeply influenced by events in neighbouring countries and the wider world. It is axiomatic to say that domestic policies are influenced by foreign relations and the state's geopolitical location, and foreign policies are deeply linked to domestic concerns. Pakistan's militant religio-political parties are not purely domestic products. Rather, their politics and focus have been the consequences of wider global politics in which Pakistan's unique location next to Afghanistan has played a central role.

Cold War, Jehad, and the Frontline State

The concepts of Jehad have been elaborated in the subcontinent for a long time, especially since the decline of the Mughal Empire and the regeneration of the role of the Ulema, who no longer had state patronage and needed to find alternative sources of income.[38] The role of Shah Walli Ullah, the eighteenth century reformer, and Ahmad Sirhindi who contested the Emperor Akbar's efforts at communal harmony, was highlighted, and attempts were made to represent the Ulema as the torch-bearers of Islam in India. In this discourse designed primarily to present the priestly class in a positive light, Shah Walli Ullah is depicted as a believer in armed revolution based on the principles of Jehad.[39]

Modern Jehad in Pakistan seems to have resulted from a confluence of several factors, including an interplay between the imperatives of a communal state with its origins in religious separatist myths, cold-war geopolitical and geo-economic realities, politics of 'spheres of influence', economic compulsions and strategies, the inability to usher in development and create economic opportunities for poor youth, uneven regional development, electoral politics (creating the vote banks of sectarian and religious parties), proliferation of arms, especially small arms and Kalashnikovs during the Afghan war, and the failure to create a liberal democratic state. However, the genesis of contemporary militant religious outfits is traced once again to the policies of the state under General Zia-ul-Haq. In 1979, the former Soviet Union invaded Afghanistan, a Muslim country on the western border of Pakistan. The invasion was immediately perceived in the United States as a threat to its interests in containing the spread of communism. As a country with a contiguous border with Afghanistan, Pakistan was selected by the US as the base from which resistance to the Soviet occupation would be launched. Apart from being a front-line state in purely geographical terms, Pakistan was also an ideal choice ideologically as 'godless communism' could be countered by invoking the sentiments of Jehad. There followed a close cooperation between the US and Pakistan in creating and sending militants across the border to fight against Soviet troops.

On 3 July 1979, Zbingnew Brezinski revealed that the administration of Jimmy Carter had created a secret fund of 500 million dollars for the purpose of the Afghan Jehad.[40] The fund was kept secret even from Congress and the American public. According to John Pilger, the purpose of the fund was to create a global terrorist movement which could eliminate the Soviet Union from Central Asia and promote Islamic fundamentalism.[41] The Central Intelligence Agency (CIA) named this initiative 'Operation Cyclone', for which a staggering amount of 4 billion dollars was allocated in the years following the Soviet invasion. A large part of this operation involved the creation of *deeni madaris* for the ideological indoctrination and military training of Mujahids (holy warriors). Pilger reveals that enthusiastic young men belonging to Islamic parties were sent to the CIA training camp in Virginia where the future Al Qaida members were trained. Other young men were sent to the Islamic School of Brooklyn, New York, where they received training in militancy. Within Pakistan, aspiring young militants were guided and trained by the British intelligence service, MI6, and the secret agency of the Pakistan military, the Inter-Services Intelligence (ISI). According to the November-December 2000 issue of the US State Department magazine, between 1986 and 1989 the US and Saudi Arabia provided 3.5 billion dollars to Pakistan for the Afghan Jehad.[42] A large portion of this money found its way into the illicit arms and drugs market, and created what came to be commonly called 'the Kalashnikov culture' in Pakistan.

In the same period, religious seminaries began to proliferate in Pakistan. Prior to 1980, there were a total of 700 religious schools in Pakistan and the rate of increase was 3 per cent a year. By the end of 1986, the rate of increase in *deeni madaris* reached a phenomenal 136 per cent. By 2002, Pakistan had 7,000 institutions which award higher degrees in religious teaching. The new schools were mostly set up in the Frontier province, southern Punjab, and Karachi. Religious leaders were provided with economic incentives to create militants for the Afghan war. Thousands of young men belonging to poor families were handed over to secret agencies which ensured their training at the seminaries and then showed them the way to Afghanistan. The other front where trained militant students of religious schools were being sent was Kashmir. The secret agencies and religious leaders made fortunes from the US money that was being funnelled into the country to create militants. Jehad thus became a roaring, highly lucrative business.[43] Apart from the religious schools, student organizations in universities and colleges recruited youths for Jehad and became the second biggest source of manpower for militant activity in Afghanistan and Kashmir.

In Afghanistan, the Mujahidin became embroiled in the inter-ethnic struggles which led to an enormous amount of bloodshed, and terror and fear, for Afghans belonging to all ethnic groups and sects. In the long war, which lasted for over two decades, thousands of Afghans were killed or maimed, and wave upon wave of refugees, mostly women and children, escaped to Pakistan creating the biggest refugee influx in the history of the country. In 1996, the Taliban, trained in the *deeni madaris* belonging to the Jamiat-ul-Ulema-e-Islam, and provided with military training and equipment by the ISI, captured Kabul and unleashed the worst reign of terror seen in this part of the world. The terror, violence, and excesses of the Taliban are recorded in detail in Ahmad Rashid's *Taliban: Islam, Oil and the New Great Game in Central Asia*.[44] In Kashmir, the militants of the Hizb-ul-Mujahidin weakened the indigenous freedom struggle of the Jammu & Kashmir Liberation Front (JKLF), and the secular resistance movement came to be couched in religious colours.

Jehad has very little, if anything, to do with religion. Muhammad Amir Rana relates a number of incidents in which the Mujahidin were involved in harassing girls, beating up a headmaster after forcibly entering a school, beating up a boy because the ball he was playing with accidentally hit two Mujahidin on a motorbike, and generally terrorizing and bullying the local people.[45] The power, that carrying a gun gives youths from the dispossessed classes makes them feel strong and masculine. Most of them join the Jehad because it is a job in a world where gainful employment is scarce and economic opportunities virtually non-existent. Several of the Mujahidin recruited from the Punjab said that they had watched Indian movies in the past and admired the heroes. They wanted to be like those heroes and had joined the Jehad for the opportunity for adventure. In a very few cases, Jehad may be motivated by a genuine but misplaced religious fervour. However, if the young Jehadis disagree with their leaders, they are immediately termed agents of the Indian secret service RAW (Research and Analysis Wing). The young men thus have no avenue of escape even if they become disenchanted. The leaders, who make enormous financial profits from Jehad, inspire the young men with tales of miracles about Mujahids whose feet shone in the dark and who were taken away by fairies and cured upon being shot and wounded.[46] The young men, who are the ones to die for the so-called Jehad cause, are seldom given a fair share of the funds that are pocketed by religious leaders. As a result of the burgeoning economy of Jehad, leaders of religio-political parties drive around in Pajeros, travel by air, carry Kalashnikovs or other expensive weapons, employ bodyguards for their protection, live in palatial houses, and conduct business on mobile phones.[47] All the symbols of modernity and vulgar consumerism, associated with the so-called hated 'west', are used and openly displayed by the leaders of religious outfits. Jehad, like all other wars, is a classed phenomenon in which the foot soldiers are exploited while the leaders make profits.

In the 1980s, the funds flowed from the US, but in recent times militant organizations like Lashkar-e-Toiba, Jaish-e-Muhammad and Harkat-ul-Mujahidin collect funds through the lectures and speeches of their leaders recorded on cassettes, which are then spread through personal contacts. A rousing speech by Jaish leader Maulana Azhar Masood on the Babri Masjid demolition, recorded on cassettes and widely disseminated, led many passionate young men into Jehad. Lashkar-e-Toiba openly displayed boxes in main bazaars and markets to collect funds, and released front-page recruitment advertisements in newspapers for Kashmir Jehad. All this would not have been possible without the connivance of the state. The government of Azad Kashmir actively participates in the activities of the militant groups.

The Punjab and the Frontier provinces are the main suppliers of manpower for the Afghan and Kashmir Jehad. The biggest recruitment centre for militancy is the Punjab which accounts for 50 per cent of all manpower. According to ten major Jehad organizations, the total number of Punjabi youths killed in militant action exceeds 12,000. About 4,000 of them were killed in Afghanistan, the rest in Kashmir. There are 5,500 religious seminaries in the Punjab out of which 3,000 follow the Deobandi sect, 3,000 are followers of the Ahle Hadees sect, 800 belong to the Barelvi school, 1,500 are Shias, and 120 belong to the Jamaat-e-Islami.[48] The Frontier Province is second only to the Punjab as a major recruiting ground on account of its proximity to Afghanistan and its ethnic solidarity with the Pashtoons. In 1979, there were 350 religious seminaries in this province, and this number had risen to 1,281 by 1999. Around 200,000 youths from the Frontier Province participated in the Afghan war, out of which around 15,000 were killed. On the Kashmir front, around 3,000 young men from the Frontier province lost their lives. Of the 15,000 who were killed in

Afghanistan, 60 per cent belonged to the *deeni madaris*, while the rest belonged to the regular schools and colleges of the province. In Kashmir, 700 students of *deeni madaris* lost their lives. In the Frontier region, the main organizations associated with Jehad are the Harkat-ul-Mujahidin, Harkat-ul-Jabbar al Islami, Hizb-ul-Mujahidin, Lashkar-e-Toiba, Al Badr, and Tehreek-e-Nifaz-e-Shariat-e-Muhammadi (TNSM). The TNSM had the largest presence in Afghanistan, where it sent 6,000 volunteers. They were disarmed and badly mistreated by the Taliban after which their support in the Frontier province dwindled.[49] Although there has been a visible reduction in Jehad-related activities since October 2001 when Afghanistan was attacked and the militants were dispersed, many are still active in the province, especially in Malakand division.

Sindh and Baluchistan account for fewer militants, partly due to their relative distance from Kashmir, partly as a result of historical contexts, and partly based on their smaller populations. In Sindh, 500 young men have laid down their lives, out of which 70 belonged to Jaish-e-Muhammad, 115 to Harkat-ul-Mujahidin, 123 to Lashkar-e-Toiba, 59 to Al Badr, 103 to Hizb-ul-Mujahidin and 38 to Lashkar-e-Islam. The rest belonged to smaller Jehadi organizations. Sindh has contributed about 25 per cent militants and 20 per cent of these never return home even if they are the sole breadwinners. Although religio-militant organizations are highly influential in rural Sindh, Karachi is the main supplier of manpower and has 2,000 *deeni madaris* to produce it. Baluchistan has not contributed substantially to militancy. Most of its militants have fought or been killed in bordering Afghanistan, while very few seem to have fought in Kashmir. The most influential party here is Maulana Fazl-ur-Rehman's JUI. Between 1990 and March 2002, 112 Baluchi youths were killed, mostly in Afghanistan. Most of the militants were enabled by the secret agencies to reach Afghanistan and Kashmir and the infiltration occurred under the cover of gunfire.

In the past, Harkat-ul-Jehad-al-Islami, Harkat-ul-Mujahidin, Jaish-e-Muhammad, Al Badr Mujahidin, and Lashkar-e-Toiba have openly admitted their connections with Osama bin Laden, and have acknowledged using the material and technical resources provided by Al Qaida. However, with time and as a result of the events of 11 September 2001, such links are denied or have become difficult due to the sea change in Pakistan's foreign policy under US pressure. The monster created by the cooperative policies of the United States and Pakistan in the 1980s has returned to haunt the two states. While the US is still far away and relatively inaccessible, the violence and terror have erupted within Pakistan, especially after the defeat of the Taliban and the return of militants from Afghanistan.

THE LIMITS OF COUNTER-TERRORISM

Terrorism and terrorists have been produced in Pakistan as a result of the state's origin in communal politics, Cold War geo-strategic interests, and the inequalities inherent within the state structure and policies. Pakistan's counter-terrorism efforts have been limited and constrained by the fact that the state has had to reverse its own policies and undo its own ideologies. It has therefore become a war against itself.

Pakistan is currently severely torn between the global pressures to end terrorism within and across its eastern and western borders, and the equally strong opposing pressures from religious and nationalist forces to refrain from submitting to American diktat. Pakistan's Anti-Terrorism Act (ATA) of 1997 is widely regarded as a highly repressive instrument designed to conduct a witch-hunt of political opponents and to suppress dissent. The ATA defines terrorism very broadly, so much so that even violence based on personal enmity is included, unlike the Indian Prevention of Terrorism Act (POTA), which is also widely seen as an instrument of state repression but refers only to acts which threaten state sovereignty.[50] The ATA refers to acts that create a sense of fear and insecurity among the population. Since 'a sense of fear and insecurity among the population' is very hard to measure, the Act lends itself to wide misinterpretation and misuse. It has been used by the state against tenant farmers struggling for land rights, journalists who reported the military's excesses against the tenants, and is being invoked against political parties like the Muttahida Majlis-e-Amal, which are agitating against the alleged humiliation of Pakistan's nuclear scientists.[51] As the standards of human rights and civil liberties have declined worldwide since 11 September 2001, and there is scant respect for due process, presumption of innocence until proved guilty, and other principles of international law and norms, there has been a corresponding decline in Pakistan. The ATA is invoked for the suppression of dissent or disagreement against the reversed policies of the state.

As a result of the attack on Afghanistan in October 2001, there has been a strong upsurge of sympathy for and solidarity with Afghans in the two Pakistani provinces neighbouring Afghanistan, the Frontier and Baluchistan. This was reflected in the results of the October 2002 election in which the MMA, an alliance of religious parties opposed to the military regime's pro-American policies, won a substantial number of seats. Historically, Pakistanis were not inclined to vote substantially for religious parties. The pattern among the smaller provinces was to vote for nationalist parties representing ethnic interests. However, the state's unstinted support for US policies and the vacuum created by its refusal and inability to deal with the two mainstream parties of Pakistan, the Pakistan People's Party and the Pakistan Muslim League (Nawaz), led to the victory of religious parties along the border regions. Some of the solidarity is also based on the shared ethnic identity with the Pashtoons across the border, with the result that there were massive demonstrations in Baluchistan and the Frontier Province against the 2001 coalition bombing of Afghanistan.

The Pakistan army's operation to 'hunt' Al Qaida suspects in South Waziristan for the last two years has been widely resented by the tribal people and the MMA. Fourteen men of the Pakistan army were killed in the Waziristan operation in 2003. In February 2004, thirteen civilians were killed in South Waziristan Agency in the tribal areas, as security forces searching for Al Qaida men opened fire on a vehicle carrying civilians. This led Qazi Hussain Ahmad of the MMA to say that the army had been pitched against the people of Pakistan in the service of the US, which is the 'biggest terrorist state of the day'.[52] There were reports that the US troops would join the Pakistan army in the hunt for terrorists in the tribal areas.[53] In March 2004, massive and bloody battles raged between the Pakistan army and suspected militants in the tribal areas. Several hundred people were killed and arrested in the search for Osama bin Laden who, it was widely believed, was being sought by the Bush administration because it was an election year. The military operation in

Waziristan, and the resulting bloodshed, was widely condemned by people from all walks of life including lawyers, High Court Bar Associations, political parties and rights activists. The government was even warned that a 1971-like situation was developing in the tribal areas where the state was pitted against society in an effort to please the US which had conferred the dubious status of 'Major Non-Nato Ally' upon Pakistan.[54] Press reports that Pakistan was sending troops to Iraq to help shore up America's illegal occupation sparked further resentment against a government becoming increasingly alienated from its own people.[55] However, the operation pleased the US authorities immensely as Colin Powell, US Secretary of State, praised the operation in the tribal areas, and the post-1999 sanctions on Pakistan were lifted allowing it to purchase military equipment and receive additional financial aid from the US.

There were press reports that the US had offered to support President Musharraf's stand on Pakistan's nuclear scientists, in return for help in finding Osama bin Laden and other members of Al Qaida. Although such reports were denied by the parties concerned, the deal was widely suspected.[56] As mentioned earlier, there was widespread public resentment against the perceived humiliation of the nuclear scientists and the unreserved support to American designs in Pakistan's tribal areas. As long as the United States continues to use the so-called war on terror as a justification for its unilateral, interventionist policies and colonization, and its support for Israel's illegal occupation of Palestinian land remains unabated, Pakistan will continue to experience a backlash against state support for America. This backlash is likely to place serious limits on its efforts to counter terrorism as Pakistan is widely perceived by its people to be in collusion with US terrorism.

A large number of the militants who have fled Afghanistan since 2001 have either re-entered Pakistan or gone to Kashmir, and now also Iraq, to continue the Jehad. As a result, Pakistan has seen an upsurge in terrorism in the last two years. In Islamabad and Bahawalpur, churches were bombed and several people killed. In Karachi in 2002, the American Consulate was bombed and fourteen members of a French multinational firm were murdered. The journalist, Daniel Pearl, was kidnapped and murdered in Karachi and a Christian human rights organization, the Idara-e-Amn-o-

Insaaf, saw seven of its members gunned down by militants. There were two attacks on the life of General Musharraf in December 2003, one of them involving suicide bombers. For the state in Pakistan, this is a case of the chickens coming home to roost.

Pakistanis in general, and religious parties in particular have resented the manner in which alleged Al Qaida operatives are hunted (a term that seems to suggest that they are animals) by the FBI in Pakistan. Every time a suspect is handed over to US agencies or is picked up by them, there is an uproar and protest. The handing over of digital maps and National Database and Registration Authority (NADRA) data to the US was widely resented in Pakistan, as was the installation of surveillance mechanisms at airports and other exit/entry points. Every action that is praised by the US and the so-called 'international community' is resented, opposed, and resisted by the religious parties as well as the public.[57] In 2003, a number of senior Pakistani nuclear scientists were apprehended for questioning regarding the proliferation of nuclear technology and know-how, the so-called 'debriefing' by the military. This action was seen as the humiliation of Pakistan's scientists who are regarded as national heroes. The condemnation of the debriefing by various political parties, including Tehreek-e-Insaaf of Imran Khan, Pakistan Muslim League Nawaz (which also took the matter to court), and the MMA was swift and severe. The MMA called a strike on 6 February 2004 to condemn the debriefing, but Abdul Qadeer Khan, the so-called Father of the Pakistani Bomb, confessed and was pardoned by the President. The whole drama was viewed with scepticism and amusement by those who always suspected and claimed that the state itself was involved in the proliferation of nuclear know-how, and that Qadeer Khan was just the 'fall guy'. The 'international community' watched and gave its nod of approval as statements emanated from Washington giving Pakistan a clean bill of health.[58]

The problem of terrorism in Pakistan is the result of the contradictory processes of state formation, wherein a state formed on the basis of a divisive ideology remained caught within that ideology, and ultimately became a victim of it. The ruling ideology of the Pakistani state needed and created enemies through its vast propaganda machine (the media and state education).[59] As a result of Cold-War imperatives, the state created what are often considered non-state actors, the militant terrorists whom the state can no longer completely control. There is a continuum of state and non-state actors as the one fed upon and strengthened the other. In Pakistan, the dichotomy between state and non-state actors dissolves as terrorism becomes both an instrument of state policy as well as the agenda of non-state actors. Even though the two may currently seem to be opposed, the links are too deep to break easily. The fact that the military enabled the MMA to achieve victory in elections by keeping the mainstream parties out and the deal on the Legal Framework Order was made only with the MMA and not with any of the other mainstream parties, is indicative of the state's inability to entirely discard the project it undertook in the 1980s.[60] Although General Musharraf promised to counter terrorism in his January 2002 speech, and banned militant outfits like Lashkar-e-Jhangvi and the Sipah-e-Sahaba, there is evidence that these groups are reconstituting themselves under different names.[61] There are frequent newspaper reports about the regrouping of the Taliban with help from elements in Pakistan's military. The International Crisis Group report seriously questions the sincerity of Musharraf's efforts in curbing madrasa-induced extremism and terrorism, despite the frequent approbation he receives from the United States for his efforts against religious extremism and terrorism.[62] The state in Pakistan is caught in a web which was woven by it during the Afghan Jehad. The need to strike a fine and difficult balance between the demands of the US and the 'international community' on the one hand, and on the other the interests of the people of Pakistan from whom state sovereignty is expected to flow, places severe constraints and limits on the efforts to counter terrorism.

III

THE CASE OF SRI LANKA: UNITARY STATE IN A HYBRID ISLAND[63]

The protracted ethnic conflict in Sri Lanka, spanning the last two decades, appears to be the result of an interplay of complex factors, which have roots in colonial history and the processes of nation and state formation. Both the state and non-state actors, have engaged in the violence, bloodshed and terror that characterize the conflict. The violence of one side seems to be mirrored and matched by that of the other, leading to a virtual partition of the Sri Lankan state along the ethnic fault lines stretching from the Sinhala dominated south and the Tamil majority areas in the north and east. Broadly speaking, four elements seem to be pivotal in igniting conflict and violence, which appear to have become endemic in the country: first, the structure and role of the state in Sri Lanka has fuelled the social conflict; second, the construction of exclusivist nationalism in a multilayered society has led to the hardening of identity postures; third, a deeply fragmented political system has led to the exacerbation of identity politics, and fourth, economic competition over scarce political and social resources has become articulated in the form of ethnic identity struggles. Each of these interconnected dimensions of the conflict needs to be examined separately, although the reader should keep in mind that there is a deep interpenetration of the issues and they are de-linked here only for purposes of conceptual clarity.

Structure and Role of the State in Sri Lanka

Like other South Asian countries, Sri Lanka is a multi-ethnic, multi-cultural and multilayered society, with a segmented and diverse population. The Census of 1981 showed that 74 per cent of the population comprises Sinahala-speaking people who are mostly Buddhists, 13 per cent are ethnically Tamil, while roughly 6 per cent are upcountry Tamils. Approximately 15.5 per cent of the Tamil-speaking people are Hindus. About 7 per cent of the population consists of Muslims, and 7.6 per cent is composed of Christians. Other religions constitute about 0.1 per cent of the population. The mix of religion and language is complex and is further complicated by the vertical fissures of caste and class within and across the communities. Religious and ethnic communities are roughly separated territorially with the Sinhalese Buddhists concentrated in the south, Tamils in the north and east and Muslims in the eastern province. These multiple and heterogeneous groups have lived, worked, played and prayed together for centuries during which migrations from India, and within Sri Lanka, created a criss-cross pattern of cultures, peoples, practices, and identities across the length and breadth of the country.

Although localized conflicts among people are a salient feature of all societies, certain characteristics that are distinctive to modernity and the formation of nations and states have led to the intensification of inter-group conflict in Sri Lanka. The modern idea of a homogenized and centralized state is one of the main underlying causes of the outbreak of group struggles. The accompanying ideology of the modern state, that is, nationalism, is strongly implicated in the genesis of the conflict.

One of the defining features of the post-Enlightenment ideology of nationalism is that older, regional, and narrower identities are suppressed, erased, and forgotten in favour of an overarching identity related to the centralized state. Official and statist forms of nationalism attempt to construct a homogenized and monolithic identity of 'the citizen' in an attempt to reduce the attraction of narrower sub-national, sub-state and older identities rooted in language, religion or caste. A certain degree of psychic violence inheres in the process of redesigning identities to fit the new concept of a modern state. Constitutionally, the Sri Lankan state is unitary, which imposes even greater homogenization as the different regions have little or no administrative or political autonomy. As a highly centralized state, Sri Lanka has tended to deal repressively with dissent and difference. The frequent imposition of emergency (for example, in 1958, 1964, 1977, and 2003) betrays a tendency towards authoritarianism when dealing with conflict. The absence of a federal structure capable of addressing issues at the regional and local levels has eroded the capacity of the state to understand or respond creatively to assertions of diversity and difference.

In Sri Lanka the modern identities drawn from the state and nation came to be monopolized by the majority community, the Sinhala Buddhists. After independence from British rule in 1948, the Sri Lankan state came to be dominated by Sinhala Buddhists who attempted to establish a hegemonic position in relation to the numerically smaller communities. One manifestation of this was the Official Language Act of 1956, by which the 'Sinhala Only' policy was adopted. This policy meant that Sinhala would be the language of state functioning and official business. In addition, Buddhism was made the state religion and given special protection and a privileged position as the religion of the Sinhalese.[64] Such discriminatory policies, which institutionalized inequality within the state structure, led to a sense of insecurity and alienation among the minority communities, in particular the Tamils who feared the loss of government jobs and access to education.[65] The fears were not unfounded as there was a steep decline in the number of Tamil recruits as a result of the policy. For example, in 1948, 54 per cent of the government recruits were Sinhala and 41 per cent were Tamil. By 1963, this ratio had changed drastically with 92 per cent Sinhalese and 7 per cent Tamil.[66] In 1958, there were riots against the 'Sinhala Only' policy, and the state declared an emergency.

Similarly, the Tamils, who were one-eighth of the population, were highly represented in the science-based universities. With the introduction of the standardization policy to university entrance examinations, the number of Tamil students became restricted as opposed to Sinhala-medium students, thereby leading to a sense of threat.[67] Furthermore, the Citizenship Act required proof of three generations of paternal ancestry in Ceylon, a measure which deprived the Tamils who had been brought from India as plantation workers of the right of citizenship.[68] The state's policy measures soon after independence, obviously designed to promote and protect the dominant Sinahala Buddhist majority, created the basis for the intensification of inter-group competition and conflict. As state identity and official nationalism came to be associated with one, numerically larger, ethnic group, the other groups, in particular the Tamils, came to be defined in ethnic terms.

As the Sinhala Buddhist politicians, priests and ideologues set about the task of constructing an essentially Sinhala state, the Tamils, who were perceived to be occupying lucrative positions in government and business, simultaneously came to be defined as the 'Other' against whom the Sinhala identity was juxtaposed. Sinhala politicians eager to win the majority vote whipped up anti-Tamil sentiments and a series of anti-Tamil riots occurred in 1956, 1958, and 1981. In the early 1970s, the stirrings of a separate homeland for the Tamils to protect their political and economic rights had begun, and the Liberation Tigers of Tamil Eelam (LTTE), a militant separatist organization was formed in 1976. In 1979, the state promulgated the draconian Prevention of Terrorism Act designed to deal harshly with the growing insurgency. The conflict between a Sinhala Buddhist-defined state and separatist Tamil guerrillas began to take on ominous proportions. The major turning point in the conflict came in 1983, when the anti-Tamil riots took on genocidal proportions, resulting in what is now referred to as a pogrom.

In July 1983, the LTTE ambushed and killed thirteen soldiers in Jaffna in what was a humiliating military debacle for the state. A day of national mourning was announced for the dead soldiers and the media highlighted the incident in ways which inflamed communal passions. For the Sinhala armed forces, politicians, and priests, the day of mourning was also a day of vengeance. Adele Balasingham provides the following chilling account of the terror unleashed upon the Tamils to avenge the death of the soldiers:

> The state funeral of the 'fallen heroes' turned into state sponsored mass violence against the Tamil people. Rampaging mobs led by politicians and priests (Buddhist monks) aided and abetted by the police and army stormed Tamil houses, shops, buildings and businesses and plundered the property and murdered the defenseless Tamils. Those who led the unruly mobs had precise information of the Tamil residences and properties. Most of them operated with voter's lists to identify the Tamil houses. It was impossible for those who lived in Colombo and in the South among the Sinhalese to escape identification. There were unspeakable horrors. Innocent Tamils were beaten and hacked to death. Hundreds of them were burnt alive. While the Tamil victims cried in agony the Sinhala rioters danced in ecstasy. In one incident in Colombo a group of foreign tourists were terror stricken and sickened as they watched a mini-bus load of Tamils being burnt alive while the Sinhala mobs were dancing in a mad frenzy. For forty-eight hours the Government maintained a calculated silence, allowing time for the violent mobs to avenge the dead soldiers.[69]

Balasingham reports that there was widespread destruction of Tamil property and massive loss of life. Businesses were destroyed and lives uprooted. On 25 July, thirty-five Tamil prisoners were attacked and killed in Welikdade prison with the collusion of the prison officers. This left a 'deep scar in the soul of the Tamil nation' and drove an irreconcilable wedge between the two groups. The struggle for a separate Tamil homeland escalated enormously after the genocide of 1983.[70] The pogrom of 1983 was followed in 1987 to 1989 by what is now referred to as the 'reign of terror'.[71] In this period, during an uprising in the south by the JVP, an organization based on class ideology, which had earlier led an insurrection in 1971, the security forces, on the orders of the government of the United National Party, picked up male youths who subsequently disappeared.

The conflict between a communal state and the sub-national guerrillas escalated substantially with dramatic acts of terror, such as the attack on the Bandarnaike International Airport in August 2001 in which half the fleet of Sri Lanka's airlines was destroyed. The LTTE scored some major victories against the state military as it became a full-fledged army funded by the Tamil diaspora and the illegal arms and drugs market. The most spectacular was their takeover in the April–May 2000 of the Elephant Pass which controls land access to the Jaffna Peninsula.

The prolonged war led to massive internal displacement, rape, abduction, killing and terrorist acts committed by both sides of the conflict. However, by September 2001, the global climate had changed drastically with 9/11 and the subsequent crackdown on 'terrorist' organizations. Since the major players in the global arena define the LTTE as a terrorist group, and support the Sri Lankan state, LTTE channels of funding and the procurement of arms began to dry up. On the other hand, the state experienced negative economic growth for the first time in 2001, and widespread calls for negotiation and peace began to be heard. In February 2002, a peace deal was brokered by Norwegian mediators calling for a truce and the cessation of hostilities.

The uneasy truce was seriously threatened when, in November 2003, the President again declared emergency and assumed three portfolios including defence and communications. The conflicts between President Chandrika Kumaratunga's Peoples Alliance and Prime Minister Ranil Wickramasinghe led to a breakdown of the government, and new elections were called in April 2004. One of the main objections of the President to the Prime Minister's peace deal was that the former had no representative on the negotiating team and that the government was handing the north and east to the LTTE on a silver platter. On the one hand, the infighting between mainstream political parties endangered the peace processes, on the other the LTTE also split up, with Commander Karun, who is believed to command around 6,000 guerrillas, acting independently against the wishes of the LTTE leader, Velupillai Prabhakaran.

The unitary nature of the Sri Lankan state, along with the enormous powers vested in the president, and the difficulties in amending the constitution, are some of the major impediments for the state-society conflict resolution. The imposition of a unitary structure on an essentially multiple and diverse society prevents the interests and rights of the myriad different communities living in Sri Lanka from being adequately protected and promoted. The very form of the state encourages centralization, homogeneity and the domination of the majority community. The attempts at devolution have not met with much success, and the creation of a federal structure would require a major constitutional amendment. Redesigning and refashioning the state seems urgently necessary, but the process requires the kind of political consensus that does not currently exist. Conflict is thus built into the very fabric of the state of Sri Lanka.

Exclusivist Nationalism in a Multicultural Society

A centralized, unitary state requires a homogenizing dominant ideology which enables it to galvanize the population around a singular notion of identity. This process is fraught with tension as diverse and multiple identities and histories need to be erased and forgotten, and the dominant version of history and identity aggressively and compulsively remembered. The repression of a long history of heterogeneity, diversity and hybridity requires a certain amount of psychological, ideological, and emotional violence as people try to cling tenaciously to multiple pasts remembered in folk tales, legends, and collective and shared cultural memories. A large part of the sense of self resides in local histories, legends, and generational stories handed down by one's ancestors as popular memory. Official, state-sponsored, and state-constructed nationalism, designed to alter historical memory and develop a monolithic new national memory by projecting present interests and anxieties on to a distant past, creates violent ruptures in the sense of Self.

When dominant and state-led versions of nationalism privilege one ethnic group over others, the stage is set for inter-group conflict over national narratives and collective memories. Minority groups, fearful of their history and identity becoming subsumed under the memories of others, develop and elaborate their own national narratives and establish their own remembering. Nationalisms are thus contested and contradictory as memories from the margins fracture and interrupt the memories of the Centre. The national narratives of each group are contradictory and contested as they deny, conceal and repress the narratives of those who constitute a minority within the subgroups. As society is layered and complex, several competing stories of the past, of greatness, heroism, sacrifice, sorrow, suffering, and pride, intermingle and compete with one another in the politics of 'the Truth'. What often gets obliterated and silenced as competing and opposing narratives are woven is the mixing, overlapping and interpenetration of the stories, tales, and narratives of the past. In fact, mixture, which connotes impurity and pollution, becomes threatening as group identities resort to notions of purity and authenticity in constructing the Self.

In Sri Lanka, the Sinhala Buddhists and Tamils constructed their own, competing pasts and identity—the Sri Lankan version of the two-nation theory. As the conflict intensified, the images and identities hardened and solidified. One of the main aspects of the consolidation of a monolithic identity is the exclusion of the 'other' within as well as outside the boundaries of the Self. Inclusion of the 'other' as a part of the self became equivalent to impurity. As Darini Rajasingham-Senanayake argues, the scientific method of arriving at the 'truth', when applied to social and cultural realities, disallows mixed categories—the logic excludes the middle term. A is either B or non-B, A cannot be B and non-B at the same time.[72] One is either Sinhalese or Tamil, one cannot be Tamil and non-Tamil at the same time. This kind of exclusivist ideology erased from memory the long history of intermarriage, hybrid cultures, mixtures and overlapping or shared identities. Neluka Silva argues that

> Hybridity is envisioned as a signifier for 'abnormality' while its binary opposition, normality, implies citizenship, stability. . . . During nationalist moments, when notions of ethnic purity, authenticity and pristine culture are validated, hybridity is disempowering. At such moments, hybridity as it appears and is lived is fraught with tension.[73]

In Silva's view, Sri Lanka has many cultures and histories, but the Sinhala and Tamil national narratives share a common plot which assumes that the two groups are mutually exclusive, and the nationalist histories they produce mirror and mimic each other in an attempt to enshrine notions of ethnically pure territory and identity.[74] Arjun Guneratne argues that the logic of contemporary nationalism compels it to read the events of the past in terms of present anxieties and this results in a picture of a world populated by two opposed groups that are represented as ancient enemies.[75] Violence and terror flow from nationalist pursuits because enemies are an indispensable requirement of nationalisms created in estrangement and alienation from an 'other'. Enemies help create threat perception and justify the amassing of arms, and provide legitimization to the pursuit of violence by all parties. As a consequence, dynastic struggles and quarrels over feudal control of labour and resources tend to be redefined as ethnic wars.[76]

The construction of mutually exclusive, opposing, and inimical groups is attributed to the colonial knowledge system, which attempted to classify and arrange colonized populations in fixed and exclusive categories that did not permit overlapping and mixture.[77] Attributing the process to a 'racial science of identity construction', Darini Rajasingham-Senanayake argues that in post-colonial Sri Lanka, nationalism is located in the politics of memory and forgetting.[78] To summarize Rajasingham-Senanayke's important arguments, the categories and classifications of colonial population mapping are modern but nationalism projects these into a distant, primordial past. Armed conflict and the consequent hardening of nationalist images and postures have created a de facto partition of Sri Lanka. The mixtures created by mass migrations and intermarriage and cultural mixing are denied as they interrupt the national narrative. The application of the scientific method of classification in the colonial census was a basic element in the 'process of colonial governmentality'. This method transformed the more fluid earlier notions of identity into fixed and impermeable categories. The process of nation building and state formation in Sri Lanka 'resulted in the bi-polar configuration of Sinhala and Tamil linguistic communities as mutually antagonistic'. Contrary to nationalist claims by ethnic groups, the north-south conflict was not a major fault line of identity and conflict of the level seen today is a modern and recent phenomenon. The transformation of a multicultural border area into an ethnic partition in armed conflict, and the accompanying destruction of hybridity and coexistence are phenomena located in the peculiarly modern compulsions of state formation and nation building. Violence, both state and non-state, has effaced a history of coexistence and hybridity, while simultaneously militarizing civil society. Nationalist myths project the two communities as locked in a perennial conflict from primordial times. Nationalist historiography, colonial topography and the census are the technologies of the governmentality of modern times. The effects of this form of knowledge have been political violence, death, loss of life, and bloodshed.[79] This post-structuralist reading of the Sri Lankan conflict in terms of colonial topography and post-colonial nationalist historiography is an important tool for the deconstruction of identity constructs epistemologically, as well as for the political project of softening ethnic barriers.

In a similar vein, Guneratne challenges the dominant cultural constructions of the Aryan–Dravidian divide. He argues that such racial classifications of two primordially opposed groups are problematic since the Sinhalese and Tamils share a large number of the elements of the kinship system. The division by language is a recent one, but kinship systems pre-date linguistic differentiations and reflect the commonalities and shared cultural constructs. Both Sinhala and Tamils share Dravidian kinship systems, and their opposition into Aryan-descended Sinahala and Dravidian-descended Tamils is a recent one. These identities are historically constructed, and the relationship of identity with territory sets the stage for conflict and violence.[80] Fictional and imagined identities have been crystallized by conflict into political entities which have effects on the lives of both Sinhalese and Tamils.

That fact that such homogenized national identities are fictional, and elide the conflicts of class, is expressed succinctly by Pradeep Jeganathan and Qadri Ismail: 'Those who speak thus of the nation, beg the question, who is that "nation" and express its will? How can we find out what the "nation" actually wants?'[81] Jeganathan and Ismail argue that the assumption that people homogenously inhabit any given piece of territory is questionable:

The probems of the nation are not, then, problems of 'Sinhalaness', 'Tamilness' or 'Moorness' *per se*. The problem rather is in the making of diverse peoples into 'Tamils', 'Sinhalas', or 'Moors'; and then in turn of making those peoples into Sri Lankans. Or put another way, there is a fundamental contradiction, a continuous oscillation between possible heterogeneity and implied homogeneity in the project of nationalism. The nation has many histories, but it claims one as it own; its people have many identities but they must inhabit one; the nation has many political coalitions within it but they are to be suppressed in the aid of one mission: nationalism. And the pursuit of this single minded, monolithic object has brought nothing but violence, terror, and destruction to us all.[82]

The connection between the invocation of nationalism and violence, terror, and destruction, is eloquently brought out by the two writers in their understanding of how difference comes to *make a difference*, as identities become politically and militarily mobilized.

In the Sri Lankan context, the complex relation between women and nationalism takes on a heightened urgency as a part of the nation-making process. Since a large number of LTTE militants are female, and many of them constitute a part of the suicide squads (the Sea Tigers and Black Tigers), there has been a debate among feminists regarding the ways in which nationalism mobilizes and demobilizes women, and invokes and contains the idea of motherhood. Although this is a major and ongoing debate, it is summarized here since an understanding of the politics of terror and nationalism in Sri Lanka cannot be understood without a reference to the militarization of the feminine and of motherhood. Neloufer de Mel has argued that the mother figure is central to the nation as 'mothers are duty bound to beget courageous sons' and the grieving mother is an evocative symbol of national pride whether the perpetrators are revolutionaries or the state.[83] De Mel has argued that the mother as nurturer and chaste woman, as well as dutiful 'housewife' is co-opted for 'symbolising this inner and sovereign cultural space of the emerging nation'.[84] At the same time, the image of a woman carrying a baby in one hand and a gun in the other combines the ideas of a sacrificing mother with sacrifice for the nation, thereby redefining the notion of motherhood without forgoing the traditional concept of femininity.

Women were recruited heavily by the LTTE when youths were no longer easily available after the Indo–Lanka Accord of 1987.[85]

The LTTE combatant is usually killed in battle, but if taken captive he or she shallows a cyanide capsule worn around the neck.[86] Dying for the nation is interpreted as ultimately upholding life—the life of the collective given through the sacrifice of individual death. This is how Adele Balasingham replied to feminist critics of the LTTE women when the former accused them of taking on masculine and militarist values and denying life and femininity.[87] However, critics claim that the politics of nationalism tends to be reactionary and contains women within specific and narrow definitions of womanhood. This assertion is supported by the manner in which Muslim women heightened their customary regulations as a continuation of Muslim identity in the face of forcible eviction by the LTTE from their homes in the northern province.[88] About 75,000 Muslims were subjected to ethnic cleansing by the LTTE, thereby forcing the exclusion of the sub-national 'other' to create the pure identity required by a defensive nationalism. Whether or not women are genuinely empowered by national conflict is still a hotly debated question, not only in places of high intensity conflict such as Sri Lanka, but in other cases as well. Nevertheless, there is a general consensus that while women are mobilized for national struggles and called upon to make enormous sacrifice, once independence is achieved, and even during the struggle, femininity and its values are deployed as an instrument of control over sexuality. Nationalist struggles include women as combatants and in other roles; the state, once formed and established, excludes them from full citizenship in its efforts to create the virtuous and moral nation.

Political violence is a process of the formation of states and nations. The nation is imagined by erasing heterogeneity and hybridity, and imposing homogeneity, if necessary through ethnic cleansing and pogroms. The state provides the territory on which the story of the nation comes to be written in blood.

Politicized Ethnicity, Ethnicized Politics

In the multicultural post-colonial societies of South Asia, democracy is generally regarded as a panacea for the ills afflicting governance. The intention of the authors of representative democracy was that pre-modern identities based on the narrow loyalties of caste, region, religion or ethnicity would erode, and in their place the modern identity of the citizen of the state would determine collective belonging. Politics would come to be based on political and economic issues instead of caste, communal or ethnic ones. It was expected that political parties would articulate economic and political interests across the divides of ethnicity, caste, and community. The larger identity of the citizen would be inclusive of all those who reside within the territory of the state, and it would be irrespective of caste, religion or language. Although this identity would be constructed in exclusive terms in relation to those residing in other states, within a single state citizenship benefits would accrue to all equally, and there would be no discrimination based on any marker of social difference whether race, gender, region or religion. These were some of the assumptions of liberal democracy, drawn from the experience of countries where the populations are relatively more homogenous and the differences of caste, colour or language are not highly marked.

These assumptions underlying liberal democracy seemed to fail in the context of the highly differentiated, multiple, and diverse societies of South Asia. Democracy itself became one of the mechanisms of reinforcing older, narrower and sub-national identities as vote banks came to be based on ethnic, caste, religious or linguistic basis.[89] As the South Asian states failed to provide the minimum standards of living and proved incapable of ensuring security, economic and social rights and welfare, the disillusionment with the state became widespread. People began to seek protection, continuity, identity, and material benefits from smaller and more personal collectivities such as the religious or linguistic community. Democracy became absorbed in South Asian societies in a manner that strengthened caste and communal identities. Increasingly, political parties that cut across the divides of caste, community and religion, failed to win votes and regional and smaller parties began to proliferate. When states themselves were formed along communal lines, such as Pakistan, there was no question of the minorities being considered equal since the very basis of the state was the protection of the interests of the majority community.

This situation was exacerbated by the fact that the political parties generally were not mature enough to handle conflicted situations wisely or with foresight. Eager to win the largest numbers of votes, political parties succumbed to the perceived desires of the majority community.[90] In Sri Lanka, the eagerness of the parties to win the Sinhala votes, led them to indulge in the appeasement of the majority community at the expense of the minorities.[91] Majorities and minorities, which in a democracy meant the largest or the smallest number of people and not the main religious or language group or the smaller religious or language group, now came to mean the latter. With democracy being rendered as a purely numerical game, the focus of the parties became winning seats and votes and making coalitions. The broader meaning of democracy, which includes strong institutions such as an independent judiciary, a supreme parliament reflecting popular sovereignty, a separation of powers along with checks and balances, and justice, freedom, equality, and rights, was replaced by the idea of reaching the magical number. This reduced the level and quality of politics to 'whoever can muster enough votes'. The kind of systems put in place in South Asia brought landlords and the clergy into power in Pakistan, religious nationalists in India, and opportunists everywhere. As the majority communities formed parties to further their own interests, the beleaguered minorities formed their own parties to protect their political and economic interests. For example, in Sri Lanka, the Muslims have formed the Sri Lanka Muslim Congress for the protection of their interests, which are threatened by the Tamils who constitute a majority in the areas where the Muslims live. The process thus repeats itself at several levels in multilayered societies. With the global decline of the politics of the Left and class-based parties, politics increasingly came to be articulated in ethnic terms.

In Sri Lanka, not only did the political parties rush to win the majority community, the infighting and bickering within the Sinhala parties also led to impediments in the peace process. For example, the UNF government of Prime Minister Ranil Wickremesinghe was roundly castigated by the ruling Peoples Alliance in 1999 and 2001 for giving in too much to LTTE demands.[92] In November 2003, as mentioned earlier, President Chandrika Kumaratunga took over three portfolios and imposed a state of emergency. This led to a serious crisis between the President and the Prime Minister over the peace process and culminated in elections being called in April 2004.

The violence during the election process has been widely reported in newspapers, and the election body took over the Sri Lankan state media, which was accused of biased coverage of the election. P. Saravanamuttu argues that no party in the south would be able to implement peace settlements even if it wanted to, as there is stiff competition between political parties for the majority vote.[93] The structural conflict inherent in the offices of the president and prime minister impedes the peace process as political parties vie with each other for majority support. Although J.R Jayewardene warned as early as 1956 that the rights of non-Sinhala people should not be trampled upon or their grievances would lead to the civil war and repeated his warning in 1966, he did not do much to remove the inequalities and stem the escalation of the civil war when he was in power and an unquestioned leader of the UNP.[94] Senaratne argues that the state tends to have a knee-jerk response to challenge or genuine grievance, and thereby exacerbates conflict instead of leading to solutions.

Shyamika Jayasundara argues that in mid-level democracies, dissident behaviour is less often accommodated than repressed and this intensifies the chances of violence.[95] Democracy bolsters ethno-political conflicts and reinforces communalism. In the case of Sri Lanka, party politics have become ethnicized and ethnicity has become politicized.

The Political Economy of Conflict

Conflicts, and the associated violence and terror, are difficult to sustain over a long period of time unless there are actors who gain from the war. The economic dimension of any conflict has to be understood along with its politics, culture, and history for a comprehensive picture to emerge. Without a regular supply of money, arms, and materials, fighting cannot go on. Arms manufacturers, smugglers, exporters, and users, all have a stake in the continuation of the conflict. The arms black market is large and crosses the borders of a single state. Some of the links between arms and drug trafficking, and smuggling have been explained in detail by Imtiaz Ahmed.[96]

Both the Sri Lankan state and the LTTE have gained financially from the war in the past. The war provides employment to unemployed youth and ensures jobs that are related to Dhananjayam security issues. According to Dhananjayam Sriskandarajah, in the 1990s, Sri Lanka evolved into a war economy sustained by high aid flows to both sides by expatriates and the diaspora. The state benefited from the war economy as Tamils were displaced from employment in the north, and the resultant vacancies were filled by others.[97] Sriskandarajah argues that ethnic and political conflicts are essentially struggles over resources. Sri Lanka currently has twenty million people differentiated along ethnic lines.[98] When the state excludes a particular group from power and access to resources (as in the Sinhala Only Policy), or promotes and supports one group over others, the struggle for rights can get articulated as an ethnic one. In the absence of organized and systematic politics of class, ethnicity may potentially become the basis on which economic battles are fought, as people turn to the immediate reference group for the security that the state failed to provide. Although people often have more in common culturally with the working people of other groups as compared with the elites of either group, they tend to rally around their own political and ruling elites for the articulation of rights.[99] Conflicts are fuelled by the inter-group struggle over scarce resources in an attempt to gain economic security through political and civil rights. Political parties that come to be based upon ethnic group identity tend to articulate the group members' rights to employment, land, college admissions, welfare, and so on. If these are not seen as forthcoming in the existing political arrangements, the demand can intensify for maximum autonomy, and ultimately secession.

Sriskandarajah rightly argues that the economy is not merely one dimension of the conflict. Rather, conflict is an inherently economic phenomenon when examined through the lens of resource mobilization for war, costs of war, incentives for war, the economic agendas served by war, economic policies designed to reduce the risk of war, peace dividends, etc. Conflict is not an interruption of peacetime, but a continuous struggle varying in intensity.[100] Although this theory of economic determinism may seem crude or extreme to some, even a cursory glance at the conflicts of today seems to uphold it. If it is not oil, it is water, if not water, it is land, but conflicts invariably seem to arise over the sharing of economic and survival resources. Of course resources are not merely material but also intellectual, social, cultural, ideological, and political over which political parties seek to gain power.[101] In a world of shrinking resources, and the control of existing resources, by some classes at the expense of others, conflict seems to be inherent in the very structure of social and political life.

In the case of Sri Lanka, it was initially a Sinhalese perception that the Tamils were predominantly over-represented in lucrative positions, and the drive to 'correct' the imbalance led to Tamil insecurities regarding employment and education.[102] The majority perceived itself to be at a disadvantage and proceeded to correct the imbalance, a move widely seen by the minority community as designed to annihilate its existence and sources of existence. Jehan Perera provides some evidence for the economic decline of the Tamil areas by arguing that the economic output of the north and east is now 60 per cent of what it used to be when the war commenced.[103]

However, the economy can also end war when it is no longer believed to be gainful. When the costs of war are calculated in material and human terms, as well as political and diplomatic terms, peace seems attractive and carries dividends. Senaratne reveals that from 1983 to 1989, which is the most destructive phase of the Tamil insurrection, and up to 1996, the war has cost Rs. 287.5 billion, which is 6 per cent of the gross domestic product and 21.6 per cent of the national budget. Between 1997 and 2001, the war cost a further Rs. 200 billion. In 2000 and 2001, the economic crisis came to a head when the LTTE captured significant territory in Jaffna and military expenses increased substantially. Sri Lanka, which had boasted the most vibrant and fastest-growing economy in the South Asian region, registered a negative growth in 2001 for the first time. The public debt had become unsustainably high at 1,414 billion, and the country experienced severe economic difficulties.[104] Additionally, there are indirect costs of war in terms of an uncertain investment climate, loss of skilled labour as nearly 65,000 people were killed in the war, frequent security checks and roadblocks leading to delays in reaching one's destination, armed desertions, and loss of manpower and productivity.[105] Among the social costs of war is the burgeoning sex-worker industry in major cities in the north and central provinces, where the armed forces were kept as stand by or had stopped over for rest and relaxation.[106] Another is the conscription of child soldiers by the LTTE.[107] It is not surprising, then, that a Norwegian-brokered peace accord was reached in February 2002 in a war-torn and war-weary Sri Lanka.

However, war enables a state to further empower itself and increase its repressive apparatus. In 2000, the World Bank reported that the per capita expenditure on defence in Sri Lanka was the highest in South Asia.[108] Sri Lanka had twenty-five years of economic liberalization but the war necessitated a reallocation of resources from welfare to warfare.[109] This also meant that the state was increasing its capacity for violence, control and terror, with the LTTE equally trying to arm itself to the teeth. Thus, while the arms industry profited, Sri Lankans killed one another on a regular basis. State terror was met by non-state terror, in an endless spiral of increasing violence, death and repression of their own people by both parties.

To a very great extent, then, war and peace are economically determined. There are those who gain from either one or the other and those who gain from both. The global, national, and local economies, all play a part in producing the conflict as well as ending it, either temporarily or permanently. In the case of Sri Lanka, the international aid flows, contributions by the diaspora, the black or parallel economy, liberalization, and inter-group economic competition, all played a role in igniting, maintaining, and reducing the conflict.

Costs of State and non-State Terror

The two-decade-long Sri Lankan civil war has taken a huge toll in terms of life, sorrow, and suffering. The loss of life and suffering have been inflicted by all sides, be it the state, a class-based organization like the JVP, or the nationalist LTTE. For example,

> the Presidential Commission into Involuntary Removal found 7,239 cases of disappearances, since January 1988 from an alleged 8,739 reported cases. Of these 4,858 were at hands of state forces while 779 were JVP instigated; journalists and scholars who have written on the reign of terror place the number of deaths at 40,000. There were 60,000 casualties in the north and east, half of them civilian with 55,000 maimed, over 750,000 people of

mainly Tamil origin displaced in a diaspora, and nearly a million Lankans, mainly Tamils and Muslims, but Sinhalese too internally displaced in refugee camps.[110]

As the conflict intensifies, postures become hardened and the resolve to win the war is strengthened.

The state's discriminatory policies and majoritarian forms of democracy, along with a unitary constitution, are at the heart of the genesis of the conflict. The state has been forced to negotiate with the LTTE not only because Sri Lanka is war weary and the economy registered negative growth in 2001, but also because the LTTE is bargaining from a position of strength. In the long run, it appears that unless serious changes are made in the very structure of the Sri Lankan state so that minority communities are adequately represented and a federal system is evolved, peace will be difficult. Additionally, the political system would have to be transformed so that it is able to accommodate the minorities in a just and equitable sharing of power and resources. This would mean that democracy would have to be more than elections, voting, majorities, and parliamentary seats. Institutions of justice and representation would have to be strengthened in such a way that the whims and fancies of a person or political party cannot deprive the minorities of their rights. A system which privileges one religious and linguistic community is not likely to lead to a viable and sustainable solution. The hybridity and diversity of Sri Lanka requires this to be reflected in the political system without reducing the diversity to mere 'vote banks' and narrow communitarianism.

The reductive, false, and binary nationalisms of Sinhala Buddhism versus the Tamil nation need to be challenged by emphasizing the essential hybridity of the Paradise Island. Exclusionary and narrow nationalisms tend to contradict democracy, which requires equality as a fundamental condition of justice. The nation as a monolithic construction cancels out the state, and narrow identities erode citizenship. The distribution of equal citizenship rights to employment, education, resources, and power would require some constraints to be placed upon majoritarianism. This is not an easy task or one that will be accomplished soon. It requires patience, vision, and statesmanship on the part of Sri Lankan leaders.

IV

CONCLUDING REFLECTIONS

An exploration of the causes and dynamics of terrorism, and counter-terror measures, shows that terrorism is not the monopoly of any group, whether religious, linguistic, national, ethnic, state or non-state. Any group or state can resort to terrorist methods based upon certain contingencies, for example, the blocking of state or group goals. The state is not necessarily a representative of the good and a victim of terror, but frequently also a perpetrator of terror, especially when it represents the interests of one class or ethnic group to the detriment of others.

Terror tends to reproduce terror. The violence of the oppressed comes to match or even exceed the violence of the oppressor. The two forms of violence may mimic and mirror each other. Matching terror tactics with terror, or using excessive force and military means to squelch dissent and disagreement, serves to exacerbate conflict. The basic causes of conflict need to be acknowledged and addressed if the grievance is not to become a festering wound and finally secession.

In countering terror, it is a gross error to overlook history and ignore the genuine grievances of the dissenting group. The policies of states can be discriminatory, leading to feelings of deprivation and injustice, which must be addressed through conflict-resolution mechanisms built into the democratic process. Denial of the existence of injustice and the tendency to deal with terror with repression only seem to worsen the situation. The means of redress for injustice, inequality or deprivation need to be a part of the systems of governance. Democracy, therefore, needs to be defined and instituted in a manner which enables it to address conflict in a systemic way, rather than allowing dependence upon a political party or individual to resolve conflicts. Constitutional amendments may be required to institutionalize the conflict-resolution methods. Instead of democracy becoming merely majority rule, the rule of law, supremacy of parliament, independence of the judiciary, rights of citizens, freedom and equality of citizens, separation of powers, and checks and balances need to be the principles of operation. Democracy means institutions and not just elections.

In multicultural and multi-ethnic societies, the federal system needs to be developed, with provincial autonomy guaranteed and limits placed on the power of the centre. The relationship of the centre with the federating units needs to be constitutionally defined and clarified so that the centre does not become too powerful and authoritarian, and the federating units do not threaten the very existence of the federation. Provisions need to be made to protect the minorities within the federating units, since South Asian societies are layered and there are sub-minorities within minorities.

Although the state is not a monolith and represents myriad voices, interests, and concerns, a certain level of conflict and violence inheres in the very nature of states. The tendency to homogenize and centralize seems to be built into the very concept of modern states. This becomes a condition of violence as difference and diversity are forcibly erased or suppressed.

The pursuit of the so-called 'national interest' by states spurs them on to violence against minorities perceived to be acting against the state-defined 'national interest'. In the pursuit of 'national security', states attack other states to annex territory or capture resources. This creates a situation of violence against which resistance is offered by those whose territory is conquered and resources captured. States have a built-in tendency to be aggressive and belligerent in the pursuit of resources and domination. Conflict seems to be woven into the very fabric of the nation-state system, internally as well as internationally. As states sacrifice human security in the name of national security, and exclude human from national, the insecurity of human beings becomes intensified. This insecurity creates its own dynamics of violence and terror.

Finally, war and conflict are forms of nation building and state formation. Pakistan was formed in conflict and a great deal of blood was spilled. Yet Pakistan's formation cannot be called a terrorist act. The emergence of Bangladesh was also a bloodstained story but it cannot be said that it was a terrorist act. Rather, terror was committed by the Pakistani military. Similarly, the USA was liberated through a war of independence and its formation cannot be called an act of terrorism. France's liberation from Nazi Germany cannot be called an act of terror. The point is that the current tendency to call all wars of liberation against occupation and repression terrorism is a gross misunderstanding of history, society, and states. Tamil Ealam may or may not emerge, but it is a struggle for state formation that has taken a violent turn as a result of the dynamics of state and non-state violence.

Terror cannot be countered by more and intensified terror. Civilians die as much in war as they do in terrorist attacks. The old adage that violence begets violence, hate begets hate is true even today. The only way to counter terrorism is to address the fundamental grievances that produced it in the first place. History is a guide to a great deal of common sense.

NOTES

1. Cited in Rohini Hensman, 'The Only Alternative to Global Terror', in Ammu Joseph & Kalpana Sharma (eds.), *Terror, Counter-Terror: Women Speak Out* (New Delhi: Kali Press, 2002), p. 23.
2. Georg Witschel, 'Global Terrorism: Trends and Response', in Sridhar K. Khatri and Gert W. Kueck, *Terrorism in South Asia: Impact on Development and Democratic Process* (Colombo: Regional Centre for Strategic Studies, 2003), p. 22.
3. Witschel, *Terrorism in South Asia*, p. 28.
4. P.R. Chari, 'Combating Terrorism: Devising Cooperative Countermeasures', in Khatri and Kueck, *Terrorism in South Asia*, pp. 427-47.
5. P.R. Chari, 'Post-11 September Global Developments: An Indian Perspective', in Dipankar Banerji and Gert W. Kueck, *South Asia and the War on Terrorism: Analysing the Implications of 11 September*, Regional Centre for Strategic Studies (New Delhi: India Research Press, 2003), pp. 51-64.
6. Witschel, *Terrorism in South Asia*, p. 27.
7. Akmal Hussain, 'Terrorism, Development and Democracy: The Case of Pakistan', in Khatri and Kueck, *Terrorism in South Asia*, p. 123.
8. Chari, 'Post-11 September Global Developments', p. 51.
9. For example, Ammu Joseph and Kalpana Sharma refer to Barbara and Rosa Ehrenreich's work to argue that 'terrorists could be motivated by the same sense of duty, honour and sacrifice as soldiers in a war. After all, both sets of men are moved by a love of country or cause that pushes them to kill others, or to die.' Joseph and Kalpana Sharma (eds.), *Terror, Counter-Terror*, 'Introduction', 2003, p. xvii.
10. Witschel, *Terrorism in South Asia*, p. 21.
11. Chari, 'Combating Terrorism', p. 431.
12. Attributing terrorism mainly to religion, and within this category to Muslims, Chari writes: 'religion has supplanted politics as the main

principle animating terrorist groups, exemplified by the Muslims outfits operating in the Middle East'. A little later in the same paper he writes: 'Religion does remain, however, a powerful subsidiary motive inspiring terrorists in the Muslim world, since its fundamental elements derive sustenance from political Islam'. See Chari, 'Combating Terrorism', pp. 431-2. In the last para on p. 432, Chari attributes some validity to Samuel's Huntington's dubious and discredited thesis of the clash of civilizations. On page 435 of the same paper, he argues that the US has a legal basis for its attack on Iraq as it was assembling weapons of mass destruction, a fantasy widely known to be incorrect. Chari uses the argument to justify an attack by India on Pakistan. On page 445, he argues that a phobia exists in the Muslim world against the US and Israel and recently India has been added to this list. The discourse is patently racist not only because of what it says about entire religious communities, but also because of what it does not say. For example, Chari fails to mention US terrorism against a number of other states, Israeli occupation of and terrorism against the Palestinians and the Indian pogrom against Muslims in Gujarat in 2002. The US, Israel and India are presented as victims and Muslims are terrorists without showing the reverse side of the picture. Additionally, entire communities and their faith are held responsible for terror without any fine distinctions. Such essentialism can only be explained as racist and a clear case in which intellectual discourse seems to follow rather than interrogate the hegemonic discourse on terrorism.

13. For some interesting reflections on how war and imperialism are essentially racist in character, see Hensman, 'The Only Alternative', p. 53. Hensman explains how no European country which was involved in the Second World War was subjected to nuclear weapons as was Japan, and napalm and Agent Orange were used in Vietnam. The guinea pigs for the experimentation of deadly weapons were invariably Asians. More recently, cluster bombs and nuclear-tipped bunker busters were used on an Asian Muslim country (Iraq).
14. The fact that the US's and UK's illegal invasion of Iraq is widely perceived as a terrorist attack is evident from the statements emanating from the Islamic Scholars Conference in Jakarta in which several scholars described it as terrorism, and Indonesia's Vice-President accused US President George W. Bush of having no conscience and blasted the US-led war in Iraq as terrorism to all mankind. See *The News*, 26 February 2004.
15. Hensman, 'The Only Alternative', p. 24. Hensman explains how the US and terrorist groups shift their definitions of terrorism based on who is the victim and who is the perpetrator.
16. See Rosalind P. Petchesky, 'Phantom towers: feminist reflections on the battle between global capitalism, and fundamentalist terrorism', in Joseph and Sharma (eds.), *Terror, Counter-Terror*, New Delhi: Kali, p. 53.

Petchesky critiques the language of cosmic 'good' *vs* 'evil' and the apocalyptic rhetoric that echoed between Bush and bin Laden. She argues that the pseudo-Islamic and the pseudo-Christian, the Jihad and the crusade, both lie.

17. See Faizi Inayatullah, 'The Process of Development of Ethnicity and Ethno-nationalism: A Theoretical Analysis', in *Pakistan Perspectives*, vol. 5, no. 2, July-December, 2000.
18. *Speeches and Statements of Field Marshall Mohd. Ayub Khan* (Karachi: Pakistan Publications, 1962), vol. 5, p. 90.
19. Ibid., 1963, vol. 6, pp. 83-94.
20. Selig Harrison, 'Ethnicity and the Political Stalemate in Pakistan', in S. Akbar Zaidi (ed.), *Regional Imbalances and the National Question in Pakistan* (Lahore: Vanguard, 1992), pp. 232-3.
21. Ibid., p. 242.
22. Shahid Kardar, 'Polarisation in the Regions and Prospects for Integration', in S. Akbar Zaidi (ed.), *Regional Imbalances and the National Question in Pakistan*, p. 313.
23. S. Akbar Zaidi, 'Sindhi *vs* Muhajir: Contradiction, Conflict, Compromise', in S. Akbar Zaidi (ed.), *Regional Imbalances and the National Question in Pakistan*, p. 340.
24. Farida Shaheed, 'The Pathan-Muhajir Conflicts, 1985-6: A National Perspective', in Veena Das (ed.), *Mirrors of Violence: Communities, Riots and Survivors in South Asia* (New Delhi: Oxford University Press, 1990).
25. Hamza Alavi, 'Politics of Ethnicity in Pakistan', in S. Akbar Zaidi (ed.), *Regional Imbalances and the National Question in Pakistan*, p. 270.
26. See Muhammad Ejaz Khan, 'Balochistan PA grills district govt system' in *The News*, 26 February 2003. According to Khan the provincial assembly vehemently criticized the district government system in the province and the resentment against it was expressed by a senior provincial minister who appealed for its abolition since it had been created under martial law. Critics levelled the charge that the whole government system had been badly affected by the district system. Similarly, the Nazims in the Frontier resigned as they felt that the provincial government did not accept their powers and jurisdiction.
27. See 'The Devolution Debate', in *The News*, 8 February 2001. Shahrukh Rafi Khan argues that the local elections had brought members of the same old feudal classes into power. See also Qamar Shirazi, 'The New District System and the Government's Horses', in *Mazdoor Jidd-o-Jehd*, 23-30 August 2001, pp. 7-8. Under the Finance System section of the Local Government Plan 2000, number 143 states: the three tiers of local government will have a tax collection machinery at their disposal and the specified schedule of local taxes for union, tehsil, and district that will fall under the control of these respective levels.
28. In his speech to the Constituent Assembly in August 1948, Pakistan's

founder Mohammed Ali Jinnah conceptualized a secular state. However, the use of the religious rhetoric in Pakistan's formation made it difficult for the state to emerge from its founding mythology.

29. Abbas Rashid, 'The Politics and Dynamics of Violent Sectarianism', in Zia Mian and Iftikhar Ahmad (eds.), *Making Enemies, Creating Conflict: Pakistan's Crises of State and Society* (Lahore: Mashal, 1997), p. 28.
30. Ibid., p. 28.
31. Eqbal Ahmad, 'The Roots of Violence', in Zia Mian and Iftikhar Ahmad (eds.), *Making Enemies, Creating Conflict: Pakistan's Crises of State and Society*, p. 19.
32. Rashid, 'The Politics of Violent Sectarianism', p. 29.
33. Ibid., p. 31.
34. Muhammad Amir Rana, *Jehad-e-Kashmir-o-Afghanistan: Jehadi Tanzeemon Aur Mazhabi Jamaaton Ka Aik Jaiza* (Jehad in Kashmir and Afghanistan: An Overview of Jehadi Organizations and Religious Parties) (Lahore: Mashal, 2002), p. 49.
35. Ibid., p. 66.
36. *The News*, 10 March 2004. According to some witnesses, untrained and trigger-happy policemen opened fire on the Ashura procession killing people which led to the killings in retaliation. Once again, the role of the state is questioned in citizen safety.
37. Rana, *Jehad-e-Kashmir*, p. 70.
38. Mubarak Ali, '*Ulema, Muashara Aur Jehad Tehreek*' (The Ulema, Society and Jehad Movement), in Mubarak Ali, *Almiyah-e-Tareekh* (Lahore: Progressive Publishers, 1993), pp. 93-106.
39. Ibid., p. 100.
40. Rana, *Jehad-e-Kashmir*, p. 17.
41. Ibid., p. 17.
42. Ibid., p. 18.
43. Ibid., p. 19.
44. Rashid Ahmed, *Taliban: Islam, Oil and the New Great Game in Central Asia* (London: I.B. Tauris, 2001).
45. Rana, *Jehad-e-Kashmir*, pp. 26-7.
46. Ibid., pp. 28-9.
47. Ibid., pp. 56-8.
48. Ibid., pp. 33-4.
49. Ibid., pp. 41-3.
50. Erum Sajjad Gul, 'Terrorism as understood in Pakistan and India, I & II', *The News*, 6 and 7 January 2004, p. 16. Also, according to commentator Praful Bidwai: 'Pakistan, for its part, has done no better with its Anti-Terrorist Act of 1997, nor indeed with other special laws like the National Security Act of 1980, or Maintenance of Public Order, 1997 (16 MPO), and similar legislations. A glance at the ATA shows that it too is replete

with draconian provisions that violate the International Convention on Civil and Practical Rights, many fundamental rights guaranteed by the Constitution of Pakistan and even the Pakistan Penal Code. . . . The ATA provides impunity to officers provided they are acting in "good faith"—always a dubious assumption. As the South Asia Human Rights Documentation Centre says: "The Act's ambiguous definition of terrorism, strict time limits for trials and investigations, use of the armed forces, together with its loose use of military and judicial personnel make it a danger to both the people of Pakistan and the institution of democracy. It seeks, through wide ranging police powers, to give the state the power to judge and sentence terrorists by effectively bypassing the safeguards of the judicial system. . . . Nawaz Sharif had the Act passed in the teeth of citizens' opposition. Ironically, in 2002, he was himself sentenced to life imprisonment for "intimidating" the special court set up under the ATA—the most famous use of the law.' 'Circle of Violence', *The News*, 12 August 2004.

51. *The News*, 7 February 2004.
52. Ibid., 29 February 2004.
53. Ibid., 1 March 2004.
54. Ibid., 25 March 2004. The opposition warned the government that it was leading the country into a civil-war like situation reminiscent of the army action in East Pakistan in 1971. The opposition members staged walkouts against the military operation in Wana, Waziristan.
55. *The News*, Internet Edition, 28 March 2004.
56. *The News*, 2 March 2004.
57. For example, the government had to answer angry legislators' questions about the killing of civilians in Wana, South Waziristan and in Quetta in February/March 2004. Angry legislators walked out of the National Assembly session to protest against the role of the state in the murder of civilians. *The News*, 10 March 2004.
58. Ibid., 6 February 2004. Christina Rocca expressed her satisfaction over the way in which Pakistan's president had handled the difficult issue of nuclear scientists involved in peddling state nuclear secrets.
59. Rubina Saigol, 'Enemies Within and Enemies Without: The Besiged Self in Pakistani Textbooks', in S. Akbar Zaidi, *The Social Sciences in the 1990s* (Islamabad: COSS, 2003, as 'History, Social Studies and Civics and the Creation of Enemies'), pp. 223-82.
60. For a glimpse of the kinds of complexities that beset the relationship of General Musharraf with the Ulema, and the bargains made in order to secure their conditional support by not interfering in their governments in NWFP and Baluchistan, see 'General and the Ulema' by Anwar Syed, *Dawn*, 8 February 2004. It is widely feared among the liberals in Pakistan that the government will succumb to pressure by the MMA with regard

to Islamization measures aimed at women and culture, in return for abandoning opposition to the General's rule.

61. General Musharraf continues to make statements about his resolve to root out terrorism from the country. On Pakistan's Independence Day on 14 August 2004, he said: 'In my view, the biggest challenge to this country is the spread of terrorism by some elements of foreign countries with the collusion of some Pakistani religious and sectarian extremists', Musharraf said and added, 'But we can't be scared of terrorism. We can't be defeated. I promise my nation that I will not disappoint you.' He lashed out at some political parties for supporting the cause of Islamic militants. . . . Vowing to take Pakistan forward as a moderate progressive Islamic country as envisioned by the Quaid-i-Azam, President Musharraf has appealed to the nation to reject forces of obscurantism and darkness and raise the voice of the moderate majority. . . . 'On this occasion of Independence Day, I appeal to the nation to rise and resolve to fight off elements, who want to push Pakistan into darkness and raise the voice of the vast majority —that is, taking the country forward and not backward', he said. The president said Pakistan is capable of moving forward on the path of progress and development. . . . 'The Quaid-i-Azam envisioned Pakistan as a moderate, progressive Islamic state; we have to take forward this vision by rejecting terrorism, intolerance and extremism. Pakistan will progress and rise every year', *The News*, 15 August 2004.
62. *Pakistan: Madrasas, Extremism and the Military*, International Crisis Group Report, 29 July 2002, ICG Asia Report, no. 36.
63. The term 'Hybrid' is borrowed from Neluka Silva's book *Hybrid Island*.
64. Selvy Thiruchandran, 'Sinhala Buddhist Nationalism', in *South Asian Journal: Quarterly Magazine of South Asian Journalists and Scholars*, Religious Revivalism in South Asia, no. 2, October–December 2003, pp. 62-70.
65. Shyamika Jayasundara, 'The Dichotomy of Security: The Case of Sri Lanka', in *Comprehensive Security in South Asia: Ethnic Dimensions* (New Delhi: Delhi Policy Group, 2003), pp. 268-92.
66. Ibid., p. 276.
67. Ibid.
68. Thiruchandran, 'Sinhala Buddhist Nationalism', p. 67.
69. Adele Balasingham, *The Will to Freedom: An Inside View of Tamil Resistance* (Mitcham, UK: Fairmax Publishing, 2001), pp. 68-9.
70. Ibid., p. 69.
71. Neloufer de Mel, *Women and the Nation's Narrative: Gender and Nationalism in Twentieth Century Sri Lanka* (Colombo: Social Scientists' Assocation, 2001), p. 16.
72. Darini Rajasingham-Senanayake, 'Identity on the Borderline: Modernity, New Ethnicities, and the Unmaking of Multiculturalism in Sri Lanka', in Neluka Silva, *The Hybrid Island: Culture Crossings and the Invention of*

Identity in Sri Lanka (Colombo: Social Scientists' Association, 2002), p. 46.

73. Neluka Silva (ed.), *The Hybrid Island: Culture Crossings and the Invention of Identity in Sri Lanka*, Preface, pp. i-ii.
74. Ibid., p. iv.
75. Arjun Guneratne, 'What's in a Name? Aryans and Dravidians in the Making of Sri Lankan Identities', in Silva, *The Hybrid Island*, p. 27.
76. Ibid., p. 27.
77. See for example, Guneratne, 'What's in a Name?' See also Rajasingham-Senanayake, 'Identity on the Borderline', pp. 41-70. Both writers point out the methods of colonial knowledge that led to the consciousness of hardened and mutually exclusive identity formation.
78. Rajasingham-Senanayake, 'Identity on the Borderline', p. 41.
79. Ibid., pp. 41-70.
80. Guneratne, 'What's in a Name', pp. 20-40.
81. Pradeep Jeganathan and Qadri Ismail, *Unmaking the Nation: The Politics of Identity and History in Modern Sri Lanka* (Colombo: Social Scientists' Association, 1995), p. 2.
82. Ibid., p. 8.
83. Neloufer de Mel, 'Static Signifiers? Metaphors of woman in contemporary Sri Lankan war poetry', in Jayawarden, Kumari and Malathi de Alwis (eds.), *Embodied Violence: Communalising Women's Sexuality in South Asia* (London: Zed Books, 1996), pp. 168-89.
84. de Mel, *Women and the Nation's Narrative*, p. 213.
85. Ibid, p. 37.
86. Ibid., pp. 209-10.
87. Balasingham, *The Will to Freedom*, pp. 286-9.
88. de Mel, *Women and the Nation's Narrative*, p. 40.
89. Selvy Thiruchandran argues that democratic structures themselves create the divisions which are consolidated through party politics. See 'Sinhala Buddhist Nationalism', p. 66.
90. Jagath P. Senaratne, 'Reflections on the Secessionist Insurrection in Sri Lanka: Consequences for Sri Lanka, and Lessons for the International Community', in Khatri and Kueck, *Terrorism in South Asia*, p. 273.
91. Jayasundara argues that the system of universal franchise favours the majority community, the Tamils organized themselves along ethnic lines. See 'The Dichotomy of Security' (New Delhi: Delhi Policy Group, 2003), p. 274.
92. P. Saravanamuttu, 'The Peace Process in Sri Lanka: How Difficult, How Different?', in Khatri and Kueck, *Terrorism in South Asia*, p. 299.
93. Ibid., p. 312.
94. Senaratne, *Secessionist Insurrection*, pp. 266-71.
95. Jayasundara, 'The Dichotomy of Security', p. 283.

96. Imtiaz Ahmed, 'Contemporary Terrorism and the State, Non-State, and the Interstate: Newer Drinks, Newer Bottles', in Khatri and Kueck (eds.), *Terrorism in South Asia*, pp. 353-88.
97. Dhananjayan Sriskandarajah, 'Economic Dimensions of Security in Sri Lanka', in *Comprehensive Security in South Asia: Economic Dimensions* (New Delhi: Delhi Policy Group, 2003), p. 186.
98. Ibid., p. 170.
99. Guneratne, 'What's in a Name?', p. 21.
100. Sriskandarajah, 'Economic Dimensions', p. 176.
101. Senaratne, 'Secessionist Insurrection', p. 250.
102. Ibid., pp. 180-4.
103. Jehan Perera, 'Sri Lanka: Confrontation to Acccommodation', in *South Asian Journal*, no. 3, January-March 2004, p. 94.
104. Senaratne, 'Secessionist Insurrection', pp. 262-3.
105. Saman Kelegama, 'Managing the Sri Lankan Economy at a Time of Terrorism and War', in Khatri and Kueck, *Terrorism in South Asia*, pp. 147-8.
106. Ibid., p. 148.
107. Saravanamuttu, 'The Peace Process in Sri Lanka', p. 299.
108. Kelegama, 'Managing the Sri Lankan Economy', p. 145.
109. Ibid., p. 149.
110. de Mel, *Women and the Nation's Narrative*, p. 235.

CHAPTER III

The State and the Limits of Counter-Terrorism – II: The Experience of India and Bangladesh

SHAHEDUL ANAM KHAN

Terrorism is the deliberate use of violence employed as an instrument of coercion in order to achieve political ends. The operative word here is 'political'. And this is what sets terrorism apart from other forms of violence. Scholars assert that while it is political motivations that stimulate terrorists, criminal activity is also often resorted to. The fundamental difference was the causes and the counter-measures thereto, which go beyond security and police actions. While terrorists seek changes at the macro level, other violent criminals seek personal economic benefits, remaining generally occupied with the micro level. The word 'political' is used here in a more inclusive sense, encompassing traditional Left–Right politics as well as religious motivations or social issues.[1]

Politically motivated terrorists act with the purpose of making the world, according to them, a better place to live in. Both liberal democracies and autocratic regimes have been the targets of terrorism equally. However, one erudite scholar on the subject, while delving into the root causes of terrorism, illustrates a very interesting fact that it was in the more liberal pluralist societies and democracies and not the oppressive regimes and harshest dictatorships in which terrorism occurred.[2]

Terrorism neither recognizes any rule or convention of war nor works within any circumscribed area. There are neither defined battlefields nor dividing lines between peace and war. In the words of George Habash, 'In this age of revolution of peoples oppressed by the world imperialist system, there could be no political or geographical boundaries or moral limits to the operation of people's war, no one is innocent, no one is neutral.'[3] One can imagine the intensity of the problem from the fact that between 1975 and 1985 no fewer than 6,200 terrorist acts were recorded all over the world resulting in 4,700 deaths and 9,000 wounded.[4] However, since th 1990s there have been fewer terrorist activities than the previous decade, but the number of casualties through terrorist acts has increased.[5]

Terrorism is a phenomenon which South Asians have lived with for a long time. As a strategy against foreign and colonial domination, it was a very handy tool. Terrorism was even sanctified as having a human face.[6] Although currently the term has gained a pejorative slant, those who were involved in terrorism in the past had been showered with accolades and were acknowledged as national heroes. Many of them are now glorified as icons of nationalism and national assertion, both in India and in Bangladesh. Chhatrapati Shivaji is not only immortalized in Indian history books, many important institutions and buildings in India are also named after him, not to speak of the Shivaji festival which even the secular political parties in India are proud to be associated with. The radical Hindu fundamentalists in India seek motivation and inspiration from his exploits against the Mughals. The tactics that he used were guerrilla in nature, and the emperor Aurangazeb branded him a terrorist and an outlaw.

Shaheed Bhagat Singh still evokes deep sentiments in the hearts of the Indians, enough to immortalize him in films and literature. In Bengal, the self-sacrifice of a young orphan while attempting to remove a symbol of colonial oppression in the form of the Lt. Governor of Bengal has become part of the folklore, often invoked as a source of inspiration. Surja Sen, commonly known as 'Master Da' in Bengal (he was a well-educated person and a college teacher, as were Charu Mazumder and Shantu Larma. This negates a common perception that terrorism is a 'trade' taken up only by the 'criminals and idiosyncratic'),[7] and Preetilata Dey, both famous for the Chittagong Armoury raid, are household names, immortalized in various ways in Bangladesh.

During the Bangladesh Liberation War, the valiant freedom fighters were termed variously as miscreants, rebels, and terrorists by the occupying Pakistani forces. Of late terrorism has become more indiscriminate. Regarding this Lacqueur says, 'Contemporary terrorism has become indiscriminate in the choice of victims. Its aim is no longer to conduct propaganda but to effect maximum destruction.'[8] Some scholars go so far as to suggest that terrorism has been 'criminalised'.[9] The idea conjured up by these two statements is that terrorism in the past was invested with a degree of ethical values. Experts opine that there is indeed a significant departure from the motives and modus operandi of the terrorism of the nineteenth century from that of the twentieth century, a difference which is marked by the absence of morality.[10] But not all 'terrorist' activities were conducted with a spirit of cool detachment and wanton destruction. A nobel laureate, once dubbed a terrorist by the West, particularly by the US, says, 'I do not, however, deny that I planned sabotage. I did not plan it in a spirit of recklessness, nor because I have any love for violence. I planned it as a result of a calm and sober assessment of the political situation that had arisen after many years of tyranny, exploitation, and oppression of my people by the Whites.'[11] This sums up the element of 'morality' and the motivation of terrorists!

At the macro level, 'terrorism occupies a broad space in the conflict spectrum, from activity barely distinguishable from crime or vendetta, through conventional terrorism in support of political and transcendental to potential "superterrorism", perhaps as a means of proxy war,' says Lesser, who goes on to assert that the nature of terrorism is changing as a strategic problem, it having become more amorphous and diffused 'beyond the question of tactics and strategic targets'.[12]

Thus, if we want to tackle terrorism successfully, we must understand its character as well as address its root causes because, in the words of an Israeli engaged in the job of hounding out Palestinians, 'Those who want victory without addressing the underlying grievances want an unending war.'[13] There are, though, three schools of thought that predominate discourses on countering terrorism, but not all of them are willing to concede that addressing the underlying causes first and foremost is the best way to go about it.[14] We must also not be overwhelmed by the phenomenon of international terrorism while going into its root causes, but instead heed the experts' caution that, 'Measuring the volume of international terrorism—the thickness of a thin crust atop a very deep pie—would tell us little about the root causes of terrorism or the nature of societies that produced it.'[15] It is also essential to distinguish terrorism from other types of violence in society, particularly from the tactics resorted to by freedom fighters and liberation movements, because it is as illogical to describe all liberation movements as terrorism, although they may resort to terrorist tactics, as it is to characterize all terrorist outfits as freedom fighters, although liberation may be their ultimate objective. What separates these two is the method.[16]

There is an unwitting propensity to use the terms 'guerrilla', 'insurgency', and 'terrorism' in a fungible manner. Although commonly equated, it remains a fundamental mistake to equate terrorism with insurgency or guerrilla warfare in general. While political terrorism prospers through the application of destructive intimidation, revolutionary war is largely waged without resorting to terror. Revolutionary warfare subsumes within itself various phases, including the insurgency phase, while guerrilla warfare is a form that is a legally accepted means of conflict. Terrorism, on the other hand, is a violent act, which may or may not be resorted to by the insurgents. By the same token, terrorism may form a tactical element in their struggle or the basic strategy on which they pursue their political agenda.[17] What obtains in India at this moment, particularly in the north-east is a 'Cusp between guerrilla warfare, revolution and of late terrorism'.[18]

The objective of this chapter is to assess the state of counter-terrorism and the limits that are being faced by India and Bangladesh, in combating terrorism respectively, i.e. the responses of the states to the phenomenon and the various impediments thereto. In doing so the chapter will first briefly look at the definitions and the problematic in understanding and combating terrorism. The next section will dwell on the state and features which are unique to India and Bangladesh, and which determine respective responses to this phenomenon. By addressing the features it is hoped that the root causes would be automatically highlighted. Finally, we will look at the responses of the states and the factors that have stood in the way of a resolution of the problem.

I

WHAT IS TERRORISM?

In spite of the fact that terrorism has a long history, the failure to arrive at a generally accepted definition belies Nietzsche's observation that only things that have no history can be defined.[19] Given the fact that terrorism is multifaceted and multidimensional, how does one define it? As underscored by scholars and analysts, 'Perception is one of the core problems in defining terrorism.'[20] Is there a pressing need for us to formulate a universally accepted definition? Mark Burgess provides the answer partially when he says: 'Arriving at a working definition also has uses other than increasing our understanding of terrorism. For, by defining terrorism one can also define the preferred means of countering it.' Sorting out the definitions of terrorism is also essential if only to distinguish it from other forms of violence.[21]

That definitions are so very dependent on parochial perception is well illustrated in the series of activities and the number of proposals leading up to the adoption of the UN resolution on terrorism. No fewer than seven draft proposals were submitted by different nations to the three subcommittees that were set up by the UN ad hoc committee in 1973 to 'examine the definition, causes, and prevention of terrorism'. So divided was the House and for so long that it was not until 1987, when the international conference, convened by the UN Secretary-General to differentiate freedom struggle from terrorism, agreed to identify terrorism with crime, that the relevant report was passed, wherein all acts of terrorisms were condemned,[22] except those fighting for the cause of self-determination against foreign and racist regimes.[23]

There is a plethora of definitions but no single one captures the entire character or nature of terrorism, and, 'Even if there were an objective, value-free definition of terrorism, covering all its important aspects and features, it would still be rejected by some for ideological reasons.'[24] There is, however, a general consensus that the lack of a universally accepted definition should not be allowed to inhibit our efforts to confront terrorist groups on the basis of a working definition. A problematic in countering terrorism is the lack of understanding of the phenomenon itself. Walter Lacqueur is of the opinion that the history of terrorism is one of the keys to understanding terrorism. The debates and discourses on this phenomenon have been many but these have been largely affected by passions and emotions. But in the same vein, he suggests, 'Past experience is no longer the only key for understanding terrorism'. Newer elements like access to weapons of mass destruction, and religious–political fanaticism should occupy our attention, although he concedes that radical Islamism has not always been the main threat and may not always be so in the future. [25]

Another impediment to understanding and combating terrorism is the fact that it is multifaceted and multidimensional and 'There is no Clausewitz not even a Jomini to provide an authoritative and systematic guide' because there is not one terrorism but a variety of it and no two terrorist activities are entirely similar in character. Coupled with this is our mental disposition against any new idea, resulting in the debate resembling, 'a parade of old hobby horses. People who have ready-made explanations of why terrorism occurs will not easily give up their beliefs, however proof to the contrary is produced'.[26] Another problematic is whether one should approach and deal with this issue as a crime or as a mode of warfare. Each has its own implications, which determines the means and manner of countering it. It is also important to determine whether terrorism is the cause of a particular conflict or the conflict has fostered terrorism. Needless to say there are objective conditions which fan the flames of terrorism and these are not universal in nature but germane to a particular country. Each is predicated on particular sets of circumstances and each has its own reasons for gestation. Thus the imperative of going into the root causes to formulate appropriate measures. Another problematic is, how far does the state go in its fight against terrorism without impinging on the basic human rights of its citizens? It would be well to keep in mind that, 'Human rights and security are not mutually exclusive concepts. More human rights do not mean less security.'[27] By the same token, one could say that more security of the state and the individual should mean less human rights. In so far as India and Bangladesh are concerned, we have to look at them quite differently, if only because their experiences, the intensity, nature, and motivations of the militant groups that they face, are different.

II

THE INDIAN SCENARIO

Terrorism in India is modulated by different compulsions in different regions. In some areas terrorism is fabricated on ideological motives but driven primarily by irredentist aspirations. In some cases religion provides militancy with the motivating force while political aspirations provide the endurance. In other parts of India, the militants employ terrorism as a technique in the insurgency phase of the conflict, to further their political cause. Terrorism in these areas stems from ethno-centric and parochial motives, seeking to break out from the majority fold, which they consider dysfunctional to their economic and political development as a separate ethnic entity.

Although India has been facing this problem in varying degrees, of intensity since independence, in recent times, the intensity has increased manifold, particularly in Kashmir. While the government has been able to contend with some of the terrorism elsewhere in India, the Kashmir issue has resisted resolution. The failure is not entirely of India's making. This is where understanding terrorism and the limits to counter it assume significance because, 'Understanding terrorism is not an easy process since the study needs to be time, issue and location specific . . . requires examining terrorist groups . . . and at the consequences of their action on our societies.'[28] India has devised its own means and methods to counter terrorism and militancy—but the government's counter-terrorism measures beg the question of how efficacious and the appropriate the responses to the problem are, which most scholars agree to be of political in character.

The causes of India's societal conflict, whether caste, ethnic or communal, go back to the terminal years of British rule. It bred from the misgivings, of some of the groups about the prospect of being marginalized in a post-colonial dispensation. The British in their last days were seen to be giving in to the pressure of the majority groups while the minorities, 'felt threatened and were afraid of being overwhelmed by the majority politics dominated by the Congress which in practical term meant the caste Hindus'. Thus the Naga National Council's demand for a special protected status for ten years following the British departure from India after which they were to decide on their political future. In Assam, the intra-ethnic cleavages between the Ahoms and the Assamese and Bengali caste Hindus were so pronounced that the Ahoms, out of fear of Bengali domination, preferred to be classified as Ahoms rather than Hindus in the 1941 census. So also was the plight of the tribes of the plains, who resented both the Congress and the Muslim League for their parochial policies. The matter was further aggravated by the Sadullah government's policy of resettling Muslim peasants in the tribal lands. The result was the first Convention of the All Assam Tribes and Races Federation, which declared Assam as never being a part of India, and demanded a 'Free State into which the Hill Districts bordering Assam be incorporated.' Similarly Mizoram, too, demanded 'autonomy and freedom'. The Dogra Maharaja's efforts to keep Kashmir 'independent' from both India and Pakistan were overtaken by the events of 1949. (Technically Kashmir was an independent state until 26 October 1949.) The Sikhs demand for an 'Independent Punjab' eventually got diluted. [29]

We can conveniently situate the Indian scenarios into what Cunningham describes as

> four predominant models of how terrorism is conceived that frame counter-terrorist responses: (1) a crime that should be handled by law enforcement and the judicial system; (2) a form of warfare best suited for a military response; (3) a liberat-ion struggle conducted by oppressed minority, political or religious groups whose desires for self determination or power should be accommodated; and (4) a violent reaction to a complex set of socio-economic, political, cultural and possibly religious variables that have both long term preconditions and short term precipitant causes that need to be addressed with a multifaceted intervention to eliminate underlying causes and cycles of violence.[30]

The Indian scenario presents an interesting picture as to why and how terrorism has festered in this country, which merits deliberation in order to understand the limits of the response of the state to terrorism. In these also lie the root causes of terrorism in India.

FEATURES OF INDIAN TERRORISM

There is no one generic problem in India. In fact there are three distinct areas or 'conflict zones' in India that are classified variously as 'High Intensity Conflict Area' (Kashmir), 'Low intensity Conflict area' (North-East), and areas afflicted by 'extremist violence' (Andhra Pradesh, Jharkhand, Bihar, Maharashtra, Chhattisgarh—Punjab is not mentioned here since there is no overt conflict situation in Punjab today). Each of these problems has its own history and causes of growth and 'demise'. Each of these exists in varying degrees of intensity and each in its own way is resisting resolution. The accretion of problems resulting from the state's failure or unwillingness to resolve them results in violence, and terrorism is resorted to when all other constitutional and legal alternatives appear to be inefficacious.

The terrorism or militancy that is being experienced in India today is either ethno-religious in character, as in Kashmir, entirely ethnic, as in the north-east, or 'charged with political fervour, seeking to effect a structural change', as manifested in the activities of the Naxalites or the Peoples' War Group (PWG). While the Kashmiris seek to come out of the system as an independent identity, the ethnic struggle in the north-east provides a mixed picture of some elements seeking changes residing within the system and some seeking to disassociate from the system itself. On the other hand, terrorism motivated by politico-ideological principles seeks to change the system itself through a class struggle.

Terrorism in India, in particular the type we see in the secessionist movements, is festering in the border belts or the peripheral areas of the Indian land mass, while the agrarian revolt exists primarily in what some refer to as the BIMARU states.[31] Even in these cases the agrarian struggle appears to be largely confined to the tribal areas and those that are largely inhabited by the Dalits, Schedule Castes and OBCs. The phenomenon is acute in areas that have unresolved political as well as boundary issues that are transnational in character. Some scholars characterize this as a 'mismatch' between the boundaries of the nations of South Asia. State contractions as a result of territorial adjustments, either because of the partition of India or through internal reorganization on linguistic lines, have caused the empowerment of some and the disempowerment of others, resulting in these areas becoming fertile ground for secessionist movements, which exhibit remarkable resistance to the process of integration.[32] The boundary problem is so vexing that some scholars suggest that in the era of globalization time has probably come where serious thoughts have to be given to the definition and re-negotiating the meaning of international boundary.[33]

The issues of identity, marginalization, and deprivation or political and cultural alienation, mutate into a common cause of discontent which predisposes some to violence. Some opine that the state has not been able to reconcile the various differences and claims and integrate the various disparate but not necessarily divisive elements. This point is made here to stress the fact that just because, 'ethno-religious and other cultural factors are the basis of secessionist feelings does not make ethno-religious cultural assertiveness illegitimate'.[34] But this begs the question that, while similar situations prevail in many other parts of India, why is it only in a few areas that the people have risen against the state? Another feature that not only compounds the situation but, to some, is also the main cause of the rise of militancy and terrorism is the issue of migration and the 'change' in the demographic character of some of the areas in the Indian north-east. This issue, whatever may be the statistical link, had been used from time to time as a rallying point by the irredentists in the north-east, particularly in Assam. Although there has been a slight attenuation of this issue, particularly in Assam, it still remains a matter of prime concern.

According to some analysts, the issue of migration should be viewed from two different perspectives. One, it is a natural phenomenon and should be tackled as such without making it an emotive issue to reap political benefits from because not all those migrating from Bangladesh end up in the Indian north-east, or are the, 'key to the crisis', that is overwhelming north-east of India.[35] If there is a Bashir in Delhi, one will find many such Bashirs in Dublin or Durham. The moot point is, what can be done about migration, or more importantly, about what Kanti Bajpai calls the 'perception of migration'. Not all scholars are willing to concede the figures that are put out from time to time of the illegal migrants from Bangladesh and Nepal into the north-east of India. That the figures given are not only far-fetched but also concocted for political profiteering is evident from Bajpai's very perspicacious observation on the subject of migration. He is unwilling to concede that there are 15 million Bangladeshi migrants in India (recent press reports put the figure at 20 million), primarily because no one is sure of the way the figure has been computed.[36] If we take the figure of 20 million Bangladeshi illegal migrants in India to be accurate, accreting over a period of twenty years, the daily outflow from Bangladesh on the average comes to around 2,000, a staggering figure indeed! The other way of looking at migration, my second perspective, is the predominant concept of countering terrorism, where the realist prescription predominates state response.

A unique feature which is highlighted in the scholarship of the Indian writers is the foreign support with which all three secessionist movements have flourished. Pakistan has been active in Kashmir, and the north-east secessionists have received support from both China and Pakistan. The Naga rebel groups straddle the Indo-Myanmar border and the ISI is alleged to be using Bangladesh to maintain links with the north-east rebel groups. While by its own admission, Pakistan is supporting the Kashmir militancy, Indian official claims of ISI support to India's north-east insurgent groups remain unsubstantiated.[37] It is, however, an inescapable reality that foreign support is a sine qua non for secessionist movements to survive and succeed. One has only to look at the Indian help in the liberation of Bangladesh, its activities in the Sindh province of Pakistan, its cooperation with the US in the latter's interference in Tibet in the 1960's, its involvement in Myanmar's ethnic problems and in CHT in Bangladesh, not to mention the support and sustenance it provided to the LTTE,[38] to recognize the fact that such movements, though specific in nature, cannot survive without foreign help, the motivations of the neighbours notwithstanding. But the point at issue is the causal link between these two—is foreign help the cause of terrorism or do incipient movements stemming from internal dynamics attract foreign support?

Another unique feature of the phenomenon is related to the state's recourse to violence and coercion in countering terrorism. The compulsions of the state merit separate study, but suffice it to say that this has in many ways hampered the state's capabilities in combating terrorism. Disappearances and custodial deaths, fake encounters, and extra-judicial killings have been flaws in the Indian government's fight against terrorists and secessionists. We will look at this aspect later in the chapter. Being unique in nature the three areas of 'high intensity', 'low intensity', and 'areas of extreme violence' merit separate deliberation.

North-East

The Indian north-east comprises an area of approximately 2,65,000 sq. km. with a population of around thirty-six million, which constitutes approximately 8 per cent of India's land mass and approximately 4 per cent of its population.[39] The diversity of the region can be gleaned from the composition of its population. By one account there are 116 tribes inhabiting the area. Within the Nagas there are 13 tribes while the Kukis subsume within its fold 37 sub-tribes. Of the 1,652 languages and dialect spoken all over India, 420 are spoken in this region. With this one must include the non-tribal populations of Assam and Tripura.[40] The percentage of the tribal population varies from 22-30 per cent in Tripura to 63 per cent in Arunachal and 94 per cent in Mizoram. While Assam has a numerically larger tribal population of 2.47 million, in terms of percentages, it accounts for only 12.8 per cent.[41]

Historically, what constitutes the Indian north-east today had never been a part of India, politically, culturally or ethnically.[42] The British, through a gradual process of subtle annexation commencing with the dislodging of the Burmese from what is now Manipur and the Treaty of Yandabo in 1926, formalized the annexation of the north-east. S. Guru Dev accurately sums up the Indian north-east today:

> India's north eastern borders lands are in turmoil; revolutionary 'liberation fronts' are cheaper by the dozens, crises of identity spawned militant ethnic groups . . . the Brahmaputra valley is the home of terrorism and Manipur, the testing ground for orthodox insurgency. . . . The Left and the Right woo the Manipuri rebels . . . Meghalaya illustrates the skillful use of attrition to create panic among the minorities and the 'under privileged,' . . . Nagaland remains disturbed and Mizoram relatively quiet but for the Hamar's ethnic ambitions, an internal problem with grave consequences. Arunachal provides a corridor for insurgents to commute between India and Myanmar.[43]

This is a region that is influenced by three sources—extra-regional, regional and internal. This is a region where the assertion of ethnic identity and aspirations of nationhood remain unfulfilled. This is a region of false promises, where bad governance is as much to blame as the centre's insensitivity to local demands. According to the experts, terrorism in the north-east is not the disease but the symptom of the disease, where distance from the heartland and limited means of accessibility have exacerbated the sense of remoteness, and which has 'various possibilities including becoming a progressive national liberation movement'.[44] While it is true that internal conflicts in India's north-east are 'overwhelmingly conceptualised within the framework of unique ethnic identities that are threatened . . . by an inchoate cultural mainstream',[45] it would also not be wrong to suggest that not all conflicts are explained by this phenomenon. In many cases the underlying motive is the internecine conflict centering on tribal, sub-tribal or tribal–outsider rivalries.

Of the three conflict zones in India, the north-east has the longest-running incidence of militancy- and terrorism-related violence. The seeds of secessionism predate the Independence of India when the Nagas attempted to assert their separate identity and through a memorandum to the British in 1937 sought a different dénouement to their ethnic distinctiveness. This zone is also the area where the severity of the violence caused by the intensity of the conflict has surpassed the figures of the rest of India. In the words of Eric Forum, the Indian north-east is in a state of 'Malignant Aggression',[46] which is witness to a variety of problems that stimulate terrorism and violence in their full manifestation.

We must however, be, careful lest we are misled into thinking that under the rubric of the north-east lies a single ethnic, economic, cultural, and political construct. The seven states, or the 'Seven Sisters', a sobriquet by which the area is commonly known, comprise a complex region, more diverse than any other part of India, even though it was carved out, from time to time, from 'Greater Assam'. Kanti Bajpai hits the nail on the head when he says, 'this is a region of great differences and to encompass all its diversity under the portmanteau term "north-east" is not terribly helpful'.[47]

India's north-east is less Indian and more South-East Asian in its ethnic and cultural make-up.[48] The problem is further compounded by the nature of the international boundaries and the indigenous attempts to establish linguistic identity. Partition rendered a distinct geopolitical entity to the north-east, starting beyond the Siliguri neck, with an external perimeter 98 per cent international and 2 per cent Indian.[49] That is why scholars contend that even after more than fifty-five years of independence, India is still in the process of coagulating as a nation attempting to seek unity in diversity rather than cast its entire people in a single mould. And this is perhaps the crux of the problem. Not all the people that constitute India today are willing to be integrated into the Indian mould. The inability to get out of it in a peaceful manner has forced some to seek alternative means, militancy being one of them. The baggage of history is still being carried along in that the colonial practice of divide and rule is resorted to by the centre to drive a wedge between the various factions of the secessionists/separatist movements.[50] It is no wonder, then, that the continuation of the colonial practices and behaviour has caused the north-east to perceive the centre as a colonial power. While the region as a whole suffers from the minority syndrome, similar syndromes pervade the political and psychological firmament within the north-east. While Bengali domination was seen as dysfunctional to Ahamiya prospects, the distrust and resentment felt by the non-Ahamiya and tribals at Ahamiya domination and chauvinism was equally strong.[51]

Two very palpable features that are common to the north-east are worth noting. One is that, except for Arunachal and Meghalaya, long-standing movements, either for autonomy or for independence, in all the other five, have graduated into violent militancy over time. Most importantly, there is violence at many levels in all these seven states. There is conflict between the centre and the states, between the states themselves, between tribes within the state and inter-state tribal conflict, between tribal and non-tribals and between indigenous groups and 'outsiders'. Mizoram is the only state where militancy has been contained. Nagaland and Assam remain the most violent states, while Tripura and Manipur are less so.

Another distinctive feature of the north-east terrorism scenario is the issue of migration, which had so far been at the core of all the problems of terrorism, secessionist impulse, and violence related to the struggle for autonomy. But migration is not a new phenomenon in the north-east, particularly in Assam. The Assamese have long been accustomed to the 'unobtrusive' migration of non-Assamese, particularly of Bengalis who provided the state with cheap labour for its plantation economy and also with entrepreneurial and professional elite. Since 1970 most of the migrants have been Bengali. The added element of difference in this case was that these migrants were mostly Muslims.[52]

A very interesting feature, which should merit the attention of those who are trying to fight this phenomenon, is the demonstration effect in the proliferation of militant groups in the north-east. Financial motivation, rather than any political agenda or gains, is what drives these militant groups. Much of the proliferation of armed militant groups is the result of the perceived success of some of the other armed groups representing various shades of ethnic identity. Much of the success is related not to politics but 'increasingly to the financial gains of widespread criminal activities that are undertaken by all militant groups in the north-east',[53] including trade in illicit weapons and drugs.

Another feature is the feeling of marginalization brought about by economic deprivation and neglect and the 'step motherly' treatment by the centre. To some, this criticism is unjustified ',ecause it is not so much the lack of funds, but the misutilization of the funds that are allotted to the area.[54] Reportedly, the region's economic plight is being exploited, most of all by the militants and the terrorist outfits themselves. In this matrix there is a close nexus between militants and politicians, which facilitates the transfer of development funds to the terrorists. In Assam, in one sector alone, as much as Rs. 60-70 crore is diverted annually to the under-ground economy of terrorism, i.e. to the ULFA.[55] There are, however, both negative and positive fallouts of these collusive arrangements. The positive impact is that the collusion, for obvious reasons, reduces the risk of militant activity. [56]

Another feature of militancy in the north-east has been the spurt of Muslim terrorist outfits, particularly in Assam, whose existence is nebulous and whose activities have been limited to propaganda and expression of their demands. By some accounts, Muslim migrants in Assam have shown signs of incipient militancy. There are between fifteen and twenty militant outfits in Assam of which the Muslim Liberation Tiger Front of Assam has called for a separate state comprising the five Muslim majority border districts of Assam.[57]

Kashmir

If the Indian north-east has been the theatre of the longest-running insurgency and terrorism in India, Kashmir has been the cause and the battleground of all but one of the major Indo–Pak wars. Like most of the major conflict situations that are prevailing in India today, the Kashmir imbroglio is another legacy of the British Raj. Jammu & Kashmir (J&K) has been caught in the vortex of terrorism for over fifteen years now, resulting in the deaths of over 32,000 including in excess of 11,000 civilians since 1990, not to mention the internal migration and displacement of the Kashmiri pundits from the valley.[58]

Terrorism in J&K can be divided into three phases starting from 1988. The first phase, from 1988 to 1990, saw the emergence of Jehadi groups calling for independence from India. The second phase, between 1991 and 1995, saw the rise and domination of pro-Pakistani militant groups and the marginalization of those indigenous militant organizations known to be more secular in their outlook. What this meant was that the militant and the terrorist groups came more and more under the orbit of the religious and radical Islamic elements in Pakistan. The third phase commencing from 1996/7 and till date has seen the emergence of foreign mercenaries who have taken control of the terrorist activities under what the Indian government terms as the direct control of the ISI.[59]

Although all the major wars (but one) fought between India and Pakistan have been over Kashmir, it would be wrong to conclude that these have been entirely due to Pakistan's support for the Kashmiri bid for self-determination. There are major strategic interests that motivate India's and Pakistan's position on Kashmir. The root causes of the Kashmir issue are too well documented to be recounted here, but it is enough to say that the matter hinges on a 'basic ideological dichotomy' between India and Pakistan. As in the north-east, there are some distinct features of terrorism in Kashmir.

The first is that while the vexing political issue of J&K's status had existed since the independence of the subcontinent, the *intifada* or the call for Jehad or terrorism has only emerged in the late 1990s. This is a conflict to which Pakistan, by its own admission, is providing political and moral support. That is what India considers a euphemism for a proxy war by Pakistan. Internal alienation brought about by political gerrymandering, broken promises, agreement obligations not fulfilled, policy of divide and rule and what some scholars characterize as an 'ethnic security dilemma', are some of the reasons why terrorism in Kashmir has continued for so long. Poor governance, administrative incompetence and corruption have compounded the situation further, causing disillusionment among the general masses.

What is most unique in the case of Kashmir, what we do not see in other similar conflict areas/situations in India, is the fact that there is a quantum jump, according to some Indian authors, in the participation of foreign mercenaries, from 15 per cent in 1990 to 40 per cent in 1994[60] and 60 to 70 per cent today.[61] Reportedly, foreign mercenaries are more ruthless and, being religiously motivated, tend to be more indiscriminate.[62] This is evident from the number of soft targets that have come under terrorist attack since 2000. There is expanded coordination among the pro-Pak militant outfits to increase their areas of operation, and also the use of unconventional weapons including IEDs, grenades, RDX, and state-of-the-art weapons and equipment. Soft targets have included political personalities, minorities, and the volunteer members of the VDC.[63]

The Kashmir scenario is, however, different from the conflict situation prevailing in the north-east or the one that had existed in Punjab. Unlike these two regions, Kashmir is a subject of international territorial dispute, and recognized as such by the UN. It has also been a point of much international focus, including that of the US, since the character of the problem is both internal and domestic than only internal. J&K has been able to draw the attention of the international community to the extent that not only has Pakistan's position been acknowledged, its support to the proxy war in Kashmir has also been condoned and tolerated.[64] Unlike Punjab, the vast majority of the population is estranged from the Indian mainstream, and its geographical location leaves it open to large-scale infiltration, and external support for the militants is comparatively easy, not to speak of the easy accessibility to the vast arms bazaar that extends from Pakistan to Afghanistan.[65] What is also noticeable is the Indian government's unsuccessful efforts post-9/11 to project the situation obtaining in Kashmir as a part of International Islamic Terrorism.

Leftist Violence, Naxalites and the Peoples' War Group

Another aspect of terrorist violence in India, with unique features and locations of its own, is the use of terror tactics by Maoist elements, whose area of operations has been more visible in Bihar and the surrounding areas. The activities of these groups display a classic case of terrorism being used as a tactic to achieve higher strategic aims. Militant and armed insurgents motivated by Maoist ideology have been conducting a violent armed campaign in Bihar for more than two decades now. Their professed objective is to 'rescue poor farmers in the state from virtual bondage by rich upper caste land owners from both the state and the Hindu and Muslim communities.' Recently there has been a proliferation of various 'senas' or private armies, mainly of upper-caste Hindus, to protect themselves from the terrorist and violent acts by the Maoist elements. Some of these groups have been named after religious personalities. Inter-sena clashes have taken the shape of caste-conflict—upper castes pitted against the Dalits and the lower castes—resulting in many deaths. The Muslims in Bihar have also formed their private protection groups. Six members of one such group, the Ali Sena, who were Muslim landowners were the victims of such an attack in a village in Ranchi in Bihar in 2002.

The People's War Group traces its birth to a village in Siliguri in West Bengal, Naxalbari, where the seeds of the peasant struggle, which grew into an insurrectionary movement, were sown in 1967 when a sharecropper was killed on a flimsy ground of stealing a few kg of rice. While the movement is now in a torpid state in its place of origin, the Naxalites continue to commit violence in their strongholds in Bihar and Andhra Pradesh. The PWG derives its motivation from the Maoist doctrine of peasant insurrection through the use of violence and terror, and acquiring 'power through the barrel of a gun'. It situates its strategy on guerrilla warfare through which it aspires to usher in a 'New Democratic Revolution (NDR)'. The PWG's immediate goal is the 'establishment of a people's democratic dictatorship (of the four classes) as the first step towards transition to socialism. The final goal was communism.'[66]

Recently, various Naxalite outfits have come together to form the People's Guerrilla Army (PGA) with the declared objective to counter the offensive of the security forces against the Naxalites.

The PGA has declared its intention to work alongside the extremists of Kashmir, the north-east, and the LTTE, and has stated its intent of having a 'fraternal relationship' with and is willing to harbour secessionist groups as far away as in Chechnya to the north and the Kurds to the west as well as the Al Qaida.[67] For some time now the PWG and other Left-wing extremist groups have been active in the subcontinent in an effect to expand and consolidate Left-wing extremist movements in different parts of India and its neighbourhood.[68]

Although the PWG/Naxalites have marginalized the local administration and terrorized certain sections of the population, it has to be said of the Naxalites that they have been able to enforce fair wages and fair interest rates in many areas of their operation. People's courts have been set up in some areas to enforce fair prices and minimum wages. This has lent a modicum of legitimacy to the struggle of the landless and the Dalits. The PWG movement, according to some scholars, does not seek to destabilize the nation. The strategy to deal with them should therefore be different from what would be used to deal with terrorism elsewhere in India, scholars assert. [69]

III

THE BANGLADESH SCENARIO

Bangladesh has been the breeding ground for indigenous terrorist activities since the days of the British Raj. However, history gives us quite a different picture of the Bengali psyche, one that was naturally disinclined to violence. It was during the British rule that anti-colonial sentiments, a result of the oppressive rule, found limited expression through peasant revolts. Anti-British movements, led by local leadership, which had developed by then, followed two distinct and different lines. One followed the Gandhian[70] precepts of non-violence while the other followed the path of the Swadeshi movement or the 'Anushilan Shamiti'. The attack on the European Club and the simultaneous attack on the Chittagong armoury were synchronous with other Swadeshi activities in the subcontinent. While this was a part of the overall liberation movement in India, there were a number of incidents that were categorized as terrorism by the colonial rulers.

The period between 1947 and 1971 witnessed a failed attempt at Pakistan's national integration. The carnage perpetrated by the occupation forces was the Bengali's modern baptism in terrorism. Post 1971 saw the people's expectations belied, the causes of which lay in a combination of factors, some beyond the control of the leaders of the time. These ground conditions were further compounded by across-the-border developments, particularly the Naxalbari movements in the Indian state of West Bengal. About the same time, the Sarbahara Party, whose birth predates that of Bangladesh, came to the forefront with much the same aims and objectives as the Naxalites. It had duplicate fronts, one was the underground element while the other was involved in open platform politics. The underground element resorted to terrorism to express its philosophy and establish its political viewpoints. The simmering dissatisfaction that manifested itself through various militant activities in various parts of the country following the liberation of Bangladesh in 1971 was basically motivated by politico-economic causes, propped up by leftist ideology. Religion had very little to do with these subaltern, subterranean movements.

The Sarbahara was an example of ideological terrorism which purported to wage a class struggle of the proletariat. Although motivated by the Naxal movements, it neither sought nor received any support from the protagonists of the class struggle from across the border.[71] The areas of its operations were mostly in the south and south-western part of Bangladesh, e.g. Kushtia, Jhenidah, Madaripur, etc., though the Atrai area of greater Rajshahi district saw an upsurge of terrorism and rural violence in 1972 and 1973, which was quite severely put down by the security forces, particularly the Rakkhi Bahini. An interesting feature of the Leftist movement was that the Leftist militants abstained from the wanton and indiscriminate use of violence although they resorted to terror tactics. Their aim was 'Robin Hoodsian'—helping the poor by taking from the rich. And these elements were the target of the Rakkhi Bahini.

Be that as it may, thus far analysts had taken comfort in the fact that Bangladesh was fortunate not to be thrown into the vortex of what can be described as classical terrorism, the likes of which is being experienced by both India and Pakistan, and till recently Sri Lanka as well. What Bangladesh had been exposed to so far were incidents where the criminals and the extremists resorted to tactics of terror to pursue their parochial aims. Although Bangladesh is yet to face the full horrors of political or ideological terrorism, the kind which we see in some other parts of South Asia, the miscreants and the lumpen elements are using the tools and tactics of terror for economic and political gains. What we observed till recently here was primarily a severe societal violence. Also, certain miscreant elements are using the swathe of political parties but are actually engaged in criminal activities.

However, it cannot be said with certainty that, given the current flux in the society, the political situation obtaining today in Bangladesh, and, in spite of being one of the most homogenous nations at birth, the hiatus that exist in its society, the socio-political condition, the spillover of international terrorism and the 'war against terrorism', but more significantly, the spillover effect from across the border, will not be in resonance, leading to a segment of the 'deprived elements' or the 'aggrieved party' resorting to terrorism as the only alternative to resolving the situation.

Bangladesh has had an insurgency situation in the CHT, and although it is currently in a state of limbo, there is no guarantee that the situation will not turn violent in the future. Although some underground elements motivated by political ideology are in a current state of torpor, they may very well exploit the current flux, perhaps with external motivations, to gain some dividends. The Swadhin Bangabhumi movement, allegedly under the sponsorship of the Indian government, has expressed its intention to carve out a chunk of the south-western districts of Bangladesh which is predominantly a Hindu-dominated region of the country, to form an independent country or merge with India. There are reportedly many radical elements with religious motivations which may seek recourse to extra-political means to bring about changes in the current state and political structures. The arrests of some Islamists at the end of February 2005, provides a new twist to the issue of religious extremism in Bangladesh.

These are just a few scenarios which might be worth addressing in the context of terrorism in Bangladesh. While dealing with the phenomenon of terrorism in Bangladesh, we must draw a line between societal violence and terrorism. Violence as a natural inclination of human beings has existed in Bangladesh, as in any other part of the world, for as long as human beings have existed as social beings, and, unfortunately, it predominates our social and political behaviour. Terrorism in Bangladesh fits the format of the 'crime' model suggested by Cunningham.[72] The next section of this chapter will thus deal with analysing the situation and assessing the prospect of classical terrorism in Bangladesh.

FEATURES OF TERRORISM IN BANGLADESH

As in India, there are some features of terrorism that are unique to Bangladesh. First and foremost is societal violence, primarily sustained and supported by the political parties, where political vendetta plays a strong motivating factor. These groups are being patronized by various political parties who utilize these elements not only to settle scores but also as rent-seeking agents. A large chunk of the parallel economy is the consequence of the pervasive rent-seeking exercise that is conducted by these outfits. [73]

The extremist elements, belonging to both the Left and the Right are active in south-eastern and northern Bangladesh. These are the PBCP (Purba Bangla Communist Party, Janajudha), the SHP (Sarbahara Party) and the JMJB (Jagrata Muslim Janata Bangladesh, considered to be an Islamist extremist group). Though many of the killings in the south are attributed to these elements, no credible action thus far has been taken. None of the leftist elements in Bangladesh are organized in any structured manner, unlike the orthodox terrorist organizations. The organizational set-up of the two recently outlawed (February 2005) Islamist groups is only now coming to light. What is of concern is whether there is a link between these groups and HuJI (Harkat-ul-Jihad-al-Islami) which is reportedly the only internationally linked and recognized, terrorist group with significant operations inside Bangladesh. According to some, these outfits are not motivated by religious or political ideology. The so-called underground terrorists or militants such as the SHP or the EPCP (ML), actually do not believe in any political ideology, rather, they are now more criminal outfits than political organizations. They call themselves political parties in order to lend a semblance of legitimacy to their otherwise criminal and illegal activities.[74]

There are reportedly outgrowths of religious organizations with radical leanings who have links with international terrorist organizations which might in the near future actuate action, either as a part of a wider radical religious movement or by themselves with their own agenda.[75] A large number of incidents of violence and terrorist activities spring from the politicization and crimialization of educational institutions where every major political party has its own well-armed student wing. Campus violence, whose fallout is reflected in the society at large, has been a distinct phenomenon since after the liberation of Bangladesh

It would be relevant to dilate on the factors in those situations that might be the cause of terrorism and violence in Bangladesh. The unstable socio-political condition, which was a natural sequel to a debilitating freedom war in 1971, has not exhibited any signs of abating. The government would like to characterize the current situation as a deliberate ploy by the opposition party to destabilize the country. A situation such as we observe today lays itself open to terrorism and violence. The absence of a national direction, a situation where the nation has leaders but no leadership, a hiatus at all levels of the society, total disharmony at the political level where democracy has lost all meaning and where the main opposition party chooses to abdicate the responsibility reposed in it by the electorate, and a slide in the law and order situation point to the possibilities of dangerous developments.

Chittagong Hill Tracts Situation (CHT)

Nealry twenty years of insurgency in the CHT came to a close on 2 December 1997 with the signing of the CHT Accord between the Government of Bangladesh and the Shanti Bahini. If that is the redeeming feature of the CHT situation in which we can take some solace after twenty years of violence, the disconcerting feature is the lack of progress in implementing the substantive provisions of the Accord. Within the Shanti Bahini there are those that have opposed the Accord from the time it was signed. The Preeti group and the pro-Accord faction are yet to hand in their weapons, which the Accord obligates them to do. The returning refugees have not all been fully resettled yet. There are a host of other provisions which because of their nature or the inaction of the relevant quarters, have resisted implementation.

Communist and Leftist Underground

To some, the 'left' ideology has all but lost its ideological and political appeal in Bangladesh. The existence of the Leftist parties as self-sustaining political entities is in danger.[76] But the disturbing factor is the existence of underground elements, with natal links with some political parties, which might turn to criminal activities mixed with terror tactics, as is presently occurring in many parts of the country. Bangladesh's south-western part has been witnessing terrorist activities by the outlawed radical political parties, particularly over the last decade. Although these elements were motivated more by money than by ideology, they have indulged in political killings also. Statistics show that at least 500 people are killed every year by the extremists and as many as 443 were killed in 1998 alone.[77] Reportedly, some of the underground elements are regrouping in these areas. Prospects of serious bloodletting have been reported in at least one newspaper.[78] If we take stock of the various underground elements, particularly those with Leftist propensities, operating in Bangladesh, certain features emerge, which are distinct in nature from similar groups operating around us. Those elements in Bangladesh that swathe their activities with the names of Left parties are motivated more by economic considerations than by any political ideology. They resort to terror tactics but do not qualify as terrorists or insurgents in the classical sense of the term, being bereft of convictions to follow or of an ideology to implement. They indulge in petty criminal activities but call themselves political parties, to lend a modicum of 'credibility' and 'respectability' to their activities.

Proliferation of Small Arms and Light Weapons

There can be no terrorism without weapons, and light weapons are the handiest tools of the terrorist. Although this phenomenon is better described as diffusion rather than a large-scale proliferation in the context of Bangladesh, it has nonetheless affected the country in as severe a way as any other country of South Asia which is beset with this problem. Bangladesh has become a transit route not only of small arms, but also of narcotics and drugs which find their routes of ingress and egress through the borders of Bangladesh. There have been reports of a large-scale influx of weapons and explosives into Bangladesh recently.[79] The recovery of arms on April 2004 was perhaps the largest single consignment ever seized by the police in the history of Bangladesh, and only confirms the country's vulnerability as a conduit of illicit weapons.

In Bangladesh, weapons have become the final arbiter of dispute settlement. Linked with this is the weaponization of educational institutions. Liberation saw the dominance of student politics in national affairs. Every major political party has its own political wing represented in all the major political institutions in Bangladesh, but they exist in a more pronounced fashion in the universities. They vie for dominance, most often through the use of force. Reportedly, a large quantity of arms has found its way into the hands of these political cadres. Campus violence has become the order of the day, the ramifications of which reflect on Bangladesh's politics and social life.

Hemmed in as Bangaldesh is by the most volatile area of this region, it can hardly remain impervious to the developments in the region. The residual fallout of the trade in illicit weapons, drugs and narcotics, as well the militancy in the north-eastern region of India, will impact Bangladesh adversely.

Radical Islamic Militancy and International Linkages

'Bangladesh is on the point of threatening the region, the Indian subcontinent, and far beyond if left unchallenged. Islamic fundamentalism, religious intolerance, militant Muslim groups with links to international terrorist groups, a powerful military with ties to the militants, the mushrooming of Islamic schools churning out radical students, middle-class apathy, poverty and lawlessness—all are combining to transform the nation'.[80] So goes a report claiming to be an analysis of the situation in Bangladesh following an equally far-fetched assessment of Bangladesh by Bert Lintner appearing in the FEER in April 2002. Whatever may be the quality of the substance of the report, certain internal developments cannot be overlooked. Even if one were to discard these elements as belonging to the fringes of the political process in Bangladesh, one must look into the misgivings that are expressed from time to time about the potential of these elements to influence the political arena.

Of late many radical Islamic elements have been arrested in various parts of Bangladesh. Following the US 'War on Terror' in Afghanistan, apprehensions were expressed that the mix of the domestic political factor and the impact of the war in Afghanistan, and the consequent political and economic instability may be exploited by the radical religious elements in Bangladesh. The apprehensions are primarily due to the character of the Four Party Alliance under the BNP government, one of the constituent elements of which is the Jamaat-e-Islami (JI), known for its anti-Bangladesh stand during the Liberation War, and its pro-Pakistan inclinations. This party now has seventeen seats in the Parliament. It is also reported that another small but, to some, an important part of this alliance is the Islami Oikkyo Jote, whose chairman, Maulana Azizul Huq, is reportedly on the advisory council of a suspected terrorist group in Bangladesh, the HuJI. According to reports emanating from official US sources, HuJI is a terrorist organization with ties to Islamic militants in Pakistan.[81] The HuJI and its link with Al Qaida became public when a fatwa declaring war against the US had as one of its signatories, one Fazlur Rahman, purportedly a leader of the 'Jihad Movement in Bangladesh'. Among the other signatories were bin Laden and Ayman al-Zawahari.

According to one report, this organization has within its fold several thousand hard-core members.[82] This group has perhaps been active since the year 2000, and local newspapers have provided it with extensive coverage. It reportedly has connections to the Pakistani HuJI and Harakat ul-Mujahidin (HUM).[83] While some ascribe the spate of communal violence following the 2001 elections to the rehabilitation of the religious right in the political arena, some others lay it squarely at the door of the HuJI. Still others are more hesitant, however, to paint the post-2001 election violence with an exclusively religious colour.

There is also a perception that Islamist extremist influence is on the rise, particularly in the rural areas, and the role of the incorruptible Leftist purists of the 1960s and the 1970s has been taken over by the 'dedicated Islamic cleric in flowing robes and beard'.[84] It is a matter of conjecture if devotion to religion will transform into violent resentment leading to the capture of state power or become a 'source of terrorism, to be exported outside Bangladesh', as some western analysts apprehend. While one may discount the reports, contemporary developments in respect of religious extremism present a very disquieting picture. There have been attempts by some fractious religious groups to organize themselves. Incidents of IEDs and the capture of large quantities of arms and ammunition,[85] as well as the arrest of persons claiming to belong to religious groups whose activities gives rise to serious apprehensions. The arrest of several persons in 2003, whose purported motivation was to wage 'Islamic Movements' in Bangladesh,[86] and the arrests of alleged radical operatives in the last week of February 2005, and the banning of two religious outfits with extremist and radical motivations, namely, the Jagrata Muslim Janata, Bangladesh (JMJB) and the Jamaat-al Mujahedin Bangladesh (JMB), have given a new perspective to the whole issue of religious militancy in Bangladesh.

Some scholars in Bangladesh, however, are averse to the use of the phrase 'religious militancy' and feel that 'militancy in the name of religion' might be more appropriate. This view stems perhaps from the notion that militancy in Bangladesh has no relationship with religion. That may be so, but whether some militancy in Bangladesh has been motivated by religious imperatives or otherwise is still an unanswered question. One understands the genuine apprehensions of those who see in the phrase 'religious militancy' the suggestion of a situation where militant activities are mandated and legitimized by religion and scripture. In this context one could take issue with those that assert: 'For the religious terrorist, violence first and foremost is a sacramental act or divine duty executed in direct response to some theological demand or imperative'. However, one cannot rule out the existence of groups or individuals that are naturally predisposed to violence and seek legitimacy of their acts in religion and the scriptures. Disconcertingly, there has also been a graduation in the manner and means of the operations of these elements. [illegible]ture of their targets and the weapons used point to their strong[illegible]s as well as the source of their weapons. The 21 August 2004 incident has confirmed the presence of a well-trained group in Bangladesh capable of conducting well-planned operations.

While it may not be possible to identify the perpetrators conclusively on the evidence that is available so far, analyses of the targets of the attacks since 1999 provide an image of the culprits and expose the character, motivations and religious inclination of those who carried out the attacks. It would be a fair assumption that the aims and objectives of the 21 August 2004 grenade attack and the January 2005 attack in Habiganj were entirely different from those that prompted the other attacks since 1999. Whether the perpetrators are the same is difficult to say. The types of weapons used in these attacks point to their common link, at least of those that have occurred since May 2004.

The twenty-one incidents of bomb blasts over the last five years, particularly on 21 August 2004, at the Awami League rally and the 27 January 2005 attack at Habiganj, which took the life of an ex-finance minister along with four others, by their timing and the nature of the targets raise some serious questions. Thus what is needed now is to get to the roots of the Islamists' links with other international militant organizations, their compulsions, as well as their convictions. This merits in-depth study in order to assess and determine their objectives and the prospect of success in Bangladesh.

What is noticeable in this respect is the reluctance of the government to acknowledge the possibility of the existence in Bangladesh of extremist groups with strong religious motivations, capable of carrying out violence such as the 21 August attack. Regrettably, this shows the government's ostrich-like attitude and a tendency to hedge around the issue. Also, the fact that none of the governments so far have been able to get to the bottom of any of the bomb incidents since 1999, and bring any of the perpetrators to book has only emboldened the extremists. It is a matter of grave concern that the identity of those behind biggest arms haul in Bangladesh still remains a mystery. At least the current LGRD minister has admitted and acknowledged the weakness of the administration in finding out the culprits behind these acts.

Apprehensions are also expressed from across the border not only of the proliferation of Islamist militant groups in India's north-east but also of the potential and possible linkages between the radical elements on both sides of the border.[87] Some even suggest that efforts may be underway to establish a separate Muslim homeland in the north-east comprising those states that have predominantly Muslim population. Jaideep Saikia sums up the anxiety when he says that, 'Islamic militant activities have begun to proliferate in the region. . . . Recent reports have also indicated that the ISI and the DGFI are reportedly encouraging the illegal influx with an eye to carving out a *Brihot Bangladesh* (Greater Bangladesh) in the region.'[88] Without indulging in a detailed critique of Saikia's assessment, one cannot but wonder at the strategic far-sightedness of those who are seeking to carve out a Muslim state in the north-east. It would not be hard for even a strategic ignoramus, to see that a 'greater Muslim Northeast' would have the same outcome as that of the Kurds: hemmed in by hostile groups, landlocked and left to the mercy of the neighbours, doomed to destruction. What strategic dividends this new configuration would bring to Bangladesh is also difficult to imagine.

According to a Dutch paper there is a swelling of the 'Radical ranks by graduates from the estimated 64,000 madrassas',[89] and this is causing concern. The perception is that these madrassas, where education is free and readily available, do not prepare their students adequately enough to enter the mainstream, and they thus fall victims to the lures of religious fanatics. It merits mention that madrassas have been in existence in what is now Bangladesh since the British period when the Indian Muslims, resentful of the British attitude towards them, deliberately shunned British education and started their own Islamic educational institutions all over the country. True, they are a source of free education and also provide a means of livelihood to the village people who, after passing out from these religious schools, find employment in a village 'makhtab' or a mosque. Almost all the mosques, particularly in the rural areas are used as schools to impart religious education. particularly the teaching of the Holy Koran. The perception that the madrassas are only for the poor is incorrect. To suggest that the madrassa is a 'factory producing terrorist' is also an absurd notion, although recent reports have revealed that that there are some madrassas which are imparting radical messages to their students. The government is in the process of making the madrassa syllabus more eclectic by including other subjects besides only religion, such as science.

No doubt there are elements within the political circle, Jamaat-e-Islam being one of them, whose stated political objective is to convert Bangladesh into an Islamic state. It is also true that the Right-wing religious parties have been represented in parliament since 1975. The open politics of the Islamist parties is perhaps a good thing on many counts. First, their participation in politics will act as a deterrent to their participation in any clandestine anti-state activities. But more importantly, these Islamist parties would not be able to make a dent in parliament without going into an electoral alliance with one of the two major parties. It is inconceivable that either of the two major parties would allow the Islamist agenda to be implemented, even if they chose to contest the election on the same platform. On the other hand, the shadowy religious element with links and funding from abroad would find it difficult to acquire popular appeal amongst the highly religious but at the same time highly secular common Bengali. Nonetheless, going by recent developments, these elements can be more than just of nuisance value to Bangladesh's state fabric.

On the growth and rise of fundamentalist groups in Bangladesh, at least three authors have provided fanciful and rather implausible information.[90] These groups have been credited with the capability not only of transforming the country into a fundamentalist state but also of exporting terror. Saika, in his ACIDIS paper written for and financed by a prestigious US institute, quotes statistics obtained from classified sources, as does Lintner. Lintner's piece was dismissed as 'infantile journalese' by most of the Bangladesh media, who said it was one-sided, motivated, preconceived, unsubstantiated and devoid of credibility because of the absence of any direct sourcing as any decent and honest journalistic work should have. Lintner was also accused of having written it the behest of those who do not wish Bangladesh well.[91] Those that the writing was intended to influence, namely the US, were equally dismissive of Alex Perry's article, as being totally unsubstantiated.[92] Some of the statistics mentioned in these works do not stand up to verification on the ground either. In Saika's piece, for example, one of the appendices contains the names and addresses of the 'training establishments' in Bangladesh of the fundamentalist and Muslim extremist elements of north-east India. Clearly this work suffers from lack of research. Enquiries and visits were made to a number of the areas in which the so-called training camps are supposed to exist, and to at least one institution which is supposedly conducting the training of the so-called Muslim fundamentalist organizations of the Indian north-east in the Cox's Bazaar region. Cox's Bazaar has featured repeatedly in the reports of certain external intelligence agencies, and picked up by various scholars later on. It is depicted as a place swarming with clandestine activities directed against a particular country. No trace of any such establishment was found.[93] It is interesting to note that soon after the coalition government in Bangladesh took over, which was immediately after 9/11, there were well-orchestrated efforts to depict Bangladesh as a radical fundamentalist country, if and possible, to have her declared a terrorist sate.

IV

CONCLUSION: RESPONSE AND THE LIMITS OF THE STATE

It is essential for us to keep in mind that while trying to address the issue of 'state and limits of terrorism in South Asia' it is well nigh impossible to overlook 'statist discourse'. We may well attempt to go beyond it but any scholarly endeavour on the issue will perforce be circumscribed by it. The state was and continues to be a part of the problem; more often it is the cause of the problem—the causal link of the issue—and in most cases it is either the unfortunate victim of terrorism or the perpetrator, nationally or internationally. The causal link between the state and terrorism is universal which cannot be done away with.

The response to terrorism in both India and Bangladesh follows the three points of view that dominate the discourse on the means and methods to counter terrorism. India's posture, according to experts,[94] has been more defensive and reactive while Bangladesh's response has primarily consisted of perfunctory palliative measures. This is an unwitting response brought about by the very nature of the state itself. But before going into the response of the state in detail, let us glance at the three major streams of opinion, i.e. the liberal, the conservative, and the realist.

The liberals put the blame for the rise of terrorism squarely on the shoulders of the state and the government. They believe terrorism is a reaction to bad governance, as well as economic, social and political deprivation, which engenders a feeling of marginalization. They see in terrorism a response to the misery brought on by the failure of the state to provide the basic needs. Since the state is the 'provider' of all that is basic, its failure makes it the target of the aggrieved who turn to violence and eventually to terror, in most cases when all other legitimate means of redress have failed. Terrorism may not always be directed against the government. but against a group or groups perceived to be responsible for the misery. The government becomes a target if it is seen to be siding with any of the disputants or adjudicating laws to curb the aggrieved.

The conservatives attribute the rise of terrorism to the process of nation building, a process that all nations have to go through. Terrorism, they aver, is a consequence of the natural 'stress and strain', that the process of nation building entails. This is more pronounced in cases where the nation has gained statehood before attaining nationhood. Efforts are made to integrate the land mass and the agglomerate constituents of the state, both physically and psychologically. In the pious efforts of the states to 'enforce the new regime', some groups are alienated while some are frightened due to what one scholar describes as the 'dilemma of ethnic security identity'. The natural consequence is resistance, which may turn violent if and when the state resorts to violence to curb violence. This is how the cycle of violence is initiated.

Between these two strands is another opinion which some consider a variant of the conservative line of thought, that is, the realist stream. Power is the motivating factor behind the realist pronouncements. Realists see terrorism as a reflection of the competition between states, where one seeks to 'control' the other through the exercise of power. Acquisition of power provides a state with the ability to actually use or threaten the use of violence. Terrorism is an expression or exercise of power through indirect means, short of use of force or direct violence. State terrorism is resorted to because, 'Terrorism is one of the stratagems available to states in their competition for power', to weaken others from within thus divesting it of its ability to compete without.[95]

The responses to terrorism consequently are as varied as the different precepts of this phenomenon. Thus, the liberals suggest that the state should first tackle the root causes of terrorism and the reasons that act as the primary incentive, to divest the secessionists or the militants of their rationale for fighting the state. The state should only apply force as a last resort; otherwise the cycle of violence would draw both parties into inextricable peril. The conservatives' stance in the matter of tackling terrorism is quite the opposite of the liberals. They prescribe the use of force ab initio to deal with violence. Conservatives consider economic, social, political, and administrative engineering a waste of time. Force must be met with force, they argue, and the more it is used peremptorily, the more would be the lives saved on both sides of the conflict. The realists' counsel is in line with that of the conservatives on the rationale that since the insurrections are externally motivated and sponsored, no amount of state building would be able to assuage the terrorists since they are bent on emerging out of the orbit of the state anyway.

We will not go into a discourse on the validity of any of these three arguments, but suffice it to say that if our response is 'exclusivist', relying entirely on any one of the three philosophies to the exclusion of the others, terrorism instead of abating will perpetuate. There cannot be one form of counter-measure to what is a set of very complex issues. One must look at these in a nuanced way. Since there is no one form of terrorism, the state is faced with two options: one, to deal by with it by force, the other, to settle the issue through dialogue and discourse. Unfortunately experience shows that it is the first option that the state finds easier to adopt.

Some also contend that the limits of counter-terrorism are inbuilt in the basic structure of any democracy, India included, and as one scholar suggests, 'since the limits are built in the basic structures itself, it may not be possible for us to meaningfully respond to the terrorist phenomenon from within the same structure'.[96] If we accept the three recommendations as effective in their own ways, then the states have primarily three forms of addressing this phenomenon—the political, the military, and the legislative. Both India and Bangladesh have taken recourse to all the three in their fight against terrorism, but the realist remedy of the use of force has perhaps dominated the activity and thinking of the leadership of these two countries.

The predilection of the state to resort to force to combat force ab initio is explained by scholars as being a legacy of imperialism. The reaction of the state is directly proportional to and dependent upon the nature of the state. The use of the coercive apparatus of the state by the British is demonstrated in the governance philosophy of the South Asian states who find it an easy tool, since the process of dialogue and flexibility and accommodations is considered a tortuous and often long-drawn process.[97] This is well reflected in the various measures that have been adopted by both India and Bangladesh.

That is not to say that the states have overlooked the political aspect of this problem. From time to time, measures were undertaken to accommodate the political aspirations of the aggrieved people. In the case of India, a large number of accords and agreements were contracted between the government and various militant and secessionist elements. While these were arrived at through a sometime tortuous process of dialogues between the parties, the agreements were not implemented in full measure. Likewise, certain laws were enacted to combat terrorism, which only exposed the coercive nature of the state and did little to counter terrorism. Bangladesh has also enacted legislation to make the fight against terrorism easier, and the recent CHT Accord indicates the state's sincerity about solving the problems of the ethnic minorities in the Hill Tracts. However, due to certain limitations, implementation remains elusive.

The following issues have proved to be limitations to countering terrorism:

Nation and State Building

More in India, than in Bangladesh, there is a strong divide between the core and the periphery, 'accentuated by the difficulties of nation and state building'. A natural corollary of this aspect is the issue of ethnicity and the management of ethnic conflict, which is viewed by many, particularly in India, as 'hegemonic and violent control exercised over minorities in the peripheral regions'. The process of nation and state building, in which both India and Bangladesh are still engaged, is fraught with inherent dangers since the process of integration and development creates a crisis of identity which the scholars term as security of identity, where 'Violent reaction arises when identities are under siege—sometimes in the form of terrorism'.[98] A case in point is Bangladesh, where the call by the late president, Sheikh Mujibur Rahman, for all to become 'Bangali', was seen by the ethnic minorities as a demand for them to shed their ethnic identities and transform into something that they were not. What followed is well known. Similarly, the crisis of identity still persists in India's north-east. This is due to the perceived attempt of the centre to subsume all groups under one entity—thus the fear of loss of identity. A glaring example where state building has trampled minority interests is the Kaptai dam in the CHT in Bangladesh.

Intra-State Conflict

Assam is an example of intra-state conflict. Assam is described as India's Yugoslavia, where many diverse groups within it are fighting one another. Within Assam there are many who suffer from the same phobia in relation to the Assamese as the Assamese feel about the migrants and settlers.

Over-centralization

Much of the motivations of terrorism have to do with the federal structure of the state also. The Indian federalist construct has lent itself to conflictive situations in the centre-state relationship. The desire for a strong centre and thereby the unwillingness to devolve power, has caused militancy and terrorism to persist. Compounding the problem is the physical size of India, which creates not only a physical distance but also a psychological gap. This results in either faulty or late reaction, and sometimes overreaction, to various situations. Scholars are also of the opinion that in an attempt to make the centre strong the whole federal concept became skewed, which intensified terrorism.[99] What over-centralization does in reality is that it leaves local issues unresolved and in many cases unattended. When the local elected representatives fail to address real issues they resort to exploiting 'non-issues' and this allows frustration to grow.[100] Concomitant, with this, the conflict that ensues takes the form of local versus central elites, and the local elites appear invariably at the forefront of the entire terrorist organization in the Indian north-east.[101]

Internal Politics

If we accept the proposition that the due political process keeps the level of militancy low, than the political games that have been played out in India have stood in the way of countering terrorism. This is more pronounced in the north-east where most governments lack political legitimacy since they lack popular support. In most cases, political parties with unnatural or artificial groupings are thrust upon the people. Leadership lacks lateral linkages since they are not germane to the system. Even if these parties manage the popular vote, it is the popular support that they are unable to acquire. This keeps the root causes and the scourge of terrorism alive.[102]

Colonial Experience and Practice

Unfortunately South Asia has retained the colonial mindset in its internal political dealings. In India this is very starkly evident in the attitude of the centre in dealing with the regional parties particularly when it comes to driving a wedge between the political parties. The policy of divide and rule is still followed with unremitting zeal, so that the ensuing confusion and flux can be further exploited. Destabilization of ministries and state governments was an article of faith carried out with military planning and precision and specific ministers of the central governments were entrusted with the task—as was done in Assam in the late 1980s.[103] It is now an established fact that in Punjab it was Mrs Gandhi who deliberately created the problem. Her reluctance to resolve the issue was part of a calculated strategy to divide the Sikhs.[104]

Method of use of the Security Forces

The induction of the military should be a last resort, not to tackle the daily law-and-order situations but to combat the terrorist. In India, as elsewhere, the military is trained for the specific job of tackling visible enemies. But the terrorists, who cannot be always perceived as enemies and who are seldom visible, are a different kettle of fish. The police, on the other hand are dreaded, and having lost the confidence of the people cannot undertake the 'hearts and mind programme', which is so important in an insurgency situation. They continue to look through the colonial prism, which creates a negative impression of the police in the minds of the common people who doubt their impartiality. It is no secret that the Indian military establishment had expressed resentment against its frequent deployment in internal security duties. This is as true of Bangladesh as it is of India. The induction of the military exposes the states' over-reliance on military solutions to what are essentially political problems. Military actions are often counterproductive.

Misreading the Actual Nature of the Problem

Nothing stands in the way of effective counter-terrorism more than the political leadership's lack of understanding of the basic nature of the issue. One must have a clear understanding of the aims and objectives of the terrorists. An administration bereft of this suffers from a lack of understanding of the militant's modus operendi, but even worse is that it leads to underestimating the capabilities of the militants. Still worse is the attempt to view everything militant as a law-and-order issue. This happened in the case of Assam where there was a clear cleavage on the very critical and fundamental issue of the Bodos, between the Chief Minister and Home Minister of Assam. These internal squabbles and hawkish tendencies were behind the emergence of an underground militant organization, the Bodo Security Forces (BdSF). Uncoordinated thinking on the part of the government is also blamed for the prolonged longevity of the Naga insurgency in spite of the many splits and coups that have occurred with the NSCN over the years.[105]

Politicized Administration

A politicized administration is a liability at any time and at any place. But this was felt most starkly in the Indian north-east, where both the fear of political reprisal and the anticipation of political patronage did not allow the government functionaries to act objectively and fearlessly. The highly politicized administration in Bangladesh has prevented the tackling of some of these issues in their seminal stages causing them to become almost intractable.

Lack of Unified Command

From the military point of view, what ails counter-terrorist operations is the lack of operational unity where the writ of the military does not reach the paramilitary forces. The idea behind creating the paramilitary forces, it is surmized by some, was to check the army from becoming ambitious, like the Pakistan army. This perhaps explains why the directors of the BSF and CRPF rejected the idea of joint training proposed by the Indian army.[106]

Lack of Intelligence, in Particular Human Intelligence

Given the disposition of the locals towards the security forces and the fractious nature of the administration, what was once taken for granted is no longer so. This is evident in Kashmir as well as the north-east.

Nexus between Politicians and Terrorist

Political patronization not only fosters terrorism but it also undermines the state's efforts to address the issue, not only by physically combating the terrorism but also by all other related actions, to get at its the root causes. In the north-east the parties in power were suspected of harbouring terrorists in their ranks. In fact, in Assam, the AGM was recognized as the political front of ULFA and several MNAs were elected with ULFA backing. An ex-governor of Manipur made charges of collusion between the NSCN-K and a ruling chief minister, and the NSCN-IM was accused of being hand in gloves with another chief minister.[107] Among other things, such a nexus causes development funds to percolate to the terrorists' coffers, which means that it is the people's money that is sustaining the terrorists.[108] In Bangladesh, the situation has come to such a pass that the miscreants have become empowered enough to sponsor MPs and politicians rather than the reverse.[109] A similar nexus between the PWG/Naxalites is known to exist in many affected parts of India, where as much as 60-70 per cent of the funds are reaching the militants.[110]

Abetment of Terror by the State

As many as 70,000 gun licenses were issued to the political cadre of a particular political party, most of them in Dhaka city alone, just before the last caretaker government took over in 2001. Convicted criminals had been given party tickets to contest seats for ward commissioners in Dhaka city, and as many as thirty-two of them were elected.[111] The government, to add to their muscle power, released, from time to time, jailed criminals. These actions of the government over the last decade have been termed by some analysts as the abetment of terror by the state.

Propensity to Hedge the Issue

The propensity to somehow 'manage' the issue rather than seeking a permanent solution has caused the terrorist phenomenon to survive in India. The paths of discourses and accords are seen as temporary holding actions. A large number of accords with the various elements in the north-east and Kashmir have remained unimplemented. The December 1999 CHT Accord has some inherent defects, which brings the intentions of the government into question.

Overlooking the Human Factor

This lacunae stems from the inability of the planners to analyse the problem in the correct perspective at the planning stage itself. Most often, Indian counter-terrorism operations had resided primarily on the political and military plane, essentially as action against criminal acts overlooking the need to tackle the problem at the individual level. What the politicians often forget is the fact that the human factor, and the population, is the 'battlefield itself'.

Expectations of Quick Result

Fake encounters, custody deaths and extra-judicial killings are instances where the hearts and minds are relegated to the background and success in counter-terror/insurgency operations is measured in term of the bodies bagged. This is considered by most as an expression of state coercion bordering on terror, encouraging the cycle of violence and further growth of terrorism.

Influx of SA&LW

It is the considered opinion of the experts that the proliferation of small arms and light weapons (SA&LW) is one of the most important causes of the rise of terrorism in South Asia. What limits to the state's efforts to counter terrorism is the easy availability of SA&LWs. Another factor is that the gap in the level of sophistication of the weapons held by the state and the non-state actors has reduced considerably to the extent that in many cases, in both India and Bangladesh, at one point of time, the militants and terrorists were in possession of weapons and equipment that were far more sophisticated than the weapons of security forces. Increased sophistication meant more casualties and, consequently, erosion of confidence in the law enforcing agencies.

Statist Posture

This attitude is the result of a particular mindset, which prevents the countries of the region from addressing these issues realistically. Statist positions blur the understanding of the phenomenon and cause one to take a narrow view of the matter. In the 'blame thy neighbour' game it is the militants whose position is strengthened.[112] However, there is a need to dispel two common misperceptions about terrorism in India, first, that a third country is responsible for the entire crisis, and second, that terrorism is an externally inspired problem, devoid of internal motivations. Neither Pakistan nor any other external agency can be totally blamed for the advent and growth of terrorism in India.[113]

Use of Surrendered Terrorists

A feature of the Indian counter-terrorism campaign was the granting of amnesty to surrendering militants, both in the north-east and in Kashmir. A good deal of government funds were spent in rehabilitating the militants in the mainstream. This generous intent of the government was exploited in ways that not only criminalized terrorism but also inflated the terrorists' ranks. The militants who had—called the SULFAs or surrendered ULFAs—apart form being used to seek the ULFAs, were also set after the families and sympathizers of the militants. The SULFAs were patronized as a private army by many of the politicians. Inter SULFA–ULFA clashes were responsible for many violent deaths in Assam. The SULFAs were engaged not only to combat the ULFAs, they were also involved in rent seeking and continued their activities after their surrender, this time with political patronage. Some scholars describe their activities as a form of state terrorism perpetrated on a 'wider section of the population'. They were used as what one scholar describes 'as means of extra constitutional counter-terrorism'. The Bangladesh government in 1998-9 granted a general amnesty to a large number of Sarbahara cadres, and as a part of the rehabilitation scheme, inducted them into the Ansar and VDP. Most of them have since gone back to their old ways.

State Terrorism

It is a universally accepted fact that technological innovations as well as industrial developments have caused states to lose their 'monopoly on violence'.[114] But also, contrary to established perceptions of terrorism, it is no longer a tool in the hands of the weak to balance the asymmetry. State terror, a result of proactive or reactive measures, due to over-reliance on the coercive tools at the disposal of the state, results in a vicious cycle of violence where violence begets violence and where the parties are drawn into a vortex aptly described as a 'black hole'. To quote a former DG of the Indian BSF, 'Terrorism has become an accepted political instrument and governments are known to tolerate and exploit terrorism. State terror by its very description, amounts to gross misuse of state authority with a view to protect national defense and state security.'[115] The challenge that faces the government is how to respond to terrorism without becoming a 'mirror image' of the terrorists it is supposed to defeat. Some assert that equating the actions of security forces with a broad brush of terrorism is also based on flawed arguments. However, 'Terrorist violence is also an instrument of states and governments, often to combat non-state terrorist,' opines Kanti Bajpai.[116] If terrorism is the use of violence to force acquiescence, the violence adopted by the state also fits the bill.

The Indian government has sought to tackle the issue of terrorism in all its forms in various ways. Over the last fifty-six years various legislations were enacted, from time to time, including the use of the military. Even now a large portion of the Indian military is engaged in counter-terror operations. Over the years the Indian security forces were reorganized and new paramilitary forces were set up for the purpose of combating terrorism. Bangladesh, too, ailing from this phenomenon since its liberation, has taken recourse to both security and legal means to address this issue. The Rakkhi Bahini, created soon after liberation, was used to combat the militants who had made it their objective to bring down the government. Very recently, the Bangladesh government has created an elite force, the Rapid Action Battalion, to stem the rising incidents of violence and terror in the country.

Some of the activities of the Indian security forces have drawn criticism from home and abroad, particularly because of the many in Punjab who were 'Reduced to Ashes', and the many who were killed in fake encounters in Kashmir, and the north-east. A recent report of the 'Committee for the Coordination on Disappearance in Punjab' (CCDP) gives a very exhaustive account of fake encounters, disappearances, torture, arbitrary arrests, unlawful detentions, and other instances of human rights violations by the security agencies in Punjab in the 1980s and early 1990s. The report brings out very clearly the state's limits in fighting terrorism and questions how far the state can go against those that are seeking its destruction. The report not only points a damning finger at India's investigative agencies but also accuses the judiciary of complicity in 'Ensuring impunity for the police in case of custodial torture and deaths'. It is also critical of the Indian National Human Rights Commission for its inaction in spite of clear evidence of 'complicity in the conspiracy of impunity' of all agencies engaged in counter-insurgency operations including the CBI.[117] India's anti-terrorist activities had at one time caused some members of the US Senate to introduce a bill calling for it to be described as a terrorist state.[118]

In Bangladesh, state terrorism had emerged in many forms and many faces. From colonial times, when the farmers in Bengal were subjected to the worst form of terrorism by the indigo planters, to the oppression by the landlords, the people have been at the receiving end of terror perpetrated by the state. The reign of terror unleashed upon the Bengalis from 26 March 1971 is surpassed only by a few similar acts of state violence in history. The emergence of state terrorism in Bangladesh is attributed to the weak state of the government institutions and their incapacity to control the variables, and to the compulsions of the dominant class—most of whom belonged to the ruling party—to control the dominated class with hegemonic passion. But the most important factor that led to state violence, according to one opinion, was the failure of a particular ideology vaunted by the party in power, which was as vague in its precepts as it was nebulous in its conception.[119]

Post-1971 Bangladesh witnessed a new phase in terrorism applied by the state. Apologists seek the shelter of the state- and nation-building process to rationalize such acts of the state. It was a time when anything resembling anti-government was construed as conspiratorial in design. Here was a situation where the urge to integrate the nation was felt acutely after a cataclysmic nine months, necessitating political control, but which in reality was a hegemonic dispensation of the dominant class, and where there was a pathological dislike by the ruling party of anything 'left', motivating the state to resort to the only instrument considered appropriate—force. It was perhaps inevitable that the pangs of gestation would throw up social and political variables to confront which the force resorted to by the state would be construed as a form of terrorism. In its effort to impose control the state organized what some describe as 'private forces'. That too perhaps can be explained. Being a newly emerged country, where the military as well as the police had participated directly in the war of liberation, there was perhaps a sort of hesitation on the part of the government as much as there was a psychological disinclination on the part of the security forces to use and to be used against the people, lest they mirror the image of the occupation forces that they had only recently helped to dislodge. This is the rationale behind the formation of several private militias like the 'Lal' Bahini and the more structured Rakkhi Bahini. Terrorism was 'officially' used to stamp out political dissenters and ideological opponents.[120] The attempt at integration and the means thereto engendered terrorism by the state in the seminal years of Bangladesh, which can be encapsulated thus: 'the integration of the dominated classes which are at once in the state of ferment . . . is being attempted not through the usual strategy of control and satiation of objective needs, but through . . . blood chilling terror unleashed by institutionalised violence', through such instruments of terror as the 'Rakkhi Bahini', 'Lal Bahini', 'Volunteers' and the like.[121]

The current discourse on terrorism gives one the impression that terrorism as a phenomenon has only evolved with the incidents of 11 September. There are ample examples and historical evidences and precedents of the use of terrorism as a tool of political control and a means of political repression, predating the formation of nation-states. A dispassionate evaluation of the characteristics and causes is needed so that a correct response is formulated to counter this phenomenon. India and Bangladesh provide two very different canvases of the terrorism phenomenon, although the root causes and the methods used by them are very similar, so are the impediments that these two countries are facing. Many of the limits are inbuilt in the system and in the attitude of the politicians and bureaucrats. While external factors exacerbate terrorism, taking refuge in this may not help us to totally eliminate the phenomenon.

NOTES

1. Paul Pillar, quoted in Mark Burgess, 'Terorism: The Problem of Definition', *CDI Paper*, 1 August 2003.
2. Walter Lacquer, *No End To Terrorism: Terrorism in the Twenty First Century* (New York: Continuum, 2003), p.14.
3. Shahedul Anam Khan, 'Terrorist Activities in Bangladesh: Ways to Combat the Growing Menace', unpublished paper, 1989.
4. Ibid.
5. Bruce Hoffman, 'Terrorism in the Twenty-first Century: Trends and Prospects', *Rands Paper* 986.
6. Lacquer, *No End To Terrorism*, p. 24.
7. Khitij Prabha, 'Defining Terrorism', *Strategic Analysis*, vol. 24, no. 1, April 2000.
8. Lacquer, *No End To Terrorism*, p. 9.
9. Ashish Sonal, *Terrorism and Insurgency in India: A Study of Human Element*

(New Delhi: Lancer Publishers, 2001), p. 2; and Rochana Das, 'Security and Terrorism: The Northeast Indian Perspective', in O.P. Mishra and Sucheta Ghosh, *Terrorism and Low Intensity Conflict in South Asia Region* (New Delhi: Manak Publications, 2003).

10. Laqueur, *No End To Terrorism*, p. 25.
11. The reference is to Nelson Mandela.
12. Ian O. Lesser, 'Countering the New Terrorism: Implications for Strategy', *Rand Paper* 989.
13. Arri Aylon, former Head of Israeli Intelligence.
14. Kanti Bajpai, *Roots of Terrorism* (New Delhi: Penguin Books, 2002).
15. Brian Jenkins, in his Foreword to 'Countering the New Terrorism: Implications for Strategy', *Rand Paper* 989.
16. Bajpai puts out some fine determinants of a freedom fighter and a terrorist, *Roots of Terrorism*, pp. 7-17.
17. For a good dilation on the subject see, Ariel Merari, 'Terrorism As a Strategy of Insurgency, in *Terrorism and Political Violence*, vol. 5, no. 4, Winter 1993, pp. 214.
18. Binalakshmi Nepram, 'Small Wars and Insurgencies in the North East', *Himalayan and Central Asian Studies*, vol. 5, nos. 3-4, July-December 2003.
19. Walter Laqueur, *The New Terrorism* (New York: Phoenix Press, 2001), p. 6.
20. William G. Cunningham, 'Terrorism, Definitions and Typologies', in *Terrorism: Concepts, Causes And Conflict Resolution* (Fort Belvoir, Virginia: Defence Threat Reduction Agency, January 2003).
21. A study carried out by Alex Schimd and Albert Jongman involving analyses of 109 academic and official definitions, brings out very interesting facts which are that the element of violence was included in 83 per cent of the definition, political goals in 65 per cent and 51 per cent emphasized the element of inflicting fear and terror. Only 21 per cent of the definitions mentioned arbitrariness and indiscrimination in targeting, and only 17.5 per cent included the victimization of civilian noncombatants, neutrals or outsiders. The study also reveals that official definitions of terrorism are fairly similar while those that are offered by academicians are more diverse, albeit containing the essential elements of the official definitions. But the consensus reflects very much the Western perception, which is at a variance with that of the Third World countries and which is not shared by the majority people on earth. See also Ariel Merari, 'Terrorism as a Strategy of Insurgency', p. 214.
22. Report A/42/832.
23. Prabha, 'Defining Terrorism'.
24. Lacqueur, *No End To Terrorism*, p. 6.
25. Ibid., p. 8.
26. Ibid., p. 9.

27. Gerard Stoudmann, Director, Office for Democratic Institutions and Human Rights (OSCE/ODIHR).
28. Sridhar Khatri, 'Understanding And Combating Terrorism In South Asia', in Moonis Ahmar (ed.), *The World after September 11: Challenges and Opportunities* (Karachi: University of Karachi, 2003).
29. See Clingendael (Netherland) Report, 'South Asia: Regional Report, Part I', March 1998, pp. 70-3.
30. Cunningham, 'Terrorism', op. cit.
31. Means 'sick' in Hindi, an acronym for the Indian states of Bihar, Madhya Pradesh, Andhra Pradesh, Rajasthan, and Uttar Pradesh.
32. Gurharpal Singh, *Ethnic Conflict in India: A Case Study of Punjab* (London: Macmillan Press Ltd, 2000), Chapter 4.
33. This interesting but sensitive point came out of the present author's discussions with Subhashis Bannrejee, Department of International Relations, Jadavpur University, Kolkata.
34. Bajpai, *Roots of Terrorism*, p. 34.
35. Sanjoy Hazarika, *Strangers of the Mist, tales of War and Peace from India's North-east* (New Delhi: Penguin, 1994), p. 3.
36. Bajpai, *Roots of Terrorism*, p. 137.
37. See, 'India's Insurgencies: A Special Report', USCINPAC (VIC), 22 April 2002.
38. Bajpai, *Roots of Terrorism*, p. 98.
39. B.V. Verghese, *India's Northeast Resurgent* (New Delhi: Konarak Publishers, 1996), p. xiii.
40. Ved Marwah, *Uncivil Wars: Pathology of Terrorism in India* (New Delhi: HarperCollins, 1995), pp. 225.
41. Verghese, *India's Northeast*, pp. 2-3.
42. Ibid., p. 10.
43. S. Guru Dev, *Anatomy of Revolt in the Northeast India* (New Delhi: Lancer Books, 1996), p. ix.
44. Das, 'Security and Terrorism'.
45. Ajay Sahani, 'Survey of Conflicts & Resolution in India's Northeast', SATP, www.satp.org; Das, 'Security and Terrorism'.
46. Quoted in Nepram, 'Small Wars and Insurgencies'.
47. Bajpai, *Roots of Terrorism*, p. 62.
48. This characterization was made by Anindyo Majumdar, Professor, Department of International Relations, Jadavpur University, Kolkata, during a discussion with the author on 16 February 2004.
49. Verghese, *India's Northeast*, p. vii.
50. The 'Inner Line Regulation', devised by the British to sanitize the 'Frontiers' is still in vogue in India today.
51. See Anindita Dasgupta, 'Migration, Identity and Conflict in Assam', *Himalayan and Central Asian Studies*, vol. 5, nos. 3-4, July–December 2001, p. 38; see also, Das, 'Security and Terrorism', p. 468; Amiyo Kumar

Samanta, 'Some trends in the Northeastern Insurgency and the Naxalite Movements', in Mishra and Ghosh, *Terrorism and Low Intensity Conflict*, p. 493.

52. W.H. Morris-Jones, 'More Questions Than Answers', *Asian Survey*, vol. 24, no. 8, August 1984.
53. Sahani, 'Survey of Conflicts', p. 46.
54. Some scholars contend that economic deprivation is not always the motivating force of the terrorist movements in the north-east and that there is no positive correlation between development and insurgency. This insight was provided by Prof. Anindyo Majumdar of Jadavpur University in discussions with the author; and Das, *Security and Terrorism*, p. 467 and Samanta, 'Some Trends', p. 500.
55. Samanta, 'Some Trends', p. 501; and Sahani, 'Survey of Conflicts'.
56. Sahani, 'Survey of Conflicts'.
57. See Sahani, 'Survey of Conflicts'; and Nepram, 'Small Wars'.
58. The figures were obtained from Government of India's Annual Report 2002-2003, on the 'Internal Security Scenario: The Overview'. However, unofficial figures put the death toll in excess of 50,000.
59. See ibid., for an assessment of the situation.
60. Gurmeet Kanwal, 'Proxy War in Kashmir', *Strategic Analysis*, April 1999.
61. Government of India, 'Internal Security Scenario'.
62. This proposition finds a rationale in various articles by Lacquer, Jenkins, Hoffman, etc.
63. Government of India, 'Internal Security Scenario.
64. Sumit Ganguly, 'Explaining the Kashmir Insurgency: Political Mobilization and Institutional Decay', *International Security*, vol. 21, no. 2, Fall 1996.
65. Ibid.
66. 'Left Wing Extremist Group', www.satp.org; Ajay Dharshan Behera, 'The Politics of Violence and Development in South Asia', in Asia.doc.
67. Ibid.
68. *The Christian Science Monitor*, 13 August 2002.
69. Samanta, 'Some Trends', pp 506-7.
70. Bajpai, *Roots of Terrorism*; Behera, op. cit.
71. These are opinion expressed by senior police and government official in discussions with the author.
72. Cunningham, 'Terrorism Definition and Typologies'.
73. Neila Hussein, 'Youth, Chandabaji and Small Arms—A Political Nexus', in Anam Khan and Afroze (eds.), *Chandabaji versus Entrepreneurship: Youth Forces in Bangladesh* (Dhaka: BIISS, 1999).
74. The basis of this formulation is the author's discussion with various law enforcing and intelligence agencies in Bangladesh. However, interrogations of some of the recently (February 2005) arrested Islamists have revealed their religio-political agenda.

75. Jaideep Saika, 'Terror Sans Frontiers: Islamic Militancy in North East India', ACIDIS Paper, University of Illinois at Urbana-Champaign, July 2003; Subir Bhowmik, 'Bangladesh: Second Front of Islamic Terror', in Mishra and Gosh, *Terrorism and Low Intensity Conflict*; and Bert Lintner, 'A Cocoon of Terror', *FEER*, 4 April 2002. See also, *The Daily Star*, Dhaka, 19, 22 and 24 August 2003.
76. This perception stems from the auhtor's discussion with Enayetullah Khan, Editor, *Holiday*, Dhaka. Coming from an erstwhile practitioner of left politics, this prognosis has credibility.
77. Farhaz Hasan, 'Outlaws on the Rampage', *Dhaka Courier*, 26 February 1999.
78. *Prothom Alo*, Dhaka, 10 April 2004.
79. *Janokhanta*, Dhaka, 21 March 2004.
80. *A Cocoon of Terror—A Review*, Agni Corporation/Stichting Werkgroep Agni, The Netherlands.
81. US State Department, *Patterns of Global Terrorism 2001*.
82. Bert Lintner, 'Bangladesh: Extremist Islamist Consolidation', SATP. The figures are so varied that it gives rise to doubts about the authenticity of the statements. A statement by the Chief of Indian Police says that there are 15,000 of them. See, *The Daily Star*, 6 April 2004.
83. US State Department, *Patterns of Global Terrorism 2004*, 29 April 2004.
84. Lintner, 'Bangladesh'.
85. *The Daily Star*, Dhaka, 27 February 2003.
86. Ibid., Dhaka, 19 August 2003.
87. See Saika, 'Terror Sans Frontiers'; Bhowmik, 'Bangladesh'; Nepram, 'Small Wars'; and Sahani et al., 'Survey of Conflicts'.
88. Saika, 'Terror sans Frontiers'.
89. *A Cocoon of Terror*, Agni Coroporation, The Netherlands.
90. Saika, 'Terror Sans Frontiers'; and Lintner, op. cit.
91. *The Daily Star*, Dhaka, 10 April 2002.
92. Ibid., 21 October 2002. See also, Alex Perry, 'Deadly Cargo', *The Time*, 21 October 2002.
93. The author visited at least six listed areas, supposedly the training establishments of the north-east Muslim insurgents but found nothing even remotely resembling training establishments.
94. Tara Katra, 'Countering Transnational Terrorism', *Strategic Analysis*, February 2000.
95. Bajpai, *Roots of Terrorism*.
96. Samir Kumar Das, 'Terrorism and the Limits of Democracy: The Case of Contemporary Assam', in Mishra and Ghosh, *Terrorism and Low Intensity Conflicts*.
97. Author's discussions with Prof. Shuvashish Bannerjee, Department of International Relations, Jadavpur University, Kolkata.
98. Lesser, 'Countering the New Terrorism', p. 97.

99. Author's discussions with Professor Bannerjee.
100. Sonal, *Terrorism and Insurgency in India*, p. 14.
101. Das, 'Security and Terrorism', p. 462.
102. Anindyo Majumder in interview with the author.
103. Bajpai, *Roots of Terrorism*, pp. 78-9; Prabha, 'Defining Terrorism'; and Das, 'Security and Terrorism', p. 471.
104. Singh, 'Ethnic Conflicts in India', Chapter 4.
105. Ibid.
106. Ibid., p. 80.
107. Samanta, 'Some Trends', p. 500.
108. Sahani, 'Survey of Conflicts'. See also, K.P.S. Gill, *The Pioneer*, 9 December 2000.
109. *The New Age*, Dhaka, 15 March 2004.
110. Alok Kumar Gupta, 'Naxalites and Private Armies: Caste Conflict in Bihar', in Mishra and Ghosh, *Terrorism and Low Intensity Conflicts*, pp. 522-3.
111. *The Daily Star*, Dhaka, 27 April 2002.
112. Imtiaz Ahmed, 'Contemporary Terrorism and the State, Non-State and the Interstate: Newer Drinks, Newer Bottles', in Sridhar K. Khatri and Gert W. Kueck (eds.), *Terrorism in South Asia: Impact on Development and Democratic Process* (Colombo: Regional Centre for Strategic Studies, 2003).
113. Report of the IPCS Seminar held on 12 September 2003.
114. Noam Chomsky, 'Wars of Terror', *New Political Science*, vol. 23, no. 1, 2003.
115. Quoted in S. Guru Dev, *Anatomy of Revolt*, p. 72.
116. Bajpai, *Roots of Terrorism*, p. 7.
117. *Frontline*, vol. 20, issue 13, 21 June-4 July 2003.
118. *Congressional Record*, p. E1913, Tuesday, 6 October 1998.
119. Enayetullah Khan, 'The Bangladesh Syndrome', *Holiday*, Dhaka, 22 April 1973 and 6 May 1973. See also, Rezwan Siddiqui, 'Kathamalar Rajneeti' (Politics of Words), Dhaka, 2002.
120. Khan, 'The Bangladesh Syndrome–IV', *Holiday*, Dhaka, 13 May 1973.
121. Idem, 'The Bangladesh Syndrome–II: The Specter of Mujibbad', *Holiday*, Dhaka, 29 April 1973.

CHAPTER IV

Weapons Technology and the Reconceptualization of Terrorism

IMTIAZ AHMED with FARID AHMED BHUIYAN

There were times in history when killing was done solely with bare hands. The Stone Age (from the Palaeolithic to the Neolithic period) probably made the first difference. People could be killed from a certain distance. The Bronze Age (before 3000 BC) brought a certain mastery in the art of defence. In fact, Homer in the *Iliad* relates how Hephaestus, the Greek god of fire, threw copper, tin, silver, and gold into his furnace to make the shield of Achilles. Yet Achilles could not be saved; the bow and arrow of his Age were enough to strike his heel, indeed, from a distance beyond the range of his eyesight. The Iron Age (before 1000 BC), however, while extending further the distance between the victim and the perpetrator, made killing swifter. This Age otherwise succeeded in combining distance with speed in the business of killing, and soon and for many, many years, one civilization after another raced with each other to find the combination best to do this.

By the eleventh century AD, the hashish-addicted (Shi'ite as well as Ismaili) Assassins became a class of their own, mastering the art of killing the 'disobedient', mainly with daggers but with a devotion unmatched in recorded history. They also had their counterparts in the Christian world, the Knights Templars. Both the Assassins and the Templars while mastering the art of killing succeeded in terrorizing the people, indeed with swiftness, secrecy, and their readiness to commit suicide when challenged. The use of weapons, even if it was only a dagger, made a qualitative difference when groups of such nature began using them. Handguns could only make the victims more numerous and vulnerable.

Gunpowder, however, came to be used in Europe only towards the end of the thirteenth century, although it took a century or two more for it to replace crossbows. In fact, monarchs were reluctant to use the new weapon because, schooled in the use of swords and crossbows, they still found it 'ignoble to kill a man from a great distance!'[1] The cost of gunpowder was also a factor. But since gunpowder had manifold uses—handguns, (primitive) rockets and more importantly cannon—and proved effective in one battle after another, including naval warfare, the replacement was matched with the development of newer techniques in the use of gunpowder in a much shorter span of time.

In the nineteenth century came the modern military explosives—TNT (trinitrotoluene), tetryl, picric acid, PETN (penaerythrite tetranitrate), and RDX or cyclonite. But it was not until Alfred Nobel (1833-96) perfected the technique of detonating high explosives that the latter became deadly. Indeed, this time *shock* was added to *distance* and *speed*. The Nuclear Age (from 1945) made a diabolic combination of all three. The inventors of the A-bomb, with scores of megatonnage bombs (many over 50 MT) in their possession, could now boast of destroying the earth with all its population not once, as the divine willed, but more than nine or ten times, and that again in a flash of seconds! Not for nothing did the 'father' of the A-bomb, Robert Oppenheimer, recite from the *Gita* when he first saw the explosion at Alamogordo, New Mexico, on 16 July 1945: 'Now I am become death, the destroyer of worlds!' Here creation got fused with destruction!

Weapons technology, the other name for killing people, went hand in hand with the civilizational quest of the humans. The latter possibly could survive and prosper even after all the dreadful killings in history mainly because the *technology* of killing transformed simultaneously. Distance, swiftness, and shock made the killing 'unreal', almost without the perpetrator feeling remorse and guilt. This was as vital to the individual as it was to the state when it came down to the business of killing. Incidentally some seventy years back, Rabindranath Tagore made a reference to this issue. In April 1932, following his aeroplane journey to Iran at the invitation of the Shah, Tagore remarked:

As the aircraft began to climb, the intimacy between the world and our five senses grew faint, till it narrowed to only one—our sight—but it was too hazy for comfort. All evidence of the certain yet diverse earth we absorb daily, now faded; a three-dimensional reality became a two dimensional picture. Creativity is manifest in varied structures seen in the totality of space and time. As these distinctions become obscure, creation turns out to be annihilation. Just then, our earth appeared to me in that light of extinction. Her identity vanished, her constant demands on the imagination ceased. In a similar state, when a man sets out to drop fiery weapons from an aeroplane, he becomes unspeakably ruthless. His cruel arm does not hesitate in doubt. He is absolutely certain of his enemy's guilt—for they are so remote from him. Men have an innate tenderness for the natural world. When the reality of this world becomes unreal, his affection withers. The advice given in the *Gita* is comparable to this aeroplane—it removed Arjuna's compassionate mind to a distant world; from its pinnacle it became impossible to perceive who lived and who died. Men have many such theoretical aeroplanes to conceal reality in their armory—in imperialism, in theories of sociology, in religions. The blows that fall from those heights come pleasantly wrapped with one consolation: *Na hanyatey, hanyamanye sharirey* (The body can be slained [*sic*] but the soul is indestructible).

The British maintain an airbase in Baghdad. The resident Christian priest told me they were currently bombing a village of a sheikh. The dead, old and young alike, were receiving these blows from the misty heights of the British Empire. It was easy to kill them—Imperialism made their humanity indistinct. . . . Moreover, from an aeroplane it was easy to bomb the desert dwellers. There was no fear of retaliation; and the dead and injured appeared as mere statistics. People who can be killed thoughtlessly have never been alive in the minds of their killers. This is the reason why men and women ignorant of Western ways of destruction are slowly becoming a blur to these masters of war.[2]

Terrorism too, for that matter, went through a remarkable change, almost in line with the development of weapons technology, in the business of terrorizing and killing people. For the contemporary terrorist the victim has finally become 'unreal'! This is true for the non-state terrorists with explosives in their hands as it is for the state terrorists with aircrafts and naval vessels loaded with precision-guided missiles. Put differently, there is hardly a difference between the airborne terrorism of 9/11 and the American bombing of Afghan towns and villages.

In South Asia the 'terror' of terrorism also got transformed in leaps and bounds with innovations and uses of modern weaponries.

Terrorism would have been a lot different if the terrorists were equipped only with rocks and daggers, or even just double-barrel guns. AK-47s, hand grenades, rocket launchers, and now more frighteningly, biological and chemical weapons like anthrax radically transformed the outcome of terrorist attacks. With this, of course, was added, albeit in line with the Assassins, the Templars, and later on the Hezbollas, the Tamil Tigers' 'civil' but deadly contribution, that is, the horrifying element of 'suicide bombing'. It seems that *contemporary terrorism* has replaced ontology with (to use a word from Derrida) *hauntology*.[3] That is, so fearsome has terrorism now become that even when it is not present it haunts us like a spectre. A reconceptualization of terrorism, for that matter, is in order.

The chapter is divided into four sections. The first section reflects on the various rituals of terrorizing people. Although the rituals can be traced back to antiquity, the marvel lies in humans' ingenuity in developing the art and science of killing and terrorizing fellow human beings, at times in deadly, *inhuman* ways. Indeed, if the state machineries were constantly in the business of devising newer methods, non-state elements were no less innovative in the art and science of killing and terrorizing the people. At the same time, with the advent of modernity, the rituals of terrorizing the people became identical, whether the terror was unleashed by the state or by the non-state in Europe, Africa or South Asia. Section two then reflects on modern weapons technology and how it has come to represent conformity, empowering the perpetrators—state and non-state—simultaneously in the business of killing and terrorizing people across the globe. Modern weapons technology and the transformation of South Asian terrorism is taken up in section three. The last section deals with the issue of what is to be done.

But before we proceed further, two theoretical positions central to this chapter must be made clear. Firstly, the chapter does not subscribe to a linear understanding of history. Rather, the intention here has been to take certain historical events in discrete social formations and point out how humans have lived and died within those socially composed events. Human ingenuity in terrorizing and killing people differed over time, although, as the paper will demonstrate, with the arrival of modernity and the development of modern weapons technology there is now conformity in not only how we live but also how we die! In sum, the paper reflects on how the development of modern weapons has contributed to a precise conformity in the art and science of terrorizing and killing people, indeed, with consequences which remain perverse and demonic. Secondly, the paper does not rule out other elements in the understanding of terrorism. The focus on weapons technology is mainly to shed light on the dire need for reconceptualizing terrorism in the light of its complicity with the modern state and modern technology and the demonic havoc that it is now capable of unleashing not only in one locality but throughout the state, region, and the world.

I

RITUALS OF TERRORIZING PEOPLE

Homer provides one of the earliest accounts of terrorizing people or, to put it slightly differently, the act of one terrorizing the many. This refers to the treatment of the Trojan hero Hector by Achilles.[4] Although Hector was defeated, Achilles refused to show him any mercy. After putting his spear through Hector's throat, Achilles left the body for his Greek supporters to strip and mutilate. He then cut the tendons of Hector's feet at the heel and with strips of oxhide he attached them to his chariot, only to drag him round the walls of Troy and terrorize the citizens of the fallen city. Whether the fear tactics numbed the citizens or made them more resolute in defeating Achilles remains less a disputable issue now that the people are reminded more of Achilles' heel than that of Hector's! But a beginning was certainly made in the ingenuity of terrorizing the people and Achilles was neither forgotten nor forgiven for that. Individual terror tactics soon caught the imagination of groups, communities, nations, and states.

Palestine is the birthplace of many noble and ignoble things, including the first battle in recorded history, that is, the one between the rebel tribes of Palestine and Syria and the Egyptian Pharaoh Thutmosis III in 1469 BC. Little known, however, is the fact that Palestine also contributed very early on to what is now known as terrorism. We know from the record of Josephus that the 'Sicarii'

(Zealots) of Palestine used unorthodox tactics to knocking down their enemies. With a small sword hidden under their coats, the Sicariis would launch their attacks in daylight, preferably on holidays when crowds congregated in Jerusalem. The victims were few but the resultant chaos was overwhelming. Other groups, including the Assassins, made further contributions to this strategy.

The Assassins, as indicated earlier, were an offshoot of the Shi'ite and Ismailis who appeared in the eleventh century and were suppressed only by the Mongols in the thirteenth century. Based in Persia, they spread to Syria and Palestine, killing prefects, governors, caliphs and even Conrad de Montferrat, the Crusader King of Jerusalem. The Assassins also tried to kill Saladin, the Syrian commander and vizier in Egypt (1137-93), but failed. Their first and foremost leader, Hassan Ibn al-Sabbah, seemed to have realized very early on that his group was too small to confront the enemy in open battle but that a planned systematic, protracted campaign of terror carried out by a small, disciplined force could prove more effective in defeating the enemy. The Assassins always operated in complete secrecy; the terrorist fighters were disguised as strangers, at times even as Christians.

Indeed, the Christian counterparts of the Assassins—the Templars—were no less fanatic and secretive. The only notable difference between them was the Templars' massive success in combining fanaticism with finance. At one stage, they became more of 'an international bank than a defender of pilgrims', a factor which turned both princes and people against them.[5] But the transformation of the Templars also provided a clue to what the result could be if armed militancy (dagger-held, it may be) is backed by fanaticism and finance. The South Asian non-state terrorist rituals were no less interesting.

The secret societies of Thugs (from the Hindi *thagi*, literally deceivers) existed for centuries in India. Colonel Sir James Sleeman, the grandson of 'Thuggee Sleeman' (Major General Sir William Sleeman of The Bengal Army who exterminated the Thugs), estimated that over a period of 300 years 40,000 fell victim annually to the Thugs. They strangulated their victims with yellow-coloured silk scarves, knotted at one end, which represented the hem of the goddess Kali's robe. The Thugs considered themselves to be the servants of the goddess Kali, and this sort of murder as a divine mission, while the booty obtained was their earthly reward. The tactics adopted by the Thugs seldom varied. The gangs, usually numbering from twenty to fifty men, moved along the roads pretending to be ordinary travellers. They would to win the confidence of innocent travellers and would, if necessary, travel many miles and for several days until any suspicion of their real intentions had been dispelled. Then, when the leader of the band judged that the moment had come to strike, they would prepare their victims' graves and each would select a victim to strangle. Usually the signal to strike was *Tamakhu Kha lo* (smoke tobacco) but at times they also used the sound of a cock crowing as the death call.[6]

The actual strangling was the work of a moment. Two Thugs usually tied the scarf around the neck of the victim, the third pulled the legs to throw him on his face, another delivered a blow in the most sensitive parts and with a jerk backwards, the neck was broken. Once the deed was done, the bodies were searched and then buried, the booty shared and the Thugs moved on in search of other victims. These expeditions were carried out during the winter season and lasted for several months. After that the gangs dispersed to their homes and resumed their normal activities. Many of them spent the summer relaxing and reassembled with the call of the leader for another expedition. Few showed any remorse for the murders they had committed, believing they were serving a religious end, and many of them were respected members of the society. The ramifications of Thugee ran deep; many influential barons, landowners, minor rajahs extended them protection as they 'drew from them a fine income in *douceurs* paid from the loot of the winter campaigns'.[7] This is also an indication that the relationship between the state (landowners, rajahs, and the like) and non-state Thugs in the business of terrorizing people is somewhat fuzzy, and the one could indeed aid and influence the other. This issue will be discussed in greater detail later in the paper.

But the Sicariis, Assassins, Templars, and the Thugs were not alone in devising unique ways of killing and terrorizing people. Following the death of the Mughal Emperor Aurangzeb in 1707, a state of total anarchy ensued for more than a century. During that period the common people were at the mercy of gangs of freebooters, and amongst them the Pindaris were the most terrifying. The name 'Pindari' comes from the liquor 'pinda', which they drank in quantities. They were comprised of 2,000 to 3,000 men from different gangs of robbers mounted on horses, and their operation area extended through central India and the Deccan. Defeated Maratha chiefs and the chiefs of Rajasthan who had not as yet crossed swords with the East India Company used the Pindaris to serve their own purposes. The Pindaris usually retired to the deserts and jungles of Rajasthan after carrying out their raids.[8]

The Pindaris moved like a tornado through the countryside annihilating everything in their path, but in the face of stubborn resistance they just melted away. In their expeditions, while marching towards the objective, they neither carried tents nor any baggage. They always moved light, 'each horseman carried a few cakes of bread for his own subsistence and some feeds of grain for his horse'.[9] They moved as secretly as possible at the rapid rate of 40 or 50 miles a day. On reaching their objective they grabbed all the cattle and property they could find and destroyed what they could not carry away. In the process they committed all sorts of atrocities to terrorize the people. By their secrecy and swiftness they always deceived the troops who were guarding the front lines of the countries invaded. They always retreated before a force could be brought against them.

The Pindaris' trademark torture was to tie a bag of hot ashes over man's mouth and nose and then thump his back, thus forcing him to disclose the place where he had hidden his valuables, a practice which subsequently caused the lungs to rot. The Pindaris mainly consisted of discharged soldiers, escaped criminals, and vagabonds who offered their swords to such acknowledged leaders as Chitu and Karim Khan. If the non-state Sicariis, Assassins, Templars, Thugs, and Pindaris mastered the art of killing and terrorizing people, the state was no less innovative in this respect.

In ancient India, rulers and feudal lords resorted to very precise methods in terrorizing the people. In punishing offenders, including criminals, rebels, and opponents, they used spikes (*shool*). The victim was forced to sit on a sharpened iron spike or *shool*, which entered the body through the lower end and come out through the upper end/head. This undignified way of execution was always a ceremony which was attended by the public as well as the ruler himself. In ancient times it is seen that in an execution the head of the victim was always the concern of the executioner but somewhat amusingly in India it was the lower end of the body that was the focal point. A disgraceful way of killing, it only reflected the perverted mentality of the perpetrators.

A different kind of execution was performed in eleventh century Central Asia. This was also a ritual carried out with the intention of terrorizing the people. In Bukhara a magnificent minaret was constructed for executing people. The victims were taken up and then thrown from the windows to die in front of the public. The minaret is still there in Bukhara and is known as the 'tower of death'.[10] It is difficult to tell whether this practice reached South Asia, although the region is full of minarets. But there were other ghoulish methods that the state resorted to for terrorizing people in pre-colonial India.

The Mughal Emperor Zahiruddin Muhammad Babur, in his memoirs *Babur Nama* described the punishment he awarded to the food taster and cooks who tried to poison him on the instructions of the mother of his arch-enemy, Ibrahim Lodi.

> Monday being court-day, I ordered the grandees and notables, amirs and wazirs to be present and that those two men and two women should be brought and questioned. They there related the particulars of the affair. That taster I had cut in pieces, that cook skinned alive; one of those women I had thrown under an elephant, the other shot with a match-lock. The old woman (Ibrahim Lodi's mother) I had kept under guard; she will meet her doom, the captive of her own act.[11]

Skinning people alive, throwing them into a hungry tiger's cage or to be trampled by an elephant, or sewing the eyelids of living human beings shut were common forms of royal punishments in medieval times. Dragging and quartering with the help of horses was also a popular punishment with the Mongols.

The colonial state, however, introduced newer methods in the business of terrorizing the colonized. If the French had the guillotine for the purpose of exterminating criminals, rebels, and noble dissenters,[12] the British made hanging the main instrument of their coercive policy.[13] The impact of hanging on the colonized population had been so far-reaching that even today, that is, after fifty years of decolonization, hanging remains a legal form of punishment in both civil and military courts of South Asia. Indeed, there is something uniquely spectatorial in the hanging of a person which makes it so convincingly terrible but lasting.

In colonized India, however, the British, in addition to hanging, used cannons and rifles to kill and terrorize the people. In fact, following the unsuccessful rebellion of 1857, also known as the Sepoy Mutiny, the British shot hundreds of sepoys from cannons mainly for revenge but also to terrorize the colonized. Indeed, so rampant was the use of cannons that some British officers protested at the bloodshed.[14] The Jallianwala Bagh massacre of 1919 brought a newer dimension to state terrorism: the random killing of unarmed people by shooting directly at them. The British military under the command of Brigadier-General R.E.H Dyer, shot 1,650 rounds of .303-inch ammunition over a crowd numbering 15,000 to 20,000 to put a stop to their anti-British (albeit peaceful) campaign. Over 1,000 were killed, including women and children. Dyer's tactics bore the marks of a firing squad, which had come into prominence ever since the military acquired rifles.

It was not long before when the non-state elements, now in possession of guns and rifles, also resorted to firing squads when dealing with the (captured) members of the coercive forces of the state. But the tactics and the means in hand were bound to catch the imagination of many. In fact, in post-independent Bangladesh, members of one students' organization shot nine of their fellow mates in a manner resembling a firing squad, and that again, within the premises of the university. The goal was to terrorize both the dissenters and the students' community as a whole. Indeed, one marvels at the ingenuity of humans in innovating rituals of killing and terrorizing people. But, then, much of those deadly rituals could not have come about without innovations in weapons technology in modern times. Now, with bombs, assault rifles, grenades, even missiles, in the hands of the terrorists, often with the direct complicity of the modern state, the terror has come to haunt not only the possible victims but also bystanders and even the perpetrators, and that again, not in one locality but across the globe. As one critic, while referring to contemporary terrorism, noted:

The problem of the global war declared by America was that it lacked a strategy. While all generals were always accused of fighting the last war during the next one, the efforts of President Bush to put together a Homeland Security system by cobbling together many intelligence agencies was as doomed as his international coalition. As with the anarchists of the nineteenth century, there was no protection against their bombs detonating in any urban centre. The problem was that a Victorian bomb might only kill dozens while a nuclear 'dirty bomb' could now kill hundreds of thousands of people and contaminate a city.[15]

Although a nuclear 'dirty bomb' in the hands of the terrorists is a distant possibility, it is this spectre that has now come to haunt us all.

Indeed, when it comes to modern weaponries and terrorism it matters little whether we live in New York or in some urban centres in South Asia. The fear is the same. Weapons technology in modern times has finally succeeded in universalizing terror. This, as discussed above, is markedly different from the pre-modern era when the lack of conformity in the art and science of terrorizing and killing people was the norm. The means adopted by the Thugs or the Pindaris never went beyond their respective localities. Only weapons technology in modern times could claim universal applicability, with the power of transforming humans into *hauntological* beings.

II

MODERN WEAPONS TECHNOLOGY AND TERRORISM

There is now multiple use of weapons technology. Historically, it was limited within the fold of the protagonist and the antagonist. Both knew each other, envied each other, and at times also respected each other. With contemporary terrorism, however, a newer dimension has come into place. The protagonist and the antagonist could now end up as both reproducers and victims of contemporary terrorism. If this is a new villain, it is a villain often within but more often unknown. It is at the same time everywhere and nowhere, and that is why deadly weapons in its hands make it even deadlier. Three types of weapons technology, each with its unique composition of speed, distance and shock, inform and empower contemporary terrorism. These may be classified as *unfair small arms*, *unfair missiles and indirect fire weapons* and *unfair bombs and explosives*. What is noteworthy here is the fact that all modern weapons are in some sense 'unfair' and are 'explosives' of one kind or the another. The distinction, however, is worth pursuing, mainly to show uniqueness in each of these components. It may be mentioned that 'nuclear weapons' have been kept outside the scope of this study mainly because only states hold absolute monopoly over these weapons and the non-state terrorists using nuclear weapons, even a 'dirty bomb', remains, as indicated earlier, a distant possibility.

Fairness in killing has bothered humans from antiquity. In fact, Moses went a step further. He banned killing: 'Thou shall not kill'. But since banning the killing of fellow human beings became an ideal difficult to realize, people of various cultures settled for the next best possible option, and that was to kill 'fairly' if killing was to be done at all. War, where most declared killings took place, came under rules and regulations. One of the earliest codifications is found in the *Mahabharata*: 'Never fight at night. Never strike a man who has withdrawn from the fray, or a man fighting with words. . . . And never strike in the back, nor on the legs.'[16] In fact, the reason why the Pandava brothers, save Yuddhisthira, landed in Hell even after waging a 'just war' was mainly because they did not fight the war fairly. Arjuna, under the spell of the arch diplomat, Krishna, took a shot at Duryodhana when he was already down and could not stand on his feet. Duryodhana's curse of Krishna for making Arjuna act unfairly still remains memorable.

Some cultures, later to be codified in some religions, made the subject matter of killing more reprehensible, indeed, to the point of including animal killing as well. Jainism and Buddhism went to the extreme of denouncing all killings, human as well as animal. Some religions, however, took measures to tell people how 'fairly' the killing of animals was to be done even if they were meant for food. Judaism and Islam made *kosher* and *halal* the only forms acceptable if animals were to end up as gastronomic delights. In many respects, fairness in killing became the yardstick of distinguishing the civilized from the barbarian. In modern times, international treaties and conventions, including the most recent one, the International Criminal Court, made it clear as to what is acceptable and what is not. 'How' you kill became as important as 'what' you kill. And the 'how' increasingly began to address the instruments or weapons of killing, keeping in mind that the technology has taken the art of killing into the realm of 'mass destruction', that is, with chemical, biological, and nuclear weaponries.

But then the human mind is so susceptible to changes that what was 'unfair' at one point of time began to be tolerated and accepted at a later stage, and in some measure this includes chemical, biological, and nuclear weaponries as well. And this is the horrifying element that humans have so far failed to rectify or even contain. In fact, in ancient times a whole range of weapons were considered unfair. According to van Creveld:

> [Every] historical period seems to have had its share of unfair weapons. In Western civilisation until about 1500 AD, the most important reason why some weapons were considered unfair was because they enabled their users to kill from a distance and from behind cover. The victim being unable to retaliate, such weapons obscured the vital distinction between war and plain murder. One such weapon was the bow, as illustrated by the story of Paris killing Achilles at Troy. Another was the catapult, which was perceived as a device that would render valour superfluous in war. In the Middle Ages knights held similar attitudes towards these weapons and this sometimes resulted in the execution and mutilation of captured bowmen. During the Renaissance, and as late as the beginning of the seventeenth century, the contempt in which firearms were held not only was responsible for many atrocities of this kind but also found echoes in the works of such writers as Arioste, Cervantes, Shakespeare and Milton.[17]

The issue of 'valour', however, did not prevent human beings from developing unfair weapons. Indeed, range, speed, lethality, and the safety of the user in using them from behind cover became a standard philosophy in developing weapons. 'Unfair weapons' became a fair tool in neutralizing the enemy. People invented mines, barbed wire, torpedoes, and the submarine. As van Creveld goes on to say:

> A particular significant category of unfair weapons and one which more than any other highlights the irrational nature of the entire issue is that of weapons considered too terrible (read: too effective) to use. An early example of this is provided by the crossbow, a weapon whose use against Christians was outlawed by the Lateran Council of 1139, though its employment against heathens was permitted and even encouraged. Others

are red hot cannon balls, explosive dropped from balloons (which, it was argued, would indiscriminately kill both soldiers and civilians), and of course the famous dumdum bullet which was originally invented by the British on the theory that savages of powerful physique could not be stopped by ordinary small-calibre ammunition. Usually the objection brought against these weapons was that they caused 'un-necessary' suffering. In practice, since what constituted 'un-necessary' was a little hard to define, quite often weapons were called unfair simply because, under the prevailing circumstances they were more helpful to the other side than to oneself.[18]

Unfair weapons were otherwise considered 'fair' when the target became the 'other'—heathens and savages, although it must be admitted that the killing of (enemy) civilians was also taken into consideration and viewed as unacceptable. But since nothing was done to control or prohibit their production or the technology that came with it, unfair weapons multiplied and literally filled up the arms market, arming the protagonists, the antagonists, and even the newer villains and dissenters.

Unfair Small Arms

Unfair small arms are all 'direct fire' weapons, meaning they are designed to shoot a projectile, usually against targets within the firer's range of vision (although the target itself may be obscured from view). Small arms are difficult to classify along strict lines of mission, use, or type of munitions. They fall generally into four categories: handguns or pistols, which are further comprised of revolvers and self-loading pistols; assault weapons, the which include submachine guns, machine pistols, and assault rifles; shoulder-fired weapons, the most common of which are rifles; and special purpose weapons, of which grenade launchers are an example. Although the shoulder-fired rocket launcher is a light anti-tank weapon (LAW) its ability to destroy concrete structures has made it popular with the terrorists and, therefore, it may also be included in the final category. Tables 4.1 to 4.6 provide good examples of some of the widely produced and used unfair small arms in the light of the categories mentioned here.

Three things are somewhat evident from Tables 4.1 to 4.6. Firstly, there is the complicity of the state when it comes to manufacturing and marketing unfair small arms, however *privatized* the

TABLE 4.1: PISTOLS AND REVOLVERS

Name	*Produced by*	*Used by*
Glock semi-automatic safe action pistols (Models 17-36)	Austria	Special forces, military and police of more than 50 countries
FN 9 mm BDA double-action pistol	Belgium	Belgian and some foreign police forces
FN 9 mm Browning High Power pistol	Belgium	Seen service in over 100 countries
NORINCO 7.62 mm Type 54 pistol	China	PLA and others in South Asia and South-East Asia
CZ Model 75 pistol	Czech Rep	Czech and Slovak forces and also sold in the West
PAMAS G1 9 mm pistol	France	French Armed Forces and former French colonies
MAB PA15 9 mm pistol	France	France and former French colonies
Walther PP, PPK, and P series pistols (different models)	Germany	Widespread use in Germany, other European countries, USA, and South America
HK 9 mm P7 pistols (different models)	Germany	Germany, USA, and commercially sold to many other countries
HK USP pistols	Germany	German Armed Forces and Police, commercial sales
IMI Desert Eagle pistol	Israel	Widespread use as a sporting and military pistol
Beretta 9 mm Model 92 pistol (different versions)	Italy	Italian Armed and Police Forces and wide commercial ownership
Astra 9 mm Model A70, A80, A90, A100 pistol	Spain	Spain and many other countries
Astra Falcon pistol	Spain	Spain and commercial sales
Sig Sauer P220 pistol	Switzerland	Swiss Army, some foreign police and special forces
Sig Sauer 9 mm P226 pistol	Switzerland	USA, UK , New Zealand, and many other countries
Sig Sauer 9 mm P228 pistol	Switzerland	Switzerland, USA, UK, and many special forces
Colt 0.45 Model M1911A1 auto pistol	USA	US armed forces and many other countries
Python revolver	USA	Wide commercial sales
Ruger 0.357 GP 100 revolver	USA	US police and government agencies
Smith & Wesson .38 Model 64 revolver	USA	Widely used by police and security organization

(*contd.*)

TABLE 4.1 *(contd.)*

Name	*Produced by*	*Used by*
7.62 mm TT-33 Tokarev pistol	Russia	All over the world
9 mm Makarov pistol	Russia	Former Soviet and Warsaw Pact armies and China

Sources: Terry J Gander, (ed.), *Jane's Infantry Weapons 2001-2002* (Surrey: Jane's Information Group Limited, 2001), pp. 221-308; Chris Bishop (ed.), *Combat Guns and Infantry Weapons* (England: Airlife, 1996), pp. 6-24.

TABLE 4.2: RIFLES AND ASSAULT RIFLES

Name	*Produced by*	*Used by*
Steyr 5.56 mm Aug rifle	Austria	Austria, Australia, New Zealand, Oman, Malaysia, Saudi Arabia and Ireland
FN FAL 7.6 2 mm rifle	Belgium	More than 90 countries
FN FNC 5.56 mm rifle	Belgium	Belgium, Indonesia, Latvia, Nigeria, Sweden, Tonga, and Zaire
Model 58 7.62 mm assault rifle	Czech Rep	Czech Army and sold commercially
Sako M76 7.62 mm assault rifle	Finland	Finland, Indonesia and Qatar
FAMAS F1 5.56 mm assault rifle	France	France, Djibouti, Gabon, Senegal, UAE
FA MAS G2 5.56 mm assault rifle	France	France and several French colonies
H & K 5.56 mm SL 8 tactical rifle	Germany	Germany and many other countries
H & K 7.62 mm G3 rifle	Germany	More than 50 countries
IMI 5.56 mm and 7.62 mm Galil assault rifle	Israel	Israel, Bolivia, Botswana, Chile, Columbia, Costa Rica, Guatemala, Haiti, Honduras, Nicaragua, Philipine, and many others
Beretta 5.56 mm AR 70/223 rifle	Italy	Italy, Jordan, Malaysia, and some other countries
Beretta 7.62 mm BM 59 rifle	Italy	Also manufactured. under licence in Indonesia and Morocco
SAR 80 5.56 mm assault rifle	Singapore	Singapore
Vektor 5.56 R4 and R5 assault rifle	South Africa	South Africa
Vektor 5.56 mm R6 compact rifle	South Africa	South Africa

(contd.)

TABLE 4.2 (*contd.*)

Name	*Produced by*	*Used by*
SANTA BARBARA 5.56 mm Model L and LC assault rifles	Spain	Spain
Sig 540 series assault rifles	Switzerland	More than 20 countries
Sig 5.56 mm SG 550, SG 551 and SG 552 commando assault rifle	Switzerland	Switzerland
7.62 mm L1A1 rifle	UK	Australia, Barbados, Canada, Gambia, Guyana, Oman, Malaysia
5.56 mm L85A1 individual weapon	UK	UK and some other countries including Jamaica
0.30 M1 Carbine	USA	Obsolete, but still in widespread use
M1 Garand	USA	More than 12 countries worldwide
7.62 M14 rifle	USA	US Navy, Israel (reserve), South Korea, Taiwan
5.56 AR15/M16 series rifles and carbines	USA	US Forces and 55 countries worldwide
Ruger 5.56 mm Mini-14 rifle	USA	Security forces around the world
AR-18	USA	Some commercial sales and police
AK-47	Russia	Over 100 countries and in guerrilla hands
AK-74	Russia	Former Soviet and Warsaw Pact forces
5.45 mm AKS 74 U short assault rifle	Russia	Former Soviet republics and some former Warsaw Pact countries
Simonov 7.62 mm self-loading rifle (SKS)	Russia	No longer used in Russia but similar models are used in many former Soviet republics, China, and several countries in Asia

Sources: Terry J. Gander (ed.), *Jane's Infantry Weapons 2001- 2002* (Surrey: Jane's Information Group Limited, 2001), pp. 5-118; Chris Bishop (ed.), *Combat Guns and Infantry Weapons* (England: Airlife, 1996), pp. 40-61.

TABLE 4.3: SUB-MACHINE GUNS

Name	*Produced by*	*Used by*
F1	Australia	Australian Defence Forces
9 mm FMK-3 Mod 2 sub-machine gun	Argentina	Argentinian forces

(*contd.*)

TABLE 4.3 (*contd.*)

Name	*Produced by*	*Used by*
Steyr 9 mm Mpi 69 and Mpi 81 sub-machine gun	Austria	A number of military and police forces
Steyr Aug 9 mm para sub-machine gun	Austria	Austrian special forces units
FN 5.7 × 28 mm P90 sub-machine gun	Belgium	Belgium, Cyprus, Saudi Arabia, USA, and a few South Asian countries
7.65 mm Model 61 Skorpion machine pistol	Czech Rep	Some Czech and Slovak units, Afghanistan, Angola, Egypt, Libya, Mozambique, and Uganda. Also used by terrorists and guerrillas
Madsen 9 mm sub-machine gun	Denmark	Denmark, Brazil (built under license) and other SE Asian and South American forces
Jatimatic	Finland	Finland, China, and various commercial sales
MAS 38	France	Obsolete, but may be found in Africa and South-East Asia
MAT 49	France	France and former French colonies
HK 9 mm MP 5K series sub-machine gun	Germany	Special forces and undercover police forces of various countries
HK 9 mm MP 5 sub-machine gun	Germany	At least 30 countries
IMI 9 mm Uzi sub-machine gun	Israel	At least 20 countries
Beretta 9 mm Model 12 sub-machine gun	Italy	Italy, Brazil, Gabon, Indonesia, Libya, Nigeria, Saudi Arabia, Tunisia, Venezuela
Spectre	Italy	Various undisclosed police and military bodyguards
Carl Gustav 9 mm m/45 sub-machine gun	Sweden	Sweden, Egypt, Indonesia, Ireland
Star 9 mm Model Z-84 sub-machine gun	Spain	Spain, military and security services in various countries
Sterling 9 mm L2A3 sub-machine gun	UK	No longer in use in UK but some 90 countries purchased it
M1 Thompson sub-machine gun	USA	Militias, irregulars and guerrillas all over the world
0.45 M3 sub-machine gun	USA	No longer in production, may be found in South America and Southeast Asia

(*contd.*)

TABLE 4.3 (*contd.*)

Name	*Produced by*	*Used by*
Ingram sub-machine guns	USA	Bolivia, Colombia, Greece, Guatemala, Honduras, Israel, Portugal, UK, USA, and wide commercial sales
Ruger 9 mm MP 9 sub-machine gun	USA	US special forces and some South American countries
PPSh-41	Russia	Rebel groups in Angola, Ethiopia, Lebanon, Somalia
PPS-43	Russia	Some irregular forces

Sources: Terry J. Gander (ed.), *Jane's Infantry Weapons 2001-2002* (Surrey: Jane's Information Group Limited, 2001), pp. 183-219; Ivan V. Hogg, *The New Illustrated Encyclopedia of Firearms* (London: Grange Books, 1993); Chris Bishop (ed.), *Combat Guns and Infantry Weapons* (England: Airlife, 1996), pp. 25-39

TABLE 4.4: LIGHT AND HEAVY MACHINE GUNS

Name	*Produced by*	*Used by*
FN 7.62 mm MAG general purpose machine gun	Belgium	More than 75 countries
FN 5.56 mm Minimi light machine gun	Belgium	In service with over 30 countries.
FN 0.50 Browning M2 HB machine gun	Belgium	Belgium and various European, South American, Middle Eastern and Asian countries
7.62 mm Model 59 and 68 Rachot general purpose machine gun	Czech Rep	Czech and Slovak armed forces
7.62 mm MG3 machine gun	Germany	Austria, Chile, Denmark, Greece, Iran, Italy, Norway, Pakistan, Portugal, Spain, Sudan, and Turkey
7.62 mm HK21 general purpose machine gun	Germany	Portugal and some African and South-East Asian countries
SIG 710	Switzerland	Bolivia, Brunei, Chile
7.62 mm L4A4 (Bren) machine gun	UK	UK and many Commonwealth countries
7.62 mm L7A2 GPMG	UK	UK and some Commonwealth countries

(*contd.*)

TABLE 4.4 (*contd.*)

Name	*Produced by*	*Used by*
Manroy 0.50 M2 HB QCB heavy machine gun	UK	NATO and other forces worldwide
Browning M2HB 0.50 calibre heavy machine gun	USA	USA and 30 other countries
7.62 mm M60 GPMG	USA	Australia, US, South Korea, Taiwan, and 20 other countries
7.62 mm RPD light machine gun	Russia	China, Egypt, North Korea, Pakistan, Vietnam and others
5.45 mm RPK-74 light machine gun 7.62 mm	Russia	Former Soviet and Warsaw Pact countries
PK machine gun family	Russia	Former Soviet and Warsaw Pact countries

Sources: Terry J. Gander (ed.), *Jane's Infantry Weapons 2001-2002* (Surrey: Jane's Information Group Limited, 2001), pp. 314-64; Chris Bishop (ed.), *Combat Guns and Infantry Weapons* (England: Airlife, 1996), pp. 72-83.

TABLE 4.5: GRENADE-LAUNCHERS

Name	*Produced by*	*Used by*
40 mm Granatpistole grenade launcher	Germany	Germany and a number of military and police forces worldwide
40 mm HK 79 add on grenade launcher	Germany	Germany, Norway, Nicaragua, and Panama
CIS 40 GL 40 mm grenade launcher	Singapore	Singapore and a number of undisclosed countries
40 AGL 40 mm automatic ground launcher	Singapore	Singapore and a number of undisclosed countries
M203 40 mm grenade launcher	USA	US and NATO armed forces, more than 30 countries
M79 40 mm grenade launcher	USA	USA and more than 30 countries
Brunswick RAW	USA	USA
Lockheed Martin Multi-purpose Individual Munition/ Short Range Assault Weapon (MIM/ SRAW)	USA	US Army
Mk 19 Mod 3 40 mm grenade machine gun	USA	Egypt, Honduras, Israel, Mexico, South Korea, and Sweden

(*contd.*)

TABLE 4.5 (*contd.*)

Name	*Produced by*	*Used by*
30 mm AGS-17 automatic grenade launcher	Russia	Afghanistan, Angola, Chad, China, Cuba, India, Iran, Iraq, Mozambique, Nicaragua, Poland, Former Soviet states, and South Africa
30 mm AGS-30 automatic grenade launcher	Russia	Russian Federation states and offered for export sales
40 mm GP-25 and GP-30 rifle mounted grenade launcher	Russia	Former Warsaw Pact countries and others

Sources: Terry J. Gander (ed.), *Jane's Infantry Weapons 2001-2002* (Surrey: Jane's Information Group Limited, 2001) pp. 158-82; Chris Bishop (ed.), *Combat Guns and Infantry Weapons* (England: Airlife, 1996), pp. 94-8.

TABLE 4.6: ANTI-TANK WEAPONS

Name	*Produced by*	*Used by*
Milan	France/ Germany	France, Germany, UK, and more than 30 other armed forces
Hot	France/ Germany	France, Germany, and more than 12 other armed forces
Aerospatiale Matra Eryx short range anti-tank missile	France	Brazil, Canada, France, Malaysia, Norway, Turkey, and a GCC country
Giat Industries Wasp light anti armour weapon system	France	French Army and one other undisclosed army
Dynamit Nobel Panzerfaust 3 light anti-tank weapon system	Germany	German Army and some other armies including Switzerland
Gill/Spike portable anti-tank weapon system	Israel	Israel Defence Forces, Finland, and Singapore
IMI B-300 light anti armour weapon	Israel	Israel, El-Salvador and Mexico
Carl Gustav 84 mm M2 and M3 recoilless rifles	Sweden	Sweden and 20 other countries
Bofors BILL RBS-56 medium range anti-tank system	Sweden	Sweden, Austria and Brazil
AT 4 84 mm light anti-armour weapon	Sweden	Sweden, USA, Denmark, Netherlands, Brazil, Venezuela

(*contd.*)

TABLE 4.6 (*contd.*)

Name	*Produced by*	*Used by*
Swingfire	UK	UK, Belgium, Egypt
Hunting Law 80 light anti-tank weapon	UK	British forces, Jordan, Oman and other countries
Talley 66 mm Improved M72 series LAW	USA	US Forces and most NATO armies
3.5 in M20 rocket launcher	USA	No longer produced in USA, but can still be found in many African, Latin American and Asian countries
106 mm M40 series recoilless rifles	USA	Supplied to more than 30 countries and can be encountered all over the world
CMS Dragon medium anti-armour missile system	USA	USA, Iran, Israel, Jordan, Morocco, Netherlands Saudi Arabia, Spain, Switzerland, Thailand, Yemen
TOW heavy anti-tank weapon system	USA	USA and more than 40 other armies
RPG-7 Knut portable rocket launcher	Russia	Widespread use in Africa, Asia and the Middle East
73 mm SPG-9 Kopey recoilless rifles	Russia	Former Warsaw pact countries
AT-3 'Sagger'	Russia	Cuba, India, North Korea, and more than 12 African and Middle Eastern countries
AT-4 'Spigot'	Russia	Russia and some former Warsaw Pact countries
9 K 111 Fagot anti-tank guided missile	Russia	Russia and former Warsaw Pact countries
RPG-18 Mukha light anti-armour weapon	Russia	Russia and former Warsaw Pact countries
40 mm RL	China	Many South Asian and South-East Asian countries

Sources: Terry J. Gander (ed.), *Jane's Infantry Weapons 2001-2002* (Surrey: Jane's Information Group Limited, 2001), pp. 380-429; Chris Bishop (ed.), *Combat Guns and Infantry Weapons* (England: Airlife, 1996), pp. 104-15.

manufacturing and marketing of such arms may be. In this respect, when some of these weapons land in the hands of the non-state terrorists the complicity of the state in the reproduction of non-state terrorism becomes all the more evident. Secondly, a cursory look at the manufacturers of small arms, and this would include their marketing as well, would show that the bulk of them are western developed countries. The complicity of the developed west, particularly judging from the rise in the use of such weapons by the non-state terrorists, indeed, in many cases of developing or underdeveloped societies of the non-West, becomes a valid point difficult to rule out. And thirdly, following from the above contentions, the state-sponsored or produced weaponries are bound to land in the hands of the non-state terrorists sooner or later.

The tables point out that AK-47 assault rifles produced by Russia,[19] M1 Thompson and M3 sub-machine guns produced by the USA, and Model 61 Skorpion sub-machine guns produced by the Czech Republic have already landed in the hands of non-state armed forces, including terrorists. Also suspect in this respect are Galil assault rifle produced by Israel, Python revolvers produced by the USA, and CIS 40 GL grenade-launchers produced by Singapore. But often governments and also the public only come to know how weaponized the terrorists have become when the latter are photographed in action. One such case was of a terrorist waving his Skorpion sub-machine gun from the cockpit of a hijacked Pakistani airliner.[20] In many cases, these weapons land in the hands of terrorists through informal, dubious trading, the complicity of the state, seizure during times of conflict, and also leftovers from war situations. This is true even of rockets, grenade-launchers and mortars. Previously, these were used by the non-state militants in what is referred to as the 'third phase' of guerrilla warfare. But now, in the backdrop of the US invasion of Afghanistan and Iraq and a vibrant informal arms bazaar, such weapons have been acquired by terrorists, many of whom may not fit the traditional profile of an insurgent. Indeed, some of the unfair small arms are now so readily available on the black market that they can be purchased almost at will, the only requirement being the availability of hard cash.

Unfair Missiles and Indirect Fire Weapons

The first missile weapon was the rock that humans hurled at animals out of fear or for food, and also at each other to settle or unsettle some matters of dispute.[21] The practice is not completely lost. Some religions have ritualized rock throwing. Every year, during the Muslim performance of Hajj, rock throwing at Satan is obligatory. The *intifada* of the Palestinians against the heavily armed Israeli forces consisted mainly of throwing rocks at the soldiers, with the latter at a loss as to how to respond effectively and humanely other than by the brute force of modern weaponries and consequently finding themselves losing the conflict on moral grounds. But then the *intifada* of rock throwing is very different from the terrorist (both state and non-state) use of missiles. The latter has now turned wholly demonic, albeit gradually and somewhat unknowingly.

The Greeks evolved three kinds of missile infantry. They were the archers, slingers, and javelin throwers. Among them, the archers were the most dangerous. Each archer carried fifteen to twenty arrows and could shoot them from a distance of 80 to 100 yards. Although these arrows could not penetrate a hoplite's shield or brass plate, they could always inflict nasty wounds on the exposed portion of his body and this capability made the archer a potentially formidable weapon system.[22] But then, viewed against present times, such missiles were playful things. Tables 4.7 and 4.8 provide a description of the mortars, rockets, surface-to-surface missiles, surface-to-air missiles and air-to-surface missiles, enough to suggest the qualitative transformation of the indirect fire weapons and missiles.

Three things are noteworthy here. Firstly, warheads of rockets and missiles and mortar shells with high explosives have the enormous capacity to destroy. Moreover, since there is a 'human' factor in the delivery of these weapons, not to mention the imperfections of technology, often the destruction is beyond acceptable limits even from the standpoint of armed conflicts. One good example in this context is the USS Vincennes, an aegis class cruiser with sophisticated equipment, shooting down an Iranian passenger airliner over the Persian Gulf. Secondly, missiles have now attained demonic quality because chemical and biological warheads can be fitted into them. In fact, this is precisely what Saddam Hussain did. He used chemical weapons on his own Kurdish people with the help of missiles and artillery guns. Thirdly, anyone acquiring indirect fire weapons and missiles can, as one critic pointed out, 'inflict unprecedented levels of destruction on any *large* armoured force on the move' [emphasis added].[23] And it is precisely because

TABLE 4.7: MORTARS

Name	*Produced by*	*Rate of fire*	*Maximum range*	*Used by*
TDA 60 mm light mortars	France	30 rpm	2060 m	France and 20 other countries
TDA 81 mm mortars	France	15 rpm	5000 m	France and several other countries
TDA 120 mm MO 120 RT	France	12 rpm	13000 m	France and 22 other countries (Belgium & Canada)
IMI 52 mm light mortar	Israel	35 rpm	420 m	Israel Defence Forces
Soltam 60 mm mortar	Israel	20 rpm	2550 m	Israel and many other countries (Guatemala, Honduras)
Soltam 81 mm mortar	Israel	n.a.	5000 m	Israel and some other countries (East Africa)
Soltam 120 mm mortar	Israel	n.a.	7200 m	Israel, USA and some other armies
Soltam 160 mm mortar	Israel	n.a.	9600 m	Israel and Honduras
RO 51 mm mortar	UK	8 rpm	800 m	UK forces
RO Defence 81 mm L16A2 mortar	UK	15 rpm	5650 m	Austria, Bahrain, Canada, Guyana, Nigeria, Oman, UAE. and many other countries
60 mm M19 mortar	USA	8 rpm	n.a.	No longer in use in USA but supplied to many countries
60 mm M224 light mortar	USA	30 rpm	1500 m	USA and UK
81 mm M29 & M29 A1	USA	n.a.	n.a.	USA (being phased out) and many other countries
107 mm M30 rifled mortar	USA	18 rpm	6800 m	USA, Austria, Belgium, Canada, Greece, Guatemala, Iran, Norway, Oman, S. Korea, Turkey, Zaire

(*contd.*)

TABLE 4.7 (*contd.*)

Name	*Produced by*	*Rate of Fire*	*Maximum range*	*Used by*
120 mm M120/121 mortar	USA	15 rpm	7200	US Army
82 mm M37 mortar	Russia	25 rpm	3640 m	Most of the former Warsaw pact countries, China (as the type 53), Cambodia and Nicaragua
82 mm 2B14 Pondos light mortar	Russia	30 rpm	7270 m	Russian Federation countries and offered for sale
107 mm M38 mortar	Russia	15 rpm	6300 m	Countries of Russian Federation, China, North Korea, and possibly Vietnam
120 mm M43 mortar	Russia	15 rpm	5700 m	Russian Federation countries and many allied countries
160 mm M1943 and M160	Russia	3 rpm	8040 m	Countries of Russian Federation, China, Egypt, India, Nicaragua, and others

Sources: Terry J. Gander (ed.), *Jane's Infantry Weapons 2001-2002* (Surrey: Jane's Information Group Limited, 2001), pp. 453-95; and Chris Bishop (ed.), *Combat Guns and Infantry Weapons* (England: Airlife, 1996), pp. 99-102.

TABLE 4.8: ROCKETS, SURFACE-TO-SURFACE MISSILES, SURFACE-TO-AIR MISSILES, AND AIR-TO-SURFACE MISSILES

Name	*Produced by*	*Maximum velocity*	*Maximum range*	*Used by*
Exocet anti-ship missile	Europe (France)	700 mph	65 m	France, Germany, Pakistan, Abu Dhabi, Argentina, Singapore, Brazil, Oman, Egypt, Iraq, Kuwait, Libya, Qatar, and Peru
SATCP 'Mistral' air defence system	France	Mach 2.6	6000 m	France, Abu Dhabi, Belgium, Cyprus, Finland, Gabon, Italy, Saudi Arabia, Spain
Bofors RBS 70 series low altitude surface to air missile	Sweden	Supersonic	5000 m	Sweden, Argentina, Bahrain, Iran, Ireland, Indonesia, Pakistan, Tunisia, UAE, Venezuela
Shorts Missile System 'Javelin' low altitude surface to air missile	UK	Supersonic	5500 m	UK, Botswana, Dubai, Jordan, Malaysia, Oman, S. Korea
Shorts Missisle System 'Starstreak' close air defence weapon system	UK	Mach 4	7000 m	UK
FIM-92 Stinger low altitude surface to air missile	USA	Mach 2.2	4500 m	USA and more than 20 other countries
Raytheon MIM-104 'Patriot' missiles	USA	Mach 5	1,60,000 m	Germany, Israel, Japan, Kuwait, Netherlands, Saudi Arabia, Taiwan, USA
Lance short-range ballistic missile	USA	Mach 3	75 m	Decommissioned but used as targets
Tomahawk cruise missile	USA	550 mph	600 m	USA
Kolomna KBM Strela-2/Strela-2M (SA-7 'Grail')	Russia	Over Mach 1	3700 m	More than 60 armies and more than 30 terrorist and guerrilla groups

(contd.)

TABLE 4.8 *(contd.)*

Name	*Produced by*	*Maximum velocity*	*Maximum range*	*Used by*
Kolomna KBM Strela-3/Strela 3M (SA-14 'Gremlin')	Russia	Mach 1.6	6000 m	More than 20 former Warsaw Pact and former Soviet client states
R11 / SS-1B Scud A	Russia	n.a	50-93 m	Iraq and North Korea
SS-1C Scud B	Russia	n.a	100-175 m	Iraq and North Korea
AS-8	Russia	n.a	5-6 m	Afghanistan, Russia and its allies
Luz-I	Israel	n.a	50 m	Israel
Arrow-2	Israel	Mach 9	90,000 m	Israel

Sources: Tony Cullen and Christopher F. Foss (eds.), *Jane's Land-Based Air Defence 1998-1999* (Surrey: Jane's Information Group Limited, 1998), pp. 16-38; Chris Bishop (ed.), *Combat Guns and Infantry Weapons* (England: Airlife, 1996), pp.116-21, Bill Gunston, *The Illustrated Encyclopaedia of the World's Rockets & Missiles* (Sydney: Lansdowne Press, 1979).

of this factor that the non-state armed groups, including the non-state terrorists, are in constant search for rockets, light anti-tank weapons and missiles to make a difference to their relatively disempowered position. The consequence of this can hardly be minimized. But then the destructive potential of the missiles ignited the imagination of many, some even with more demonic intent.

The 9/11 attack on the United States showed how innovative were the terrorists in devising a weapon. No bombs or guns were used, yet the terrorists destroyed the twin towers of the World Trade Center and a portion of the Pentagon, and killed over 3,000 people. According to one estimate, the terrorists spent only US $500,000 to execute their plan but destroyed property worth over US $40 billion.[24] In fact, the innovation consisted in hijacking passenger aircrafts and using them as *missiles*. In the process the terrorists did not hesitate to sacrifice the lives of innocent passengers and also their own. This is where modern technology combined with suicide bombing becomes deadly. More on this issue later.

But how did America respond to the terrorism of 9/11? Alas, and somewhat ironically, by resorting to state terrorism. Precision-guided missiles and aerial bombing pounded the cities, hills, and villages of Afghanistan, mainly to locate and kill the alleged 'godfather of 9/11'—Osama bin Laden. In fact, in the initial stages of American bombing, many of the Afghans, devoid of modern communication, including radio and television, hardly had any idea as to what had befallen America and the cause of its anger. If distance made the people's life unreal and made them dispassionate killers, it also blurred the distinction between civilian and military casualties in the place where missiles and bombs were dropped.

Mahathir Mohammad, while criticizing the United States and its allies for their action, went on to say:

> We see states launching massive retaliation, not just to curb suspected terrorists, but his family, his home, his village and his town. . . . It would be ridiculous to think that such attacks do not terrorize the innocent. . . . It would seem that the great exponents and practitioners of democracy believe that the way to spread the doctrine and break down resistance is by terrorizing the world.[25]

With modern missiles and bombs the state and non-state terrorists may have succeeded in 'knocking' down the door of the intended victim and bringing him to book, but in the process they have also succeeded in 'knocking out' the whole neighbourhood and the world around. Targeting a perpetrator has gone out of hand, thanks to the over-zealous members of the victimized state.

Unfair Bombs and Explosives

A name that is very difficult to erase from the science of explosives is that of Alfred Nobel. Nobel had 355 patents for various inventions and discoveries to his credit, but that was hardly his claim to fame. He only became famous for his expertise in inventing and developing explosives. Nobel publicly declared that he worked with explosives for their potential in positive human uses like blowing up mountains to construct roads and bridges, demolishing unnecessary constructions, mining, etc. During his lifetime, however, he found his invention being abused. Explosives became a formidable weapon of war. The burden of guilt arising from the mass destruction possibly compelled him to introduce the Nobel Prize.

But it would be naïve to believe that Nobel did not foresee the outcome of his invention. For, those who ventured to write his biography did mention that the passion for explosives was in Nobel's blood.[26] His father, Immanuel Nobel, was a technician and an inventor, and was also involved in explosives research. In 1842, Immanuel left for St. Petersburg in Russia, where he was involved in making torpedoes and mines for the Russian navy. From there he kept pushing young Alfred to different parts of Europe and America to learn business. In 1859, Immanuel Nobel returned to Sweden and established an explosives factory. Alfred Nobel joined his father's factory as an assistant and carried out research with nitro-glycerine. In 1864, there was an accidental explosion in the factory which it was completely destroyed. Alfred's brother, Emil, died in that explosion. Immediately after this incident there were quite a few more accidents with nitroglycerine. Many held young Alfred responsible for the explosions and in general considered him an enemy of the people. This ill-feeling from outside ultimately led him to invent a more stable explosive, which could be carried from place to place safely. Within years he established a huge centralized industrial empire and made a fortune out of his various inventions, including explosives. Without any formal training in chemistry, Alfred Nobel started working with explosives, and through sheer diligence reached the position where we can see him today. The invention itself, however, remained as destructive as ever.

In the twentieth century, particularly during the Cold War, there was stiff competition between the Capitalist and Communist blocs in the development of explosives. If the United States came up with its fearsome explosives called C4 (consisting of RDX, other explosives, and plasticizers), the Czechs, then under the hegemony of the Soviet Union, came up with their own version called Semtex, equally stable and destructive. The difference between the two is minimal. C4, for instance, requires a detonator for use and has a soft, dough-like texture, so that it can be moulded into shape without the risk of exploding.[27] Moreover, it is odourless and free from metal compounds and therefore undetectable by detectors. Critics allege that C4 explosives, tracked to a manufacturer in Israel, were used in the nightclub bombing on the Indonesian island of Bali in 2002.[28] The explosives killed nearly 200 people, mostly Australians.

Semtex, on the other hand, got its name from Semtin, the village in East Bohemia where Brebera, a Czech citizen and a Communist Party member, invented it. A compound of RDX and PETN, Semtex can slip through airport detectors as easily as a pair of nylons.[29] It is far stronger than traditional explosives like TNT, and is easily available on the black market. One estimate suggests that some 40,000 tons of Semtex are stockpiled worldwide and have already made their way into the hands of militants and terrorists, including the Irish Republican Army (IRA) and various terrorist groups in Iraq and the Middle East.[30] So easy is its availability that in September 2002, the Czech police found 33 kg. of Semtex, enough to destroy a building ten to fifteen storeys high, in a filling station near Prague. It may be mentioned that its use in terrorism is mainly in the making of car bombs, although it is widely believed that Semtex was used to destroy Pan Am Flight 103 over Lockerbie, Scotland, which killed 270 people. There is no denying, however, that Semtex is a favourite weapon of the terrorists.

In the field of explosives, however, what has lately caught the attention of security scholars and strategists is the improvised explosive device (IED). IEDs can be almost anything, made from all kinds of materials and initiators. As 'homemade' devices, the IEDs are designed to kill and destroy, either by using only explosives or in combination with toxic chemicals, biological toxins or radiological materials. Furthermore, IEDs can be produced in varying sizes and can be made to function differently using various kinds of delivery methods. To name a few, pipe bombs, dynamite bombs, bazooka rockets, grenades, and landmines—all are explosives used as IEDs, mainly by non-state terrorists, including suicide bombers.

The above description of some of the explosives may give the impression that only sophisticated explosive compounds can create a terrible impact. This may be true to some extent, but not in all cases. In a relatively peaceful situation, where concerns for explosives are less obvious, ammonium nitrate (fertilizer) mixed with other chemicals like nitromethane, something that is commercially available, could do the trick! Indeed, it could be as devastating as sophisticated explosives and serve the purpose of the terrorists. In fact, it is generally believed that Timothy McVeigh, a Gulf War veteran, used ammonium nitrate with three drums of nitromethane to blow up the Federal Office Building in Oklahoma City in 1995. But then a sophisticated input in explosive making, particularly in detonation, could make the bomb demonic.

Two things are worth pointing out here. Firstly, with each technological innovation there is always the likelihood of the terrorists acquiring the technology and making the weapon more deadly. For instance, at the present stage of technology terrorists do not need to be present to blow up a passenger airliner. They could use a barometric detonator which would detonate the bomb automatically when the aircraft reached a certain height. Indeed, it is possible that such a detonator was used to blow up the Pan Am aircraft over Lockerbie, albeit with the use of Semtex explosives, as indicated earlier. Put differently, explosives may be an old technology, but if this technology is used innovatively to exploit the new vulnerabilities arising from newer technologies, it can become a destructive weapon.

Secondly, non-state terrorists are at times one step ahead of the state in the creative use of weapons. One good example is the IRA's bomb-making innovation and the manner in which it routinely succeeded in outsmarting the British military. The competition is well illustrated by Hoffman:

In hopes of obviating, or at least reducing, [the] risks, the IRA's bomb-makers invented a means of detonating bombs from a safe distance using the radio controls for model aircraft purchased at hobby shops. Scientists and engineers working in the scientific research and development division of the British Ministry of Defence (MoD) in turn developed a system of electronic countermeasures and jamming techniques for the army that effectively thwarted this means of attack. However, rather than abandon this tactic completely, the IRA began to search for a solution. . . . [The] IRA's own 'R&D' department toiled in cellars beneath cross-border safe houses and the back rooms of urban tenements for five years before devising a network of sophisticated electronic switches for their bombs that would ignore or bypass the army's electronic counter-measures. Once again, the MoD scientists returned to their laboratories; emerging with a new system of electronic scanners able to detect radio emissions the moment the radio is switched on—and, critically, just tens of seconds before the bomber can actually transmit the detonation signal. . . .

For a time, this mechanism in its turn proved effective. But then the IRA discovered a means to outwit even this countermeasure. Using radar detectors like those used by motorists in the United States to evade speed traps, in 1991 the group's bomb-makers fabricated a detonating system that can be triggered by the same type of hand-held radar gun used by police throughout the world to catch speeding drivers. Since the radar gun can be aimed at its target before being switched on, and the signal that it transmits is nearly instantaneous, no practical means currently exists either to detect or to intercept the transmission signal.[31]

Indeed, so stupefied were the members of the MoD by the IRA's successive innovations that one staff officer of the British army's 321 Explosives and Ordnance Disposal Company frankly admitted: 'We are dealing with the first division . . . I don't think there is any organization in the world as cunning as the IRA. They have had twenty years at it and they have learned from their experience. We have a great deal of respect for their skills . . . not as individuals, but their skills.'[32] In fact, in an unstable, conflict-ridden environment the genius of the mind often slides back to demonic deeds, for there is little to lose and apparently everything to gain. But apart from diabolic innovations, the birth of 'suicide bombers', in the midst of modern weaponries is what has radically transformed the outcome of terrorist activities.

Albert Camus in the middle of the twentieth century made a bold reflection on life and death. He said: 'There is but one truly philosophical problem and that is suicide. Judging whether life is or is not worth living amounts to answering the fundamental question of philosophy. All the rest—whether or not the world has three dimensions, whether the mind has nine or twelve categories—comes afterwards.'[33] Little did he realize that by the end of the twentieth century there would be numerous of them, with some even having the courage to blow themselves into pieces along with their targets. Traditionally, the aim of the terrorist was not to commit suicide. Even the Assassins and the Templars committed suicide only when challenged. But to make the body itself a part of the weapon and that again with the knowledge that the body would be ripped off while creating havoc in and around the target is something of an innovation, arising no doubt from the 'absurdity' of earthly life in the midst of all the violence and the kinds of weaponries, particularly explosives, that are now at one's disposal. Also the sense of martyrdom and an assured reward after death seem to have played a role in the making of suicide bombers.[34] If anything, a suicide bomber has derailed all counter-terrorist efforts, for when a person is ready to die with explosives strapped to his or her body, there is no way to stop that person from terrorizing and killing many more. In the process, the age-old distinction between victims, witnesses, and perpetrators gets erased. Living becomes an exercise in *hauntology*.

The dynamics of weapons technology in areas of unfair weapons, missiles, and explosives, indeed, by way of hyping up *distance*, *speed*, and *shock*, have not only transformed the art and science of terrorizing and killing people but also succeeded in making death too numerous to the point of questioning the very survivability of humans. The following lethality index (Table 4.9), albeit a theoretical one, is a good pointer in this context.

It should not go unnoticed that it is the modern state, obsessed with modern weaponries, that has raised the lethal toll to unacceptable, dehumanized levels. No one can guarantee the lessons the non-state terrorists will take from all this. Judging by past records, there is hardly any hope in containing the diabolic transfer of weapons technology from the state to non-state terrorists. It may be pointed out that more than 500 million small arms and light weapons are now in circulation around the world, that is, for every twelve persons there is one weapon. Moreover, in the last fifteen years small arms and light weapons alone have caused almost four million

TABLE 4.9: THEORETICAL LETHALITY INDEX (TLI)[35]

Weapons	*TLI*
Hand-to-hand (sword, pike, etc.)	23
Javelin	19
Ordinary bow	21
Longbow	36
Crossbow	33
Early nineteenth-century rifle	36
Late nineteenth-century breech-loading rifle	153
Springfield Model 1903 rifle (magazine)	495
World War I machine gun	3,463
World War II machine gun	4,973
French 75 mm gun	386,530
105 mm howitzer, M-1	657,215
155 mm 'Long Tom'	1,180,681
V-2 ballistic missile	3,338,370
20-KT nuclear airburst	40,086,000
One-megaton nuclear airburst	695,385,000

Source: Trevor N. Dupuy, *The Evolution of Weapons and Warfare* (Virginia: Da Capo Press, 1984), p. 92.

deaths, out of which 90 per cent were civilians and 80 per cent women and children. Terrorism, it seems, is now dictated not by a cause or political outcomes but by the weapons in one's possession, and that again on a global scale.

III

MODERN WEAPONS AND SOUTH ASIAN TERRORISM

Modernity empowers itself not so much from innovations as from replications. It is an empowered entity the moment it appears itself as a 'model' for others to copy. When modernity caught the imagination of the South Asians, they found solace in the predominantly western idea of nationalism. The colonial state was good in undermining whatever was indigenous to South Asia, referring to them as 'traditional' and 'backward', but was less equipped to respond when the colonized copied from the West, and that included the idea of nationalism as well. Things are not so different when it comes to terrorism.

Terrorism in South Asia began with the colonial state. This does not cancel out the rituals of terrorizing people in pre-colonial times, only that such rituals lacked coherency and the means varied from one locality to another. In fact, there are qualitative differences between pre-colonial and colonial/post-colonial or modern terrorism. Two are easily highlighted. The first is with reference to the role of the state. The state became a central actor in reproducing terrorism in modern times. Even with non-state terrorism, the complicity of the state, particularly in the production and use of weaponries, remained overwhelming. In marked contrast to this, much of the terrorist activity in pre-colonial times resulted from the idiosyncrasies of the ruling elite or individuals who had succeeded in amassing a following. The second is in the arrival of conformity in the use of weapons, that is, in the very *means* of unleashing and reproducing terrorism. As indicated earlier, modern weapons made a difference to terrorism in that the same categories of weapons are now being used to terrorize people, not only in one locality but throughout South Asia and the world. This also contributed to the creation of an ever-proliferating weapons market, including links to what can be referred to as 'subaltern globalization' (i.e. the dubious and shadowy networks across nations and regions, of smugglers, narco-traffickers, money launderers, arms dealers, and the like).[36]

The Bengal terrorists of the colonial era were largely a product of modern science and ideas imported from Europe. The chief ideologue, Aurobindo Ghosh, was educated in the West and turned to terrorism after his return to India, and the renowned bomb maker, Hem Chandra Das, learnt political theory and explosive chemistry from the Russian, Nicolas Safranski, and others and joined the terrorist group after his return from Paris.[37] More importantly, the weaponries used by the Bengal terrorists included cocoa tins filled with picric acid and Osborne .38 and Webley .45 calibre pistols,[38] all of which were produced or manufactured in the West. This resulted not only in the conformity of weapons technology between the state and non-state elements of terrorism but also gave way to a precise conformity in the art and science of terrorizing and killing people. With identical goals and means, including the complicity of the state, terrorism in South Asia entered a precise *modernist* phase.

State terrorism in post-colonial South Asia bore a remarkable similarity, whether reproduced in Pakistan, India, Sri Lanka, Nepal or Bangladesh. The use of the coercive forces, including the military, of course with certain variations and degrees, remained almost identical in each of these countries. The state terrorism that Pakistan had unleashed on the people of Bangladesh in 1971 probably would stand as an extreme case, with allegations of genocide and the death figure rising to some 3 million,[39] but some of the methods used in terrorizing and killing people in 1971 Bangladesh were also to be found in India's counter-terrorism in Kashmir, Sri Lanka's counter-terrorism in Jaffna or Nepal's counter-terrorism against the Maoists. More importantly, the weapons reproducing state terrorism in each of these countries were almost identical (like machine guns, mortars, artillery guns, tanks, including fighter aircrafts, and in some cases, naval guns); indeed, even the tactics, battle drills, and operational skills of the counter-terrorist forces against the non-state dissenters remained almost the same.

Non-state terrorists throughout South Asia are no different either when it comes to the use of weaponries and strategies of violence. There has been a precise conformity in the way they operate, thanks largely to the weapons at their disposal. In Bangladesh, for instance, there are about 2,50,000 illegal firearms,[40] almost all in the hands of the (local) terrorists, popularly known as *mastans*. According to some unconfirmed reports, a substantial number of illegal firearms enter the country every day through its borders, indicating the existence of an informal arms bazaar in the region. Small arms are also manufactured locally in illegal factories within the country. Some researchers indicate that there are 1,000 illegal arms factories in Bangladesh, running mainly with foreign spare parts.[41] During 2001-2, the use of illegal weapons became so rampant that the government of Bangladesh had to launch a military operation named, 'Operation Clean Heart' to bring the perpetrators to book. Indeed, one of the major tasks of the joint forces in this operation was to recover illegal firearms. In this operation a total of 2,016 firearms of different categories were recovered, amongst these were six AK-47, two M- 16 rifles and a few sub-machine guns (SMG). There were also many local guns in that cache, which were either smuggled in or produced within the country. But that is not all. On 27 June 2003, the police recovered 62,112 rounds of Chinese rifle bullets and 120 kg. of explosives from an abandoned truck in the precincts of a house at Jogarpara village of Kahalu police station in Bogra. Subsequent raids in the neighbouring areas yielded more ammunition and explosives, which were later found to be the deadly RDX. The total amount recovered currently stands at about one lakh bullets and nearly 200 kg. of explosive. And then again, on the night of 1-2 April 2004, the police and coastguard forces seized illegal arms from a government-owned jetty on the Anwara coast of Chittagong. The seizure has been described as the 'largest single' arms consignment to have been intercepted by the law enforcement officials in Bangladesh. Table 4.10 provides a detailed inventory of the arms and ammunitions seized in Chittagong.

There are different schools of thought about the latest arms seizure. Some opine that the arms were meant for the ULFA, others say that they were meant for the Tripuran rebels. Some even include the Nepalese Maoists and the Kashmiri militants as possible buyers. The most plausible theory, however, is that the consignment was shipped from Hong Kong and was destined for the Tamil Tigers, but following a chase by the Indian or Sri Lankan navy the suppliers decided to hide the weapons in a safe warehouse in Bangladesh until it was safe to ship the consignment to its original customers. Looking at the composition of the weaponries, this could indeed be true. What is, however, more frightening is the existence of a sophisticated network of illegal arms trading stretching from Hong Kong to South Asia, and even beyond. Moreover, there is no

TABLE 4.10: WEAPONS SEIZED IN CHITTAGONG[42]

Item	*Quantity*
7.62 mm T-56-1 SMGs	690
7.62 mm T-56 SMGs	600
40 mm Rocket Launchers T-69	150
40 mm Rockets	850
9 mm Semi Automatic Spot Rifle	400
Tommy Guns	100
Grenade Launcher	2000
T-82-2 Hand Grenade	25,020
7.62 mm Bullets	739,680
7.62 mm Pistol Bullets	4.00, 000
Wireless Set	1

guarantee that some of these weapons would not slip into the local market and reach the hands of the local *mastans* and non-state dissenters.

Amongst the various categories of weaponries, IEDs are more readily used, terrorizing and killing people in the most heinous manner. In fact, over the last four years more than 100 people were killed and over 500 injured in bomb explosions in Bangladesh. A chronology of bomb blast incidents is found in Table 4.11.

A closer look at the various targets shows that no credible pattern can be traced from the incidents. Although in the beginning it seemed that Left and secular forces, including religious minorities, were the target, more recently, with the killing of the journalists claimed by pro-Left radical forces, it now seems that perpetrators of various shades and colours are using explosives against their victims. Interestingly, none of these incidents were officially solved and many, as one newspaper commented, 'point a finger to the intelligence agencies for their impotence and utter servility to the powers-that-be'.[43] Furthermore, there has been a routine blame game, with the government blaming the main opposition party, and the latter

TABLE 4.11: BOMB BLAST INCIDENTS IN BANGLADESH[44] (1999-2004)

Date	*Target*	*Killed*	*Injured*
6 March 1999	Pro-Left cultural rally	10	100
8 October 1999	Ahmedia Mosque	8	30
20 January 2001	Communist rally	7	50
14 April 2001	Cultural function	10	50
3 June 2001	Church	10	n.a.
16 June 2001	Awami League office	22	n.a.
23 September 2001	AL public meeting	8	100 +
26 September 2001	AL public meeting	4	n.a.
28 September 2002	Cinema/Circus	3	100 +
6 December 2002	Cinema halls	27	200 +
17 January 2003	Fair	7	20
1 March 2003	Police sergeant	1	n.a.
11 March 2003	Police constables	2	n.a.
12 January 2004	Muslim shrine	12	30
15 January 2004	Journalist	1	n.a.
21 May 2004	Muslim shrine	3	n.a.
28 June 2004	Journalist	1	1

likewise blaming the government for the violent incidents. This has further complicated the origins and growth of terrorism in Bangladesh, including the easy availability of modern weaponries.

The situation is more volatile in Kashmir. According to one former official of the Government of India, over 38,000 terrorist incidents took place in Jammu & Kashmir between January 1988 and October 1998.[45] Incidentally, most of these terrorist acts were directed against civilians, over 20,000 of them. The remaining 18,000 terrorist incidents took place against the members of the security forces. In fact, during January 1988 and December 1999, the terrorists killed a total of 11,814 persons, of which 9,733 were civilians and the rest members of the security forces. This, however, does not include the number of deaths from the violence perpetrated by the state or the coercive operations undertaken by the security forces in the name of counter-terrorism. Such a high degree of casualties, particularly in the hands of non-state militants and terrorists, could not have occurred without the easy availability of modern weaponries.

Kashmir is a hot place for weapons. A protracted alienation-cum-conflict in that area, aided no less by various external forces, including Pakistan, found Kashmir harbouring not only radicals, militants, and terrorists, but also modern weaponries of all kinds. Table 4.12 provides a list of weapons which the Indian security forces seized from the Kashmiri militants and terrorists between January 1988 and December 1999.

The amount of explosives found in ten years is staggering. In fact, in recent times, most of the casualties among security personnel in Kashmir resulted from improvised explosive devices, including remote-controlled ones.[46] But what has lately transformed the terrorist landscape in Kashmir is the arrival of the suicide bomber, suggesting that the latter phenomenon is not restricted to the infamous 'Black Tigers', the suicide squad of the Tamil Tigers in Sri Lanka, but that it has spread elsewhere in South Asia.[47] Although it is too early to say whether such a squad exists in Kashmir, it is nonetheless true that the entry of the suicide bomber, with RDX strapped to his or her body, is bound to transform the meaning of 'terror' there. As one critic commented:

[T]he fear of the suicide bomber will have its greatest impact on the security

TABLE 4.12: WEAPONS CAPTURED BY THE INDIAN SECURITY FORCES IN KASHMIR[48]

AK series Rifles	21,165
Sniper Rifles	312
Pistols/Revolvers	8,363
Machine Guns	1,167
Rocket Launcher	923
Grenades	38,611
Rockets	2,964 * (only 1998)
Rocket Boosters	1,786
Mines	5,874
Grenade Launchers	268 *
Mortars	88 *
Ammunitions	30,56,000 rounds*
Explosives	20,382 kgs*
Bombs	1,957 *
WT Sets	1,974 *

Notes: * Indicates that the figures for 1999 are not included.
Between 1996 and 1999, the explosive seized included 2,075 kg. of RDX. Figures for the other years are not available.

of the leaders in the state. Though many of them have been provided adequate security and bulletproof cars, the witnessing of a suicide bomber armed with RDX blowing up everything near him, as has occurred in other parts of South Asia will have an impact. This fear will result in the leaders feeling insecure and lead to further strengthening their security, which will cause inconvenience to the general public, and also alienate the leaders from the masses. . . .

In the wake of suicide bombing, a sarcastic smile or a wink, when being checked or interrogated, would cause more damage than a 20 kg RDX blowing up a security vehicle. . . .

Even a small quantity of RDX can throw a jeep 30 meters into the air or cause damage to not only the target, but also to the surroundings and a bulletproof car can easily be made into pieces. More than the blast, the sight of a vehicle disintegrating into pieces or a security post being destroyed would cause maximum psychological damage. A suicide bomber can walk or cycle up to any governmental or security installation, and blow up the entire structure. Even if the suicide bomber is caught before reaching its target, the triggering of the bomb, would serve its purpose, depending on the quantity of the RDX, he or she is carrying.[49]

As indicated earlier, when such a milieu comes to haunt the life and living of the people, humans end up as *hauntological* beings.

IV

CONCLUDING REMARKS

Contemporary terrorism, in the wake of its complicity with the modern state and modern weaponries, has come to haunt people not only locally but also nationally, regionally, as well as globally. When it comes to the production and use of the weaponries, a precise conformity informs and reproduces terrorism in modern times. Small arms, missiles, indirect fire weapons, bombs, and explosives now terrorize and kill people not only in Kabul, Karachi, Baghdad, Bali, Colombo, Nairobi, Jerusalem, Delhi, Dhaka, Srinagar, Gauhati, Tel Aviv, Madrid, Mymensingh, Bogotá, Rome, New York or London but practically anywhere and everywhere in this world. Indeed, in terms of its means, terrorism has entered a modernist phase of conformity and specterality. At the same time, the spectacular growth in the development of weapons technology in modern times, combining *distance*, *speed*, and *shock* in ways unparallel in history, has made killing so 'unreal' that perpetrators—state and non-state—can now turn demonic without any remorse and guilt. This has allowed not only newer production and proliferation of the weapons but also their use against innocent people in both developed and developing countries. The complicity of the modern state remains deeply entrenched in this.

Modern weapons technology is not only science-dependent; it is also a profitable vocation at the disposal of the state. Research, production, and supply, all are mostly sponsored and regulated by the state. The state also controls the strategic materials within its territorial bounds, indeed, to reproduce, what Dwight David Eisenhower once called, a military-industrial complex (MIC). In fact, modern weapons production is an industrial process which depends on various inputs and factors of an economy. These include, as one commentator pointed out, the overall level of industrialization, the existence of an adequate economic infrastructure, the supply of skilled labour, the existence of backward and forward linkages with other industries (for instance, the supply of raw materials, subcontracting and marketing of spin-off products), the level of state support and protection, and the existence of a market for the goods.[50] These factors almost intrinsically put the state at the centre in weapons production. The power of the state should not be limited to empowering state terrorism, however. Indeed, when it comes to non-state terrorism, the connivance of the state is not only in fomenting terrorism but also in arming terrorism.

As major weapons producers of the world, the developed countries of the West are particularly to be blamed for the contemporary weaponization of terrorism. According to a report published by the International Institute of Strategic Studies (London),[51] USA, Britain, Russia, France, China, Ukraine, Germany, Italy, Israel and Brazil are the ten top arms sellers. If the leaders of these countries are asked why they sell arms, they probably will reply 'if we do not sell we will not be able to produce and have them' or 'if we do not sell, someone else is going to sell', or 'if we do not sell we are going to see more unemployed workforce'. In fact, there is intense competition amongst the arms producers, interestingly leading to an ever-proliferating informal arms bazaar beside the visible and monitored formal market. The informal trading in modern weapons sustains bloody conflicts around the world, deteriorates law-enforcement situations in both developed and developing countries, and sustains terrorists, drug traffickers, money launderers, and the like, around the globe. Besides the informal market, states sometimes supply weapons to insurgents and terrorists to make another state a 'failed state'. Weapons are also supplied by the state to non-state entities on ideological grounds or in a 'balance of power game'. Covert gunrunning by intelligence or other government agencies to insurgent groups has historically been a major source of illicit arms. The weapons supplied by the CIA to guerrillas in Afghanistan, Angola, and Central America during the 1980s not only sustained brutal fighting but also destabilized some of the neighbouring countries in the region. But the CIA alone need not be blamed for this. Intelligence agencies of other states, like the KGB of the erstwhile Soviet Union, MI6 of Britain, Mossad of Israel, ISI of Pakistan or RAW of India, also supplied modern weapons to non-state dissenters, including militants and terrorists.

It is not difficult to see that the recipient countries alone cannot stop the flow of arms unless it is stopped at the suppliers' end. While the developed countries are the major weapons producers, there are also many countries which are used simply as transits for arms trading. To stop the proliferation, measures should be taken to devise a Non-Proliferation Treaty on Small Arms at both regional and international levels, including the United Nations. In this context, the United Nations Small Arms Conference of July 2001 is certainly a step in the right direction. The European Union has also tried to take a positive step by introducing a code of conduct in the sales of arms. The intention is to have a more responsible export of arms, but the Americans are reluctant to commit themselves to such an international agreement. Even though the code has been signed there are still many shortfalls, including establishing effective monitoring of sales and transfers by a member state. Moreover, arms can still be exported to regimes that would use them and violate international humanitarian laws. But as a starting point, the initiative of the European Union must be welcomed. It is high time that South Asia, independent of global influences, undertook such initiatives. The latter ought not to be limited to governments alone.

Viewed against recent experiences, the non-governmental or civil initiative is vital here. In fact, when civil bodies formed the international campaign to ban mines in 1992, many viewed their goal—a treaty banning the production, trade and use of anti-personnel landmines—as too idealistic, since mines have been an integral part of the military around the world for decades. But the global campaign catalyzed by the non-governmental civil bodies ultimately resulted in such a treaty in 1997. Many governments have already committed to the ban and signed the treaty. Bangladesh is also a signatory of the landmine treaty. A campaign to curb unfair weapons is as feasible as banning landmines. The mine campaign benefited from the fact that the MIC in general did not have a vested interest and therefore did not oppose the campaign to the end. Similarly, the arms industry will not benefit much from illicit transfers, and also, the possibility that the demonic consequences of the weapons could actually haunt their neighbourhood could in fact bring them into a position where they would refrain from hindering efforts to curb the production and trading of unfair weapons. In the case of South Asia, a regional civilian watchdog to monitor arms production and trading should be immediately set up, with or without the blessings of the government.

Finally, there is an urgent need for innovations in political resistance. Externally, states and governments, including their citizens, must resist the temptation of depicting or making 'the other state' a failed state. A violent failed state is bound to influence and destabilize the region and beyond. Since people of such states have little to lose by carrying and using an assault rifle or, even worse, strapping their bodies with some IEDs, there would be little hesitation on their part to stretch their operation beyond the immediate locality, particularly if there is an understanding that the land beyond is also culpable in producing their plight. More importantly, if the non-state dissenters are serious in their campaign to overcome the violence and terrorism of the modern state, they must engage themselves in a way as not to fall prey to the power of modern weaponries. Any turn to militancy using modern weaponries would only empower the modern state and its machineries and would make the former's goals a Sisyphean task.

NOTES

1. Bernard and Fawn M. Brodie, *From Crossbow to H-Bomb: The Evolution of the Weapons and Tactics of Warfare* (Bloomington: Indiana University Press, 1973), p. 43.
2. Rabindranath Tagore, 'Airborne', from *In Persia*, translated by Debjani Sengupta. See, *Sarai Reader 03: Shaping Technologies*, Delhi: CSDS, February 2003, pp. 74-5.
3. See, Tom Lewis, 'The Politics of "Hauntology" in Derrida's Specters of Marx', in Michael Sprinker (ed.), *Ghostly Demarcation: A Symposium on Jacques Derrida's Specter of Marx* (London: Verso, 1999), pp. 134-67.
4. See, Andrew Sinclair, *An Anatomy of Terror: A History of Terrorism* (Oxford: Pan Books, 2003), pp. 1-2.
5. Ibid., p. 33.
6. Sir Francis Tuker, *The Yellow Scarf : The Story of the Life of Thuggee Sleeman or Major General Sir William Henry Sleeman, 1788-1856* (London: J.M. Dent and Sons Ltd., 1961), pp. 65-6.
7. Ibid., p. 60.
8. Sita Ram Pande, *From Sepoy to Subedar* (Delhi: Vikas Publications, 1970) p. 33.
9. Ibid., p. 33.
10. The photograph of the Tower of Death can be seen on the website, www.webcorp.com/images/uzbekimage3.htm
11. See Zhiruddin Muhammad Babur, *Babur Nama*, vol. 1 (tr.), Annette Swannah Beveridge (New Delhi: Oriental Books Reprint Corporation, 1979) pp. 542-3.

12. Doctor Joseph Ignace Guillotin (1738-1814) was a physician by profession. Ironically, his name got entangled with a device which became the symbol and chief instrument of the Reign of Terror in the French Revolution. The 'Guillotine', the beheading device, was in fact adopted for humane and egalitarian reasons. Dr Guillotin belonged to a small reform movement in France which sought to banish the death penalty altogether. At that time, executions in France were cruel public events held in town squares and the entire town gathered to watch a quartering. Upper-class criminals bought their way into a less painful death; decapitation was their exclusive privilege. Dr Guillotin urged the National Assembly to decree that all executions should be carried out in the same manner; he did this as an interim step towards completely banning the death penalty. Guillotin did not invent or develop the 'guillotine'; such devices were already in use in Germany, Scotland and Persia for executing aristocratic criminals. On the basis of Dr Guillotin's demand the government commissioned engineers to modify the earlier version of the device under the advice of professional executioners.

    The first guillotining took place on 25 April 1792, of Nicolas Jacques Pelletie, at Place de Greve on the Right Bank. The most famous victims of the guillotine were King Louis XVI and Queen Marie Antoinette. During the Reign of Terror (June 1793-July 1794) French aristocrats and political opponents were guillotined at wholesale public executions. When the Jacobins were overthrown in July 1794, Robespierre, Saint Just and many other Jacobins were among the 105 guillotined during the three-day insurrection. All these executions became more of a public celebration. Beheading by the guillotine remained the legal method of execution in France until 30 September 1981, when France abolished the death penalty by law. See, Richard T. Bienvenu, 'Guillotine' in *The Encyclopedia Americana* (Internaitional Edition) vol. 13 (Danbury: Grolier Incorporated, 1986), p. 580 and Nathaniel Cantor, 'Guillotine', in Emanuel Friedman (ed.), *Collier's Encyclopedia*, vol. 11 (New York: Macmillan Education Company, 1986), p. 522.
13. In England hanging was carried out in public till 1868. From then on executions were carried out within the walls of county prisons. A few witnesses, including reporters, were admitted up to about 1910, but thereafter executions were carried out in complete secrecy. Public hangings apparently met the needs of justice but they also served the purpose of terrorizing the common masses. Prior to 1800 the English state could use almost any place for an execution and the court could order that the hanging be carried out near the place of the crime. However, most executions were carried out in the recognized place, often on market days in the county towns, so as to draw the biggest audience. Crowds, which were supposed to be frightened and be deterred by the spectacle, actually turned out more for the morbid excitement and a day out. It may be

mentioned that the modern expression 'Gala Day' is derived from the Anglo-Saxon 'Gallows Day'. See, 'The history of judicial hanging in Britain', Website: http://www.richard.clark32.btinternet.co.uk/hanging1.html

14. See, *The New Encyclopaedia Britannica*, vol. 6, Micropaedia (Chicago: Encyclopaedia Britannica Inc., 1986), p. 289.
15. Andrew Sinclair, *An Anatomy of Terror*, p. 366.
16. See, *The Mahabharata: A Play*. Based Upon the Indian Classic Epic by Jean-Claude Carrière. Translated from the French by Peter Brook (London: Methuen Drama, 1985), p. 155.
17. Martin van Creveld, *Technology and War: From 2000 B.C. to the Present* (London: Brassey's, 1991), p. 71.
18. Ibid.
19. It may be mentioned that other countries also produce variations of the AK-47. See, Ned Schwing, *Standard Catalogue of Military Firearms: 1870 to the Present*, 2nd edn. (Wisconsin: Krause Publications, 2003), p. 243.
20. See, Chris Bishop (ed.), *Combat Guns and Infantry Weapons* (England: Airlife, 1996), p. 28.
21. Trevor N. Dupuy, *The Evolution of Weapons and Warfare* (Virginia: Da Capo Press, 1984), p. 2.
22. In ancient warfare, archers fought individually, they could not use the heavy infantry's tactical formation. As they wore no armour, they could easily run away from the heavily equipped enemy hoplites, and by maintaining their distance they could avoid shock action and use their missile weapons effectively. Such methods of the archers, in fact inspired the idea of modern 'light infantry tactics.' See, Archer Jone, *The Art of War in the Western World* (Urbana: University of Illinois Press, 1987), pp. 2-10.
23. Eliot A. Cohen, 'A Revolution in Warfare', in *Foreign Affairs*, vol. 75, no. 2, March-April 1996, p. 44.
24. See, Imtiaz Ahmed, 'Contemporary Terrorism and the State, Non-State, and the Interstate: Newer Drinks, Newer Bottles', in Sidhar K. Khatri and Gert W. Kueck (eds.), *Terrorism in South Asia: Impact on Development and Democratic Process* (Colombo: Regional Centre for Strategic Studies, 2003), p. 372.
25. Cited from 'Mahathir Attacks State Terrorism', BBC News: World Edition, dated 22 October 2003.
26. For the life of Alfred Nobel, see, Erik Bergegren, 'Nobel, Alfred Bernhard' in Emanuel Friedman (ed.), *Collier's Encyclopedia*, vol. 17 (New York: Macmillan Educational Company, 1986), p. 569.
27. Website: http://tvone.nzoom.com/programmes/spooks/episodeguide_gg_ep1.html
28. Website: http://sf.indymedia.org/news/2002/10/1536683
29. Website: http://www.survivalguide.com/terrorist_weapons/explosives.htm

30. See, Report by Michael J. Martinez, 21 August 2003, website: ABCNEWS.com
31. Bruce Hoffman, *Inside Terrorism* (New York: Columbia University Press, 1998), pp. 180-1.
32. Cited from ibid., p. 182.
33. See, Albert Camus, *The Myth of Sisyphus* (London: Penguin Books, 1975), p. 11.
34. David Brooks, 'The Culture of Martyrdom: How suicide bombing became not just a means but an end', *The Atlantic Monthly*, June 2002. See also, John Daly, 'Suicide bombing: no warning, and no total solution', *Jane's Terrorism & Security Monitor*, 17 September 2001.
35. TLI includes the relative effectiveness capability of historical weapons, based upon such considerations as range, rate of fire, accuracy, reliability, radius of damage, etc. For a detailed exposition see Dupuy, *The Evolution of Weapons*, p. 92.
36. For a detailed exposition of 'subaltern globalization', see Ahmed, 'Contemporary Terrorism'.
37. For a closer exposition see, Peter Heehs, *The Bomb in Bengal: The Rise of Revolutionary Terrorism in India 1900-1910* (New Delhi: Oxford University Press, 1993).
38. Ibid.
39. The conservative death figure is 300,000. See, Imtiaz Ahmed, *State and Foreign Policy: India's Role in South Asia* (New Delhi: Vikas Publishing House, 1993), p. 264.
40. This was disclosed by the former Chief Advisor Latifur Rahman in an interview with *The Daily Star*. See, 'Prevalence of illegal arms now greater than that in "91 & 96"', *The Daily Star*, 6 August 2001. Cited from Syed Tamjid ur Rahman, *Illegal Use and Trade of Small Arms & Light Weapons: An Assessment of Present Status of Bangladesh* (Dhaka: South-Asian Partnership Bangladesh, September 2002), p. 12.
41. Syed Tamjid ur Rahman, ibid., p. 13. See also, Ajay Darshan Behera, 'Light Weapons and Security in South Asia: Exploring the Linkages', in Navnita Chadha Behera (ed.), *State, People and Security: The South Asian Context* (New Delhi: Har-Anand Publications, 2002), p. 193.
42. Compiled from various newspaper reports.
43. See, *The New Age*, 22 May 2004, p. 1.
44. The table has been prepared from *Star Weekend Magazine* (*The Daily Star*), 12 March 2004, and *The Daily Star*, 21 May and 28 June 2004.
45. See, B. Raman, 'Pakistan-Sponsored Terrorism in J&K', *South Asian Analysis Group Papers*, Paper No. 192, 30 January 2001.
46. *The Indian Express*, 25 May 2004.
47. The suicide bomb has also cropped up in post-9/11 Pakistan. See, Suba Chandran, 'Suicide Terrorism in South Asia: From Promised Land to

Presumed Land', *Peace & Conflict: An IPCS Bulletin*, New Delhi, vol. 6, no. 6, 2003.

48. Raman, 'Pakistan-Sponsored Terrorism in J&K', op. cit.
49. See, Suba Chandran, 'The First Suicide Bomb in Kashmir', *Terrorism Project*, Article no. 353, IPCS (The Institute of Peace and Conflict Studies), New Delhi, 11 May 2000.
50. Keith Kruse, *Arms Trade* (Cambridge: Cambridge University Press, 1999).
51. International Institute of Strategic Studies (IISS), *Military Balance 2000-2004*, London, 2004.

CHAPTER V

Terrorism and Subalternity – I: The Misgovernance Syndrome in Sri Lanka

JEHAN PERERA

When Sri Lanka gets into the international media it is usually on account of its ethnic-related violence. This has included mob riots in which there has been government complicity, the loss of a thousand soldiers in a single day with the fall of major army bases, and the destruction of half of the country's fleet of international aircraft at its international airport. The major part of this violence has pitted the Sri Lankan government against the Liberation Tigers of Tamil Eelam (LTTE), which has been fighting for an independent Tamil homeland. The LTTE is an organization which has its own army and lays claim to be the sole representative of the Tamil people on whose behalf it is fighting a war of independence. It has a leader of cult status and an army of over 10,000 soldiers, each of whom has sworn to commit suicide by swallowing a cyanide capsule rather than surrender.

More recently, Sri Lanka has also enjoyed a measure of international publicity on account of its peace process, which commenced in earnest on 22 February 2002, when a newly elected government headed by Prime Minister Ranil Wickremesinghe signed a ceasefire agreement with the LTTE leader Velupillai Prabhakaran, with Norwegian facilitation. The ceasefire between the government forces and the LTTE continues to hold more than three years later, despite significant problems affecting the peace process and even leading to the LTTE pulling out of peace talks. The first weeks of April 2004, immediately after a general election which led to the defeat of Prime Minister Wickremesinghe's government, saw the first major armed clashes after the signing of the ceasefire. But these clashes were not between the government forces and the LTTE, instead they were intra-LTTE fighting following the break away of its eastern leadership on the grounds of regional differences. While the clashes led to casualties on both sides and to the displacement of thousands of civilians, they ended soon with the collapse of the breakaway group.

The difficulty of a negotiated peace in Sri Lanka has been compounded by the inability of the political elite representing the country's distinct ethnic communities to agree on a power-sharing formula over the past five decades. In Sri Lanka the democratic principle of one person one vote has led to the domination of the numerically smaller Tamil population by the numerically much larger Sinhalese. But while the Sinhalese are a majority in the country, taken as a whole, the Tamils are a majority in the north and parts of the east of the country. If Sri Lanka had been provided with a federal constitution at the time of independence from the British, the Sinhalese and Tamil leaders might have been able to politically bargain with each other from their power bases at the centre and region respectively. Instead Sri Lanka was provided with a unitary form of government which vested all power at the centre and therefore in the hands of the Sinhalese.

Despite its present primacy, the ethnic conflict has not been the only major conflict in Sri Lankan society. There are other major sources of conflict constituting deep-seated cleavages in society which have fragmented society and undermined social cohesion. Twice in the past three decades the country has gone through class-based and Marxist-inspired insurrections in which tens of thousands of Sri Lankans have lost their lives. Interestingly, both of these insurrections have been confined to the Sinhalese section of the population, with no Tamil or Muslim involvement.

The first insurrection by the People's Liberation Front (JVP) took place in April 1971. Thousands of poorly armed JVP cadres simultaneously attacked police stations throughout the Sinhalese-majority areas, and an estimated 10,000-20,000 of them died in the government crackdown that followed, most within a span of a month. The efforts by the government to institute radical political and economic reforms led to actions that antagonized the Tamil section of the population. One example was the change in criteria for university admissions that saw the proportion of Tamils plummeting within a couple of years to make space for disaffected Sinhalese youth. The disgruntled Tamil youth deprived of university education in the decade of the 1970s, was in the forefront of the Tamil militancy.

The second JVP insurrection took place in 1988-9, and unlike the first one, which was more or less over in less than a month, this one stretched over two years of violence, terror, and disappearances with an estimated 30,000-60,000 killed. But like the first one, it ended with the capture and execution of the leadership. There was no political solution, only a military one.

Both JVP insurgencies were grounded in the sense of alienation and deprivation of the rural Sinhalese youth, who saw themselves being left out of the development process that was largely confined to Colombo and its environs which account for most of the country's industrial capacity. About 85 per cent of industrial production in the country is concentrated in the Colombo-centred Western Province, leaving only 15 per cent for the remaining seven provinces.

This paper will make the following points:

1. The rise of terrorism in the north and south of Sri Lanka has been due to the lack of responsiveness of the political system to the deeply felt grievances of sections of the polity. The result has been the legitimization of violent means for obtaining changes in the prevailing order.
2. With regard to the ethnic conflict, which has pitted the minority Tamil community against the state and has sought the establishment of a separate state, this unresponsiveness is caused by two factors. One is racism, which has led to the perception of the other community's position as unreasonable. The second is a political system that has concentrated political power in a single institution, which is invariably dominated by the majority Sinhalese, leading to an effectual tyranny of a permanent majority.
3. It is likely that a government faced with an insurrection against its authority will first seek to employ repressive law-and-order methods to quell the uprising. This would enable the state to remain unchanged. A military solution would give the state the

space to change in a minimal fashion, which would take the edge off the causes that led to the insurgency.

4. It is the failure of law-and-order methods that induces the state to attempt fundamental political reform. However, the attempt to achieve fundamental reforms cannot be internally sustained without external pressures, such as those generated by actual victory on the ground of the insurgent forces. If the state is enlightened, it will accept the new reality, and find ways to legitimize and reabsorb the insurgency into a reordered state.

CEASEFIRE 2002

The question is whether a negotiated peace which entails mutual compromise is possible in Sri Lanka. On the one hand, the LTTE's highly military nature, a fragmented Sinhalese polity, and economic vested interests put roadblocks on the path to political reforms and compromise. On the other hand, a general war-weariness among the general population, economic debilitation, and the threat of the US-led war against terrorism puts pressure on the conflicting parties to compromise and resolve their disputes through political negotiations. However, the ceasefire agreement of February 2002 that the Sri Lankan government and the LTTE signed under Norwegian government auspices appears to offer the real prospect of a final end to violence as a means of conflict resolution. On the other hand, demonstrating the fragility of the ceasefire even at its outset, the US embassy in Sri Lanka, under the hand of its ambassador, Ashley Wills, issued a statement which claimed,

> We have heard credible reports that the Liberation Tigers of Tamil Eelam (LTTE) are engaged in activities that could jeopardize the recent indefinite ceasefire accord reached with the Sri Lankan government. These reports recount increased LTTE recruitment in Sri Lanka's north and east, including of children, as well as kidnapping and extortion, especially of Muslims. To be fair, we understand that incidents of recruitment, kidnapping and extortion have apparently decreased in recent days, a trend that we hope will continue. There also have been credible reports of LTTE resupply operations since the ceasefire. Continued smuggling of weapons by the LTTE could undermine the trust needed to move from a cessation of hostilities to a lasting peace.
>
> The U.S. understands that both sides, not just the LTTE, have

responsibilities under the terms of the ceasefire accord. In the current international context, however, in which terrorism is being condemned in more and more countries, the LTTE should be especially vigilant about observing the terms of the ceasefire accord. If it does not, it will increase its international isolation and do harm to the group it claims to represent, Sri Lanka's Tamils, who earnestly want an end to the war. On the other hand, if the LTTE chooses the path of peace, ends its reliance on terrorism, accepts that an independent 'Eelam' is both unattainable and unnecessary, and honors democratic and human rights norms, the U.S. will respond Positively. We urge that the government and the LTTE take advantage of the ceasefire accord, and work with the Norwegian government to negotiate a permanent settlement of the conflict.[1]

The reference in the US statement to the Muslims brings to the fore one of the submerged aspects of Sri Lanka's ethnic conflict. The Muslims, who are mainly Tamil-speaking, nevertheless consider themselves to be a distinct ethnic community. Although 8 per cent of the Sri Lankan population, they are spread throughout the country, which has weakened their bargaining strength for regional autonomy, unlike the 12 per cent of Tamils who are regionally concentrated in the north and east. But the Muslims are a majority in pockets of the east. Along with the Tamils, they have been victims of government-sponsored land settlement schemes that settled Sinhalese in areas of the east that they once predominated. However, they have also suffered grievously at the hands of the LTTE, the most striking occasion being when nearly 1,00,000 Muslims were expelled from Jaffna and other parts of the north in 1990 with just two hours' notice. The Muslims were forced to leave without even being able to take along their movable property, such as jewellery. During the period of armed conflict they were reluctant to voice their sentiments, but now, with the advent of the ceasefire and increased international attention, they have been demanding the same rights and privileges as those to be accorded to the Tamils.

TRACING THE ORIGINS OF ETHNIC CONFLICT

Sri Lanka has a plural society of several different ethnic communities numbering 18 million. The Sinhalese form the main ethnic group with 74 per cent of the population. The majority of the Sinhalese are Buddhists and are mainly concentrated in the south, west, and central parts of the country. The Sri Lanka Tamils with 12 per cent of the population form the next major ethnic group. They form a majority in the north-east of the country. The Muslims form the third major ethnic group with 8 per cent of the population with a concentration in the east. The Up Country Tamils, who are of recent Indian origin, form the fourth major community with about 5 per cent of the population. They live in the central hills of the country and have not been involved in the separatist conflict. Most of the Tamils are Hindu by religion. While a minority of both Sinhalese and Tamils, comprising about 7 per cent, are Christian by religion, they are not considered to be a separate ethnic group.

The population census of 2001 carried out after an interval of twenty years was not conducted in most of the north-east province, which is contested territory and claimed by Tamil nationalists as the 'traditional Tamil homeland'. However, estimates indicate that the Sri Lanka Tamil population has dropped to a little under 11 per cent of the population in the intervening period.[2] Among the salient points brought out by the census is the intermingling of the Sri Lankan population, with Colombo, the main city located in the south-west of the country registering a Sinhalese population of only 41 per cent, the majority being from Tamil-speaking communities.

Sri Lanka's ongoing ethnic conflict and the separatist war it has given rise to can be described as the country's most intractable and destructive problem. The war, which steadily escalated between the Sri Lankan government and the LTTE, is generally counted as having started in 1983. It caused an estimated 65,000 deaths and major damage to personal and public property, with the total loss between 1993-8 estimated at 1.27 times the GDP as at 1998.[3] A total of some one million persons have been uprooted and displaced internally as a result, at some time or the other, with another half million leaving the country to claim refugee status abroad.

Ironically Sri Lanka has had a relatively long tradition of modern democracy, stretching back to the British colonial period. The country was one of the first in the world to enjoy universal suffrage in 1931. But the inability of the political elites belonging to the different ethnic communities to share power equitably among themselves led to a series of broken agreements and to acute mistrust between the communities. The difficulty of protecting minority interests in a parliamentary system in which majority–minority relations are strained is exemplified by Sri Lanka's modern political history. Jayadeva Uyangoda writes that:

Sri Lanka's post-independence legislative past does not offer positive examples of constructive management of tension among communities that had placed competing demands on the state. Our history of governance during the past fifty years is replete with ill conceived legislation and public policy measures of regimes responding to agitation by majoritarian political mobilisation. Those measures were marked by very little attention paid by policy makers to their negative consequences for the larger goals of democratic nation building. Politicians waiting to catapult themselves into power have quite heroically made use of such agitation to propel their own projects forward. The language legislation in 1956 is a classic case in point. By satisfying the agitation made on behalf of the majority Sinhalese community, that policy measure effectively alienated all the ethnic and linguistic minorities from the Sri Lankan state.[4]

In tracing the history of the ethnic conflict there are two major considerations. The first is that the ethnic conflict is essentially a twentieth-century phenomenon having its origins in rival elite competition. While the conflict cannot be fully understood in isolation from events that span over two millennia, the memory of these events is but a contributory factor and not the cause of the conflict. The fear of the Sinhalese of absorption by Tamil culture is one that has historical memory. As K.M. de Silva observes:

There is the Sinhalese sense of historical destiny, of a small and embattled people who have preserved Theravada Buddhism when it was obliterated in India under a Hindu revivalist tide, and whose language despite its roots in classical Indian languages, is uniquely Sri Lankan. Linked to this is their perception of the Tamils as a traditional 'national' enemy against whom they have fought at various times over two thousand years of a common history.[5]

Second, even though the origin of the conflict was competition between a small faction of the population, the intensity of the emotion it has succeeded in generating among the general population through appeals to ethnic identity, has transmuted elite conflict into a conflict between two 'incipient whole societies' or nations. To fully appreciate this phenomenon it is necessary to trace back in some detail the crucial events that gave rise to the present polarization.

HISTORICAL DETERMINANTS

The textual source of nationalist Sinhalese inspiration has been the *Mahavamsa*, a Sinhalese chronicle written in the fifth century AD by Buddhist monks at a time when the Sinhalese Buddhist kingdoms were under attack from the Tamil Hindu kingdoms of southern India. The chronicle recorded history back to fifth century BC, to the time time of the Buddha's dispensation. It records that on the day of Buddha's death, Prince Vijaya, the ancestor of the Sinhalese, landed on Lankan soil from northern India. On his deathbed, the Buddha summoned Sakka, the king of the gods, and instructed him that 'Vijaya, son of Sinhabahu, the lord of men, is come to Lanka from the region of Lala together with seven hundred followers. O lord of gods, my dispensation will be established in Lanka. Protect him well, his followers, and also Lanka.'[6]

The Sinhalese are therefore especially susceptible to the persuasion that they were a chosen people with a mission, the preservation of Buddhism in Sri Lanka. Thus was Sri Lanka both 'Dhammadipa' (island of the Faith) and 'Sihadipa' (island of the Sinhalese). Further, that their enemies, while being in general any alien non-Buddhist, were in particular the Tamils. The reason for this again is rooted in the *Mahavamsa*. As Gananath Obeyesekere has observed, 'The historical events as depicted in Sri Lanka's chronicles had until the sixteenth century one unvarying pattern; with a few exceptions Sri Lanka was consistently invaded by a South Indian peoples who were generally Tamil speakers.'[7]

By appealing to the *Mahavamsa*, Sinhalese nationalism laid the groundwork for an ideology that is based on race, language, and religion to forge an identity which superseded other less inclusive identities. It was also one which, because of the numerical strength it could mobilize, the Sinhalese political elite was to find most useful to embrace with the approach of independence in the age of mass politics. The opening was provided by the apprehensions and actions of the Tamil political elite who, nurtured in the protected but non-democratic environment of colonial rule, saw themselves as the major losers in an independent democracy based upon majority rule in which the Sinhalese voting strength would be preponderant.

Interestingly, however, the earliest voting experience in the second decade of the twentieth century did not show such an ethnic-oriented pattern. In 1911, the British took the initial tentative steps towards self-government in Sri Lanka by creating the 'Educated Ceylonese Seat'. This was an all-island constitutuency with the entitlement to vote limited to those with appropriate occupational and educational qualifications. At the first election, Ponnambalam Ramanathan, a Tamil, defeated Marcus Fernando, a Sinhalese, by 1,645 votes to 981. When the second elections were held in 1917, Ramanathan increased his majority by trouncing J.S. Jayewardene, a Sinhalese, by 1,752 votes to 48. Had anti-Tamil sentiments been uppermost amongst the Sinhalese electorate, the Sinhalese candidate would not have fared so badly, especialy since there were more Sinhalese than Tamils in the electorate (1,748 Sinhalese against 1,346 Tamils). At this time inter-caste rivalries were the more salient feature of political life. The Sinhalese candidate at the 1911 elections belonged to a rising minority caste, and this weighed against him.[8]

By the 1930s the British had begun to advocate territorial representation and universal suffrage as essential to the achievement of democratic government. The Sinhalese accepted this set of principles as progressive as it would redress their then severe under-representation in the legislature *vis-à-vis* the minority communities, especially the Tamils. The chief anxiety of the Tamil leadership was that with the ratio of Sinhalese to Tamils being increased from two to one (under the Manning Constitution of 1924) to five to one (under the Donoughmore Constitution of 1931), they would be unable to safeguard their positions in both the legislature and the civil service. This is reflected in the argument that a leading Tamil politician of the time, G.G. Ponnambalam made in an address to the Governor in 1935. He claimed that:

> There should be a more equitable and balanced distribution of political power among the various communities than obtains at present, and that the Ceylon Tamil Community should have adequate representation in the State Council in keeping with its historical past and its present importance.[9]

At this time the Tamil elite's perception of pluralism was that of a sharing of power at the centre among communities, and was based neither upon equal suffrage on the basis of individual votes nor upon a holding of power at the periphery. Indeed, in 1926, when S.W.R.D. Bandaranaike, a future prime minister, proposed federalism as a solution to the island's diversity and ethnic mix, the Tamil leadership showed no interest in it, for their eyes were set on the capture of power in Colombo. Like his predecessor Ponnambalam Ramanathan, G.G. Ponnambalam, in pleading for a 'more equitable', 'balanced', and 'adequate' distribution of legislative seats, was in fact arguing for the preservation of the privileged position of the Tamil elite. As Jane Russell has noted,

> Much of the apprehensions with which the Ceylon Tamil elite viewed the new constitution, and their consequent preoccupation with the number of seats accruing to them, stemmed from the prospect of the middle classes losing their numerically disproportionate position in the public service to the majority community.[10]

This demand saw its peak in the call for the Sinhalese to be confined to half the seats in the legislature, with reservation of the other half for the minorities, better known as the '50-50 demand'. The Tamil political leadership could have phrased their demands in a manner that was less narrowly designed to protect the privileges of their class, and emphasized instead the central issues of vital concern to the Tamil population as a whole. These would have included their rights to self-government, development of the economic resources of the Tamil areas, and the preservation of their identity as a people. Such an appeal may have received a more sympathetic response from the British constitutional commissions, if not from the Sinhalese political leadership. The British rejected the demand for communal representation for minorities and heeded the plea of the Sinhalese for territorial representation which would give them the legislative strength denied them for so long.

TAMIL GRIEVANCES

By the time of independence in 1948, Sinhalese and Tamil nationalisms were solidly entrenched forces, but their numerical preponderance giving the Sinhalese the advantage. The concepts of a plural polity, a Sri Lankan nationalism, and a secular state were among the first to be undermined by the Sinhalese majority. The first victims were the Up Country (Indian) Tamils who were relatively recent immigrants from south India—since 1826—to the island and worked on the tea plantations in the central highlands. Most of the land utilized by the British for the plantations was thick forest that had normally belonged to the Sinhalese king and the aristocracy and there had been little or no actual utilization. The Up Country Tamils became identified with the British as joint confiscators of these traditional Sinhalese lands.

In 1948, these Tamils, nearly a million in number, were deprived of their citizenship. In the following year they were deprived of their franchise. The articulated governmental justification for this action was that the Up Country Tamils were aliens dumped on Sri Lanka by the British, whose loyalties lay in south India, and to whom Sri Lanka owed no responsibility. But a further motivation was that the Up Country Tamil vote would swamp the Sinhalese vote in many electorates. Indeed at the general election of 1947, the Left parties made an unexpectedly strong showing winning around a third of the parliamentary seats, many of them from plantation areas.

Interestingly, the Sri Lanka Tamil Leader G.G. Ponnambalam, who by this time was a cabinet minister in the government, voted in favour of the Citizenship Act, although its end result was the disenfranchisement of most Up Country Tamils. This was not surprising in view of his class interests and the perception of many Sri Lanka Tamils that the Up Country Tamils were indeed aliens. But the more percipient of the Sri Lanka Tamils saw ominous signs in this use of the Sinhalese voting strength. Their apprehensions were not lessened by the transfer of population from densely populated Sinhalese areas to the Tamil-speaking northern and eastern provinces under state-aided colonization.

The vision that captivated D.S. Senanayake, independent Sri Lanka's first prime minister, was of a self-sufficient Sinhalese peasantry reclaiming the heritage bestowed upon it in a bygone age by the ancient Sinhalese kings from the jungle. But this in turn threatened to make the Tamils minorities in areas where they were presently the majority. The call for the 'preservation of the traditional homelands of the Tamils' made its appearance at this stage. Mainstream historians see this concept of 'the traditional homelands' as a recent construct without real historical root. K.M. de Silva says, 'the historical evidence the Tamil advocates of a "traditional homeland" provide in support of their case is so flimsy that only "true believers" can accept them'.[11] It is linked to Tamil aspirations, as a measure to strengthen their claim.

It was the enactment of language legislation that finally convinced the Tamils that their ambition to share power at the centre was illusory, and that their interests could not be secured within the framework of a unitary state in which the Sinhalese majority would dominate the centralized decision-making processes. The agreed policy among leaders of all communities prior to independence was that the Sinhala and Tamil languages would replace English as the official languages of the country. Yet, in 1955 the Sinhalese political leadership had abandoned the two-language policy and adopted the policy of Sinhala as the only official language.

The catalysts behind this move were Buddhist activists and the Sinhala-educated intelligentsia. Since the advent of colonial rule they had not exerted influence on a national scale. The dominance of English as the language of administration shut them out of rewarding careers. In addition, they were aware, as much as those Tamil leaders who pleaded for 'adequate representation' in the legislature in keeping with their 'present importance', that Tamil-speakers enjoyed a disproportionate representation in government, business (Muslims, together with Tamils), and the professions. S.W.R.D. Bandaranaike articulated these concerns by linking economic domination with language. In Parliament, in 1955, he said, 'The fact that in the towns and villages, in business houses and boutiques, most of the work is in the hands of Tamil speaking people will inevitably result in a fear, and I do not think an unjustified fear, of the inexorable shrinking of the Sinhalese language.'[12] This statement should be placed in the context of Sinhalese fears of being submerged in a regional Tamil majority that included southern India. In 1944, J.R. Jayawardene, in a speech in the State Council had said:

> The great fear I had was that Sinhalese being a language spoken by only 3 million people in the whole world would suffer if Tamil is also placed on an equal footing with Sinhalese. The influence of Tamil literature, the literature used in India by over 40 millions, and the influence of Tamil films and Tamil culture in this country, I thought, might be detrimental to the future of the Sinhalese language.[13]

With this in mind the Sinhalese nationalists aimed for the revocation of the informal language settlement arrived at a decade earlier that Sinhala and Tamil should eventually replace English as the national languages, and insisted instead on 'Sinhala-Only'. In 1956, after a sweep of the polls by the political party headed by S.W.R.D. Bandaranaike, the Official Language Act declaring Sinhala to be the only official language was passed with a large parliamentary majority.

Language is a way of creating unity within a group; it is also a way of maintaining boundaries between groups. The threat to language is, therefore, a potential threat to group identity. The sense of impending threat to the Tamil identity in an independent Sri Lanka was articulated by S.J.V. Chelvanayakam in 1947. He warned that, 'The Tamil language is in danger of being annihilated. The Sinhalese leaders are plotting to make Sinhala the only official language in the country, and to relegate the Tamil to the Northern and Eastern provinces and to make it a purely local language.'[14] Two years later Chelvanayakam was to become leader of the Federal Party, which would dominate Tamil politics until it became the leading component of the Tamil United Liberation Front (TULF) in 1976.

TAMIL NATIONHOOD

In explicitly mobilizing communal solidarity, and subsuming cross-cutting loyalists in the region, caste, and class, the language issue made the Sinhalese–Tamil cleavage the most decisive one in Sri Lankan society. The power of ethnic-based nationalism over other considerations was clear in the Tamil reaction to 'Sinhala-Only'. The Tamil electorate decisively rejected the Tamil Congress because it saw in the language issue a question of discrimination in employment and education, and swung towards the newly formed Federal Party which gave Tamil identity and political autonomy the foremost importance. No longer would the Tamils articulate their demands merely in terms of the rights of minorities; they would do so in terms of nationhood.

An example of the self-perception of the Tamils was the assertion made at the Presidential Address of the Federal Party in 1961:

> We are a nation by all standards. We inhabit a geologically compact and well-defined territory. We speak a common language. We are proud inheritors of a common heritage and culture as ancient as man himself.

And above all, we are bound together by the feeling of oneness which is a necessary ingredient for nationhood, that consciousness which you and I and all of us share whatever part of the country we may live in.[15]

However, the Tamil claim to nationhood was still articulated within the framework of a united Sri Lanka, albeit federal as opposed the existing unitary structure. It required two more watershed events before the mainstream Tamil political parties were to finally opt for secession. The first was the association of Buddhism with the state in the constitution of 1972, which stated that: 'The Republic of Sri Lanka shall give Buddhism the foremost place and accordingly it shall be the duty of the State to protect and foster Buddhism.' The principle of a special status for Buddhism was reaffirmed in the constitution of 1978 which has prompted K.M. de Silva to say that 'Even if Sri Lanka has not become a theocratic state in fact, it has ceased to be a secular state in form.'[16]

The elevation of Buddhism reinforced the psychological grievances of the Tamils—ever mindful of Sinhalese claims to exclusive possession of the island—at this attempt of the State to create a single culture overriding communal cultures, yet drawing most of its symbols from the heritage of the Sinhalese Buddhists. National identity too easily became conflated with the identity of the majority Sinhalese, with the abandonment of the concept of a multi-ethnic polity being justified by the democratic sanction of numerical superiority.

The second watershed event was the educational policy begun in 1970, of squeezing out Tamil students to make room for Sinhalese under the rationale of affirmative action for the educationally underprivileged. Tamils have historically placed great stress upon educational attainments as a vehicle for social mobility outside their arid Jaffna heartland. Up until 1970, when university admissions were based on merit, Tamils occupied an average of 30-50 per cent of the places in the highly sought after medical, engineering, and science faculties. But such a distribution of educational opportunity did not correspond to the distribution of political power. In response to Sinhalese pressures, especially the trauma of the 1971 Sinhalese youth insurrection, the government that year adopted a scheme of 'standardization' under which to enter the universities, Tamils had to score higher than identically situated Sinhalese students. By 1974, the proportion of Tamil students entering universities had been halved, to 15-25 per cent in the relevant faculties. [17]

The extent of Tamil bitterness at standardization induced the government to modify the scheme in 1975, but the psychological damage had been done. The seeds of separatism planted in earlier times of confrontation with an intolerant Sinhalese nationalism now took firm root during these years of frustration. The first political killing of a government official, the (Tamil) mayor of Jaffna, occurred in 1975. One of those involved in the killing was Velupillai Prabhakaran, the leader of the LTTE, then a small militant group and now the major actor on the Tamil side of the divide.

In 1976, the TULF, an umbrella organization of the major Tamil political parties adopted a resolution that stated that the party was committed to the 'restoration and reconstitution of the free, sovereign, secular, socialist state of Tamil Eelam based on the right of self-determination inherent to every nation'. Further, it declared that such a state had 'become inevitable in order to safeguard the very existence of the Tamil nation in this country'.[18]

Like the Sinhalese, the Tamils, says S. Arasaratnam, are 'equally susceptible to mobilization and manipulation by traditionalist and parochial appeals'. For they had a memory of shared historical experience. Even from the evidence of the ancient Sinhalese chronicles, the Tamil presence on the island can be shown to extend back to the earliest times. Perhaps the most powerful identifying factor was the independent political power the Tamils were able to wield in the north of the island until the Portuguese conquest in 1621.[19]

These factors have contributed to a distinctive self-definition of the community that has been reinforced by the repeated and indiscriminate targeting of Tamil lives and property by Sinhalese mobs. Following the first ever Sinhalese–Tamil riots in 1956, which accompanied the introduction of the 'Sinhala-Only' bill in Parliament, there have been serious outbreaks of mob violence directed against Tamils in 1958, 1977, 1981 and the pogrom of July 1983. The last, which took place in the heart of Colombo, was sparked off by the killing and mutilation of the bodies of thirteen Sinhalese soldiers after a Tamil ambush in Jaffna. For one week Sinhalese mobs roamed the streets of Colombo and its suburbs looting and destroying Tamil homes and businesses, and killing Tamils. The President delayed in declaring a curfew, and there are other indications of complicity of sections of the government in these riots. For instance, the thugs had voter lists in their possession, which they used to identify Tamil-inhabited houses. In many instances, police and army did not intervene to save Tamils.[20]

The degree of ethnic polarization reached such a fever pitch that many of these anti-Tamil actions, particularly directed against the economic base of the Tamils, were tactically approved by the Sinhalese incensed by Tamil separatist success and governmental impotence in suppressing the terrorist violence. The government acknowledged a death toll of nearly 400, but unofficial sources claimed that as many as 1,500 Tamils were killed and millions of rupees worth of property destroyed, while the figure popularized by the Tamil diaspora is as high as 4,000. The government also admitted that the program was organized, but attempted to place the blame upon an 'international communist conspiracy' and not, as it more accurately should have, largely upon factions within its own ranks. In summary, a combination of factors, with the entrenched resistance of the Sinhalese to accept the Tamil claim to nationhood and sporadic riots, saw an increase in the popular support for Tamil nationalism inextricably linked with separatism.

CONSTITUTIONAL REFORM

A weakness of the Westminster system in general, which relies upon the unitary form of government, is that in ethnically divided societies, it permits the largest ethnic community to obtain the largest number of seats in parliament, and then take unilateral decisions that affect the smaller ethnic communities. In Northern Ireland this system enabled the Protestants to rule over the Catholics, and to discriminate against them. The framework document that led to the Northern Ireland peace agreement in 1998 has several novel mechanisms to ensure that both Protestants and Catholics share equally in the power to make decisions that will bind both communities. Certain key decisions requiring 'cross-community' support (that is, both Protestant and Catholic support) have been designated in advance, to include the election of the Chairman of the Assembly, the First Minister, the Deputy First Minister, standing orders and budgetary allocations. In other cases, such decisions could be triggered by a petition of concern brought by a significant minority (30 out of 108) members of the Assembly.[21]

In the Northern Ireland context, the principle of parallel consent means that certain key decisions can be taken only if a majority of both unionists (Protestants) and nationalists (Catholics) vote for the decision. The principle of weighted majority means that at least 60 per cent of the assembly must vote in favour of the decision, together with at least 40 per cent of each of the unionist and nationalist members voting for the decision. A further protection against the 'winner takes all' mentality that plagues Sri Lanka, and which drives the opposition to despair and even revolution, has been developed in the Northern Ireland peace agreement. It is to share ministerial positions on the proportional basis of the number of seats won by each party in the Assembly. Not only does this permit the smaller communities to share executive authority, it also enables rival political parties to share power.

In Sri Lanka, the centralized state bequeathed to the newly independent country in 1948 effectively transferred political power into the hands of the Sinhalese majority. This power was immediately used to restrict the membership of the polity by denying citizenship rights to the 'Indian Tamil' or Up Country Tamil population and by seeking to correct 'historical wrongs' done to the majority. This followed a pattern in which the politicization of ethnicity has occurred in contemporary plural societies, and the claims to group entitlements in current mass politics provide the initial basis for collective identity, mobilization and action.

The skewed distribution of political power in Parliament also led to economic disparities emerging between the Sinhalese and Tamil-majority parts of the country. While social welfare benefits such as health and education were relatively equitably distributed throughout the country, the same did not hold true for large-scale economic investments. With few exceptions, these prized projects, which provided opportunities for political patronage and development, were located in the Sinhalese majority parts of the country. Ruling party politicians engaged in tussles to obtain these projects for their own electorates. As the Tamils from the north in particular were rarely represented in the higher rungs of the government, their case went by default. The deprivation of the Tamil majority areas has continued and escalated due to the war situation that has prevailed over the past eighteen years. A recent study has shown that the output of the north-east is a mere 60 per cent of what it used to be in 1983, when the war commenced.[22]

Several serious efforts made by government leaders to work out a solution with the Tamil political leaderships failed due to the inability of the government leadership to obtain the backing of their own party let alone the opposition. The most outstanding instance was the agreement reached in 1957 between Prime Minister S.W.R.D. Bandaranaike and the leader of the largest Tamil party. The Prime Minister unilaterally abrogated the agreement when it proved generally unpopular in the country. Buddhist monks even demonstrated in numbers against the agreement which gave autonomy to the Tamil areas. A similar agreement arrived at in 1965 by Prime Minister Dudley Senanayake suffered the same fate, but this time due to strong divisions within the ruling party itself.[23] The salient feature of both these agreements were to provide a degree of autonomy to the northern and eastern provinces and to permit them to merge or work together if they so desired. Self-rule, regional autonomy and merger of the two provinces remain the key issues dividing Sinhalese and Tamil sentiment to this day.

The Tamil position that is constantly reiterated is that of the Thimpu principles. At the Thimpu talks held in 1985 in Nepal, the Tamil delegation, consisting of the EPRLF, EROS, PLOT, LTTE and TULF, issued the following statement:

It is our considered view that any meaningful solution to the Tamil national question must be based on the following four cardinal principles.

(1) Recognition of the Tamils of Sri Lanka as a nationality.
(2) Recognition of the existence of an identified homeland for Tamils in Sri Lanka.
(3) Recognition of the right of self-determination of the Tamil nation.
(4) Recognition of the right to citizenship and the fundamental rights of all Tamils who look upon the island as their country.

Different countries have fashioned different systems of governments to ensure these principles.[24]

The 13th Amendment to the constitution which gave effect to the devolution provisions of the Indo–Lanka Peace Accord of July 1987, sought to devolve power to provincial councils throughout Sri Lanka. It contained three lists which enumerated areas of power to be devolved to the provinces, retained at the centre and a concurrent list of shared functions, which were ultimately controlled by Parliament at the centre. However, continued centralization of power was represented by the executive presidency. Rohan Edrisinha says:

> Perhaps the greatest obstacle to practical devolution was the first phrase of the Reserved List, which provided for 'National Policy on all Subjects and Functions' to be determined by Parliament. This phrase completely undermined powers apparently devolved to the provinces. Since the inauguration of the 13th Amendment, Parliament has used this rubric often to encroach into the provincial sphere.[25]

So far the most radical proposals for ending the ethnic conflict through a constitutional arrangement has been the 'Devolution Package' of August 1995, proposed by the government as a draft document. This sought to redefine 'the constitutional foundation of a plural society'. The provincial councils of the 13th Amendment were renamed as Regional Councils with added powers. Edrisinha goes on to say that:

> The deletion of Articles 2 and 76 of the constitution, which entrenched the unitary character of Sri Lanka, removed an unnecessary obstacle to substantial devolution. The abolition of the Concurrent List was another positive feature, as were other attempts to remove ambiguity in the division of powers. These included the clarification of the role of provincial governors and the awarding of greater revenue raising powers to the regional council.[26]

However, a major weakness in the proposed regional councils would have been the ability of the executive president to dissolve a council in case of emergency. Further its framers failed to respond to the larger issues, such as those of self-determination and nationhood, and obtaining the concurrence of the LTTE, which rejected the devolution package as being insufficient.

RISE OF THE LTTE

The frustrations and repeated political failure of the democratic and mainstream Tamil political parties to redress Tamil grievances led in the 1970s to demands for a separate Tamil state, articulated by the Tamil political parties themselves. This was followed by armed resistance and ultimately civil war. In 1972, the Tamil political parties joined to form the Tamil United Front and threatened to take 'non-violent direct action against the government . . . in order to win the rights of the Tamil nation on the basis of the right to self-determination' if the government failed to amend the constitution to take their aspirations into account. As mentioned earlier the first political assassination took place in 1975 with the assassination of the mayor of Jaffna, Alfred Duraiappah, a government supporter. The leaders of the Tamil political parties refrained from explicitly condemning the use of violence which, however, was described by the government and by most mainstream Sinhalese politicians as being 'terrrorism'. As a result the government permitted the steady erosion of the norms of democracy, and the use of brutal methods of police repression to eradicate terrrorism, while Tamil politicians expressed intolerance of any deviation from the nationalist line. The rise of militant Tamil nationalism can be traced back to this period.

In 1976, the Tamil United Front was renamed the 'Tamil United Liberation Front'. At its first national convention held in Vaddukoddai it resolved 'that the restoration and reconstitution of the free and sovereign secular socialist state of Tamil Eelam based on the right of self-determination inherent to every nation has become inevitable in order to safeguard the very existence of the Tamil nation in this country'.[27] Thus, the uncompromising stand for an independent and sovereign state of Tamil Eelam has its democratic antecedents. The hardline LTTE emerged as the main armed movement among the Tamils, gradually establishing its control over most of the Jaffna peninsula.

Rohan Gunaratne has summarized one view of the LTTE:

> Elements of the LTTE mindset are: its claim to the be the sole representative of the Tamils; intolerance of dissent within the Tamil community; liquidating the alternative Tamil leadership; massacring non-Tamil civilians;

reneging on three peace agendas/undertakings; and the inability to compromise on [its leader] Prabakaran's avowed goal of Tamil Eelam.[28]

A contrary view has been presented by S.J. Emmanuel:

The government failed to recognise the political face of the LTTE and talked to them only as a militant if not terrorist group. This was a misapprehension. The government will do well, even concurrent to the understanding of a militant leadership, to clearly recognise not only the peace aspirations of the Tamil people, but also that of their de facto leadership.[29]

In the initial phase of Tamil militancy in the early 1980s, there were several Tamil militant organizations in the fray against the Sri Lankan government. However, the LTTE proceeded to decimate them one by one. In addition the LTTE targeted leaders of the Tamil political parties as well. This ensured for them the mantle of the 'sole representative of the Tamil people', a designation that they continue to insist upon. It was undoubtedly in recognition of the LTTE's superior bargaining strength relative to the other Tamil political parties and organizations that most of them came together under the umbrella of the Tamil National Alliance in 2001. They also agreed to contest the general election of December 2001 on the slogan that the LTTE would be the sole representative of the Tamils. This stemmed in part from their judicious observation that the unity of the Tamil people should not be sundered in negotiations with the government. Undoubtedly there was also a measure of LTTE coercion in these parties being prepared to relinquish their own representative status. Every one of the Tamil political parties contesting the elections had lost its leaders to the LTTE. At the general elections of April 2004, several of the Tamil political parties contested once again under the banner of the Tamil National Alliance and increased their tally of seats in Parliament, capturing virtually every Tamil majority constituency in the north-east.

Many, if not the overwhelming majority of Tamil people, support the notion of the LTTE being the sole representative of the Tamil people at the negotiating table with the government. The reason is their belief that the LTTE is best positioned to obtain for the Tamil people the full measure of their democratic rights. However, sole representative status in governing a people (as distinct from negotiating a settlement) can ultimately only be earned at free and fair elections, and not by fiat. Today, after more than two decades of armed struggle, the LTTE has achieved a more superior negotiating position *vis-à-vis* the government than any of the democratic Tamil political parties. It has obtained the recognition of its equality at the negotiating table from the government which enabled the lifting of the ban once placed upon it. At the peace talks in Thailand in 2002, the government even referred to the LTTE as partners, a clear acknowledgement of its equal status at the negotiating table and in the peace-building process.

But two years after the signing of the Ceasefire Agreement the LTTE also has reasons to be discontented. The LTTE's primary justification for pulling out of the peace talks in April 2003 was the lack of implementation of the promises made during the six rounds of negotiations that took place between September 2002 and March 2003. The LTTE has felt acutely frustrated by its inability to gain access to international funding which would make it the benefactor of the Tamil people. The new institutions of governance that were agreed to be set up for the interim period in the north-east have yet to be implemented. The political crisis that pitted the president against the government stalled any further possibility of establishing those institutions on the ground. After the general election, the LTTE is likely to press the new government to deliver on these institutions.

In March 2004 the LTTE faced an unprecedented challenge when its eastern commander decided to break away from the organization and set up his own eastern administration. The LTTE was able to overcome the challenge to its hegemony amongst the Tamil population in the north-east relatively easily within a month. This is another indication that the LTTE will be a permanent feature of the political landscape of Sri Lanka, and particularly the north-east, for a long time to come. Despite its major flaws, it is likely that the great majority of Tamil people continue to see no alternative to the LTTE. Nor would they wish the LTTE to be marginalized or weakened in any way. This is because the LTTE is potentially the best guarantor that the Tamil people will eventually obtain a fair share of rights and political power in Sri Lanka, alongside the Sinhalese and other communities. Through its military power, and preparedness to use it, the LTTE has closed the previously enormous gap between the bargaining strengths of the Tamil minority and Sinhalese majority.

The inability of the government to deliver a peace dividend to the people of the north-east even after nearly two years' of ceasefire should show the Tamil people that their well-being is not a priority concern of the government in Colombo, and further, that what is rightfully theirs has to be wrested from an unwilling or uncaring government. The track record of successive governments shows that none of them have been prepared to give voluntarily, one reason being the nature of opposition politics which sets up Sinhalese fears against the Tamils. This means that everything has to be bargained for or forcibly extracted. Due to their lack of an alternative way of obtaining their rights in the country, it is reasonable to believe that the Tamil people will be reluctant to do anything that might endanger the LTTE's bargaining power in relation to the government. Therefore, a major reason for their silence in the face of the LTTE's abusive behaviour towards the people is their wish to ensure that that the LTTE retains its strength until a just solution is entrenched in the country. Others might see the factor of fear as the main reason for the relative silence of the Tamil people. But as the other factors discussed above demonstrate, fear is not the only reason.

However, the position of sole representative is untenable in a democracy. If the multiplicity of voices emerging from the south of the country speaks of the weakness of democracy, the single voice emanating from the north suggests an authoritarian regime. When the LTTE made its historic decision to pursue the path of peace talks, it implicitly accepted travelling towards democracy. It was listening to the voice of the war-weary people. It would also have been aware that the path of a negotiated peace with international mediation would end in the regaining of democracy. The only viable model of governance that is acceptable to the international community at this point in time is democracy. But this did not deter the LTTE from pressing for a ceasefire and for peace talks. At the general election of April 2004, the LTTE openly backed the Tamil National Alliance and saw it obtain virtually all Tamil majority electorates in Parliament in the north-east, though with a high level of intimidation and vote rigging. Independent election monitors ruled that the elections in the north-east were not free and fair.[30]

CHANGED STRATEGY

A major breakthrough in the peace process occurred when President Chandrika Kumaratunga invited the Government of Norway in February 2000 to act as a third-party intermediary with the LTTE. Prior to this invitation few Sri Lankan politicians were prepared to publicly admit the need for foreign assistance in resolving the conflict. The Norwegian intervention in the Sri Lankan ethnic conflict would count as the most significant event bearing upon a negotiated settlement in over a decade. The last such external intervention was the Indo–Lanka Peace Accord which ended in 1990 with the withdrawal of the Indian Peace Keeping Force. However, much more than that ill-fated accord which the Sri Lankans saw as being in the nature of an Indian imposition, the Norwegian initiative appeared to be an expression of the government and the LTTE's willingness to have the Norwegians play the role of intermediary.

Despite the progress in the peace process since December 2001, there remain concerns about the sustainability of the peace process. Sections of the opposition, who now form the United People's Freedom Alliance government, vigorously opposed the ceasefire agreement as being unconstitutional, a 'sell-out', and as paving the ground for a renewed LTTE military campaign for separation. Spearheading the opposition to the ceasefire agreement was the JVP, a Marxist-oriented political party which attempted to violently overthrow the government in 1971 and again in 1988-9. On both occasions the JVP was militarily suppressed at a huge cost of life, estimated at around 15,000 and 30,000 respectively. Today the JVP is a coalition partner with the Sri Lanka Freedom Party which is headed by President Chandrika Kumaratunga.

The JVP's position draws upon a perception shared by many Sinhalese that the devolution of power is a means of dividing the country along ethnic lines. The fears of the division of the country in the minds of a sizeable proportion of the Sinhalese constitutes a major obstacle to a negotiated solution with the LTTE. Clearly the preferred option of this section of the population is a military solution that would eliminate the LTTE and thereby end the threat to the country's unity.

A second obstacle is the continued rivalry between the government and opposition parties in the Sri Lankan political mainstream, in which the ethnic conflict becomes yet another means of one side embarrassing the other for narrow political gain. Godfrey Gunatilleke writes:

A clear lesson emerging from past failures is that no effort at resolving the conflict will succeed unless there is a broad-based consensus within each community, Sinhala and Tamil, around a solution that is perceived by both as equitable. The internal power struggles within both the communities—Sinhala and Tamil—have continuously thwarted such a process of consensus building. The negotiations took place in a changing configuration of political power with the constant prospect of changes of government, in which the ethnic issue was perceived as being a crucial factor. The history of negotiations up to 1990 show that each of the two major Sinhala-dominated political parties, SLFP and UNP, have endeavoured to reach a political settlement when they have been in power and have opposed or thwarted a settlement when are in opposition. The party in power then opts for an easy way out of the dilemma by withdrawing its proposal. It justifies its action on the ground that they cannot obtain the support of the people.[31]

Gunatilleke continues:

The other feature in the Sinhala–Tamil relations was the incapacity or unwillingness of the Sinhala leadership to resist the well organised, highly vocal pressure groups within their own constituency. This became a recurring characteristic of Sinhala–Tamil negotiations. [As for Bandaranaike himself, his] convictions were not deep enough to oppose the Sinhala leaders who would not concede that the Tamils had genuine grievances or that their aspirations for a share of power were reasonable. Above all, the Tamil issue seemed to be at the periphery of the political agenda, and largely for demographic reasons the dissatisfaction of the Tamils seemed manageable. What pre-occupied Bandaranaike and other Sinhala leaders was the socio-economic socialist agenda and its impact upon the population as a whole.[32]

For many years now, community leaders and political analysts have been calling for a consensus between the two major political parties for a solution to the long-drawn-out ethnic conflict. But in doing so, they may have glossed over the political realities that have kept the two dominant parties apart on the issue. The hard fact is that the Sinhalese community, which by far forms the largest segment of the electorate, is still more or less evenly divided on the question of political reforms that could lead to a political settlement of the ethnic conflict. The general election of 2 April 2004 revealed

Sri Lanka to be a fragmented polity, both politically and ethnically. The main casualty was the United National Party (UNP), which was the main constituent party in the UNF coalition government which sought to lead the country to ethnic peace through compromise. The shocking defeats suffered by the UNP in its urban stronghold of the Colombo district, where it came third in some electorates behind the Buddhist monks of the Jathika Hela Urumaya, reveal that the UNP suffered an erosion even of its urban middle-class support base. The election results indicated that the UNP failed to keep its traditional urban Sinhala Buddhist middle-class base. The fact that the UNP fell to third place behind both the UPFA and JHU in the suburbs of Colombo suggests that the Buddhist monks broke into the UNP's vote, rather into the UPFA's vote, as had been anticipated. This leeching away of the UNP's middle-class base is not due as much to economic factors as it is to the unhappiness with the concessions made to Tamil nationalism in the course of the peace process.

The governmental strategy following the December 2001 election marked a complete shift from that of previous governments, which was to confront the LTTE at every level. The government, led by former Prime Minister Ranil Wickremesinghe during its two years in office was non-confrontational in its approach to the LTTE. This governmental strategy was based on an assessment of the former failures to succeed through confrontation. After the collapse of the peace talks with the LTTE at the very beginning of its term of office in April 1995, the former government declared a full-scale war for peace. The two-pronged military and political strategy was aimed to weaken and sideline the LTTE. But both types of confrontation failed. Instead of being militarily weakened, the LTTE emerged militarily strengthened from the major confrontations of the past.

The government under Prime Minister Wickremesinghe absorbed two important lessons from the former governmental failures. The first was that head-on confrontation would not bring a solution to the ethnic conflict. Accordingly, political and structural reforms de facto rather than de jure, would have to be agreed to by the general population with whom as little information as possible is shared. However, the alternative of explaining everything in detail to the people in order to get them to vote in favour of the settlement was likely to cause too much controversy. There is deep-rooted resistance in the Sinhalese community to fundamental constitutional reform that would lead to power-sharing across the ethnic and regional lines.

Therefore, the measures adopted by the government at the outset of the ceasefire were taken with only a minimum of consultation with the other political parties, the general population or the civil society. These included lifting the security barriers, ending the economic embargo of the north-east and lifting the ban on the LTTE. The success of these measures, however, set a precedent where the government kept on making decisions without either consulting or adequately informing the other stakeholders in society, who, effect, therefore, became passive bystanders in the peace process.

The absence of broad-based consultations and the highly top-down nature of the peace process was a primary reason for its rapid progress at the outset. However, this strategy had several negative results. One major weakness in the current peace process was the lack of a wide base of informed public discussion regarding the peace process. This resulted in a limited output of creative ideas from the ranks of the country's intelligentsia and other socially active sectors. For instance, although the government and LTTE agreed to explore a federal solution, there has been little public discussion on this issue in either academic forums or the media. The limited representation of Muslim interests in most civil society discussions added to the lacuna regarding appropriate representation and pluralism in the envisaged interim arrangements.

The lack of adequate public participation in the peace process was further reflected in the slowing down of civil society activism in relation to the peace process. Although there is an increased amount of funding for peace work, made available by international donors, the capacity of civil society and NGO groups to absorb this failed to increase at a proportionate pace. The involvement of the business community in actively supporting the peace process also declined over time.

A major weakness in the peace process was the exclusion of the opposition. This led to politically motivated criticism of and lack of support for the peace process by the opposition, as it felt no sense of ownership of the process. While this lack of opposition support did not prevent the government from taking bold decisions at the outset, with more complex decisions, the lack of opposition support in Parliament became a major problem, which was accentuated by the fact that the government did not have an integral element of governance under its control, namely the Presidency. This made it difficult for the government to take actions that required the President's consent, as she was bound to refuse them. Therefore, in its two-year period in office, the UNF government of Prime Minister Ranil Wickremesinghe was unable to set up an interim council for the north-east, as it had promised in its election manifesto. The territory militarily controlled by the LTTE, and to which the government's military forces have no access, accounts for about a half of the north-east province, but it controls a much smaller population, amounting to about 25 per cent. The inability of the Sri Lankan state to wrest back control over these areas over the past fifteen years is a key feature of the current situation. A viable strategy for the government would be to accept the situation of dual military power—so long as there is no major fighting between the two armies—one controlled by the government, the other by the LTTE. However, recognizing the fact that the LTTE is unlikely to be content with remaining confined in its political power to the areas currently under its direct military control, it will have to be given greater scope for such power in the north-east areas under government control as well. It is likely that the device of an interim council with a high degree of autonomy will provide the LTTE with this political power.

There was little reason to doubt that the LTTE's proposals in terms of the interim administration they sought for the contested north-east of the country would be ambitious. This was to be expected, as in the case of any first offer in a negotiation. No party that makes a first offer would ask for less; instead they would ask for more. However, in its proposals the LTTE refrained from frontally addressing emotive issues. It made no mention of its own military or the right of the Sri Lankan military to be present in the north-east, or the Sinhalese settlements in the north-east. The LTTE's proposals also did not call for a change in the national flag or anthem or the special place accorded to Buddhism in the Sri Lankan Constitution. Any mention of these could have generated an emotional response from Sinhalese nationalists.

However, a closer scrutiny of the LTTE proposals would reveal that they were maximalist in spirit, as was to be expected from an organization that waged war for the cause of complete Tamil separation from Sri Lanka. The proposals, in sum, call for the establishment of an Interim Self Governing Authority (ISGA) for the north-east in which the LTTE would have an absolute majority of members without an election. Thereafter the proposals indicate that complete autonomy is sought in virtually every aspect of the political and economic life of the people.

The LTTE proposals call for separate institutions to be set up for the north-east in respect of police, judiciary, elections, taxation, local and foreign grants and loans, and trade, among others. There is an assurance that internationally mandated standards of human rights, accountability, multi-ethnic representation, and free and fair elections will prevail. But all the institutions that are to be set up to ensure such good governance practices will be under the sole control of the ISGA which will have an absolute LTTE majority, without having to be subjected to the basic requirement of an election at the outset.

In a society where the spirit of power-sharing is yet to be learnt and practised, obtaining an absolute majority without being subject to the discipline of an election is a potential license for unilateralism. When this potential is coupled with autonomy, the result can be a high degree of control. It is noteworthy that the LTTE's proposals make no provision for integration with the nationally prevailing structures. Viewed in this context it is not surprising that the Sri Lankan government's response to the LTTE proposals was cautious and restrained. The government's immediate response was to say that there were fundamental differences between the LTTE's proposals and those submitted several months earlier by the government.

In its own proposals regarding an interim administration for the north-east, the UNF government specifically excluded matters pertaining to police, land, revenue, and security from the purview of the interim administration. But in the LTTE's counter-proposals, all the above with the exception of security, are considered to be the specific domain of the ISGA. Further, in the government's proposals, while an absolute majority was indeed conceded to the LTTE without having to be tested at an election, provision was made for a minority veto on matters that affect the interests of the Muslim and Sinhalese communities living in the north-east.

On the ground, the Muslims and Sinhalese of the east, who presently constitute over 60 per cent of the population, have strongly protested their inclusion into an LTTE-dominated administration. The Muslims in particular have been vociferous in their opposition because in the Sri Lanka Muslim Congress they have a political party which draws virtually all its strength from the east. The SLMC's first response to the LTTE's proposals was to say that they did not meet Muslim aspirations.

The government's cautious response to the LTTE's proposals was also due to its apprehensions about a backlash against them from Sinhalese nationalists bolstered by opposition political parties. The unfortunate history of post-independence Sri Lankan politics is that opposition parties have seized upon governmental concessions to Tamil parties as betrayals of the Sinhalese to mobilize popular opposition to the government. A major problem is that federalism is not a familiar concept to Sri Lankans. It is not surprising that Sri Lankans know little about federalism when for the past 170 years, since the Colebrook–Camaroun reforms of 1833, Sri Lanka has had a centralized administration. Therefore, there is little practical expertise in this field within the country. Most local commentators on the ills and pitfalls of the federal system have lived most of their lives in one of the most centralized systems of government in the world, which is what the Sri Lankan system has been since the Colebrook–Camaroun reforms. The critiques and fears of federalism come from theory and not from actual experience. This may explain why there is so little constructive discussion about the most appropriate form of federalism for the country.

The powers of regional units in federal systems over police, land, taxation, and judiciary claimed by the LTTE are basic to most federal systems. Of course, in democratic societies federal powers are not only a matter of regional elites wresting powers from central elites, which is presently the case in Sri Lanka, where the interim administration would see the LTTE get power legally transferred to it from the central government. But in true federal systems, there are elaborate systems of checks and balances, which include accountability to higher levels of authority and, ultimately, to the people themselves at free and fair elections. This is a reality that the LTTE needs to realize and respect in the negotiations on the interim administration proposals. In particular, subjecting the LTTE to the discipline of free and fair elections needs to be a prerequisite for the grant of legitimate state powers.

On 3 November 2003, however, a mere three days after the LTTE's submission of its interim administration proposals, President Chandrika Kumaratunga took over three ministries of the government, including the defence ministry. This was done without consultation with the prime minister, but with the constitutional powers vested in her. The president's move plunged the country into a political crisis. She justified her actions on the grounds that the country's unity had been threatened by the prime minister's handling of the peace process, which had led to the strengthening of the LTTE and to the weakening of the government's own position. The LTTE's interim administration proposal was cited by the President and her colleagues as being an example of the dangerous future that lay ahead for the country if the government were to continue with the peace process in the manner that it had been conducting it. As Uyangoda has noted:

> Sri Lanka is in a new stage of rebuilding both the nation and state. As the experience of that failed past demonstrates, the difficult challenge in governing a plural society is about how to correct, through public policy, the injustices of one community without creating new injustices to others. Justice and fairness to all communities in the polity requires a pluralist framework of public policy. This is where political leadership, who incidentally depend on the votes of the majority community should possess the intellectual and political capacity to insulate themselves from sectarian populism of the organised fringe.[33]

It is clear that in the future the building blocks of a negotiated solution would be the non-negotiables of the two sides. On the government side, it would be the unity and territorial integrity of the country. On the LTTE side, it would be the Thimpu principles, which lay claim to the Tamils being a nation with a homeland and the right of self-determination. The constitutional and political arrangements suggested by these determinants would be a variant of federalism and confederalism. Asymmetric federalism, which would provide the Tamil-dominated region more powers than other regions of the country, was suggested by former Prime Minister Ranil Wickremesinghe. It is likely that the devolution of powers to the Tamil-dominated region would be more substantial in contested areas such as education, land, industry, and security. Provision would also have to be made for the protection of the rights of the Tamil-speaking Muslim minority and Sinhalese in the north and east who will come under Tamil majority rule. Further, given the ethnic mix outside the north-east, and the large numbers of Tamils and Muslims outside the north and east, mechanisms to ensure power sharing at the centre and the rights of ethnic minorities countrywide would also need to be found.

The challenge for Sri Lanka today is to find a suitable structure of governance in which two or more peoples can coexist, cooperate, and be partners within a single state without the members of one group being able to unilaterally impose their wishes on the members of the other groups. Sri Lanka's experience with the unitary and centralized system of government is that it has enabled an ethnic majority to monopolize power in a unitary framework and rule over the ethnic minorities. There is a compelling need for a decentralized and plural polity to replace the prevailing constitutional structure. Apart from addressing the grievances of the ethnic minorities, the rise of regional centres of power is likely to change the all or nothing nature of elections. A genuine sharing of power away from the centre, and distributed among the regional and ethnic communities, is the best recipe for a reduction in the level of political violence in society.

NOTES

1. Embassy of the United State, Colombo, Press Release, 11 March 2002.
2. S. Kohobanwickrema, 'A lost referendum', *Island*, 15 December 2001.
3. National Peace Council, *Cost of the War*, Colombo, 2001.
4. Jayadeva Uyangoda, 'Public Policy in Times of Social Tension', *Daily Mirror*, 9 January 2004.
5. K.M. de Silva, *Reaping the Whirlwind: Ethnic Conflict, Ethnic Politics in Sri Lanka* (Penguin, India, 1998), p. 19.
6. Chandrasena Pannila (ed.), *The Mahavamsa* (Colombo: The Anula Press, 1958), Chapters 7-11, p. 42.
7. Gananath Obeysekere, 'The vicissitudes of the Sinhala Buddhist identity through time and change', in Michael Roberts (ed.), *Collective Identities*,

Nationalism and Protest in Modern Sri Lanka (Colombo: Marga Institute, 1979), p. 282.
8. *Ceylon Journal of Historical and Social Studies*, vol. 10, p. 61.
9. Jane Russell, *Communal Politics under the Donoughmore Constitution 1931-47* (Colombo: Tissara Prakashakayo, 1982), p. 187.
10. Ibid., p. 192.
11. K.M. de Silva, *Reaping the Whirlwind*, p. 153. See also, A.J. Wilson, 'Race, Religion and Caste in the Sub-nationalisms of Sri Lanka', in Roberts, *Collective Identities*, p. 468.
12. Ceylon Department of Information, 'Towards a New Era', Selected Speeches of S.W.R.D. Bandaranaike in the Legislatures of Ceylon, Colombo, 1961, p. 395.
13. Russell, *Communal Politics*, p. 286.
14. Ibid., p. 287.
15. Robert N. Kearney, 'Modernization and Political Mobilization in a Plural Society', in Roberts, *Collective Identities*, p. 431.
16. K.M. de Silva, 'Nationalism and the State in Sri Lanka', paper presented at the Asian Regional Workshop on Ethnic Minorities in Buddhist Polities, Colombo, 1985.
17. C.R. de Silva, 'The Impact of Nationalism in Education', in Roberts, *Collective Identities*, p. 451.
18. International Alert, *Sri Lanka: Emergency*, London, 1986.
19. S. Arasaratnam, 'Nationalism in Sri Lanka and the Tamils', in Roberts, *Collective Identities*, p. 56.
20. Personal observations of the present author who I was then in Colombo conducting field research on the ethnic conflict.
21. Agreement between the Government of the United Kingdom of Great Britain and Northern Ireland and the Government of Ireland, April 1998.
22. National Peace Council, p. 28.
23. A.J. Wilson, *S.J.V. Chelvanayakam and the Crisis of Sri Lankan Tamil Nationalism, 1947-77: A Political Biography* (London: C. Hurst & Co., 1994), pp. 86, 105.
24. Rohan Edrisinha, 'Trying Times: Constitutional efforts to resolve armed conflict in Sri Lanka', in *Accord, Demanding Sacrifice: War and Negotiation in Sri Lanka*, ed. Jeremy Armon and Liz Philipson, Conciliation Resources, London in association with Social Services Association, Colombo, Issue 4, August 1998, p. 35.
25. Ibid., p. 29.
26. Ibid., p. 33.
27. Godfrey Gunatilleke, *Negotiations for the Resolution of the Ethnic Conflict*, Marga: Monograph Series on Ethnic Reconciliation, no. 1, 2001, p. 21.
28. Rohan Gunaratne, 'Impact of the Mobilised Tamil Diaspora on the Protracted Conflict in Sri Lanka', in Kumar Rupesinghe (ed.), *Negotiating*

Peace in Sri Lanka: Efforts, Failures and Lessons (London: International Alert, February 1998), p. 303.

29. S.J. Emmanuel, 'Kumaratunga–Prabhakaran Talks: A Northern View', in Rupesinghe (ed.), *Negotiating Peace*, p. 273
30. PAFFREL interim statement on the General Elections 2004, *Daily Mirror*, 4 April 2004.
31. Gunatilleke, *Resolution of the Ethnic Conflict*, p. 51.
32. Ibid., pp. 11-12.
33. Uyangoda, *Daily Mirror*, 9 January 2004.

CHAPTER VI

Terrorism and Subalternity – II: The Marginalization Syndrome in Nepal

DHRUBA KUMAR

Nepal has a history of intermittent political conflicts and active but sporadic armed insurrections. Political violence and systemic repression were recurrent phenomena both under the Rana oligarchy prior to 1951 and during the partyless Panchayat regime between 1960 and 1990. As dissents, protests, and political oppositions were illegitimate, the only viable option for the dissenters of the regimes then was the extra-systemic opposition through underground political movements. In fact, the first ever politically motivated organization with a clear objective of ending the Rana system and reinstating the legitimate leadership of monarchy with the rule of the people's representatives was formed in 1931 with the birth of Prachanda Gorkha, which was influenced by the Bangabhanga movement in Calcutta, British India. The Prachanda Gorkha had decided to pursue violence as a means to resolve the problem of inequality and repression by assassinating all the top members of the Rana family, including the prime minister.[1] Perhaps Prachanda Gorkha was the first political organization to advocate violence as a means to serve political ends in the history of Nepal.

Therefore, the violent policy of Prachanda Gorkha was not only depicted as state treason by the Ranas after all the members of the group were arrested and sentenced to life in prison, it was also alleged that it was 'conspiracious and terroristic' by none other than the father and the founder General Secretary of the Communist Party of Nepal in 1949—Puspa Lal Shrestha. The rationale for denouncing the Prachanda Gorkha movement as 'terroristic', as explained by Puspa Lal, was that it had failed to organize people for the cause.[2] Many in Nepal today have also observed that the Maoists, as the members of the Communist Party of Nepal (Maoist) in their present incarnation since 1995 are called, have also duly failed in organizing people in their mission to overthrow the monarchical state by senseless violence in the name of the 'People's War' with militarily dominant but politically deficient programmes. Their extortions, torture, and indiscriminate killings of the common people in their bid to spread fear and paranoia in society have perceptively caused them to shift from their initial programme of political restructuring of the state to the objective of survival as a political group through violent means. The presence of the Maoists as a violent counter-state force with the mounting threat of systemic destruction without being able to provide a convincing alternative to prevailing order has embedded their dissenting identity with terrorism.

'Terrorism', as the tactic of political violence, indeed, had a hesitant beginning in Nepal in the post-1960 political environment, setting high targets for the resolution of domestic conflicts. The bomb attacks or attempted assassinations of King Mahendra (January 1962) and King Birendra (March 1974), and the hijacking of the RNAC aircraft (June 1973) under the direction of the Nepali Congress party in exile exemplified the extreme measures taken by the disbanded political party with a clear objective of restoring democracy which had been denied through a royal coup in December 1960. On the other hand, the violent communist uprising that begun with the beheading of some landlords in the Jhapa district of eastern Nepal in 1971, under the influence of the Naxalite movement in India, was another instance of political extremism bordering on terroristic means to attain its goal. The bomb blasts in front of the gate of the royal palace, at the reception counter of the five-star Annapurna Hotel, and inside the Rashtriya Panchayat (National Assembly) enclave in 1985 heralded the inauguration as well as the termination of another terrorist attack by an obscure political group, the Janabadi Morcha. These mostly localized and dramatic incidents were not sustained further, except for the sporadic armed rebellions of the Nepali Congress till 1976. Of these, the Nepali Congress movement for the restoration of democracy immediately after the coup had a large following, exerting tremendous pressure on the king and even on the Nepali military sphere engaged in containing the armed rebellion before the outburst of the Sino–Indian War in October 1962.[3]

The Nepali Congress armed struggle, however, had not taken terrorism as a means to force the issue. It had a clear and defined objective and engaged the security apparatuses of the government. It had never indulged in senseless killings of ordinary people to raise the threshold of threat to the state. The bombing episodes against the kings were the handiwork of highly motivated youths, for which B.P. Koirala took moral responsibility as the president of the party.[4] Koirala had justified violence, contextualizing it as a means of political struggle in a situation where the regime was thoroughly repressive and autocratic.[5] Situating the Nepali Congress programme of revolution against the monarchical regime, Koirala had explained the issue of hijacking suggesting that he undertook that decision only because he had not been paid back, as promised, by the Bangladeshis for the stock of arms he had supplied them during their liberation war in 1971, as he needed money to reacquire arms to launch a rebellion against the Panchayat regime in Nepal.[6] Disputing the charges of state treason at the Special Court, Koirala had defended his case with the assertion that he was a revolutionary, not a terrorist. To him, revolution was such a situation in which the active opposition of the mobilized people would put tremendous pressure on the government compelling it to restore the democratic rights of the people. The target of the revolution, according to him, was the political system, unlike individuals who are the targets of terrorism.[7] The Nepali Congress leaders, who were arrested under the charges of state treason immediately after they returned home from exile on 30 December 1976, enjoyed a large domestic followings. Their arrest and trial gave incredible momentum to national politics culminating in nationwide anti-government protests and rallies. Consequently, the government in Nepal had to not only withdraw the state treason cases against them but also agree for a national referendum for the choice of a political system by the people in 1979 against the burgeoning mass upheavals.

Contrarily, the failure of the violent Jhapa movement of the CPN (Marxist-Leninist) to garner the support and endorsement of the people and other radical communist groups had led to their suppression and dispersion. The murderous campaigns against the 'class enemies', was not supported, particularly by the extremist CPN (Fourth Convention) group, which castigated the Jhapa movement for the 'terrorist tactics adopted', depicting it as a 'form of semi-anarchy' which 'cannot be called Marxist-Leninist'. Actually the Jhapa movement was the first Maoist uprising, which the Maoists, involved in the current 'People's War', had denigrated and which many of the former Maoists constituting the current CPN (UML) party had initiated. It is thus interesting to note that the CPN (Marxist-Leninist) that currently wears the Unified Marxist-Leninist (UML) tag and the first political party to officially designate the Maoists as 'completely terrorists', happens to be the offshoot of the Fourth Convention formed in 1974.[8] The CPN (UML) coalition government instituted *Dhami* Commission had called the Maoists' activities 'politically disguised terrorism' which should be dealt with accordingly, with the forging of a national consensus between different political parties.[9]

Situating terrorism in the context of Nepal is therefore a relative and a relational concept. No definitive meaning can be imparted to the violent activities carried out by the Left-splintered groups in the country because this social phenomenon is described much in relation to political constructs and is therefore subjective in comprehension. From the perspective of the group glorifying violence as an endemic struggle against the state because the latter is, by definition, an embodiment of violence and should therefore be negated by violence, terrorism would be justified against the supra-historical cause of the state being an expression of violent enterprise. Violence is therefore inevitable in the context of articulating political space by the impoverished people living under the exploitative situation and oppression rendered by the agencies of the state. The creative potential of violence involving a majority of the people thus becomes an agency for social transformation, in which violence would become a means for attaining the desired goal.

The Maoists in Nepal who are indulging in anti-state violence have understandably defined their acts as revolutionary violence with a missionary zeal to transform the state from being exclusive to becoming inclusive, from being oppressive to becoming responsive, and from being unitary to becoming a federal republic. They claim that the reason for their violence is the consequence of the challenges for livelihood and is aimed against the perennial situation of poverty, exploitation, and oppression. The 'People's War', according to them, is the culmination of a sustained support of the masses against oppression. Thus, under the rubric of mass revolt, their targets and execution of violence cannot be depicted as terrorism. But the regulatory function of the state's statutory law does not recognize their claim. The attitude and the reaction of the state agencies in accordance with the statutes of the country count in identifying whether the action taken is simply criminal or terrorism. As the sub-national or non-state violence is usually anti-state, the state in question naturally becomes a party to defining its role and response to its antagonist.

Although simply branding the violence caused by the non-state as terrorism is a common practice of the state, there is, however, the absence of any normally acceptable definition to determine what action is terrorism and what is not. To go back to assassination attempts by the Nepali Congress rebels on the kings of Nepal; were these attempts terroristic or revolutionary? The simple definition, according to the statutory law of the land, would definitely categorize them as terrorism of a high order involving regicide with empirical evidence requiring no theoretical amplification. Yet theoretically, it would be difficult to prove these acts were terroristic simply by negating the motives. Although the immediacy of the impacts of the actions and on-the-spot behaviour of the bomb throwers were undoubtedly terroristic in category; these acts were inadequate to explain the concept of terrorism because those endorsing 'violence from below' might vigorously contest statist definitions. This issue is of particular interest and import in the context of the Maoists' insurgency when violence has become a everyday experience for the people of Nepal for the last nine years, since they gained the rights to freedom of expression and legitimate political opposition under the democracy that the people of Nepal had succeeded in restoring in the country in 1990. With the change in the political–legal frame post 1990, a political resolution to the societal challenges facing the country could have been sought through the intensification of systemic opposition without the violence and armed struggle that is abnegating the democratic system restored through popular struggle.

Terrorism, unfortunately, appeared with all its cruel manifestations in Nepal when the country was facing the challenges for democratic consolidation. To articulate the views for the destruction of multi-party democracy along with constitutional monarchy violently undermining the laws governing the state was presumably irreconcilable. Thus, the expression of terrorism and understanding its characteristics are complex as well as problematic because the definition of terrorism does not rest only on the conceptualization of the issue. It is behavioural in essence. The pattern of behaviour of persons indulging in violence can be one explanatory tool for understanding whether the 'violence' in question constitutes terrorism. Accordingly terrorism is defined as the 'warfare deliberately waged against civilians with the purpose of destroying their will to support either leaders or policies that the agents of such violence find objectionable'.[10] The underlying notion of control that this definition of terrorism imparts has perhaps led to another definition suggesting that 'the proximate aim is to instil terror; the ultimate end is control'.[11] Perhaps the cold-blooded murder of a seventy-nine year-old man by slitting his throat for refusing to give a donation, the gunning down of the chairperson of the Maoists' Victims Association for burning the effigies of the top Maoist leaders in Kathmandu, setting vehicles carrying medicines to villages on fire, or not allowing ambulances conveying maternity patients to proceed to hospitals in the name of *bandha*, resulting in maternity deaths, are cases of instilling terror as well as assuring control on the society the Maoists are supposed to win over to their cause.

Can the frequency of such occurrences be considered politically motivated and thus defined as revolutionary acts or essentially explained as outright terrorism? Are these acts an expression, of enhancing the self-esteem of the people committed to violence in the league of Frants Fanon, and generating the 'sentiment of glory' for the people in search of self-identity, which Sorel had championed?[12] Imprecision on the definition of terrorism should not, however, cloud the intellectual judgement on such acts of violence by simply blanketing them with political connotations. Neither can intensification of such violent acts be simply explained as a means of gaining political space by the non-state, making people easy prey for counter-state activities. Spreading fear instead of generating hope can never be the essence of revolution. The distinction is that terrorism breeds fear whereas revolution breeds hope.

The henious crimes committed by the Maoists cannot be defined as acts serving the cause of a revolution championed behind the façade of subalternity. The Maoists' violence cannnot be described and defined as the acts of the powerless against the powerful and 'violence from below' when poor villagers are mercilessly killed, their households looted, their children kidnapped and forced to join the guerrillas, and village schools turned into rebel training camps where education denied. Nor can the Maoists' activities be understood as the struggle between the dominant and subordinate groups or the 'politics of the people' against the hegemonic state elites.[13] This is not the effort made by the disempowered group of poverty-stricken and marginalized people for their empowerment. Rather, the Maoists' violence has further disempowered the people from their rights to security and rights to development. Thus, when the counter-state activities of the Maoists are screened, they essentially lack the phenomenon defined in Gramscian fashion, implying the constitution of a majority of social force within the society,[14] that is, the subalterns composed of peasant and artisans ignored in the elitist historiographies of the state.[15] Despite the Maoists, claim of a nationwide following, they have yet to become the 'weapons of the weak',[16] thus, far removed from the historiography of subalternity. The context of marginality as well as subalternity is removed from the Maoists' violence as their activities have not attracted but repulsed the people on the periphery.

The objectives of this paper are, therefore, two-fold. Instead of searching for the reasons of insurgency and violence as explained by the observers of the Nepali political scene—both national and foreign—and depicted by the state agencies, we will broadly attempt to understand how the Maoists' have rationalized the 'People's War' and its cause. Second, by inquiring into their case, we will attempt to examine the Maoist insurgency, contrary to the explanation posited by them with an alternative perspective grounded in the reality and practice of insurgency. To begin with, the first section briefly discusses the manifest causes of insurgency and justification deployed for the violent transformation of the state from the divergent perspectives. It locates the structural causes to situate the Maoist insurgency within the parameters of the state-society relations complicated by the process of marginalization. The next section narrates the principled positions that the Maoists' have taken and explained for upholding the armed insurrections and their programme of restructuring the state. The third section follows with an analysis of a crucial question: whither Maoists insurgency? This section analyse the effects of the Maoist insurgency on the national scene, which here is depicted as the marginalization of the marginalized. It is argued in this section that the militaristic pursuit of the Maoists in the conduct of the 'People's War' has largely condemned the affected or the marginalized people socially, economically, and politically, forcing them to live as destitute, in whose cause the Maoists have understandably taken up arms. Although the Maoists have achieved considerable military acumen through their violent activities in the past nine years, they have, however, transformed themselves into a terror trove as far as the general masses are concerned. This contradiction is dealt with in the final section of the chapter, by analysing the gap between the political programme and the military pursuits of the Maoists and recapitulating the discourse on the 'People's War' with the evidences garnered.

INTERROGATING POVERTY-MARGINALIZATION-VIOLENCE LINKAGES

Drawing on the living experiences of the causes and consequences of political violence and being witness to the history unfolding, it would be difficult to pass a clinically detached judgement on the why and how of the Maoists insurgency. This chapter is thus written as the present author's understanding of conversations with the unfolding violence wreaked in the name of the 'People's War'. It is also a reflection on the events that have caused untold miseries in the lives of the people whose only fault was being poor and powerless. Thus, when asked about the causes of such an unfortunate turn in Nepali history, the intelligentsia, political leaderships, industrialists and businesspersons, along with commoners, invariably identify poverty, destitution, discrimination, and marginalization. Understandably, poverty as a concept encompassing the sense of denial and deprivation has been recognized for a long time as a causal factor driving desperate men to take up arms and organize violence. The centrality of poverty and inequality has been contextualized as a cause of conflict and violence when grievances relating to social, economic, and political deprivation become acute in countries facing underdevelopment and social exclusion as in happening in Nepal.[17]

This mass-level analysis of violence has been intricately linked with the activities of the non-state against the state in search of justice, equity, security, and empowerment. The causes of conflict and violence are usually located in the structural condition of the state leading to political, economic, social, cultural and perceptual incongruities in state-society relations. At the institutional-political and cultural–perceptual levels, most of the analyses veered towards identifying the root causes for the rise of the Maoist insurgency in Nepal as the dominance and hegemony of the minority but politically powerful groups over the majority of the powerless people through their systemic marginalization. One of the crucial historical markers of the process of marginalization deliberately pursued by the dominant elites in post-unification Nepal after 1769 was the confiscation of the land of the vanquished people and its redistribution among them as *Birta* and *Jagir* and enriched the power and dominance of the ruling class by virtually reducing the common people to a state of destitution and submission.[18] The confiscation of the land was not only prioritised for the rulers' enrichment; it was also a property to be distributed to the army supporting them, who in turn had sustained the Hindu religious identity of the state celebrated by the ruling class.[19]

Another historical marker of marginalization was the institutional-political construction of the state rooted in the principle of social exclusion which the Hinduized caste system codified in the *Muluki Ain* 1854 has perniciously influenced. The process of Hinduization of the state has become the critical intrusive category conforming to the pattern of 'monoethnic and monoreligious' hegemony of the political elites by legitimizing their role through constitutional, electoral, and developmental processes in a multi-ethnic and multireligious society. At the cultural–perceptual level, the dominance of Hill Hinduism is pronounced with the marginalization of the *Janajatis* (ethnics) on the basis of culture, *Dalits* (untouchables) on the basis of caste, and *Madeshi* (Tarai people) on the basis of geography.[20] Through the institutional and cultural means employed by the state an asymmetrical power relationship in the state–society interaction is created in articulating hierarchical social order by the powerful groups to restrict the access of outsiders to power through social closure. Dor Bahadur Bista has succinctly described this phenomenon as the *apno manchhe* (one's own men) syndrome leading to the evolution and consolidation of patriarchal and patrimonial systems.[21] The most articulated form of contention has therefore emerged in the context of marginalization ranging from caste, class, geographic to gender discrimination. The discourses burgeoning in Nepal have led to identifying the structural incongruity embedded in the political order, pointing towards the ritualization of policies induced by the rulers through legitimizing the mechanics of state-craft.

Although poverty, inequality and marginalization in Nepal as the causes of the deepening crisis have been recognized for some time,[22] and the concept of the 'failed development' syndrome is simply tied to the symptom manifested in the Maoist insurgency,[23] correlating these as precipitants of the conflict is still difficult. Such a situation can definitely be acknowledged as the crucial factor for significantly increasing grievances with the possibility of causing the poor people to resort to violence. The rapidly deteriorating life-chances of the people with the loss of resources for sustainability and the absence of hope for renewal have further exposed their vulnerability in relation to their survival. The struggle for survival can reasonably be expected to be more determined and violent. But in the case of Nepal, such argument would be presumptive rather than persuasive. First, there is no prior evidence of a poverty–insurgency linkage in the history of Nepal except from the pursuit of territorial conquest by the Gorkhali rulers.[24] That was definitely a case of organized violence (aggression/war) from above not below. Second, poverty, destitution, deprivation, and exploitation had forced people to migrate from their domiciles instead of fighting back either at the local or at the national level, which is vividly expressed in the narratives of the novel *Basain*.[25] This tradition has continued today as a consequence of the Maoists 'People's War' due to which the number of the internally displaced people (IDP) has been recorded as high as 2.5 million.[26] Third, the organizing ability of the poor people in the country is yet to be proven. Even peasant movements that were politically driven, motivated by the vicissitudes caused by divisive communist activities, as exemplified by the Jhapa uprising along with the Piskar and Chhintang events, were violently crushed by the government.[27] Fourth, the cultural and social attributes of the people who tend to believe in fatalism makes it difficult to imagine that the poverty-stricken people of Nepal can transform themselves from being victims to perpetrators of violence.[28]

As noted earlier, the process of marginalization dates back to the days of the formation of the Nepali state. This persistent phenomenon was, in reality, the cause of political opposition bringing the forces of political parties into play, with occasional struggles, culminating in the *Jana Andolan* in 1990 to change the status quo. The mass movement of 1990 has recognized the forces of opposition by creating a situation for mediating societal demands as politically legitimate. The Maoists, who initially participated in the open political fray through the parliamentary process, had also pursued their oppositional role by placing a socially tenable 40-point memorandum before the government.[29] But suddenly they chose violence as inevitable to change the status quo. The 40-point memorandum of demands mostly embedded with societal grievances, was politically relevant. These demands were also inclusive of the concerns of the major political parties and governments, as well as the people at large. Except for two or three demands,[30] a comparable identification of the socio-economic problems can also be found in the consecutive Five-Year-Plan documents produced by governments since 1956, and the 40-point demands posed by the Maoists in 1996. Between these two dates, a period of four decades, the social and economic problems facing the country have been the same, the contending issues are the same, and the commitments made by different governments are identical. The problems are poverty and underdevelopment, social inequalities and marginalization, discrimination and destitution, social craving and denial.[31]

The 40-point demands that the Maoists put to the government

under the banner of the United People's Front Nepal (UPFN) party was not only a consensus document amongst them, but it could also have been used to form a broad national consensus through popular mobilization for an endurable negotiated settlement of societal grievances, albeit with some difficulties on the issues pertaining to radical socio-political reform. The reformative agenda of the Maoists constituting their demands could perhaps have been pursued more conveniently by engaging the state, particularly on fourteen demands related to the people's livelihood, thus exposing the government's rigidity. But the Maoists ultimately discarded this non-violent option of negotiation in favour of armed struggle citing the government's neglect as an excuse and that the desired systemic reform could only be achieved through the 'People's War' and the establishment of the 'new state'.[32]

The imperative of the 'People's War' and the inevitability of the armed struggle has long been an issue of ideological contention and debates even between and within different communist factions in Nepal. The Maoists, who had resisted from participating in the *Jana Andolan* in 1990, as a part of the mainstream political forces but had gone their own way in organizing the people's movement, neither recognized the success of the *Jana Andolan* nor endorsed the 1990 Constitution because their earlier demand for election to the constituent assembly had gone unheeded.[33] Notwithstanding their reluctance to contest national elections, they had, however, formed the UPFN in January 1991 as a national front of the CPN-Unity Centre to expose the inadequacy of the multiparty system while simultaneously adopting a resolution to form the people's army and advance their revolutionary programme at the first national convention of the Unity Centre along with the decision to participate in elections.[34] They were rewarded with nine seats in the 1991 election, to become the third largest party in the House of Representatives.

The Unity Centre, however, did not last long enough to pursue its revolutionary programme in the Parliament as a consequence of its split and the complete ruin of the faction contesting the mid-term elections in 1994. Another faction of the Unity Centre that was denied rights to contest the elections by the Election Commission went underground and emerged as the CPN (Maoist) party in 1995, which in its March Plenum of the Central Committee, had decided for the armed struggle, 'targeting confiscation of lands from the feudals and landlords and distributing them amongst the landless and poor peasants'. It was further noted that the Maoists' Central Committee meeting nearly a year later in January 1996, had concluded with the decision to launch the 'People's War' on 13 February 1996.[35] If this was the case, the 40-point memorandum of the Maoists submitted to the government on 4 February with an ultimatum for a response by 17 February 1996 had no rationale other than to distract the people from the impending 'People's War'.[36] By implication, this means that the Maoists' armed struggle was apparently caused by factors other than poverty, destitution, discrimination and marginalization, despite these being contingent to their pursuing their goal domestically.

THE MAOISTS' POSITION

While reinterpreting the Maoist violence with hindsight, one cannot negate the critical influence of the ideology based on Marxism–Leninism–Maoism, in which the CPN (Maoists) are indoctrinated, and through the lens of which they understand and explain their own domestic situation and the world order. With these ideological moorings, the Maoists have firmly projected themselves as the vanguard of the international communist movement. Being a member of the Revolutionary Internationalist Movement (RIM), the Maoist movement has explained the 'People's War' as a part of the international communist movement the fate of which will be decisive not only for the CPN (Maoists) in Nepal but also for the world. The then General Secretary of the CPN (Maoists), Prachanda (Puspa Kamal Dahal), who has admitted that there was international involvement in the preparation and execution of the 'People's War' right from the beginning on ideological ground,[37] arguably has taken a lesson from the international communist experiences in support of his contention that an 'objective revolutionary situation always prevails in oppressed countries' and Nepal is not an exception. Accordingly, the launching of the 'People's War' was explained by the ideological formulation of the historical situation defined under the 'semi-feudal and semi-colonial' condition of the country which, according to Prachanda, was ripe for revolution.[38]

A consciously and carefully constructed explanation for the

imperative of the 'People's War' is presented by the Maoists' ideologue, Baburam Bhattarai, in his much publicized pamphlet 'The Political-Economic Rationale of the People's War' which coherently articulates his case suggesting that the revolution has become a necessity since all the possibilities of reform in the system have been exhausted. The post 1990 polity has failed to resolve the central problem concerning the national question generated by semi-feudalism and semi-colonialism. It has entrenched and expanded 'regional disparities and spatially uneven development' with 'growing social inequality resulting from the process of concentration and centralization inherent in the dynamics of capitalism'. Bhattarai testifies the reason for the initiation of the 'People's War' with empirical evidences asserting that:

> [The] People's war was initiated with a proclaimed aim of establishing a new democratic socio-economic system and state by overthrowing the present socio-economic structure and state. [This] move should be understood in the context of Nepal's gradual decline . . . in terms of various criteria of development. Seventy-one per cent of its population falls below the absolute poverty level; nearly half of the national income is in the hands of the richest 10 per cent. . . . More than 60 per cent of the total population is illiterate, more than 90 per cent of the population lives in rural areas and 81 per cent of the labour force is engaged in backward agricultural occupations. Ten per cent are unemployed and 60 per cent are underemployed or in disguised unemployment. . . . It is no secret that the present reactionary state has been peddling various attractive slogans along with Five-Year Plans since the last 50 years, but the problems has been further aggravated with deteriorating socio-economic condition of the country after the completion of each plan period. . . . In this context it is necessary to identify the root cause or causes of this condition. . . . [Thus] history compels us to dispense with the feudal, comprador, and bureaucratic capitalist classes hindering the development of Nepal and to hand over the responsibility of organizing a new and higher form of social system (the new democratic system) to the progressive classes (i.e. workers, peasants, petty bourgeoisie, and national bourgeoisie). The People's war is the inevitable instrument of this historic New Democratic revolutionary transformation.[39]

Further, in an interview to Li Onesto, Prachanda complimented Bhattarai while replying to the question about explaining the objective condition and the material basis for initiating the People's War in Nepal:

First of all, I want to respond to this question in ideological terms. Nepal is a semi-feudal and semi-colonial country, and MLM (Marxism-Leninism and Maoism) suggests that in oppressed countries like this, an objective revolutionary situation prevails. This is the ideological basis from which we started to study the concrete situation, because the main thing is ideological clarity, and through the course of class struggle, mass movements, mass struggle and mainly ideological struggle inside the communist movement, we came to the conclusion that a situation prevails in Nepal for initiating the People's War. . . . Nepal is a small and poor country. More than 85 per cent of the [Nepali] population lives in rural areas [and they] are very oppressed. Feudal relations—the feudal forms of exploitation and oppression—are very severe in rural areas. People suffered very much from different kinds of oppression and exploitation. [Under different governments, the historical experiences of Nepal led it to] become a semi-feudal country [during the British presence in India]. When the British left India, Nepal became a semi-colony of Indian expansionism.[40]

The political and economic rationale provided for the launching of the 'People's War' is quite understandable as the situation in the country has not improved, despite the indications of certain growth pockets. For example, the inequality of income distribution has widened the gulf between the rich and the poor. Records show that the richest 20 per cent of the people possessed 44.8 per cent of the GDP in comparison to 5.9 per cent by the poorest 20 per cent between 1984-5 and 1995-6.[41] Data for the year 2000 shows close to nine million people as income-poor in Nepal.[42] It is commonly acknowledged that poverty is largely a rural phenomenon in Nepal where 85 per cent of the people live in rural areas and the incidence of rural poverty is 44 per cent, in comparison to 23 per cent in urban areas. Poverty in the mountainous region is significantly higher than the national average, and in more remote mid-and-far western regions it is as high as 70 per cent.[43] Although the national per capita income is $236, income inequality has sharply increased between the urban and the rural population. A representative data set based on a nationwide household survey in 1997 suggests that the country's average per capita was $142 with a regional variation of $298 for the urban areas and $131 for rural areas. In comparative terms, the people living in Kathmandu—the capital of the country—were most affluent, with a per capita income of $446, against $146 in the eastern Tarai, $110 in the mountains, and $107 in the western Tarai.[44] According to ICIMOD, the hill and mountainous districts of the mid and far-western Nepal are the worst cases of under-development where extreme poverty and deprivation persist.[45] Bhattarai, thus, has noted that:

> The most disadvantaged regions within the country include those inhabited by indigenous people. . . . They have been left behind in the historical development process because of the blockade of their path to independent development and the imposition of socio-cultural oppression along with economic oppression, with the backing of the state, by forces that came from outside. Thus, it is quite natural that the question of oppression of the eastern, central and western hills, where Mongoloid people are numerically predominant or of the Tarai regions where Austro-Dravidian people still survive appears as a form of national oppression. In these areas, the regional and the 'national' questions are intertwined.[46]

The premium on development, though, has been the most important concern of every government formed in Nepal, the practice, however, has belied the popular expectations. Governments under democracy were privileged by the popular mandate, which they used to fulfil their personal aggrandisement. By adopting several resolutions in the House of Representatives to increase the perks and privileges of parliamentarians and other high officials, including the facility for tax-free vehicle imports by introducing the Pajero culture, in connivance with the major opposition communist party in 1996, the government performed disappointingly in a situation of burgeoning Maoist insurgency which began the same year.[47] Perhaps the poverty of the power elites and their economic insecurity caused by the competitive political environment under democracy tempted them to use state authority for their personal aggrandizement rather than addressing the challenges facing the country. Such a policy of organized political opportunism was also exemplified by the passing of a bill on the provision of pensions for parliamentarians.

The presence of the communist parties in both the houses of the parliament and even in successive governments, either in minority or coalition forms, made no material difference to their bourgeoisie democratic counterparts in the sphere of policymaking. Moreover, it was observed that the representatives of the CPN (UML) particularly in contravention of their Leftist ideology, had converted the parliament into a 'milch cow'.[48] By that time, as per the official data, the national poverty record was 42 per cent of the total population, which was numerically around 9-10 million. Despite the programme of poverty alleviation and economic development, poverty, by then, had actually increased 'at an annual rate of more than three per cent and the number of poor has absolutely doubled in the past 20 years'.[49] Unemployment and underemployment have sharpened the income inequalities as 3,00,000 people join the labour force per annum of which hardly 15 per cent manage to get employment.

The situation was further problematized by the dominance of the same religious and caste group in representing the state. Political upheavals in Nepal remained mostly state-and-power centric despite struggles being conveniently projected as democratic struggles against despotic regimes. No substantial changes occurred in the state-society relationship even under the democratic regime in the 1990s, except that from being partyless it became a party system. Except from electoral majoritarian rulership, the governance under democracy did not reconceptualize the role of the state. The failure to re-conceptualize this role, which is intricately linked with the state of poverty and the social exclusion restricting representation, had constricted the process of democratization, thus forgoing the decentralization of power. Poverty under democracy did not only subsume the income inequalities, it also became a symbol of denial of security, autonomy, and self-esteem to the people whose contributions for democratic restoration in the country were no less significant that those of the leaderships of political parties. Their growing sense of betrayal by the political parties and marginalization of their status in the process of creating a cohesive domestic identity clashed directly against their multicultural identities, and against the homogeneous control and access to economic and political power by the corrupt political elites, who replicated the 'thatched huts and stucco palaces' tradition with the denial of rights and resources to the majority to dissuade them from the political authority.[50]

The politics of consolidating power by the dominant group and its refusal to broaden the base of participation and representation of the majority has resulted in the development of a belief in the inability of the state to integrate its socially divergent groups. The challenge to integration, however, is not an unintended but intended effect of the process of institutionalizing polity with the upholding the sectarian interests. The nuance of tensions can therefore be found in the institutional-political and cultural-perceptual variations of the people sharpened by the sense of marginalization. The process of marginalization as a cause of triggering the Maoist insurgency can therefore be explained within the framework of the nature of the state that evolved under the monarchical system of governance since the formation of the Nepali state and the historical undercurrents of the struggle between the different forces of inclusion and exclusion. The evident marginalization of the majority of the people through desecularizing the state with continued discriminatory practices in preserving political power in the hands of the three dominant high-caste people, primarily the Brahmins, Chhetris and Newars, in bureaucracy, political parties, parliament, government and judiciary, etc., has become the focus of contention. Table 6.1 is thus a quantification of the misrepresentation of nationalities in the state structure.

Towards this end, the Constitution of Nepal 1990, has not only become a bone of contention in theory, it has also become a controversial document in practice. Although the Constitution 1990 forbids the formation of ethnic, and religious, regional political parties from contesting elections (Article 112 [3] of the constitution) on the basis of which the Election Commission had denied registration to the three Mongoloid political parties to contest elections, the former has, however, permitted the regional based Sadbhavana Party representing the *Madeshi* people and the Shiv Sena Nepal—an overtly Hindu religious party—to contest elections. Although none of the political parties advocating sectarian, religious and partisan interests had made any imprint on the electoral politics in the 1991, 1994, and 1999 national elections, and the preference for mainstream politics was displayed by the voting behaviour of a certain consistency, the electoral process was considered thoroughly discriminatory and a contest for mis-representation rather than representation of the popular will.[51]

Evidence from the surveys of five districts situated in different geographical terrains suggest that the contesting political parties had made the electoral process the first victim of the election campaigns. Power centrism and power play were the two prominent characteristics of the electioneering, leading to the marginalization

TABLE 6.1: INTEGRATED NATIONAL INDEX OF GOVERNANCE BASED ON SOCIAL GROUPS 1999

Institutions	*Dominant Group*		*Marginalized Group*				*Total*
	B+C+T*	*Newar*	*Madeshi*	*Janajati*	*Dalit*	Others	
Judiciary	181	32	18	4	0	0	235
Constitutional Bodies	14	6	3	2	0	0	25
Cabinet	20	3	5	4	0	0	32
Parliament (Both Houses)	159	20	46	36	4	0	265
Public Administration	190	43	9	3	0	0	245
Political Leadership	97	18	26	25	0	0	166
DDC/VDC/Municipalities	106	30	31	23	0	0	190
Industry and Commerce	7	20	15	0	0	0	42
Academic Leadership	75	11	7	2	1	1	97
Cultural/Professional	85	22	0	6	0	0	113
Science/Technology	36	18	6	2	0	0	62
Civil Society	41	8	4	1	0	0	54
Total	1,011	231	170	108	5	1	1,526
Percentage	66.5	15.2	11.2	7.1	0.3	0.1	100
Population %	31.6 %	5.6 %	30.09 %	22.2 %	8.7 %	n.a.	100
Differences %	+34.9 %	+9.6 %	-19.7 %	-15.1 %	-8.4 %		

Note: *B+C+T = Brahmin, Chhetri and Thakuri.

Source: Parsuram Tamang, *Racism and Discrimination in the New Millennium Nepal*, (Kathmandu: Nepal Tamang Ghedung, 2001). See also, Govinda Neupane, *Nepalko Jatiya Prashna* (Kathmandu: Centre for Development Studies, 2000).

of the actual voters in the winding spree of winning the elections in which 'violence, death, abduction, kidnapping, booth capturing, intimidation and coercion of polling agents and voters' with the use of state machinery are the main feature. The real voters never saw the ballot papers but votes were cast in their names each time the elections were held. In the electoral contest for the 'winner takes all' majoritarian political system, the 'political parties had become the new incarnation of the traditional feudal lords denying rights to the minorities for their representation in the political mainstream'.[52] Perhaps for this reason, political representation in Nepal has remained top heavy with the composition of the dominant caste groups, as in other spheres of the national system. Table 6.2 shows the dominance of the high caste people in Nepal's electoral history and the national polity.

TABLE 6.2: CASTE/ETHNIC COMPOSITION OF LEGISLATURES

(in Percentage)

	Democratic Phase	*Panchayat Phase (1960-90)*			*Post-1990 Democracy*		
Ethnic/Caste	*1959*	*1964-79*	*1981*	*1986*	*1991*	*1994*	*1999*
Brahmin	27.5	23.5	14.81	21.44	36.60	44.39	46.34
Chhetri	31.2	35.5	34.82	38.68	17.07	18.53	17.07
Newar	03.7	13.0	08.15	06.60	06.80	06.34	06.34
Hill Tribes	15.6	14.9	21.48	17.51	16.60	11.70	12.19
Tarai Castes	22.0	11.4	18.10	13.86	21.01	18.53	17.07
Others	00.0	01.0	02.60	02.19	00.50	00.48	00.97
Total	100.0	100.0	100.00	100.00	100.00	100.00	100.00

Sources: Results of House of Representatives, 1991, 1994 and 1999, Election Commission, Kathmandu; Harka Gurung, 'Representing an Ethnic Mosaic', *Himal*, May/June 1992.

The figures in Table 6.2 exemplify the popular alienation with the post 1990 situation, which the Maoists, who were also denied the right to contest 1994 elections, had tried to exploit in their effort to expedite their programme. Given the predominance of the high-caste group in every national sphere, the Maoists have identified their social and economic programmes with ethno-politics and political programmes with the aim of empowering the minorities and gender groups.[53] The Constitution is again at the heart of contention as it posits the concept of 'Hindu State' against the 'multiethnic and multilingual' characteristics. Although the Constitution has apparently recognized minority rights, there is, however, little discernible impact in practice. The limits to minority rights under democracy despite pressure for the democratization of the social sphere, have exacerbated social tensions as the electoral-majoritarian multi-party democratic process clashes with the actual-majoritarian demands for broader representation.

Discrimination against minorities is recorded as a historical marker by the Nepal Federation of Nationalities (NEFAN) identifying 26 provisions in the constitution and 49 legal Acts that discriminate against indigenous nationalities.[54] Despite the constitutional advocacy of equality of all citizens before the law, gender insensitivity has also been exposed by another study conducted by the Forum for Women, Law and Development (FWLD) suggesting that 18 laws/ sections/rules, 2 rules in their entirety, and 67 schedules/annexes/ forms in 54 different laws, including the constitution, have upheld discriminatory provisions against women.[55] Similarly, no fundamental change in the situation of the Dalits can be observed during the post 1990 set-up in the sphere of their cultural and caste-based oppression. Conversely, the mounting evidence of repression against their resistance in the name of preserving 'traditional practice', in accordance with the amended *Muluki Ain* 1992,[56] has sharpened the frustration of the Dalits who constituting 13.6 per cent of the total population of the country.[57] For these people, the Nepali state remains not only oppressive but it has also become increasingly theocratic in practice.

The political programme of the Maoists, which is concomitant with establishing a New Democratic state by defeating the forces of semi-feudalism and semi-colonialism, thus articulates these societal grievances. Explaining the main objective of the 'People's War' as a process of liberating people from both oppressive and exploitative situations, they have primarily developed their policies and programmes comprehending the situation faced by the ethnic and disaffected people. Although the Maoist insurgency is neither for separatism nor for secessionism, its leadership had earlier promised the right to self-determination to the ethnic people by conceding the right to secession.[58] Though initially appealing, this policy of appeasement of equating the Maoist-ethnic compact is understood to have fanned the flames of ethnic conflict in the country, where more than ten ethnic fronts are operating with a prominent demand for declaring Nepal a secular state.[59] In their much-publicized 75-point programme, the Maoists have committed to de-link the state from religion by guaranteeing equal treatment to all nations/ nationalities and languages, gender equality with regard to parental property rights, and resolution of ethnic problems within the framework of national autonomy in the New Democratic/People's Democratic System.[60] This altered scheme has been introduced in a country which is presently debating these issues seriously but is still to be embroiled in the kind of deep ethnic, religious, and even class, cleavages deemed necessary for the eruption of large-scale violence. Neither the passions nor the emotions of the ethnic/indigenous people are tied to the violence attributed to the Maoists, whose methods of violence are indiscriminate. This has also led to a division of the ethnic movement into pro and anti-Maoist camps in the shape of NEFAN and ANNA (All Nepal Nationalities Association) respectively.[61]

With the introduction of the URPC 75-point programme as a sounding board for the future of the statecraft embedded in the federal structure constituting the four-tiered central, regional, district, and village/town organizations, the Maoists have divided the country into nine autonomous regions of which six have been formed on the basis of ethnicity and the remaining three on regional classifications.[62] It would be of interest to note at this juncture that the Maoists have announced the formation of these autonomous regions one after another in rapid succession between 9 January and 2 February 2004, of which two are headed by politburo members and six by central committee members with one yet to be nominated. With the principle of 'Politics in Command', the Maoists have clearly stated that the basic policies of the state would be democratic centralism with the leadership of the proletariat in every sector commensurate with mass line and supplemented by the unified People's Liberation Army under the control of the Chairman of the Central Committee of the Communist Party. On the economic front, the state priority would be agrarian revolution with the 'land to the tiller' as the central tenet, the abolition of the feudal remnant practices and the *Guthi* system developed by the Newars for their community works, along with the labour-intensive industrialization of the country.

Of late the Maoists have also focused heavily on the abolition of monarchy as a core issue of their struggle, particularly after the palace massacre on 1 June 2001. By spearheading the argument that the struggle has been ongoing to completely establish, first a bourgeois democratic system, and second a capitalist republic, the Maoists have asserted that the elimination of the monarchy and its control of the armed forces is inevitable. Arguing that constitutional monarchy is incompatible with a semi-feudal society, the Maoists have concluded that the Nepali monarchy has been the crux of all the social problems, as it is the source of oppression, without the abolition of which it would be impossible even to develop a capitalist system.[63] On the external front, being members of the Coordination Committee of Maoist Parties and Organizations of South Asia (CCOMPOSA), the Maoists have planned to turn the South Asian region into a 'Soviet Federation' after the completion of revolution in all countries of the region.[64] An ambitious plan championed by the Maoists who at the same time are unleashing their armed struggle. It is difficult to understand how such a rationalization can explain the necessity of the 'People's War' to the people of Nepal whose experiences are not merely the subtraction of ideological abstraction. Attempting to explicate the persistent social anomalies as the reasons for the initiation of the armed struggle is therefore not helpful in understanding the Maoists' decision making. A more plausible, though unconfirmed, reason for the Maoists to opt for armed insurgency could be the insistence and advice of the RIM to foreswear or boycott the elections in lieu of violence. Prachanda has also implied about this possibility in his interview to Li Onesto.[65] Perhaps the Maoists are also tempted to ethnicize their 'class struggle', with the advice of their partners in the international communist movement, by dividing Nepal into autonomous regions while drafting their wish list to rule the country accordingly. But how the Maoists would achieve their desire to emerge as the ruling class without laying the groundwork for ethnic or regional autonomy and developing a mechanism for sustaining the process is yet unclear.

GUNS SETTLING ARGUMENTS: AN ALTERNATIVE PERSPECTIVE

The flare-up of the Maoist violence in Nepal is intriguing in the context of the gathering strength of the Left forces in the country against the background of the Leninist extinction around the world in the 1990s. Retrospectively, when communism was sweeping the world along with decolonization and self-determination as the currency of a decisive struggle in the 1950s, the Left in Nepal was too weak to raise its head during the decade of the first democratic experiment in the country. The then Communist Party of Nepal, as a monolith, had contested parliamentary elections in 1959 winning just 4 seats (7.2 per cent) against the 74 seats (37.2 per cent) won by the Nepali Congress. When parliamentary elections were held again in 1991 after a lapse of thirty-two years, of the more than a dozen communist splintered groups, four had emerged by contesting the elections and winning altogether 82 seats to the House of Representatives with a total of 36.49 per cent of the votes against 37.75 per cent of the popular votes gathered by the Nepali Congress party, which won the elections with 110 seats. The Maoists, who had contested the elections under the façade of the UPFN, won 9 seats (4.83 per cent of popular votes) and became the third largest party in the House of Representatives.

The formidable presence of the Left forces in the parliament was considered a by-product of the past thirty years of the authoritarian Panchayat regime that had helped the subversive Left activities to grow and evolve as cadre-based organizations nurtured by the anti-systemic grievances. The democratic space gained through the *Jana Andolan* 1990, therefore, was thought to be favourable ground for the Left forces to play their agency role of openly mobilizing popular aspirations by addressing societal grievances. It was thought that the 'logic of appropriateness' for mass mobilization by the Left forces would prevail in formulating social policies by making constructive choices in the course of transforming and moulding society towards their professed ideals through democratic bargaining by internalizing the rules of engagement of the parliamentary system. It was also expected that by shedding their stereotype image of dogmatic political groups the Left forces could also optimize the public sphere obtained in the post 1990 situation by articulating more fundamental social agendas.

But this was not to be. Against their anticipation of exposing the inadequacy of the parliamentary system for which they had joined electoral politics, the Maoists, as the force representing the Unity Centre, were jolted by the results of the local elections in 1992. This virtually uprooted them from their grass-roots organizations, demystifying their political programme of deepening the Marxist-Leninist-Maoist ideology suitable to the specific political, economic, and cultural conditions of the country.[66] Despite this failure, they tried to build and consolidate the party on ideological grounds in order to make it capable of implementing a political programme by resisting the onslaught of the state machinery. The hurdle in their path, however, was the inbuilt contradiction within the party—the personification of ideology by the communist leaderships. As an amalgamation of the marginal and the small splintered groups, the CPN (Unity Centre) was notoriously split-prone from the beginning. The CPN-Marxist (the remains of the oldest Communist Party in Nepal), the Nepal Workers and Peasant Party (Rohit), and the Marxist-Leninist-Maoist (under Krishna Das), had earlier joined and left the Unity Centre even before the commencement of the 1991 elections. Unity, disunity and reunity are not only characteristics of the communist factions, they are also an expression of the continuing struggle based on personal and ideological choices and interpretations of the trends setting the socio-economic and political courses in the country.

Controversies over the ideological-and organizational-based struggle and the consequent personality clashes and disagreements within the Unity Centre, particularly after the 1992 local elections, resulted in the purge and ouster of nearly 50 per cent of the Central Committee members which finally ending in its severe split before the mid-term elections 1994.[67] Talking about the two-line struggle (parliamentary *versus* revolutionary) in the party, Prachanda has argued that constant debate on the question of the people's war has marred the party. Some would have preferred the party's presence in the parliament with the simultaneous launching of the people's war, arguing that the presence of the party in the parliament would 'help strengthen the people's war'.[68] This 'rightist' tendency, however, did not prevail. But the evidence of the Bhattarai faction of the Unity Centre's registration bid as a national party, the ban by the Election Commission and the party's filing of a writ petition to the Supreme Court against the decision, suggest that the election option was not closed by the party's decision but by the decision of the Election Commission.

Some trends setting in the country between 1990 and 1996 were also not favourable to the Maoists. First, the electoral politics have proved that the CPN-Unity Centre was a poor cousin to its formidable rival Communist Party—the CPN (UML). It was least comparable to the democratic Nepali Congress party which had earlier swept both national and local elections. The formation of the minority government by the CPN (UML) in the aftermath of the 1994 mid-term polls, along with the rehabilitation of the Rashtriya Prajatantra Party (RPP)—the political party formed by the former panchayat elites—with twenty seats in the House of Representatives, and the disappearance of the CPN-Unity Centre from the House had perhaps led the Maoists to conclude these were crucial indicators of the changing political equation detrimental to their interests although vindicating their ideological reservations about the achievements of the 1990 *Jana Andolan* as being incomplete and inadequate. The process of nationwide electoral mobilization by the major political parties had also simultaneously displaced the Maoist organizations in the countryside. The consequence was the popular preference for the two-party dominant system and the deep-ening feelings of marginalization of the agency role of the Maoists who had nurtured the belief that they were the catalyst that had brought about the end of the Panchayat regime in 1990 through decisive street agitations.

Second, the competitive political environment of the 1990s had nurtured a sense of inequality in inter-party relationships, particularly between the major and minor communist parties. The dominance of the CPN (UML) in the public sphere, whom the Maoists view as 'reactionary, revisionist and reformist', and that party's ambition to emerge as an indisputable party leading to its unsavoury behaviour towards the minor communist parties (as the UML's hijacking of the UPFN's agendas by signing the 6-point agreement with the Nepali Congress, although the agitation was led by the Unity Centre) manipulating them to serve the CPN (UML's) interests, proved frustrating and deepened the schism in their relationship.[69]

The third and most crucial reason for the further alienation of the radical faction of the CPN-Unity Centre from the parliamentary process was the systemic persecution of the party cadres by the major political parties at the local and regional levels with the active aid of the government. With the experience of the party facing stiff challenges from the extremist groups of the of the UPFN during the election campaigns in western Nepal by the Nepali Congress, it resorted to impersonal measures in its drive to mobilize the party base in the Maoists' strongholds after coming to power in the 1991 elections. Confrontations between the local and regional party cadres expanded to the extent of brutal police assaults even on an elected

MP of the UPFN. The severe measures taken by the state against the UPFN cadres between 1991 and 1995, such as harassment, arrest, torture and, in some instances, rape and killings climaxed in the *Sija* campaigns by the Maoists in their efforts to reorganise the party, which were countered by the oppressive police operation, Romeo. This suppressive measure taken by the government as a matter of fact hardened the Maoists' resolve and pushed them from the mainstream to the extreme. Although point 15 of the 40-point memorandum submitted to the government by the Maoists had clearly warned the government to refrain from repeating such heinous acts, the latter's neglect of the demands vindicated the Maoists' decision to settle the arguments with guns rather than further dialogues and discourses.[70]

The governments formed by the major political parties had substantially eroded the support base of the Maoists from their areas of primacy through the electoral process and policy of persecution. Despite this, the governments had failed to pacify the restive people, who had vividly experienced the consequences of the violent state repression, either with relief or the resumption of dialogue. The obvious repercussion was the growing conviction among the people facing the harsh reality of police brutality that there was no respite for their continuing owes. The core leadership of the Maoist party had perhaps more conspicuously articulated this frustrating environment by purposefully interpreting the situation as the congenial in the context for rebellion. In their experience of electoral politics, the Maoists had found themselves outmanoeuvred, particularly by the CPN (UML) which used the underlying struggle to emerge as an unassailable communist party with an expanding party base by first minimizing the influence of other Left parties and secondly by presenting itself as an alternative to the Nepali Congress Party committed to parliamentary democracy. The Maoists were put in a precarious position both in their base areas and in the competitive political environment, forcing them to resort to arms as a remedy for the weakening situation and the inadequacy of their position in comparison to the established parties.

Perhaps, with limited party base and regional influence, the Maoists may have concluded that it would be practically impossible for them to emerge as a viable alternative to a dominant two-party system. Their ideology also remains the most unarticulated, even between the Left groups for proportionately expanding the political base and maintaining party cohesion threatened by the internecine rivalries for party fragmentation. The weakening of the Maoists' party after the split, and the situation of hopelessness caused both by the denial of participation and by the derecognition of the group as a national party, and the constant surveillance and harassment by the mainstream parties and governments, had left them with no other option to preserve their identity and survive but to make 'revolution' by articulating public interests. They faced the stark choice of either dissolving the thrust of the movement they had long prepared for as a party or go for a momentous change through violence as a strategy to optimize the prospect of their success in the future.[71] They chose violence, meaning it as communicating the historicity of their actions in their desire to emerge as an alternative to the two-party dominant political system.

It is, therefore, not the marginalization of the masses and the poverty and destitution of the people that led to the Maoists' insurgency and violence. Rather what compelled them to take up arms appears to be the marginalization of their position and agency role as a political party intricately linked with their ability and access to power. The pursuit of power, which is the function of centrality in politics reified so poignantly in the Maoist discourses, has relatively slipped from their reach in open competitive politics creating the condition of marginality. Violence thus becomes the useful means for the Maoists by which they can have access to the political process and power.

Violence as a choice for participation in the political process by the Maoists, who have finally articulated their trust in force and coercion rather than in dialogue and other peaceful procedures, however, has an unprecedented impact on Nepali state and society. In recovering their self from the political oblivion caused by the competitive environs by modulating the voices of the oppressed and marginalized groups in their fierce attempts to bridge the power differentials, the Maoists have contested the state not only with weapons but also with other means: the use of the media and information technology. The prominence of fax and e-mail as formidable weapons to announce Nepal *bandhs* with grievous impact on the socio-economic activities of the country allows the world to see the tragedy that Nepal faces. The Maoists have lawyers, human rights organizations, NGOs, intelligentsia, sympathizers and the press arrayed against the state as advocacy groups. The churning and dissemination of information in 'speaking truth' for those otherwise dismissed by the state as 'terrorists' have a meaningful impact on a society struggling to comprehend the implications of violence in everyday life.

The 'People's War' that entered its ninth year on 13 February 2004 is the longest protracted struggle that the Nepali state has ever faced. This most murderous phase in the history of the country has resurged with vigour. The thoughtfully planned and coordinated actions in the district headquarters of Bhojpur where 33 security personnel were killed and property worth Rs. 25 million damaged was followed by similar attacks on the Myagdi district headquarters on 20 March with casualties of over 26 civilians and 154 others killed, with scores of people missing.[72] 'War' casualties are increasing. Prior to these events, more than 10,000 people including security forces were killed.[73] The body count since 27 August 2003 (the day the Maoists withdrew from the last negotiations with the government), according to a military briefing, has reached 1,711, of which the dead Maoists number 1,567.[74] Between 13 February 1996 and 18 March 2004, the security forces have killed nearly 7,000 'Maoists'. A comparable figure of the persons killed by the Maoists till 4 February 2004 is 2,834, of which the number of the common people killed by the Maoists is 1,657.[75] Tracking the consequences of the 'People's War' is hazardous because it ranges from the physical, material to the psychological. In the nine years of insurgency, the Maoists have thoroughly shaken the state. The political–legal frame of the state presently remains in tatters and the shattered economy has no other choice but to opt for a dependent militarization of the state. But the glaring examples of the impact of violence on the people and their sufferings are crystallizing on the national sphere along with the ruthlessness of the bloody conflict.

When initiating the 'People's War', the then General Secretary of the CPN (Maoist), Prachanda, had firmly argued that his party's policies were against arson, looting, destruction of private properties and individual bloodshed.[76] But the conduct of the 'People's War', has given the lie to his commitments. As the INSEC 2004 data shows, poor peasants/agriculture workers, schoolteachers, and students are in the majority of those killed by the Maoists in their areas of operation. In the course of their violent forays, contradictions to the motives and ideals of the 'People's War', the Maoists have deliberately taken action to spread terror as much as possible by targeting the common people to bring them into submission. Perhaps the 'People's War' which was initiated primarily with the objective of 'confiscating the land of the feudalists and redistributing it to the people'[77] had failed to inspire the people resulting in the glaring failure of the Maoists to intermingle with the masses as the 'fish in the water', forcing them to move as armed bands to survive in the villages for both food and shelter.[78] The villagers' helplessness have therefore occasioned with the reprisals of the security forces treating them either as the Maoist suspects or sympathizers.

The Maoists, on the other hand, have also justified their brutal actions against the villagers as punishment for the 'enemies of the revolution', accusing them of being informers, spies or political opponents. In the course of eliminating the local resistance, the Maoists have put a premium on violence tormenting the lives of the people, reproducing segregation from their strongholds, if not the cleansing of their opponents.[79] Individual survival has therefore become the main priority of the people as the violence escalates. Several reports of killings of the poor and common people for their refusal to give in to the extortions, levies, and other demands of the Maoists are surfacing. The gruesome murders of the schoolteachers for not complying with the 15 to 25 per cent levies imposed on their salaries or for teaching Sanskrit in class in defiance of the Maoists' orders spread fear like wildfire. Coupled with this, the Maoists have kidnapped schoolchildren forcing them to join either the people's army or the militia, resulting in both teachers and students deserting schools. Over 3,000 schoolteachers have been displaced from the districts and villages, leading to the closure of some 700-800 schools, particularly in mid- and far-western Nepal, owing to the disturbances caused by the Maoists,[80] including arson and destruction. In some instances, these schools have been turned into battle fields with intense fighting between the Maoists and security forces resulting in the deaths of children. Some school buildings have been converted into military barracks by the Maoists or the security forces.

Along with the spread of Maoist activities and terror throughout the country, many of the villages have become inhospitable places for their own inhabitants with the rise in extortions, abductions, killings and forcible evacuation of the people. The number of the IDPs and those migrating to India is swelling although there are no definite government records. A recent sample survey conducted by the Community Study and Welfare Centre in five severely affected districts—Rukum, Rolpa, Salyan, Dang, and Achham—of mid-western Nepal has concluded that between 3,50,000 and 4,00,000 people from these districts have been displaced.[81] Earlier, a similar survey of fifty-three districts conducted by an NGO found that 4,27,500 landowning people and more than 2.5 million people homeowners have been displaced. Almost 70 per cent of the cottage industries in the rural areas are closed and agricultural production has declined drastically due to the absence of labour forces.[82] Over 6,00,000 people had already migrated to India to escape from hunger and reprisal. Citing an officer of the border checkpoint, it is estimated that 500 people are migrating into India by crossing the border from Mahendra Nagar in western Nepal regularly. The exodus is caused by the Maoists' rampage as well as creeping famine, blockade of supplies, looting, killings and forced expulsion from villages.[83] The 'one house, one-person policy'—according to which every household should provide the Maoist party with one person to join the fighting force—has further forced the people to leave to escape the Maoists' ire.[84] This increasing Maoist pressure on the common people has led to the forced closure of 327 schools in Achham district denying educational opportunities to 45,000 students, and the Maoists' 'special military campaigns' to recruit new blood has led to a mass exodus.[85]

In addition to this, the most tragic aspect of the Maoist violence is coping with challenges by those who have directly experienced violence in their lives, particularly women and children who are disproportionately affected by the murderous campaigns. The number of widows and orphans has increased. The widowed women's support base also wanes as time passes and for the most part they are forgotten except by their immediate family. Women and children living in the villages without the protection of able-bodied men have routinely become vulnerable to harassment and intimidation in their social relationships. Although the records of the number of women killed by the Maoists are scant, numerous cases of torture, molestation, and, in some instances, murder after rape are, however, documented.[86] Women left behind by their fleeing husbands for fear of reprisal by either the Maoists or the security forces have become the heads of households without any substantial means to support the family. Data on child victims, as per one account, is 300 dead with more than 1,000 disabled by the landmines and socket bombs laid and left by the Maoists. The number of dislocated children has also simultaneously increased to 10,000.[87] The observable characteristics displayed by the victims of violence are traumas and shock.

Numerous children who have lost their parents, lost education opportunities, and lost the care and support of their families have become child labourers working in tea stalls, brick kilns, stone quarries, spinning mills and carpet factories. Some have either joined the stock of *khate* (street urchins) in the urban centres or become an additional burden for relatives.[88] There are also unconfirmed reports of children being used by the Maoists as porters, informers, messengers, carriers of deadly landmines and other weapons, and even in combat situations. The Nepal Human Rights Commission has published records of missing persons, attributing the disappearance of 111 persons without a trace to the Maoists.[89] These record are based on the names of the missing persons registered by family and friends with the Commission. It is assumed that hosts of disappearances may go unreported primarily because of the fear of reprisal and from sheer ignorance. The cases of abduction by the Maoists have increased recently, for forcible recruitment in either the people's militia or the people's army. For instance, within a week in January 2004, the Maoists abducted more than a hundred persons, including some fifty school children, from different villages of Bardia district whose whereabouts are still unknown.[90]

Besides this, the Maoists have pursued their policies of paralysing the state with the destruction of private and public property. Although a comprehensive audit of 'war' has yet to be made because of ongoing violence, the absence of data, and the pitfalls in quantification methodology, some preliminary studies have estimated the cost of damage and destruction of public property and lootings of banks at Rs. 25 billion.[91] The Maoists have particularly targeted telecommunication installations, bridges, roads, hydel power plants and public buildings in their mission to foil the government's efforts to control their activities. The fallout of the Maoists' specific targets of infrastructure destruction has been the complete stoppage of development activities and supply systems. Even the minimal presence of the state in the very needy regions of the country has been compromised. The withdrawal of police posts, banks, and residual government offices from the conflict zones to the district headquarters has put the people at risk from the Maoists on the one hand, and on the other left them with a feeling of dispossession by the state. By withdrawing even the minimum presence of the state machinery from the conflict zones the state has blundered as this has provided the control access of the civilian population to the Maoists and hence defeating the insurgency with counter-insurgency is now difficult.

On the national level, the extortion spree of the Maoists has become a greater cause of concern. They have not spared private/boarding schools, publishers, business houses, civil servants, politicians or even tourists/trekkers. Donor agencies and NGOs have also become prime targets of the Maoists' fund-raising activities. Similarly, the imposition of the war tax has squeezed commercial activities and supplies in the regions dominated by the Maoists leading to a price spiral. How widespread these donation/extortions and fund-raising activities of the Maoists are/was disclosed when *Kantipur* publications was asked for monetary assistance of Rs. 4,00,000 as well as a 'donation' of Rs. 8,00,000 by the CPN (UML) party. It is also understood that a large number of Nepalis working abroad, particularly in India and Hong Kong, are the constant source of finance for the Maoists. The looting of the banks has added to the Maoists' finances thus making them perhaps 'amongst the richest terrorist groups' in the world, with an estimated accumulation of between US $64 and 128 million from various sources.[92] With the raising of the threshold of the fear of reprisal, the Maoists have made the situation in the state favourable for their financial activities against the greater cost of the shrinking of the economy of the country.[93]

The stark problem confronting the country is the chaos the Maoists have succeeded in creating in the state to which they have also laid claim. Although they have spontaneously expressed dissent against oppression, domination and marginalization through violence, thus turning the tide of suppression against the oppressors, the process of institutionalizing the movement has, however, left little scope for radical reform and has succeeded in dismantling the democratic space by stifling the chances of co-opting the societal grievances articulated by the marginalized. The marginalized are further dislocated from the state as a consequence of contradictions arising out of the violence celebrated by both the non-state and the state, and the weakening of their resolve to stand behind the people in the quagmire of the contest for national power.

The trappings of power of the state that the Maoists have reverence for, as demonstrated by their claim of 'naya satta' (new regime) with the establishment of autonomous regions, has sharpened their inclination towards militaristic approaches in settling their disputes with the 'purano satta' (old regime), thus dragging the country into an infinite struggle for power which the Maoists, in theory, revile as the original sin. The 'People's War', which began as a resistance movement, has now graduated to a strategic offensive wherein the primacy of politics has become secondary to military means in resolving the contradictions and problems facing the state. The Maoists' murderous campaigns indiscriminately victimizing the common people across the country have elements of criminality rather than revolutionary seal as the planting of bombs in schools and explosions in public places exemplify. Profiling the people's war and the consequent violence as a programme for transforming the state by changing the power holders as the highest purpose of the struggle suggests that the Maoists are also caught in the trap of the problems of power and the innate desire to possess and practise the glory of power. But the power as such can only be obtained through further destruction of social cohesion and the destitution of the people, as is glaringly exemplified by the existing regime.

The Maoists in Nepal appear to have learnt from, and taken, literally, Mao's dictum 'political power grows out from the barrel of a gun', than from the Maoism that broadly suggests the radical transformation of the social organization of power. Denying the means of livelihood, education, and health services are the three crucial anti-Maoism policies pursued by the Maoists, which is evidenced by the ravages of the 'People's War'. This ambivalence of the Maoists has forced a re-examination of the prior assumptions about the 'People's War' and a search for a new way in understanding the Maoist movement in Nepal. The popular consciousness among the Maoists is Maoism as their dominant ideology informed by the problems of power in social relationships. Their programme of New Democratic Revolution through the 'People's War' is to fundamentally change the superstructure of the state that has constrained the social relationships of production and development.

The process of revolutionary transformation, therefore, would be the interplay of destruction and creation, where force would primarily mean to destroy the 'old system' to be replaced by the 'new system'. The 'People's War' would be a continuous process, to resolve the contradiction arising out of the bourgeois democratic revolution emerging after the destruction of the old system, clearing the pathways to establish the socialist system attended by a revolutionary land reform and change in the relationship of production.[94] The objectives set by the Maoists can therefore be achieved only through 'seizing' the state power by force. In the making of the revolution, Bhattarai has scrupulously suggested that the sacrifices made by the people and the price paid for it (the People's War) was definitely worth the objective.[95] The Maoist guerrillas' execution of their military prowess can be observed in their ability to cause shattering impact and destruction on the targets of their attack, particularly the district headquarters. But the militarily dominant strategy of the Maoists has intensified state resolve to suppress the growing Maoist menace by branding it as 'terrorism', making a political solution to the issues raised by the conflict more difficult. Through their claims of the existence of 'two states and two armies', and obtaining 'strategic parity' with the 'old regime' presumably by fielding 2 divisions, 7 brigades and 17 battalions the People's Army, along with more than 1,00,000 people's militias, the Maoists have been able to militarize the social sphere provoking a military response by the state. Increasing insecurity has led the state to turn against its own citizens. As a consequence, the socio-political agendas either of reform or revolution have been repulsed or relegated to the periphery.

BETWEEN PRECEPT AND PRACTICE

The Maoists claim that the major thrust of their political programme is directed towards the establishment of New Democracy based on the concept of democratic centralism in organizing the state. The establishment of the new democratic system would be after the destruction of feudalism, with the overriding concern being the abolition of the monarchy, which is continuing the traditional system of exploitation and oppression. The Maoists have also interpreted the dominance of Hinduism, the high-caste group, and male dominance as features of the semi-colonial order. According to the Maoists, the struggle they are spearheading is targeted against the existing state, the 'old state', which upholds these historically outmoded and contradiction-ridden features blocking the progress towards the evolution of the 'new state'. In their programme the Maoists have expressed their determination to forge an alliance of all the progressive forces for the united struggles against the forces of 'semi-feudalism and semi-colonialism'. They believe that the 'new state', constituting the progressive forces, would wage a struggle against caste, ethnicity, gender, and regional oppression.

This forging of a 'new state', however, is predicated on armed struggle. Though there is an abundance of theoretical literature on the imperatives of the armed struggle, particularly that produced in China by Mao arguing it as a necessity for establishing a new democratic state, the Maoists have not been able to succinctly justify the need of the 'People's War' in the context of Nepal.[96] Despite the general explanation they have posited for the launching of the 'People's War', as noted earlier,[97] the Maoists have not been able to convincingly explain the imperatives of the 'People's War' within the context of the post-1990 Nepal which, despite the fragility of democratic consolidation, has provided freedom of political association and the right to dissent. Perhaps the Maoists, as their experience shows, are not confident that with the relative significance of the post 1990 development they will realize their objectives of democratizing society. Their scheme, no doubt, has the element of complete rejection of the post-1990 political arrangement which is marred by internal contradictions and unresponsiveness to societal demands. The democratic process was in such disarray that the initial thrusts of the guerrillas were enough to erode the state power, dismantling the local and national governments by effectively challenging the legitimacy of the 1990 constitution.

With their military forays the Maoists have achieved success, perhaps too easily, in exposing not only the decadent practices of the parliamentary political parties but also the fragility of the existing unitary state. Guerrilla tactics therefore have become a powerful incentive for the Maoists to strike at the political and military ends of the 'old state' further exacerbating the vulnerabilities and tensions inherent in the regime structure. On the other hand, the policy of intentional and deliberate killings designed to generate widespread terror in the society has completely undermined the programme sketched in New Democracy, allowing the military domain to supersede the political motive underlying the concept of the 'People's War'. For the Maoists, violence therefore becomes the currency of power and terrorism as a means to realize it. Their threat of reprisals and the indiscriminate use of force have largely paralysed the public sphere. This strategy has, however, defeated their purpose of establishing New Democracy with the objective of either 'completing a bourgeoisie democratic revolution' or establishing the dictatorship of the proletariat. This precept of 'revolution' has also led to a scrutiny of the 'People's War' as certain developments have exposed its behavioural ambiguities.

First, although the narratives of the Maoists' revolutionary rhetoric show that monarchy is the bastion of regression and repression in the country, their ambivalence towards this traditional institution has been significantly exposed following the 1 June 2001 palace massacre. One of the crucial contradictions between the Maoists precept and practice of the 'People's War', thus, was their self-confessed existence of an undeclared 'alliance', between the Monarchy and the Maoists during the reign of the late King Birendra. The Maoists ideologue, Baburam Bhattarai has surmised that duly because of this 'undeclared alliance' the late king had refused to mobilize the armed forces against the Maoists. According to Bhattarai, 'the relative *patriotism* and *liberal* political character of the late king were instrumental in developing an "undeclared working unity" between the late king and us as we share similar views on numerous national questions'.[98] Asserting that the 'crucial contributions of the Shah kings, from Prithvi Narayan to king

Birendra, have been to defend the *sovereignty* and *independence* of the country struggling first against the British colonialism and later the Indian expansionism . . . the Nepali people have [developed] ceaseless faith on them'[99] [emphasis added].

Endorsing the views of Bhattarai in totality, Prachanda, the chairman of the CPN (Maoist), in a statement on 11 June 2001, said that the 'reason behind the massacre of King Birendra and his entire family was his reluctance to mobilize the Royal Nepal Army to crush the People's War [against the wishes of the] imperialists and expansionists'. These statements and opinions were definitely not an obituary for a fallen patriot; they were not the product of confused minds. Rather, they were, in their own words, their 'un-hesitant' acceptance of the national reality.[100] Earlier, in an article published in one of the Maoist weeklies, Bhattarai wrote that the monarchists must understand the truth that only communists are capable of fighting and systematically defeating imperialism and expansionism in the world of the twenty-first century. It should also be realized that only those monarchies and monarchists who had cooperated with the patriotic communists have continued to survive, particularly in the Third World countries like Cambodia, Laos, and Mongolia. Perhaps for this reason it is expected that there should be a natural proximity between the nationalist king along with nationalists and the communist forces who are in the forefront of waging the struggle against imperialism and, specially, against Indian expansionism, the comprador of the bourgeoisie Nepali Congress party.[101] But their tacit acceptance of the role of monarchy ended with the slaying of King Birendra, when they concluded that the history of Nepali monarchy was over as the incident had led to the birth of a republic in the country.[102] The Maoists contend that with the demise of 'traditional monarchy' in the country, even an institution somewhat assertive on the question of nationalism has disappeared. Along with this, the Nepali ruling class, despite being the parliamentarian and neo-monarchists has thus dissolved into a position of comprador. Therefore, there is a need to forge unanimity between people of different ideological persuasions in order to steer the country towards a republican system.[103]

In the aftermath of the palace massacre the Maoists have pursued a stringent military policy causing the state to respond with the declaration of national emergency, the adoption of anti-terrorist laws, and military mobilization. The situation becomes nastier with the series of Maoist attacks on the police and military posts, damage and destruction of public property and infrastructure, and the rising graph of fatalities. On the other hand, they have also demonstrated a corresponding flexibility in their posture while formally negotiating with the governments. Initially emphasizing on the one-party system to be established by the communist government, the Maoists had argued for the formation of a consociational multi-party system and competitive polity after 2001. They proposed a round table conference inclusive of all the democratic and progressive forces to draft a consensual Interim Act and form an All Party Interim Government under the leadership of the revolutionary forces (read the Maoists).[104] Although the Maoists had also proposed to talk directly with the king, they however agreed to negotiate with the king's representatives.

On the last leg of talks with the government on 17 August 2003, the Maoists again demanded the abolition of the monarchy, but simultaneously scaled down their demands for the resolution of the problems provided the king agreed to be the titular head of the state. Though the Maoists had argued for their unconditional election to the constituent assembly in assertion of the popular sovereignty of the people, they were prepared to came to an understanding to retain the monarchy even under that dispensation.[105] The Maoists also conveyed their willingness to accept the constitutional monarchy if the king dispensed with the control of the army.[106] The failure of the negotiations and the resumption of violence did not end the back-channel contacts, however. It is understood that high-level contacts with the Maoists have continuously been maintained despite the official policy of branding them as terrorists and putting a bounty on their heads. It is widely believed that the Royal Palace has continued to maintain its links with the Maoists: King Gyanendra himself reportedly met the Maoist leader and spokesperson of the party, Krishna Bahadur Mahara, at Bardiya National Park, Thakurdwara Nepalgunj, where the last round of talks was held.[107] This report is yet to be contradicted either by the Palace or by the Maoists. It is also widely reported that the Maoists' military commanders and the commanders of the security forces are in constant touch even while playing hide-and-seek with each other.

Second, the leaders of the mainstream political parties also had their secret rendezvous with the Maoists. The former Prime Minister Koirala had a meeting with Maoist leaders like Prachanda and others in New Delhi through an influential Indian intermediary. During that meeting, Koirala and Prachanda had agreed on three crucial points for persuasion: first, the common platform for the struggle would be to bring the army under the control of the parliament in completing the process of establishing a bourgeois democracy instead of a people's republic. Second, the Maoists agreed to be flexible on the question of election to the constituent assembly against their previously rigid position on the issue. And third, they agreed to cooperate with all the parliamentary parties for the consolidation of multi-party democracy in the country. These positions of the Maoists were later publicized in a letter sent to seven political parties by Chairman Prachanda in May 2002.[108] Following this, there was a meeting of minds between the Maoists and the leaders of different political parties. The leaders of the six parliamentary parties had agreed to the agenda of constitutional amendment on two important issues. They had agreed with the Maoists to make the army completely responsible to the elected parliament and government and to include the provision of national referendum in the constitution to ease the process of constitutional amendment whenever desired by the people. This agenda was close to being placed as a bill in the parliament with a certainty of being adopted by the majority consensus as legislation, when, unfortunately, the sudden dissolution of the parliament in May 2002 blocked the process of a seemingly peaceful resolution of the conflict with the required constitutional reform in the existing system.[109]

Similarly, the CPN (UML) General Secretary Madhav Nepal, along with other leaders of the party, had meetings with Prachanda, Baburam Bhattarai, and others in Siliguri and Lucknow in India. At the Lucknow talks in late November 2003, the Maoists however, reiterated their position on election to the constituent assembly preceded by a round table conference and the formation of an Interim Government, instead of an All Party Government, by replacing the existing one, as proposed by the CPN (UML) leaders.[110] Conversely, the CPN (UML) rejected the Maoists' proposal of a joint struggle for establishing the republican system.[111] This change in position can be understood as a consequence of the dissolution of the parliament and dismissal of the elected parliamentary government.

Third, since the assertion of executive power by the king on 4 October 2002 transformed the political equation in the country, relegating the parliamentary forces from the centre to the periphery, the Maoists have re-evaluated their own position *vis-à-vis* the emasculated parliamentary parties whose inaction is 'gradually turning into a cause of their own extinction'.[112] The virtual powerlessness of the political parties, once they are thrown out in the streets, is evident in the absence of popular support to their urgent call for reinstatement of the dissolved parliament. The fixture therefore is that the Monarchists and the Maoists are confronting each other with their arms might, treating the only legitimate political force as the tail end. This has led the Maoists to surmise the situation faced by the political parties in the country as:

> The inability to grasp the fact that in Nepal there is no other alternative to either rally behind the leadership of the proletariat to complete the bourgeois democratic revolution or to completely capitulate to the military fascism based on the coalition of feudalism and imperialism has become the destiny of the parliamentary forces. . . . [I]n essence and in class terms the political struggle in the country is bipolar.[113]

Perhaps this is the repositioning of the Maoists' claim to power against the political parties when they chose to negotiate directly with the monarchy without taking the parties into confidence. The Maoists achieved this feat by using violence as a means to emerge as a potential force in the fluid political landscape of the country. They have also replicated the hegemonic attitude towards the political parties by clearly asserting the power of violence in settling the course of the political process. Terrorism, therefore, becomes a strategy of the politically weak reverting from the periphery to the centre as a claimant to power, which is not anti-political. But the political parties appear to be ambivalent about recognizing the Maoists as a political force because they certainly feel that the Maoists have relied on guns to dictate their agendas rather than on popular support. Thus, they feel that alliance with the Maoists can be forged only if the latter agree to the non-violent mobilization of the masses. Besides this, the political parties have their own agenda to pursue in their struggle for the restoration of democracy, which they feel has popular endorsement despite the absence of active support.

The coalition of five parliamentary political parties has promoted its own 18-point programme by prominently arguing for confining the title of Sri 5 only to the three members of the royal family—the king, queen and crown prince. They have also advocated for the royal family to abide by the law of the land as well as for bringing the Royal Nepal Army under the firm control of the elected parliament.[114] Though essentially radical, these postures of the political parties have sensitized the popular feeling as the rift between the palace and the parties grows. Notwithstanding their tenuous career in the past twelve years of democratic rule, the governments formed under the political parties had addressed some serious agendas concerning social discrimination and gender disparities, such as Kamaiya abolition, Dalit upliftment and property rights for women, despite their faulty implementation. The political parties are also confident of their ability to pursue more progressive programmes of empowering the citizenry legitimately rather than under duress. They have therefore maintained a comfortable distance from the Maoists whose political opportunism has turned the country into a bloody mess.

The implications of these developments can be seen as the Maoists' attempt to gain for themselves a comfortable position in the context of the triangular contest for power by trying to align themselves with monarchy as well as the political parties at a time of their own choosing. In this ménage a trios, the Maoists have perhaps succeeded in widening the differences between the monarchy and the political parties to meet their own political ends, by employing the military means and by defeating the parliamentary forces considered as the primary obstacle against achieving New Democracy. But as the top Maoist leaders have evidently expressed high esteem for the institution of monarchy, defining it as both a patriotic and a nationalist institution which has the unflinching loyalty of the people of Nepal, their pursuit for the establishment of New Democracy by dethroning monarchy remains inexplicable. The Maoist leaders have attributed monarchy under the Shah dynasty since 1769 with the qualities of patriotism, nationalism, anti-imperialism, anti-expansionism, and liberalism, and as the defender of the sovereignty and independence of the country, an institution which commands the 'ceaseless faith' of the Nepali people. How, then, can such an institution be considered and explained as the mainstay of exploitation and oppression, and thus to be, struggled against by the people? The Maoists have also failed to explain why the devout people should choose a republican system by replacing monarchy, as the former system is as strange to them as the concept of Maoism itself. The persistent conceptual anomalies Maoists' in the case of monarchy have been further exposed by their insistence on a constituent assembly with a 'human face' retaining monarchy under that dispensation even while demanding an unconditional sovereign/popular verdict on the issue.

Further confusion and contradiction is evident in the Maoists' explanation for the necessity of the 'completion of bourgeois democratic revolution', which would replace the establishment of New Democracy. Their refreshing commitment to the multi-party political system, for making a joint endeavour with other political parties through a round table conference, forming an All Party Government under their leadership, and election to the constituent assembly to complete and consolidate the cycle of bourgeois democracy is a rediscovering of the need of forming alliances with the parliamentary parties. The centrepiece of the necessity of this coalition of interests is again perhaps the institution of monarchy that has delegitimized the popular interests. But there is a chasm between the intensification of their search for a political alliance to promote their agenda and the actual behaviour: they are intolerant even of the ordinary democratic practices of providing freedom of speech to the cadres belonging to other political parties and the practice of forced expulsion of the people influenced by ideology other than their own from the areas they under their control. The demand of complicity does not suit the Maoists' search for a political alliance. The fear of their political programme grinding to a halt could be the most ominous situation for the resurrection and continuity of violence as there would be no other rational means for the Maoists to make their national presence other than terrorism. And in their endeavour for terrorist violence, the Maoists would not be alone.

They have nurtured a nexus with regional terrorist organizations in South Asia, of which the prominent ones are the Maoist Coordination Centre (MCC), People's War Group (PWG), Akhil Bharatiya Nepali Janatantrik Morcha of India, all actively supporting the Maoists across the border in Nepal. So long as this support continues unabated, terrorism of the Maoist variety is a phenomenon Nepalis will have to live with.

CONCLUSION

The course of the nine years of Maoist violence can be described in terms of both successes and failures. First, never in the history of Nepal has the state faced such a long and enduring violent internal conflict cracking the political structure of the state with unexpected consequences of domestic polarization. Nor has the institution of monarchy ever been the centrepiece of controversy and public debate. Second, by dismantling the constitutional process by mixing force with the manipulation of the persistent contradictions underlying the political equation, the Maoists have succeeded in rejuvenating several moribund social issues to create a chasm in state–society relations. Third, even though the enormity of the problems caused by the Maoists' violence remains unstated, the ensuing conflict has made a return to the old order of status quo impossible. Coupled with the Maoist problem, the assertion of power by the monarchy has galvanized the society to the extent of leading to the high-charged debates on monarchy by none other than the framers of the Constitution 1990, on the question of popular sovereignty. The power vacuum that the monarch has created with the assumption of the executive power of the state has been instrumental in setting off the raging debates on the inadequacy of the Constitution 1990, a corrective for which is articulated through election to the constituent assembly.[115]

Although the debates in the constituent assembly for the drafting of a new constitution may have different connotations and interpretations, the agenda asserted by the Maoists making it a bone of contention, has become a pointer to the urgency of the state-restructuring process. This has led to the possibility of the refurbishing of the constituent assembly as a mutually compatible agenda for persuasion between the agitating political parties and the Maoists provided the counter-state claims of the latter for the existence of 'two states and two governments' are moderated or relinquished. Though the Maoists, through the militarily dominant nature of their struggle, have been able to disrupt the political process, they cannot seriously question the legitimacy of the existing regime without the firm support of the political parties who still hold the trump card of popular will for re-invigorating and continuing the democratic project in Nepal. Although alienated, the political parties are adherents of the principles of constitutional monarchy with a popular sovereignty committed to the state-ordering process. Therefore, the interests of the political parties and the Maoists can converge on a socio-economic agenda, but not on the politico-military agenda of violence as an instrument for seizing state power.[116]

On the other hand, the prospects of the Maoist successfully organizing violence by creating waves of a popular uprising against the state have become bleaker. The absence of the government in the areas controlled by the Maoists, has made life difficult for the people living there because of the unsustainability of the regions without external inputs to which the Maoists have not been able to provide an alternative. The economic vulnerability of most of the areas where the Maoists hold sway has increased with the drying up of development projects and public finance and even a temporary job loss for the local people adds to their already miserable situation.[117] The loss of agricultural productivity due to the absence of a labour force has created the problem of subsistence for the people in the villages. The Maoists are also finding it difficult to recruit people for their militia or guerrilla units as able-bodied people have escaped from the villages either in search of greener pastures or from fear of forced conscription by the Maoists. Perhaps because of the difficulty in finding volunteers, abductions of schoolchildren and teachers and their forcible recruitment have increased.[118] The Maoists are also increasingly recruiting girl students between the ages of fourteen and eighteen as civilian cadres, militias, and guerrillas in the name of gender empowerment.[119] But the compulsory 'one house, one person policy' adopted by the Maoists to maintain their fighting force can be seen as a consequence of their decreasing influence on the people caused by excessive coercive measures. The widespread fear of the Maoists in the villages caused by unwarranted extortions and mischief even when informed of the villagers' inability to provide food and shelter, is eroding their credibility even among the people sympathetic to their cause.

The moot question therefore is, how should the Maoists' violence be explained and understood? Can the Maoist violence be construed as 'violence from below' and understood as having an element of subalternity and the consequence of the marginalization of the masses? These terms sound fine when taken as an explanatory cause of the conflict and violence as their echo can be heard around the world. Thus when violence is pursued as a vocation by the non-state under the guise of defence against structural violence in justification of securing elementary human needs, it draws both appreciation and admiration inadvertently conferring legitimacy to the violence. But the assumption of violence from below underlined by the persistence of the deplorable poverty, grievances and marginalization of people compelling them to resort to arms requires to be validated. Arguments generally posited to account for violence from below are that it involves the majority of the people—the oppressed and exploited—in an effort to emancipate themselves from the bondage of power and authority. Such violence internalized as revolutionary in nature and eulogized as constructive and creative is also explained as being characterized by spontaneity and sacrifice. The Maoists' violence, however, is not spontaneous but an organized and prompted violence to emerge as a political collectivity making a common cause with the destitute.

In Nepal a convenient refuge for the justification of violence is the context of marginalization. Violence is the site for expressing the collective grievances of the people, making it reciprocal to the actual violence caused by the suppression of their right to be heard by the state. Violence therefore becomes a process of the assertion of endangered identity by the people. And as a consequence of the people's refusal to confine them to the usual boundary of the existing social order, the violence committed by the non-state magnifies to the state of terrorism. The Maoists have tried to justify violence contextualizing their activities against the background of the historicity of the practice of social exclusion by the state. But their actions seeking justification only relate to an end which lies in the future. This future, however, will be determined by the popular uprising with the creative potentiality of transforming the society rather than romanticizing violence underscored by destructive activities. As has been empirically observed, *people* in the 'People's War' have become fodder to be used and ruined, and left to bear the brunt of the conflict. Both by supporting and by sustaining the appalling and haemorrhaging effects of violence, the acclaimed spontaneity of the 'revolution' in the making has shrunk to the fold of terrorism.

The indiscriminate killings of poor peasants, uprooting of the poor and helpless from their domiciles, arson and looting, forcible recruitment of children in the 'People's Army', kidnapping of government officials and bargaining for the release of imprisoned Maoist leaders, along with extortions and bank robberies, cannot be characterized as a case of subaltern resistance. Nor can these acts be explained as an uprising of the marginalized people. The Maoists' signature on Nepali soil is therefore terroristic rather than revolutionary, because the pattern of their observable behaviour is not commensurate with their revolutionary cause. These acts are not the exemplary conduct of revolutionary violence about which the Maoists are apparently enthused. These dastardly murderous activities, deliberately initiated to spread terror among the common citizenry forcing them to submission, have trivialized the Maoists' rationalization of violence as a response to the structural violence perpetrated by the state. The context of marginality and subalternity is, therefore, detached from the violence celebrated by the Maoists in Nepal, as their outrageous actions have not inspired but added to the despair of the people. On the other hand, the decision of the political parties to act in concert by repulsing violence has openly demonstrated the people's power in the streets.

Although the Maoists as a group of people alienated from the political mainstream have demonstrated that they are capable of making history by fomenting terror elevating themselves to the symbol of authority, at the same time, they have relegated the humanitarian appeal of 'revolution' to the sirens of litany by practising inhuman methods. Their false belief that violence is the only justifiable alternative against the reactionary regime and armed struggle the only means for, the seizure of the state power has defeated the purpose of popular mobilization for the success of their political programme of liberating the people from human bondage. The long-run success of the struggle, however, is commensurate with the political programme not *apolitical* violence that victimizes the poor and impoverished which is incommensurate with the Maoists' claim of 'revolution'. The political programme remains democracy and the deliverance of development lifting the veil of denial and destitution from the Nepali society.

NOTES

1. Khadga Man Singh, 2031 BS [1975], *Jailma Bish Barsha* (Twenty Years in Jail—An Autobiography) (Kathmandu: KM Singh, 1975). See also, Rajesh Gautam, *Prachanda Gorkha: Ek Addhyan* (Prachanda Gorkha: A Study) (Kathmandu: Centre for Nepal and Asian Studies, 2001).
2. Puspa Lal, *Nepali Jana Andolan: Ek Samichhya* (Nepali People's Movement: A Critique) (Kathmandu: Naya Janawadi Prakashan, 1979).
3. B.P. Koirala, *Atmabritanta* (An Autobiography) (Lalitpur: Jagadamba Prakashan, 1998), pp. 303-4. See also, Bhola Chatterji, *Palace, People and Politics: Nepal in Perspective* (New Delhi: Ankur Publishing House, 1980), p.129.
4. B.P. Koirala, *Rastriya Ektako Nimti Awhan* (The Call for National Unity) (Varanasi: Tarun Prakashan, 1978).
5. B.P Koirala, *Kranti Ek Anibaryata* (Revolution, a Necessity) (Varanasi, India: Tarun Prakashan, 1972).
6. Koirala, *Atmabritanta*, p. 332.
7. Koirala, *Rashtriya Ekatako Nimti Awaham*, p. 13.
8. A Task Force commissioned by the CPN (UML) in 1971, with an influential leader of the party, C.P. Mainali, as convener, to study the Maoists' problem had determined that the activities of the Maoists were 'terroristic'. Following this Bam Dev Gautam, the then deputy prime minister and home minister of the CPN (UML)–RPP coalition government, was the first high government official to brand the Maoists as terrorist and had tried to introduce an 'anti-terrorist bill' in the parliament with cabinet support, C.P. Mainali, another leader of the same party to recommend a hard-line approach towards the Maoists, ironically had started his political career as one of the prominent leaders of the Jhapa movement and become famous for his jailbreak during the Panchayat regime in Nepal. Ironically, these leaders of the movement are presently of the opinion that the 'Jhapa movement was an ultra-left deviation'. For an overview of the history of the Communist movement in Nepal, see Bhim Rawal, *Nepal ma Samyabadi Andolan: Udbhav,*

Bikas ra Bartaman Abastha (The Communist Movement in Nepal: Origin, Development and Current Situation) (Kathmandu: Samana Prakashan, 1988).

9. With the then Member of Parliament Prem Singh Dhami, as convener, the CPN (UML)–RPP coalition government in 1997 formed the commission.
10. Caleb Carr, *The Lessons of Terror* (London: Little, Brown, 2002), p. 6.
11. Eugene V. Walter, *Terror and Resistance* (New York: Oxford University Press, 1969), p. 13.
12. Frantz Fanon, *The Wretched of the Earth* (Middlesex, England: Penguin Books, 1978). See also, Georges Sorel, *Reflections on Violence*, translated by T.E. Hulme (New York: Peter Smith, 1941).
13. Ranajit Guha, *Dominance without Hegemony: History and Power in Colonial India* (New Delhi: Oxford University Press, 1998), p. x.
14. Antonio Gramsci, *Selection from the Prison Notebooks of Antonio Gramsci*, edited and translated by Quintin Hoare and Geoffrey Nowell Smith (New York: International Publishers, 1971), p. 52.
15. Sumit Sarkar, 'The Decline of the Subaltern', in *Subaltern Studies*, in his, *Writing Social History* (New Delhi: Oxford University Press, 1997), pp. 82-104. See also, Gayatri Chakravarti Spivak, 'Subaltern Studies: Deconstructing Historiography', in Ranajit Guha (ed.), *Subaltern Studies IV: Writing on South Asian History and Society* (New Delhi: Oxford University Press, 1985), pp. 330-63.
16. James C. Scott, *Weapons of the Weak: Everyday Forms of Peasant Resistance* (New Haven: Yale University Press, 1985).
17. The *Poverty Reduction Strategy Paper* of the government has also identified the 'persistent poverty and inequalities' as providing a fertile breeding ground for the national crisis. The weak impact of various development activities, inadequate delivery of social services, slow pace of decentralization, and inadequate community involvement, and the inadequate resource allocations for the remote areas and regions are stated as the causes for the Maoist insurgency. Accordingly, the mid-western and the far-western regions being sparsely populated had lower political representation in the parliament and lacked the ability to influence resource allocation decisions. Thus these two regions received only 11 to 12 per cent of total government expenditures between 1996/7 and 2000/1. See, NPC, *The Tenth Plan: Poverty Reduction Strategy Paper 2002-2007* (Kathmandu: HMG/National Planning Commission Secretariat, July 2003), pp. 34-5. Despite this ascertained fact, the report, however, has overlooked the more crucial fact that two elected prime ministers from these regions had served the country during the period mentioned, and they were no less influential than their parliamentary colleagues.
18. Lionel Caplan, *Land and Social Change in East Nepal: A Study of Hindu-Tribal Relations* (London: Routledge and Kegan Paul, 1970); Mahesh C.

Regmi, *Landownership in Nepal* (Berkeley, CA: University of California Press, 1977); Bhim Bahadur Pandey, *Tyshbakathko Nepal*, pt. 1 (Nepal of Those Days) (Kathmandu: Centre for Nepal and Asian Studies [2039 BS] 1982).

19. Mahesh C. Regmi, 'Preliminary Notes on the Nature of Rana Law and Government', *Contributions to Nepalese Studies*, June 1975, p. 105.
20. Harka Gurung, *Trident and Thunderbolt: Cultural Dynamics in Nepalese Politics* (Lalitpur: Social Science Baha, April 2003), p. 11.
21. Dor Bahadur Bista, *Fatalism and Development: Nepal's Struggle for Modernization* (Hyderabad: Orient Longman, 1991), pp. 97-100.
22. Piers Blaikie, John Cameron, and David Seddon, *Nepal in Crisis: Growth and Stagnation at the Periphery* (New Delhi: Oxford University Press, 1980); David Seddon, *Nepal: A State of Poverty* (New Delhi: Vikas Publishing House, 1987).
23. Devendra Raj Panday, *Nepal's Failed Development: Reflections on the Mission and the Maladies* (Kathmandu: Nepal South Asia Centre, 1999), p. 9.
24. Mahesh C. Regmi, *Kings and Political Leaders of the Gorkhali Empire 1768-1814* (Hyderabad: Orient Longman, 1995), pp. 49-63.
25. This novella, written by a Nepali born and domiciled in Guwahati, Assam (India), is a reflection of the plight of the Nepali people displaced and dislocated from their home and traditionally settled in various parts of India (including Bhutan) for the bare necessities of their livelihood or, in modern terms, in search of greener pasture. According to available data, the most deprived region of Nepal today, on the basis of poverty and deprivation, is the Karnali Zone, which is neither represented in the state's governance structure nor integrated with other regions of the country by means other than the seasonal air link. Had pervasive poverty, deprivation and popular alienation been the causes of conflict, all, five famine-stricken infested districts of the Karnali Zone would have been the most fertile ground for the Maoists insurgency rather than the districts of Rukum, Rolpa, and Dang of the Rapti Zone. See, Shaubhagya Shah, Karnali: Pida Ra Muktika Upaya (Karnali: Pain and the Means of Relief), *Himal Khabarpatrika*, 29 May-14 June 2000, pp. 12-14. See also Lil Bahadur Chhetri, *Basain* (Lalitpur: Madan Purashkar Pustakalaya, 1958).
26. CESOD, *Impact of Conflict on Agricultural Production and Small Landowners in Nepal* (Kathmandu: Centre for Economic and Social Development, 2003).
27. *Rajbandhi Upachar Thata Bimochan Ek Charcha: Jhapa Bidroha 2027-2030 BS* (Kathmandu: Nava Yuba Samuha, 1981), pp. 63-70.
28. Bista, *Fatalism and Development*, 1991.
29. Pancha N. Maharjan, 'The Maoist Insurgency and Crisis of Governability in Nepal in Dhruba Kumar (ed.), *Domestic Conflict and Crisis of Governability in Nepal* (Kathmandu: Centre for Nepal and Asian Studies, 2000), pp. 191-3.

30. Demand number 10 for drafting of the constitution by the electing Constituent Assembly; number 11 for the abolition of privileges enjoyed by monarchy; and number 12 for bringing the armed forces under the control of the elected agency of the government. See Maharjan, ibid.
31. Dhruba Kumar, 'Proximate Causes of Conflict in Nepal', a paper prepared for the project, 'Causes of Conflict and Means to Resolve Them: Case Study of Nepal' undertaken by the Graduate Institute of International Studies, Geneva, Switzerland, 7 December 2003, p. 6.
32. 'Theoretical Premises for the Historical Initiation of the People's War', *The Worker*, no. 2, June 1996.
33. As a convener of the United National People's Movement (UNPM), Baburam Bhattarai forward put the 10-point demands on 14 April 1990, immediately after the formation of the Interim Government, of which demand number 3 relates to election to Constituent Assembly. See, 'Samyukta Jana Andolanka Dasha Sutriya Tatkalin Magharu' (The Ten Point Demands of the United National People's Movement), in Baburam Bhattarai, *Bartama Nepal Kamunist Party (Maobadi) ko Tarfa Bata Prastut Prastabko Sarsanchhep* (Text of the Summary of Proposal Presented by Nepal Communist Party [Maoist] in the Talks), *Rajdhani* Daily, 28 April 2003, pp. 53-4.
34. Pancha N. Maharjan, 'Role of Extra-Parliamentary Political Party in Multi-Party Democracy: A Study of CPN-Unity Centre', *Contributions to Nepalese Studies*, July 1993, p. 222.
35. Deepak Thapa with Bandita Sijapati, *A Kingdom Under Siege: Nepal's Maoist Insurgency 1996 to 2003* (Kathmandu: The Printhouse, 2003), p. 53.
36. The establishment has found an easy excuse to blame the Maoists for the failure, on account of the deadline set by them, four days prior to which they started the violent armed struggle, on 13 February, giving no time for the government to thoroughly consider their demands and invite them to talk. The fact, however, is that the then Prime Minister Sher Bahadur Deuba, to whom the demands were personally submitted by Baburam Bhattarai, Chairman of the Central Committee of the United People's Front Nepal, had left for New Delhi, India on 11 February 1996 without even acknowledging the case.
37. CPNUC, 'Rajnaitik Pratibedan', Political Report of the Communist Party of Nepal-Unity Centre in Political Documents Presented and Approved by the National Unity Convention (Kathmandu: CPN-Unity Centre 1991), pp. 1-10; Arjun Karki and David Seddon (eds.), *The People's War in Nepal: Left Perspectives* (Delhi: Adroit Publishers, 2003), pp. 88-9.
38. Karki and Seddon, *The People's War*, p. 80.
39. Baburam Bhattarai, *The Politico-Economic Rationale of People's War in Nepal* (Kathmandu: Utprerak Prakashan, 1998).
40. Karki and Seddon, *The People's War*, pp. 77-8.

41. HDC, *Human Development in South Asia 2001* (Karachi: Oxford University Press, 2001), p. 94.
42. UNDP, *Nepal Human Development Report 2001: Poverty Reduction and Governance* (Kathmandu: United Nations Development Programme, 2002), p. 18.
43. The World Bank, *Nepal: Country Assistance Strategy 2004-2007* (Kathmandu: The World Bank, 2004).
44. NSAC, *Nepal: Human Development Report 1998* (Kathmandu: Nepal South Asia Centre, 1998), p. 114.
45. ICIMOD, *Districts of Nepal: Indicators of Development* (Kathmandu: International Centre for Integrated Mountain Development, 2003), p. 22.
46. Bhattarai, *The Politico-Economic Rationale.*
47. Pitamber Sharma, 'Jana Andolan pachi Bampanthi Partiharuko Bhumika: Euta Unpechhit Tippani' (The Role of the Communist Parties after the People's Movement: An Unexpected Critique), *Himal Khabarpatrika*, 27 February-13 March 2001, pp. 11-12.
48. Ibid., pp. 12-13.
49. NSAC, *Nepal.*, p. 128.
50. Mahesh C. Regmi, *Thatched Huts and Stucco Palaces: Peasants and Landlords in 19th Century Nepal* (New Delhi: Vikas Publishing House, 1978), p. 152.
51. Dhruba Kumar, 'Social Structure and Voting Behaviour in Nepal', a draft report prepared for the Project 'Electoral Politics in Nepal', undertaken by Nepal Centre for Contemporary Studies, Sanepa, Lalitpur, Nepal, 30 June 2001.
52. Ibid., p. 13.
53. Krishna B. Bhattachan, *Indigenous Nationalities and Minorities of Nepal*, a report submitted to the Minority Rights Group, MRG International, London, 2003; idem, 'Possible Ethnic Revolution or Insurgency in a Predatory Unitary Hindu State Nepal', in Dhruba Kumar (ed.), *Domestic Conflict and Crisis of Governability in Nepal* (Kathmandu: Centre for Nepal and Asian Studies 2000); idem, 'Ethnopolitics and Ethnodevelopment: An Emerging Paradigm for Nepal', in Dhruba Kumar (ed.), *State, Leadership and Politics in Nepal* (Kathmandu: Centre for Nepal and Asian Studies, 1995). See also, Harka Gurung, 'Nepal: Maoist Insurgency and Indigenous People', *Nepali Journal of Contemporary Studies*, September 2003; Sudheer Sharma, *Ethnic Dimension of the Maoist Insurgency*, a report submitted to the DfID, Kathmandu, May 2002; Mahendra Lawoti, 'Maoists and Minorities: Overlap of Interests or a Case of Exploitation?' *Studies in Nepali History and Society*, 8 (1), 2003.
54. Bhattachan, *Indigenous Nationalition of Nepal*, p. 25.
55. FLWD, *Discriminatory Laws in Nepal and Their Impact on Women: A Review of the Current Situation and Proposals for Change* (Kathmandu: Forum for Women, Law and Development, 2001).

56. Gurung, 'Nepal: Maoist Insurgency', pp. 3-4.
57. CBS, *Population Census 2001: National Report* (Kathmandu: Central Bureau of Statistics, 2002).
58. *Mahima* Weekly, 14 February 1998.
59. Sudheer Sharma, *Ethnic Dimenion of the Maoist Insurgency*, p. 17. See also, Sudheer Sharma and Sri Bhakta Khanal, 'Maobadiko Sampradayik Saathgaath' (The Maoists' Communal Hobnobbing), *Himal Khabarpatrika*, 13-27 February 2002, pp. 26-9.
60. URPC, 'Programme of United Revolutionary People's Council Nepal' (a resolution adopted at the formation of the 37-member United Revolutionary People's Council with Baburam Bhattarai as convener), November 2001.
61. Sudheer Sharma, *Ethnic Dimension of the Maoist Insurgency*, p. 13.
62. Sharad KC, 'Maobadibata Jatibadtira!' (From Maoism to Ethnicism!), *Himal Khabarpatrika*, 28 February-13 March 2004, pp. 28-31; See also, Sudheer Sharma, *Ethnic Dimension*, p. 18.
63. Baburam Bhattarai, *Barta ra Tatkalin Nikashko Prashna* (Kathmandu: Prabhaha Prakashan, 2003), pp. 28-31.
64. URPC, Point 74.
65. Karki and Seddon, *The People's War*, pp. 88-9.
66. CPNUC 'Rajmtaitik Pratibedan'. Also, in the 1992 elections to the local bodies, the CPN-Unity Centre gained berths for 1.3 per cent of members in the municipalities and won 3.54 per cent of the total seats for the elections to the District Development Committees (DDC) and 5.09 per cent of the total seats in the Village Development Committees (VDC).
67. CPNUC, *Nepal Kammunist Party (Ekta Kendra) ko Ekta Mahadhiveshan dwara Nirbachit Bhinnamat ka keshharu tatha Rastriya Ṡallahakar Parishadka Adhyakashya dwara Sampurna party Sadasyaharulai Appeal* (Appeal of the Chairperson of the advisory commission of the 'minority faction' of the CPN-UC to all party members) (Kathmandu: CPN-Unity Centre, 1994).
68. Karki and Seddon, *The People's War*, p. 87.
69. The street agitations against the government's misrule concerning several issues were actually led by the CPN-Unity Centre putting the government in difficulties. The CPN (UML), though earlier providing moral support to the protest movement had withdrawn that support after events turned violent and joined hands with the ruling Nepali Congress party by signing the agreement thus relegating the issues raised by the Unity Centre to the dustbin as the six-point agreement was never implemented. See, Sridhar K. Khatri, 'Political Parties and the Parliamentary Process in Nepal: A Study of the Transitional Phase', in Khatri et al., *Political Parties and The Parliamentary Process in Nepal* (Kathmandu: Political Science Association of Nepal, 1992), p. 27; Maharjan '*Role of Extra-Parliamentary Political Party*', p. 226.
70. Kumar, 'Proximate Causes of Conflict', p. 10.

71. In the words of the Maoist leadership, the 'war to break the shackles of slavery . . . and to establish a New Democratic state would be uphill, full of twists and turns and of a protracted nature, this along is a path of people's liberation and a great and bright future.' See, 'March Along the Path of People's War to Smash the Reactionary State and Establish a New Democratic State', a leaflet distributed on the day of the initiation of the People's War, 13 February 1996.
72. *Rajdhani* Daily, 24 March 2004.
73. *Brief to U.S. Assistance Secretary of State*, a Policy Brief presented by the Director General of Military Operation of Royal Nepalese Army to the visiting US Assistant Secretary of State, Christina Rocca at the RNA Head Quarters, Bhadrakali, Kathmandu on 17 December 2003.
74. *Kathmandu Post*, 19 March 2004.
75. INSEC, 'Preliminary Data: Number of Victim Killed by State and the Maoist in connection with the "People's War", 13 Feb. 1996-4 March', Kathmandu, Informal Sector Service Centre, www.insec.org.np, 2004.
76. Prachanda, 'Ka. Prachandasanghako Taja Antarbarta' (The Latest Interview with Comrade Prachanda), *Mulyankan Monthly*, April-May 1996, pp. 11-14.
77. Ibid., p. 11.
78. The Maoists' have actually become an extra burden for the poor villagers, who are struggling to meet their own bare necessities, because they are forced to provide both food and shelter to a platoon or more of Maoists whenever they knock at their doors. The villagers have to oblige the Maoists' for their fear of being manhandled, tortured or even killed. The case of the killing of a priest in Jajarkot exemplifies the Maoists' ruthlessness. The Maoists abducted the priest when his son—who was a Maoist—surrendered to the police by handing over his rifle. They demanded a compensation of Rs. 2,00,000 for the gun lost to the police. Since the priest had no to to pay, he remained in Maoists' custody and died. See Sudheer Sharma, 'The Maoist Movement: An Evolutionary Perspective', a paper presented at the Seminar on 'The Maoist Movement in Nepal: Context, Causes and Implications', organized by the School of Oriental and African Studies, London, 2-3 November 2001, p. 6.
79. NHRC, *Janayuddhako Karanle Yatana ra Apangtabare Aadhyan: Maobadi Janayuddhako Sandharvamá Manab Adhikarko Ullanghan* (A Study on Torture and Disability Caused by the People's War: The Violation of Human Rights in the Context of the People's War) (Kathmandu: National Human Rights Commission, 2002).
80. NPC, *The Costs of War in Nepal: A Research Study* (Kathmandu: Nepal Peace Campaign, January 2004).
81. Tula Adhikari and Dinesh Gautam, 'Bisthapitko Pida' (The Plights of the Displaced People), *Rajdhani* Daily, 13 February 2004.

82. CESOD, *Impact of Conflict.*
83. Karuna Thapa, 'Nirjan Bannene bhayo Gaon' (Deserted Villages), *Himal Khabarpatrika*, 16-30 December 2002, pp. 10-13. See also, *Himal*, 'Anikalbata Bachau' (Save from Famine), *Himal Khabarpatrika*, 17 November-1 December 2002, pp. 18-23; K.C. Sharad, 'Maobadi Ra Surachya Faujpachi Anikalko Achkram' (Famine Strikes after the Maoist and Security Forces), *Himal Khabarpatrika*, 17 September–1 October 2002, pp. 12-14.
84. *Rajdhani* Daily, 14 March 2004.
85. Rabi Dhami and Rabindra Nath, 'Achhamma Maobadiko Sanya Abhiyan: Anna Ra School Dui Banda' (The Maoists' Military Campaign in Achham: Closure of Schools and Food Supplies), *Himal Khabarpatrika*, 2-15 December 2003, pp. 16-17. See also, Kashiram Dangi, 'Bidhyarthilai Bokaiyo Bandook' (Students are [forcibly] given Military Training), *Nepal* Fortnightly, 28 February-13 March 2004, pp. 28-31.
86. Amnesty International, *A Deepening Human Rights Crisis: Time for International Action* (London: Amnesty International Secretariat, 2002); INSEC, *Nepal: Human Rights Yearbook 2002* (Kathmandu: Informal Sector Service Centre, 2002); Gautam (2001), op. cit.
87. Data cited in Ekindra K. Kunwar and K.P. Dhungana, 'Tuhuro Banayo Yuddhale' (The Orphans of War), *Rajdhani* Daily, 31 January 2004.
88. Gauri Pradhan, 'Thula Yuddha Ladachhan, Balbalika Mulya Chukaunchhan' (Big Fights, Children Pay), *Kantipur* Daily, 19 February 2003.
89. NHRC, 'Rastriya Manab Adhikar Ayogko Awhan' (The Call of the National Human Rights Commission), *Kantipur* Daily, 10 December 2003.
90. *Rajdhani* Daily, 31 January 2004.
91. Dhruba Kumar, 'Consequences of the Militarized Conflict and the Cost of Violence in Nepal', *Contributions to Nepalese Studies*, July 2003, p. 207.
92. Bert Lintner, 'Maoist Moneybags', *Far Eastern Economic Review*, 24 October 2002, p. 25.
93. Kumar, 'Consequences of the Militarized Conflict', pp. 206-7.
94. Bhattarai, *The Politico-Economic Rationale*.
95. Bhattarai, 'Interview' in *Nepali Times*, 13-19 July 2001.
96. Shyam Shrestha, 'Maobadi Janayuddha: Ke Yeshle Deshma Kranti Lyaula?' (Maoist People's War: Will it bring revolution in the country?), *Mulyankan Monthly*, April-May 1996, pp. 4-7. See also, Shrestha, 'Maobadi "Janayuddha" ko Mulyankanma Prakashit Samichyabare', Comments on the 'People's War', 2 pts., *Mulyankan Monthly*, August-September and October 1997, pp. 18-21, 42-7; Mohan Bikram Singh, *RIM Ra Maobadiharuko Kathita Janayuddha* (RIM and the so-called People's War of the Maoists) (Kathmandu: Jana Shichhya Griha, 2002).
97. Bhattarai, *The Politico-Economic Rationale*.

98. Emphasis added. See, Bhattarai, 'Naya "Kot Parva" Lai Manyata Dinu Hunna' (New 'Kot Parva' Should not be Recognized), *Kantipur* Daily, 6 June 2001.
99. Ibid.
100. Ibid.
101. Bhattarai, 'Belabhakhatka Kura: Sabaile Gambhirata Purbak Sochhunuparne Bela' (Timely Matter: All Should Think Seriously), *Janadesh Weekly*, 22 February 2000.
102. Bhattarai, 'Akashmik Dhangle Ganatantrako Janma Bhayako Chha' (Suddenly the Republic has born), *Rajdhani* Daily, 29 June 2001.
103. Bhattarai, 'Rastriyata Ra Ganatantra: Rastriya Sahamatiko Mul Aadhar' (Nationalism and Republic: the main foundation of National Consensus), *Kantipur* Daily, 3 August 2001; Bhattarai, 'Bartaman Gatanakram lai Kashari Herne?' (How to look at current Events?), *Dishabodh* Monthly, July/August 2001.
104. See also, Bhattarai (2003), op. cit.
105. Personal Communication, Kathmandu, 24 November 2003. The last round of talks was held on 17 August and the Maoists unilaterally pulled out of the talks on 27 August 2003.
106. The spokesperson of the CPN (Maoist) and one of the members of the Maoist negotiation team, Krishna Bahadur Mahara, is attributed with having publicly announced this while at a meeting for the Bheri-Karnali Autonomous Region in mid-west Nepal on 22 January 2004. See, Rameshowar Bohara, 'Paramsenadhipatitwa Tyage Rajtantra Swikarna Sakinchha: Maobadi' (Monarchy can be accepted if the King dispense with the Supreme Commander-in-Chief of the Armed Forces, says the Maoist), *Rajdhani* Daily, 23 January 2004.
107. *Deshanter Weekly*, 8 February 2004.
108. Jaya Prakash Anand, *Akhtiyarko Thuna: Mero Samjhana* (In the Custody of Commission for Investigation of Abuses of Authority: My Reminiscence) (Kathmandu: Madhesi Manab Adhikar Sanrachyan Kendra, 2004), p. 150.
109. Krishna Khanal, 'Kina Chahiyo Sambidhan Sabha nai Yetibela? (Why is the Constituent Assembly needed now?), *Mulyankan Monthly*, December 2003, p. 11. See also, Shyam Shrestha, 'Sambidhan Sabhako Auchitya' (The Imperative of Constituent Assembly), in Rajendra Maharjan (ed.), *Rastriya Sankat Ra Sambidhan Sabha* (National Crisis and Constituent Assembly) (Kathmandu: Mulyankan Prakashan Griha, 2004), pp. 44-5.
110. 'Lucknow Barta', *Mulyankan Monthly*, December 2003, pp. 5-7.
111. Tirtha Koirala, 'Amelako Lucknow Yatra' (The Lucknow Trip of UML), *Nepal* Fortnightly, 2-16 December 2003, p. 37.
112. Prachanda, 'Let's Concentrate Total Force to Raise Preparation for the

(Strategic) Offensive to a New Height Through Correct Handling of Contradiction', Supplementary Resolution to 'Current Situation and Our Historical Task', presented by Chairman Prachanda and adopted by the Politburo of the Central Committee of the CPN (Maoist) in October 2003, *Maoist Information Bulletin*, no. 6, 25 October 2003.

113. Ibid.
114. NC, *Santipurna Samyukta Janaandolan 2060* (Peaceful United People's Movement 2060) (Kathmandu: Nepali Congress Central Office, 2003).
115. Khanal, 'Kina Charhiyo', pp. 8-12. See also, Rajendra Maharjan (ed.), *Rastriya Sankat Ra Sambidhan Sabha* (National Crisis and the Constituent Assembly) (Kathmandu: Mulyankan Prakashan Griha, 2004).
116. During the four months of 'ceasefire', between July and October 2001 and again between February and August 2003, the Maoist leaders were trying their best to win public opinion to influence and persuade the leaders of political parties through informal mediation by the intelligentsia for the formation of a united front against monarchy. Besides the native forces, the Maoist leaders had also knocked on the doors of foreign diplomatic missions, including the American Embassy, to sell their agenda.
117. According to the Financial Controller-General's Office, out of the 75 administrative districts in Nepal only 11 are income surplus in terms of revenue-regular expenditure besides development expenditure.
118. Contrarily, recruitment in the Royal Nepal Army and the Armed Police Forces has provided rural youths a chance to be enlisted in government forces. According to *Brief*, the size of the army is 72,000 (see, *Brief to U.S. Assistance Secretary of State*), and 6,400 more recruits were added to the army more recently. The size of the newly created Armed Police Force is 18,000 and the Civil Police 48,500. As these agencies of the state are gradually absorbing unemployed youths from the villages, the consequence is the natural dent in the Maoists' manpower resources in the villages.
119. There are contrary arguments on the role of women in the Maoists' 'People's War' concerning whether it is victimization or empowerment. Among the few specific studies published on women's role in the 'People's War', some suggest that 'The supposition that janajati women [non-Hindus] make up the majority of Maoist women remain unsubstantiated. . . . It has generally been observed that most female Maoist cadre in rural areas are very young, usually under the age of 20 [and] unmarried.' According to Comrade Parvati, however, 'they soon face internal party pressure to get married. This results in marriage against their wishes or before they are ready to get married.' By focusing their recruitment efforts on unmarried women, 'the party may control marriage choices to a large extent, and also manipulate marriage alliances for political

purposes. The leadership may view marriage as a means of controlling female cadres and making it more difficult for them to leave the party, whereas women with existing marital ties . . . are seen as more likely to have conflicting allegiances. . . . Maoist attitudes towards gender relations are [thus] contradictory.' See Judith Pettigrew and Sara Shneiderman, 'Ideology and Agency in Nepal's Maoist Movement', *Himal South Asian*, January 2004, pp. 19-29. For a contrary view, see Hisila Yami, 'Janamukti Sena, Shahi Sena Ra Mahila' (People's Liberation Army, Royal Army and Women), *Kantipur* Daily, 23 February 2004, p. 6.

CHAPTER VII

Terrorism and Subalternity – III: India and the Sub-nationalist Movements in Mizoram and Nagaland

Sanjoy Hazarika

In a great arc moving across the Hindu Kush, the Pir Panjal of Jammu & Kashmir and the Himalayas from Afghanistan through Nepal to the Patkai range on the Indo–Myanmar border, and in small but violent pockets in Sri Lanka and its spillover into India's Tamil Nadu state (and earlier in the Punjab), powerful armed movements are vigorous and active, seeking a diverse range of goals. These goals are as different as the ethnic and national groups from which these armed campaigns spring. There are those who are defined as 'terrorist' groups, especially since they come directly into conflict with US interests and those of its allies in the North Atlantic Treaty Organization (NATO); groups as the Al Qaida of Osama bin Laden figure on this list as do numerous armed organizations in the Middle East and South and South-East Asia, including the Liberation Tigers of Tamil Eelam of Sri Lanka and the Lashkar-e-Toiba and Jaish-e-Muhammad of Jammu & Kashmir.

The detailed categorization was spelt out by the US Administration after the country was stunned by the events of 9/11 and broadened over the years with more organizations added to an ever-growing list. This has been discussed in other chapters and one does not wish or plan to go into these specific issues here. But what about those combatants who do not fall into the category of 'terrorists', as Washington sees them, although governments in South Asia are determined to push for such categorization, especially India.

The media too is quick to jump on the government bandwagon, confusing terrorists with militants or insurgents. The problems of definition exist and the media often makes the mistake of taking the government's point of view too literally, and takes sides in conflicts where the 'terrorists' are seen as violators of the human rights of 'innocents' and a threat to the existence of the state.[1] In turn, the state's forces are portrayed in a 'heroic' mode, upholding the flag and Constitution at the cost of their lives at the hands of 'villainous' groups which are controlled by outside powers: in the case of Kashmir, that power is seen as Pakistan while the tentacles of the Inter-State Services Intelligence agency purportedly reach through Bangladesh to the north-east. Of course, independent media groups also report violations of rights by security forces, especially in Kashmir although often the issues are portrayed in simple black-and-white terms—good versus bad.

What is important to note, though, is that the 'terrorist' label is applied too easily these days, especially when US interests are involved. The Osama bin Laden group targets US strategic and economic interests wherever it can,[2] in alliance with a motley crew of Islamic factions in different parts of the Middle East and Asia as well as the armed groups in India's Jammu & Kashmir state, which include the *fidayeen* or suicide squads of largely non-Kashmiris (meaning non-Indians) who include well-trained Pakistanis. Those using the classical tactics of ambush and hit-and-run as well as of explosives against military and even civil targets include local Kashmiri groups.

Their aims of independence for Kashmir as well as hurting India appear intertwined, although the first slogan does not resonate these days as strongly as it did in the 1990s—there is a growing public weariness with conflict and its many children: despair, hurt and grief, terror and extortion, corruption and lack of economic growth, collapse of governance, and not the least, of infrastructure, and basic essential services and facilities such as hospitals, the school system and roads.

What is important to note here again is that the fighters from across the border include large numbers of people of Punjabi origin (the dominant ethnic and linguistic group of the Pakistan-held part of Kashmir) while those inside the valley in India are predominantly Kashmiri by origin.

The Maoist movement in Nepal has exploded over the past years with little sign of abating and greater indication that this struggle will be bloody and long.[3] Scores of policemen or Maoist fighters are killed in battles on remote hilltops, their bodies scattered on wet earth and under pouring rain.[4] It is an unforgiving fight, which has pitted villagers against each other and brother against brother. Those involved in the anti-government fight include Nepalese of different ethnic/tribal stock.[5]

The Sri Lanka experience is being studied in detail elsewhere, although no survey of terrorism or militancy in South Asia would be complete without a look at the Sikh separatist movement of the 1980s, which was ultimately ruthlessly crushed by the state in the 1990s, albeit with significant support from the much-harassed and alienated Punjabi villagers of different caste groups, who were angered by the continuous intimidation from the armed factions, a fall in economic status as well as the molestation of women by these groups.[6] Yet, that experience has devastated many innocent families, thrown up hundreds of cases of 'missing' young men, who have been taken away by security forces. There has been widespread grief and bitterness.

This chapter focuses on the anti-state, armed, ethnic-sub-nationalist movements of the north-east of India, spawned by a number of complex factors. These include a questioning both of what is viewed as an uncertain colonial legacy, a questioning of the legitimacy of the successor Indian state, a sense of deep alienation from New Delhi but increasing intolerance of smaller or 'equal' ethnic groups by larger ethnics. The latter process is reflected in the example of numerous armed groups in the north-east which were, as it were, born to fight the legitimacy of the Indian State.[7] Over the decades, several of these organizations appear to have lost track of the highway and their high goals. They appear to have meandered into the side alleys of bitter and fierce jousting and fighting against ethnic rivals, squandering energy, time, and people in fights for ideological, monetary, territorial, and armed control.

There are at least as many of languages or dialects as there are ethnic groups. The population is reasonably small—about 35 million of a total of one billion for India overall, or less than 4 per cent of the national population.[8] Yet, there are barely six scripts among them all—Assamese and Bengali are dominant. The substantial

Hindi speakers and Nepalese speakers use Devanagari. The region has borders with four nations: Bhutan, Tibet (China), Myanmar, and Bangladesh. The link with India, as one has underlined often before, is perilously tenuous, in physical and emotional terms as well as economic: only one per cent of the borders of the north-east is with India. The rest are with other countries. One slim land corridor represents the Indian connection the Chicken's Neck also called the Siliguri Corridor—barely 20 km wide at its narrowest. As the crow flies, Shillong, capital of Meghalaya and one of the prettier hill cities of India, is closer to Hanoi than it is to New Delhi. And therein lies much of the tale.

The roots of the region's growing and undiminished complexity are to be found in the geographical, cultural, political, and historical spaces which make up the north-east.

The region, as has been remarked elsewhere, is both extremely difficult and very vibrant. It is home to some 350 ethnic communities in 8 states, a number of whom have both kinship and historic ties to South-East Asia—whether it is the Tai-Khamtis of Arunachal Pradesh who trace their origins to Putok in northern Myanmar, or the Lisus of the same state, who have large communities both in northern Myanmar and in China's Yunnan Province (where they have a sub-prefecture and are among the larger of that state's many minority groups). The Ahoms of Assam, whose forebears ruled the state for 600 years between 1226 and 1826,[9] migrated from the Shan area bordering Myanmar and Thailand in the thirteenth century, while the Khasis of Meghalaya, who speak a variety of Mon-Khmer, are said to be descendants of travellers from Cambodia and migrated to the Shillong Plateau via the Brahmaputra Valley. The Ahoms, defined as one of the many Other Backward Castes (OBC) of the country, are small in number, largely economically backward though politically influential—a far cry from the time when they ruled Assam.

The Monpas of Arunachal Pradesh have kin in Tibet; the Khasis and Garos of Meghalaya are separated from their communities in Bangladesh by a line drawn, at the time of Partition, by Sir Cyril Radcliffe who was in a hurry to finish his job and leave the sub-continent. Sir Cyril left a lingering legacy of devastation, suspicion, sundered families and economies, and broken relations, visible in the poverty and backwardness of the border areas, for example, of Meghalaya, where the presence of the government is visible by its absence. Before-independence, trade flourished here with meat, fish, and oil, as well as consumer goods from the plains, being exchanged for vegetables, fruit, and handmade fabrics and household goods. Today, thanks to the line of Partition that cuts across homes, hearts, and societies, not to speak of states, the process of marginalization and alienation continues unabated.

These processes have had a sharp impact on the 'nation-building' concepts and campaigns led by mainland India and its political heart, New Delhi. But the pattern of these processes within the region itself have been different, underlining the important role of inter-regional political approaches and ethnic aspirations. An example of this can be seen in the contrast of militarization and conflict in two parts of the north-east. In neither place would the term terrorism be appropriate for these are ethno-centric political movements, undergirded by the force of arms aimed against the Indian state and not seeking any religious or particular truth as espoused by Islamic fundamentalists. In the north-east, for example, the phrase or term 'terrorist' is notable in the main by its lack of use. However, it is used occasionally by the local media and even this is infrequent. In the 1960s and 1970s, the peak of period insurgencies in Nagaland and Mizoram, the anti-state fighters were described variously as 'hostiles' or insurgents or the underground.[10] There was of course also an 'over ground'—the group that had left the path of violence and gone over to the state and is regarded as 'anti-national' by those who carry the torch for the movement.[11] A 'middle ground' also existed: this group maintained contacts between the government and the 'underground', conveyed messages and kept an informal dialogue of sorts going.

These three levels of militant activity continue across many parts of the region. Until the end of the last century, the word terrorist was hardly used even by Indian government forces that fought these groups in not less than seven of eight states. More often, the vocabulary would reflect local public sentiment: 'misguided elements', extremists or 'rebels' would be favoured and would be approvingly reflected in the media. Then there would be a different lexicon for the organizations themselves fighting for independence.

Thus, in Nagaland, there are not less than five 'governments', with insurgent groups asserting their right to such positions and nomenclature.

One is the state government; the second is the central government of India, represented by the governor and central forces. Then there are three 'underground governments'. Two of them have the same name although they belong to rival groups of the National Socialist Council of Nagalim (Nagaland): Government of the Peoples Republic of Nagaland. A third is the older Federal Government of Nagaland, which is led by the original faction that declared independence but is now a rump group. They collect taxes (even from government officials, professionals, and politicians), have the equivalent of presidents and prime ministers and even have a council of ministers as well as a parliament and maintain standing armies.

Naga fighters for sovereignty are called 'national workers' and are respected on the whole—it does not matter which faction they belong to. Of these, one has been resolved politically (Mizoram) and the second is in the process of negotiations with an on-again-off-again dialogue (the Nagas). Other militarized conflicts in the region, as the once-insurgent United Liberation Front of Asom, now regarded as a low-level law-and-order problem, remain as far from a settlement as they ever were because their principal players remain locked in armed conflict with the state and are banned by New Delhi. The reference here is to the states of Manipur, Tripura and Assam. Barring Mizoram, the Centre and its agencies have armed themselves with sweeping powers, especially under the Armed Forces Special Powers Act which gives authority to soldiers to enter homes, search, arrest, and detain without warrants and even kill—without any punitive retaliatory action being available to victims of such assault. Indeed, if one considers the process of terror—'fear and awe' as perhaps the American military would put it—then it is the Indian state that has struck this chord in the hearts of individuals and people in these states.

There are countless individuals from Nagaland and Manipur who speak of recurring nightmares of fleeing from the armed forces, their fears triggered by the whine of a jeep engine.[12] Their fears and traumas, their hidden terror, remain untouched and unhealed by trained counsellors. They have not been compensated: their attackers and those who brought fear into their lives are untouched and probably living 'normal' lives far from the north-east, while their victims continue to cower and shudder at raised voices and at the sight of uniforms and armed men.

In this paper, the dominant focus will be on Mizoram and Nagaland.

I

MIZORAM: COMING TO TERMS

After nearly two decades of conflict and bitterness, between 1966 and 1986, the Mizos came to terms with the reality of India. The fighters who once sought independence from Delhi cut the best political and economic deal that they could for the Mizos. The Mizo uprising, led by Laldenga, a former government clerk, and his Mizo National Front in February 1966 shook the Indian state as much as any other event in its history. The rebels almost overran the district capital of the then Lushai Hills, Aizawl, but for one tough Assam Rifles unit which held out and a number of other towns, such as Lunglei. Indian Air Force planes strafed Aizawl and the rebel positions, and reinforcements were rushed to the town to evict the insurgents who declared they were fighting for independence.[13] One cannot recall a similar event in India since 1947—barring the fall of Kohima to Naga fighters in 1956—even in the Kashmiri and Punjabi movements, when the headquarters of a district was virtually taken over by an armed group demanding separation.

The insurgency lingered in the Lushai Hills, later called the Mizo hills, until 1986, creating terrible social upheavals, bloodshed, victimization of innocents, and militarization of the area, the second hill region after the Naga insurgency of the 1950s to engage in a continuous armed fight with the Government of India. One of the most prominent aspects of the fighting was the decision by the central government early in the conflict to hit hard at the roots and traditions of the Mizos by forcibly evicting them from homes and villages where they had lived for generations.[14] This was a relentless systematic displacement or movement of population, which tore the basic fabric of Mizo society apart as families were uprooted from their settlements in a matter of hours at gunpoint, herded into trucks with what little personal goods they could gather and taken to a point along the main road where they could be controlled and kept under constant surveillance.

These new settlements were called 'regrouped villages', and the process of moving the tiny clusters of hill hamlets was known as Regrouping. This brutal assault on a proud and sensitive people had its origins in a similar plan tried by the British in Malaysia to crush a guerrilla revolt in the 1950s. The trauma of that time has rarely been experienced by most Indians, and those who suffered at the time—a victim likened the experience, after witnessing the torture of his father by troops, to living in a 'concentration camp'[15]—continue to carry the scars, both physical and psychological. Among the greatest sufferers of the conflict in Mizoram, as elsewhere in the world, were women and children: in many cases women became heads of households when men went 'missing', as either combatants or detainees. Till today, many victims of the fighting have rarely visited a counsellor or a counselling centre because their problems were regarded as psychosomatic or physical and their wounds remain unhealed.

Yet for the most part, despite these tragedies, the 'underground', as the Mizo fighters were known, followed a code of conduct which had been set by their comrades in neighbouring Nagaland—families of armed combatants as well as of civilian officials were not to be targeted. Indeed, at times, officials were tipped off about possible ambushes and told to avoid certain routes at specific times. An unofficial truce held during the Christmas period—something that is barely possible in the kinds of conflicts that rage across the world, whether in Afghanistan and Central Asia or in South-East Asia and the Middle East.

Yet despite all these problems, the MNF under Laldenga was able, over a period of ten years, to finally close the chapter of violence and confrontation. Laldenga was helped by a number of factors. One was the support that the insurgent leader enjoyed in his organization as well as among the Mizos at large: The second was the public weariness with a long-drawn conflict which showed few signs of ending positively for the Mizos, given the overwhelming strength of the Indian military, among the largest in the world, and at that time engaged locally only in Mizoram and the Naga Hills. The army and the paramilitary forces appeared prepared to take losses and other costs and continue to fight indefinitely because of the political support behind them and New Delhi's refusal to let any part of India go. The third was a practical realization among insurgents and their people that it was best to end the fight and get maximum advantages from the Government of India, in terms of amnesty as well as economic, social and political benefits for the Mizos.[16] In exchange for a cessation of hostilities, laying down of weapons, and acceptance of the Indian Constitution, Mizoram was upgraded from a union territory to a state, Laldenga became its chief minister as the ban on the MNF was lifted, and an amnesty was declared for cadres who were then rehabilitated. The MNF has since split, been voted to power twice and defeated not less than three times in its embrace of democracy and efforts to rule the state.

Other substantial reasons for these changes include the pressure from civil society groups, especially the Church, which wanted a cessation of hostilities and bloodshed. There is also a practical, no-nonsense approach among the Mizos, which is based on a clear assessment of ground realities. In this, perhaps they are different from several, other ethnic groups in the north-east—where the past, the present and the future come together in a merging that makes it impossible to get out of emotional and 'historic' time warps and a sense that any settlement less than the most difficult and that set by the movement's leaders fifty years or so back would be regarded as a 'sellout' or unacceptable. Often they fall into their own trap of rhetoric and unreality.

The settlement between Laldenga and the Government of India, hammered out over months of discussions in New Delhi, Mizoram as well as overseas, brought about three immediate results: it took the Mizos into the 'Indian' fold and once there, there has been no looking back; it closed the chapter of violence and bloodshed, bringing peace and stability to a deeply wounded land and people; and democracy and politics began to flourish at different levels, with mixed fortunes for various players, including the MNF which had seemed so powerful with its armed cadres.

In the playground of democracy, open public opinion counted for much more than it had ever done in the years of conflict, demolishing myths such as the MNF's halo of invincibility and political rectitude: rifts emerged, splitting the organization and leading to its fall from grace and government within three years of the settlement. 'This went to prove that guerrilla leaders who consider themselves indispensable to the lay people seldom inspire respect and confidence once the gun is out of their hands. In a democracy, people cannot be ruled by violence,' remarked Gen. V.N. Sharma, former Chief of the Army Staff.[17]

In addition, other developments have taken place—the Mizos, who are now a majority in their own state (until 1972, it was a district of Assam and alienated as a result of a famine in 1959 which paved the way for Laldenga's rise and that of the MNF), have confrontations with at least two of the small ethnic groups that have sprouted their own militant organizations—the Hmars and the Reangs.[18] About 40,000 of the latter have been living in refugee camps in neighbouring Tripura for the past five years, since they fled an anti-Reang campaign by the Mizos angered by the killing of a forest official. Then there are uneasy relationships with three other small ethnics; the Chakmas, Maras, and Lais, each with a population of about 50,000 and located in the state's south, bordering Bangladesh and Myanmar.

Mizoram thus affords a clear illustration of what was originally viewed as a bilateral problem becoming internalized and then being submerged into an intra-ethnic power play where the ethnic majority (in this case, the Mizos) has sought to assert its power and control over smaller ethnics in much the same way as Assam tried with the Mizos before the uprising. Yet, as has been stressed earlier, at no point was the Mizo uprising defined as a 'terrorist' revolt, either at the time of its conduct or in the analyses and popular writings of the movement. One reason, of course, is that the movement preceded the worldwide political upheavals that spawned the use of the word and, for the main, it is seen as denoting Islamic fundamentalism. As in the case of the Nagas, the malcontents were described variously as 'hostiles', 'UGs', 'insurgents', or extremists.

The respective cases of Nagaland and Assam are quite different in that their struggles span periods when the practise of terrorism and the use of the word has became quite widespread. The Naga insurgency is perhaps the longest-running armed conflict of the twentieth century, which has spilled into the twenty-first century. Its fighting groups have battled the Indian government, with assistance from Pakistan and China in one phase (as did the Mizos in the 1970s until the fall of East Pakistan led to the end of that support). They have conducted a ceasefire and cessation of hostilities at least once (which lasted for eight years in the 1960s and 1970s). One faction negotiated an agreement which was denounced by most Nagas and led to a sharp split in Naga ranks. Today a ceasefire remains in place with the two major factions of the National Socialist Council of Nagalim, one led by Th. Muivah and Isak Chisi Swu while the other is headed by S.S. Khaplang.

II

NAGALAND: CONCEPTS OF NATIONHOOD

To place the Naga situation in a historical context it is necessary to state that for centuries the Naga groups had little exposure to the outside world. The Naga tribes are located in the states of Nagaland, Manipur, and Assam, as well as Arunachal Pradesh in India. They are also found in neighbouring Myanmar. But their interactions with non-Naga groups remained limited. They were never, as far as we are able to deduce, under any 'Indian' ruler, although there were occasional campaigns by the Manipur Maharaja to the south against them.

There were armed incursions into the Assam plains during the period of the Ahoms, a barter trade for salt, and, when the British decided to expand into Naga territory, armed clashes with the new intruders.[19] The results were predictable: despite suffering some initial reverses, the British defeated the Nagas but followed a policy largely of non-interference in their affairs, although a few officials were deputed to ensure that things remained under control. British and American missionaries followed the presence of the colonial force, as in other parts of the world, bringing education as well as the Bible.

But no account suggests that the Nagas, though fiercely independent—with their village republics and strong tribe affiliations —were a united nation. The concept of nationhood presupposes a basic political format: of defined borders, of a common political system and leadership, of currency and a common army to defend such a system. That concept came much later with the growth of political awareness. In the case of the Nagas, a group of tribes independent of each other, armed with an oral history given to them by the British, have slowly emerged as a political entity in the middle part of the twentieth century with common goals, pole-vaulting earlier processes of assimilation and state formation in mainland India. This is a unique phenomenon and the Naga case, as much as any other in the region, exemplifies the historic and notional concepts of territory and nationhood.

The anthropologist, B.K. Roy-Burman, speaks of the need to recognize what he defines as 'peoplehood'.[20] Into this concept is woven the political identity as well as cultural and other traditions of ethnic groups, their attachment to land and the forests as well as the idea of their own well-being. In some cases, it is a way of defining themselves through the perception of 'the other'—in the case of the Nagas, it is first seeing themselves as different and separate from the rest of India and then as entities different from their immediate neighbours, Assam, Manipur and Myanmar.

In the twentieth century, Nagas who travelled abroad during World War I, especially in the Labour Corps, were exposed to the global social currents and political changes. They set up the Naga Club in Kohima upon their return, and in 1929 struck their first united political blow aimed at recapturing past history. When the Simon Commission came to India that year, a group of Naga elders called on it and presented a memorandum which said in part, that when the British left, they should leave the Nagas as they were before the colonial power came to the hills.[21]

One sticking point in the current situation is that of territory and land. The British decision to transfer extensive forests, which the Nagas claim as their traditional lands, to the jurisdiction of the Assam districts of Goalpara and Nogaon (earlier Nowgong) in the nineteenth century is strongly opposed by Nagas as illegal.[22] At the same time, the Nagas cite this move as historic evidence of their demand and, therefore, reason or cause for their transfer back to Naga control, a position that is fiercely resisted by Assam which is one-third of its size at independence, fearing it would be reduced to a fraction of its former self! Colonial power, which is seen as the cause of the current problems of the Nagas, is then conveniently used to legitimize and buttress arguments on the larger Nagaland or Nagalim theory. Legitimacy is sought to be borrowed from those very histories that are otherwise rejected.

In the 1940s, Naga opinion got a visionary and leader in A.Z. Phizo, who asserted that his people had never been part of India and had never been conquered by any Indian empire or even the British.[23] Phizo took over the reins of the NNC and met officials in Assam to persuade them of his convictions and dreams: that they should be as independent of India as India was to be of Britain.

The Naga case for a greater homeland disparages India's development of the north-eastern state structure and specifically the mapping of the boundaries of the provinces, particularly Nagaland, Manipur, and Assam. It says that these are neocolonial structures that were imposed on an unsuspecting community unaware of its legal rights. Blame is placed also on the British for dividing the Nagas between Myanmar and India, and there are demands, even today which seek clarification from London on the status and rights of the Nagas.[24]

This is an issue on which the National Socialist Council of Nagalim (NSCN), especially the Muivah-Issak Swu group which is the largest and most powerful, places much importance. The NSCN says that India as the successor state made the same mistake as the colonial power by rejecting Naga demands to sit at a separate table. These demands were dismissed as unacceptable, without historical substance, and tantamount to treason. When Phizo and the NNC persisted with their campaign and the first clashes erupted in the Naga Hills, New Delhi rushed troops to tackle what was a political challenge and the tragedy of the area began to unfold, page by page, chapter by chapter.

Within the various echelons of the Indian state, there is strong support for calling out the army where the police fail. According to Gen. V.N. Sharma, in such situations, 'army sub-units get good training for war when employed in a hostile guerrilla environment over a period of time. Every soldier and junior officer has to hone his combat and leadership skills in a threatened environment, and yet learn to carry out civil action and tactfully handle innocent civilians if their support is to be retained.'[25]

While it is not critical to place all developments in the Naga story here, some need to be stressed. The repercussions of the decision to deploy the army, albeit to recapture Kohima which had fallen to the rebels in 1956 (an operation which was accomplished in a few weeks), are to be seen in the continued bitterness and suspicion that many Nagas harbour towards the Indian State, and in the disastrous human rights record of the security forces, especially in their treatment of women and captives—often the innocent were victims of assault and torture. This is a long list of damage and harm which has been extensively recorded by individuals and groups such as Nandita Haksar, Ram Kumar, The Other Media as well as the Naga Peoples Movement for Human Rights and international organizations like Amnesty International.[26]

There are few Naga families which have not felt the impress of the Indian state or suffered an injury, bereavement or significant loss as a result of security operations—and now because of the infighting among the Naga groups, although this is far less than the pressure exerted by the army and paramilitary forces. Despite this, for many years, the Nagas maintained a code, as did the Mizos, of not targeting civilian officials and their relatives. In recent years, there has been a change in this approach with attacks on or kidnappings of senior state officials in Nagaland as well as in Manipur. Large amounts in 'taxes' are paid every year to the various underground factions, particularly the NSCN (I-M) and its bete noire, the NSCN (Khaplang).[27] One of these factions is estimated to have raised about Rs. 50 crore from such extortions in the state of Nagaland alone, which funds the upkeep of its army as well as the political structure.[28]

It must be clarified here that the structure of the Naga political movement, even though it has, for the most part, depended on arms to establish its demands, does not come close to the broad definition of terrorism. All three major groups (the first split occurred in the 1970s and the second in the 1980s) have a system of political administration with a cabinet headed by a president or chairman; there is also a prime minister with a council of ministers (*kilonsers*). There is the equivalent of an assembly or parliament known as the Tata Hoho, patterned on the traditional tribal councils known as hohos which acted as a forum for the discussion of issues important to the village and individuals. The army too has a clear chain of command and it has always been under the control of the civil wing of the movement.

Thus, while a broad democratic foundation lies at the heart of the movement, in the vision of its founders and idealists, much of this has been hurt in recent years by the control that small groups exercise in each of the three Naga factions. These factions are dominated by one of the major ethnic groups that make up the Nagas, and the controlling team within each organization often brooks no opposition and is unprepared to accept a democratic and open approach to issues. This could be partly because each side believes that its ideological perception is the correct one although personal prejudices among the leaders also play a part in the development of these confrontations.[29]

Again, the label of terrorism is difficult to pin on to an ethnic-inspired movement like the Nagas. Terror was experienced by civil populations in the Naga and Mizo Hills during the security operations. While these could be attributed to the immediate provocation of the armed revolt by both groups, fear and apprehension among the innocent were caused by the security operations against the militants, not the other way around.

There was popular backing for the Naga and other armed movements because the cause was held to be national and the struggle initially subsumed traditional divisions of tribe and other rivalries. In addition, the public was opposed to and further embittered by the violence unleashed by an insensitive central government and its security forces. Yet, as mentioned earlier, the 'underground' remained committed to an unwritten code of conduct—civilians were rarely if ever attacked; senior officials were untouched if they were travelling with their families; and there was a Christmas truce where a ceasefire was observed by all sides.[30] This was, to make an understatement, gentlemanly conduct when compared with other guerrilla movements in South and South-East Asia, not to speak of Central Asia and the Middle East, which stand out because of their violence and which, in turn, invite brutal retaliation, especially in the case of Israel and the Palestinians.

The use of terror tactics—which is significantly different from terrorism as an ideology per se—such as ethnic cleansing, when civilians become 'collateral' or even deliberate targets, began in the 1990s with brutal assaults on the members of ethnic groups identified by militant organizations as either collaborative with the Indian government or another faction or simply because they were settled on lands over which the militants wanted control as a strategic or territorial space. This was visible in the Naga–Kuki clashes of Manipur and then later in the Kuki–Paite fighting in the same state.[31] In Assam, especially, militant groups such as the banned National Democratic Front of Bodoland and the now legal Bodoland Tiger Force have used IEDs which have blasted civilian targets. These groups have also been involved in alleged massacres and indiscriminate shootings at bazaars to intimidate other tribes and settlers, such as the Santhals.

Despite being a part of India since 1947 and the formation of a separate state in 1963, the feeling of separateness runs deep among the Nagas. There is also a strong desire, as expressed in not less than four resolutions of the state legislature as well as the statements of the 'underground' organizations and civil society groups, for the Nagas to live under one administrative unit. This has broad acceptance among the Nagas although some see the difficulties of establishing a larger Naga state over the fierce opposition of their neighbours, particularly Assam and Manipur.[32]

Ruthless tactics passed off as 'disciplinary measures' have occasionally formed part of the way the Naga military has kept its cadres in line. When separate incidents of rape were reported in Nagaland in the past years involving cadres from both factions, the principal accused were executed.[33] Yet, if anything, the basic democratic approach of the Naga organizations has led them to accept two steps which reflect the desire for a long-term settlement, renouncing violence as a way to settle disputes. New Delhi by accepting this approach has also signalled that it believes that the problem cannot be resolved through military means for it remains, in essence, a political issue.

The first step has been separate ceasefires with the two main groups and a detailed break-up of how these ceasefires are to be conducted. This break-up includes the relocation of fighters in designated camps, no parading or travel with weapons outside these camps and intimation to be given to local Indian force commanders when travel to places outside the designated camps is proposed. Many of these clauses have been observed in their breach, yet the ceasefires continue to extended for year every year, hinting at both their fragility and the recognition of their need.

The second step has been unconditional talks aimed at a future settlement. There have been seven years of negotiations and hard bargaining with emissaries of the Government of India with the NSCN (I-M), though no formal negotiations have yet begun with the Khaplang group, which is viewed by the Centre as considerably weakened in the past year in its war of attrition with its rival. Most of the meetings have been held overseas, at locales such as Amsterdam, Florence, Kuala Lumpur, and Bangkok. The main negotiator for the NSCN (I-M) is Th. Muivah, the General Secretary, while former Home Secretary K. Padmanabhiah has been the Prime Minister's representative.

While the talks have stuttered along, the biggest gainer are the people of Nagaland who are seeing a genuine though shaky peace for the first time in over twenty years, especially the younger generation whose lives have been marked by conflict, uncertainty, and tragedy. Clashes occasionally erupt among the rival factions but the standoff with government forces or active operations by the latter has closed. The relief is palpable, with restaurants remaining open till 9 p.m. (this is considered very late) in the commercial town of Dimapur in the plains and some shops in Kohima stay open till 6:30 or 7 p.m. In the past Kohima, the capital, would shut down by 4 p.m.! However, it is also widely acknowledged that the dominant I-M group is seeking to make further inroads into areas of the state where it was not strong earlier at the cost of the other groups.

A sticking point—and possibly a breaking point for the negotiations—remains that of territory. The NSCN (I-M) demand at the negotiating table is of bringing together 'traditional Naga lands', including those parts in Assam, Manipur, and Arunachal Pradesh where Nagas currently live.[34] This is stoutly opposed by the first two states although Arunachal has not as vehement. The northern part of Manipur which borders Nagaland, is dominated by Nagas. It includes the Ukhrul district from where Muivah, a Tangkhul Naga and the most influential and charismatic of contemporary Naga leaders, hails.

While accounts persist of a reported offer by India to the Nagas to merge parts of northern Manipur with Nagaland, it has not been officially confirmed. The Nagas as of now are insisting on the whole cake, not just a large slice of it, although in politics, many things remain in the transient land of negotiability through different instruments, including a conciliatory approach that could consider the possibility of an interim accord which would pave the way for a final settlement in the future.

The 'Nagalim' demand is the view of the I-M and has broad support in Naga society and even from the rival faction. However, the original founding political organization for Naga independence, the NNC, says that this is unnecessary and that the borders of Nagaland as they exist are appropriate and well-defined.[35] The latter position is not accepted among the Nagas and draws furious reaction from the NSCN (I-M).

The divisions and contradictory pulls and pressures which exist within the large Naga political mosaic are real and visible. Thus, Nagas say they will not compromise on sovereignty although the main group (while still stressing this!) is conducting talks for a long-term solution. Many Nagas are aware that there cannot be a solution, once the militant groups embrace New Delhi for talks, outside of the Indian framework. Although the rhetoric still blazes, the public's emotional and physical fatigue is growing with a cause that seems to have no conclusion and for which they are still paying taxes to the ubiquitous underground, straining financial resources in middle-class homes and fuelling resentment among the young and unemployed.

The Naga, and Mizoram examples focus on the importance of means and ends. Ultimately, violent means to achieve a seemingly desirable and peaceful end do not work because the organizations involved turn on their own supporters and people apart from the devastation wrought by the state. As in the case of Mizoram, bilateralism gradually appears to be turning into internalization of the problem—it is not with Delhi you must settle, but first form a common platform among your own people by ending the inter-faction, inter-tribe conflicts; sort out the problems with the neighbours—although the NSCN leadership is astutely telling New Delhi that this is a problem for the latter and not for itself, recognizing the pitfalls inherent here.

The genuine popularity and support which the groups enjoyed earlier (including foreign patronage which has stopped from China and reduced vastly from Pakistan) has waned and fratricidal conflicts have weakened the movement. This is not just true of the Naga movement but also in Assam, Manipur and Tripura. In numerous cases the 'underground elements' have the active collaboration of the state and its various players, including intelligence agencies and politicians.

The public is divided. While the support among Nagas for a separate land where they run their own affairs remains strong, many, especially the young who have lived outside the state and region, do not see how this can happen in the near future. There are demands for better infrastructure, education, health facilities and other basic human rights. There is a growing reluctance to assist insurgent groups with funds (giving money is viewed as a safety clause—as part of the effort to for self-protection) although the fear of the gun still helps to release money. A well-known fact is that funds from central government projects are siphoned off to underground groups and strengthen their anti-government stance![36] A top police official who worked in Manipur as a special adviser during a term of central rule said in 2002 that, 'the militant groups reportedly interfere in the award of contracts and are also known to enter offices carrying files to secure signatures of officers in [*sic*] gunpoint'.[37] Indeed, the state government of Nagaland in April 2004 issued a decree that any officer found paying such taxes or protection money to militant groups would be punished. This is unlikely to happen in a place where the government itself is seen as bending over backwards to help the NSCN (I-M), and where it has publicly proclaimed the solution of the 'Indo–Naga' problem as its top priority in an official statement of its common minimum programme.[38] It should be noted that this particular phrasing of the political and armed conflict in Nagaland is the way the issue is defined by various armed groups and their civil society supporters.

In this situation, the challenges to the state are becoming subsumed by a witting, or at times unrehearsed, collaboration between the militants and various state actors in order to fulfil short-term goals rather than political and ideological beliefs. Thus the NSCN openly campaigned, according to media reports, for an independent candidate in the May 2004 general elections in Manipur, intimidating voters and other candidates. The organization attacked the Bharatiya Janata Party of the then Prime Minister Atal Behari Vajpayee, accusing it of breaking its promises and being untrustworthy.

Although the NSCN and other armed groups continue to insist upon 'sovereignty', such active involvement in local politics—a unique feature of the politics of both Nagaland and Manipur for decades, where 'mainstream' politicians maintain good relations with members of the underground and each side uses the other at times of their specific need—undercuts this position. With every formal or informal step in this direction, the distance to sovereignty or independence grows greater and the internalization of a bilateral process becomes stronger.

The ethno-centric movements of the north-east—and one is referring to two of the bigger movements—cannot be viewed in the limited straightjacket approach approved by the United States and its allies. The north-east's very diversity militates against such compartmentalization. It is appropriate here to reflect on the failure of governance which has led to the collapse of institutions and which in turn are sought to be replaced by those supported by the 'underground' or traditionally acceptable to the people, such as local governing councils which do not have the mandate of the Indian Constitution but have the backing of the public. In Manipur, for example, the Tangkhul Hlong, an assembly of tribal leaders (comprising only men and, thus, in the view of this author, undemocratic and unrepresentative), considers issues before the community. There are traditional courts (four regional and one supreme court) which adjudicate on issues relating to the community but their mandate is limited to solving problems such as land disputes, marital problems and inter-tribe or inter-village difficulties.

Again in Manipur, security forces recently launched an operation to dislodge three armed groups—all of which are banned—which had controlled ten villages, including police stations and government posts for over five years.[39] In Manipur, this distinct separation of political insurgency from the politics of the state is visible in some pockets, earlier defined as 'liberated zones' and located on the Indo–Myanmar border, where rapid exit and access to the other country is easy for the militants. More than 600 persons fled the operations and many of them say that they are afraid to return home. To them, and to tens of thousands of others, internally displaced by local conflicts and strife, the basics of survival in a continuing militarized zone as well as recovering from the trauma of the wounds of conflict are as important as the struggles themselves.

The ethno-centric armed and political sub-nationalist movements of the region reflect efforts by peripheries to strike back at the 'mainland', and sometimes at each other, asserting a right to an identity which is at conflict with the state and the notion of state as prescribed by New Delhi. But over the process of decades, they have become absorbed in the processes of state politics and power play while losing their substantial support base as well as their original vision, goals, and integrity. Thus, in those states where armed groups have been active for decades and violent confrontations with the security forces have also continued for a similar period of time, confrontations which have harmed innocent people—men, women and children—the most, there appears to be a comfortable co-existence between militants, non-militants, politicians, and officials. This forms part of an extensive network of patronage which is 'typically founded on ethnic solidarity'[40] and which too has become embedded in the system.

III

WHAT IS TO BE DONE?

The current situation, especially with regard to the Naga talks, needs to be assessed in the light of continuing demands for a larger Naga homeland. While talks between the central government and the Naga leaders are likely to continue, there needs to be a better understanding by all groups, states and players involved that changing state boundaries in the north-east is not just complex but fraught with explosive consequences. Few governments seek solutions that will provoke not merely ill will but also strong public reactions which could destabilize existing conditions. There needs to be a much stronger emphasis on people-to-people contact, reduction of old prejudices, and openness, especially between majority and ethnic minorities. This is the basis for better development, governance, stability, and equality. It can happen through non-government groups and civil society organizations.

But to give a sense of realism to hope, some important steps need to be underscored. One, since the main leaders of the NSCN (I-M) returned to their home territory in Nagaland in December 2004 and have held consultations with Naga civil society groups, it is appropriate and imperative that they too use their presence to reach out to opposing groups within the state as well as to civil society in the neighbouring states, especially of Manipur, Assam, and Arunachal Pradesh. This would help them in their own discussions with New Delhi in seeking a settlement with the Indian government. Apart from the Naga political leaders, those in civil society in Nagaland and other states must begin a transparent and frank dialogue which will enable better understanding between different ethnic groups. This is the only practical way to reduce the tension that erupts whenever territorial issues come up.

A second step should be the appointment of an expert committee to study the border problem and the contesting claims and counter-claims and submit a report within a year to the centre, the negotiating parties, and the involved states. This report should form the basis of a long-term settlement of the sensitive border question.

A third step should be the recognition, without prejudice to a future political settlement, of the traditional residency of those ethnic groups who have lived in these places for decades. Political solutions which have not been based on a broad consensus have not worked in a complex region such as the north-east.

The end of 2004 was characterized by an on-again-off-again effort by the United Liberation Front of Asom (ULFA), through a prominent literary figure, to conduct negotiations. ULFA insisted on 'sovere-ignty' becoming a core issue of discussions. The Government of India stuck to its agenda of talks without preconditions. It is important that ULFA and New Delhi talk, at some level, with or without conditions. Only direct meetings and negotiations conducted quietly, without the glare of publicity and away from the pressure of expectations can help bring both sides closer together. ULFA suffered heavy blows to its cadres and prestige in December 2003, when it was driven out of its established camps in Bhutan, along with two other militant groups, by the Royal Bhutan Army. Yet it retains a certain hold and resonance in the Brahmaputra Valley, despite the fact that the Assam government had once proclaimed that more than 1,000 militants had been killed, over 300 had surrendered and some 3,000 weapons had been recovered.[41] This emphasizes a very simple fact: military pressure may yield temporary results but it can never put in place a long-term peace which needs political initiatives.

The NSCN and the ULFA are among the largest militant groups in the region. There are many others and the twenty-odd in Manipur have a total of strength of about 8,000 according to one official estimate. However, the Government of India is by far the most powerful entity. If civil society is expected by the latter to put pressure on the NSCN and ULFA to move in the direction of a peaceful political settlement, then it is only right and just that New Delhi, with its overwhelming presence, also takes specific steps to reduce the size of its military in the area and change those laws that give sweeping and unchallengeable powers to security forces and no voice to the innocent. In addition, there must be efforts to launch talks and negotiations with all armed groups/insurgent parties. The conflict between the rights of the state and the rights of its people cannot endure in perpetuity and continuing tragedy.

It is routine to read in the press in Imphal or Dimapur or Guwahati that young men especially are picked up or pulled out of buses, homes or offices or even while out walking, who then turn up dead after some time. Human rights violations and authoritarian practices over decades have inured citizens to violence, except those immediately impacted by it. Political leaders are largely silent on such issues, signalling their consensual approach, living on elements of comfort in a dark and divisive frame. This is another aspect of the decades of armed insurgency, another side to the unhappy acceptance and tolerance of the otherwise intolerable.

Military prowess cannot sustain democracy and governance; it can only contain forces arrayed against the state. In the process, new forces and groups emerge. Thus, the quagmire that exists in the north-east cannot be sorted out in clean strokes because the mess is so pervasive. There is opposition to draconian laws; but there is support for the armed forces in their fight against insurgents. This may not be seen as a contradiction but two separate faces of an approach to the existing and extremely difficult situation: what people are saying is that it is okay to the fight armed groups that are attacking the state; what they are also asserting is that it is absolutely wrong for the state and its agencies, using existing laws and the purported threat of extremism, to shoot, maim, attack, and intimidate the ordinary populace.

Simple political steps, such as those outlined above, which will reduce friction, strengthen democracy, and give governance a chance. Simple, specific economic steps such as flood-proofing in a region like the Brahmaputra Valley, a flood-endemic zone where a majority of the region's population lives and where ad hoc responses are the answer every year, will improve rural incomes and livelihoods. Economic packages of billions of rupees, which are often waved as a *mantra* by successive Indian prime ministers, cannot work in a political vacuum and in a picture that does not assure essential rights, including the right to survival.

Without these dialogues, which go beyond official discussions, the north-east cannot grow economically, as it must in a rapidly changing neighbourhood and world, nor will it break out of the vortex of blame, bloodshed, hatred, confrontation, and exploitation which has wounded it for decades and destroyed the hopes of generation after generation.

It is time to end the violence and restore peace with justice, dignity, and honour for all sides. And for this to happen, people-to-people dialogues and political initiatives based on mutual respect and transparency are a must. They may take time to fructify but there are no short cuts.

NOTES

1. Various Indian newspaper and news agency reports.
2. Statements of Al Qaida.
3. Various issues of *Himal Magazine*, Kathmandu.
4. Author interviews with Nepali journalists, scholars and officials, 2002, 2003.
5. Ibid.
6. Indian media reports, issues of *Faultlines*.
7. Sanjoy Hazarika, *Strangers of the Mist, tales of war and peace from India's North East* (New Delhi: Penguin, 1995); B.G. Verghese, *India's North East Resurgent* (New Delhi: Konarak, 1997).

8. *Handbook of the North Eastern Council*, Shillong, 2002.
9. Edward Gait, *A History of Assam*, Second Edition (Guwahati: Lawyer's Book Stall, 1926 [rpt. 1994]); see also, H.K. Barpujari, *Comprehensive History of Assam*, vols. 1-5 (Guwahati: Publication Board of Assam, 1990-4); Hazarika, *Strangers of the Mist*, and Verghese, *India's North East*.
10. See *The Assam Tribune* and *Shillong Times*, especially 1960 to 1986, for coverage of armed movements by the Nagas and Mizos.
11. The section on the vocabulary of the underground is drawn from the author's extensive travels and discussions with former members of militant groups, officials, scholars, and journalists, over the past years.
12. Interviews with the author.
13. Author interviews with Mizoram officials, Indian army officials.
14. Hazarika, *Strangers of the Mist*.
15. Author's friend in an interview, May 1970.
16. Author's interviews with Laldenga, Chief Minister Zoramthanga, and former Chief Minister Lalthanhawla.
17. Gen. V.N. Sharma, 'North East Imbroglio' in 'Our East and North East', *New Approach*, Kolkata, 2002.
18. This section is based on media reports, interviews with Mizoram government officials, and scholars.
19. See Gait, *A History of Assam*; also, Barpujari, *Comprehensive History of Assam*.
20. This phrase emerges in various published remarks, lectures and papers by Roy-Burman in the 1980s and 1990s.
21. Hazarika, *Strangers in the Mist*; Verghese, *India's North East Resurgent*.
22. See documents of Naga National Council, National Socialist Council of Nagalim.
23. Nari Rustomji, *Imperiled Frontiers* (New Delhi: Oxford University Press, 1983).
24. See statement issued at end of consultations between civil society groups and the NSCN (I-M) in Bangkok, 2002.
25. Sharma, 'North East Imbroglio'.
26. For detailed accounts on human rights violations see publications by the Naga Peoples Movement for Human Rights.
27. Government officials in Nagaland and New Delhi.
28. Ibid.
29. Based on author's discussions with representatives of various factions, scholars and non-government groups.
30. Interviews with officials and leaders of the armed factions.
31. Media reports of the clashes, especially *Imphal Free Press*, Imphal, *The Assam Tribune*, Guwahati, *The Telegraph*, Kolkata.
32. See news coverage of riot in Manipur against extension of ceasefire from Nagaland to other parts of the north-east (2001).

33. News reports in the Nagaland media.
34. Interviews of Isak Chis Swu, Chairman NSCN (I-M), and Th. Muivah, General Secretary with Hazarika and other media specialists, 2003.
35. Author's interview with NNC Chairman Adinno Phizo in London, May 2003.
36. Interviews with scholars, officials, church leaders, NGOs.
37. E.N. Rammohan, 'Manipur: A Degenerated Insurgency', *Faultlines*, vol. 10, ed. K.P.S. Gill and Ajai Sahni, New Delhi: Bulwark Books for the Institute of Conflict Management, 2002.
38. Common Minimum Programme of the DAN government in Nagaland, 2003, published by Department of Information and Public Relations, Kohima.
39. *The Assam Tribune*, May 2004.
40. Sanjib Baruah, *Durable Disorder, Understanding the Politics of North East India* (New Delhi: Oxford University Press, 2005).
41. S.K. Sinha (Lt.-Gen., Retd.), former Governor of Assam, 'Violence and Hope in India's North East', *Faultlines*, vol. 10, ed. Gill and Sahni, New Delhi: Bulwark Books for the Institute of Conflict Management, 2002.

CHAPTER VIII

Unthinking the Terrorism – Globalization Nexus

NIRA WICKRAMASINGHE

> What does one do when one is a historian, if not challenge chance, posit reasons—in other words, understand? Yet understanding does not mean flight into ideology, nor providing an alias for what remains hidden.
>
> MICHEL DE CERTEAU, *The Writing of History* (New York: Columbia University Press, 1988), p. 117

> In other words they (the new global terrorist groups) want to roll back globalisation, while making use of the instruments of globalisation.
>
> MARY KALDOR, 'Terrorism as regressive globalisation' www.opendemocracy.net 25 September 2003

The concern in this chapter is to reflect on the relationship between what is today described as 'terrorism' in South Asia by governments, the media, scholars, and the public and what in public discourse and in the work of some scholars is termed 'globalization'. The argument that the nature of armed struggles against states in South Asia is undergoing significant changes in our era of 'globalization', an era believed to be spawning the promise of either a 'world without borders' or a world of greater divides, has been made by scholars at different poles of the ideological divide. Both Rohan Gunaratne and Mary Kaldor, who epitomize two of the most common interpretations of terrorism-globalization linkages, would argue that a new form of terrorism has emerged in the age of globalization and apply this template quite indiscriminately to all regions including South Asia. They understand globalization as being about a world of things in motion, characterized by disjunctive flows that generate acute problems. They read it as a both factor enabling violent conflicts and shaping new trends in armed struggles.[1]

This paper will attempt to show the inadequacy of analyses that encompass the world at large through vague, sweeping, and ahistorical concepts such as 'terrorism' and 'globalization' in efforts to advance our understanding of social and political phenomena. The paper moves through three arguments. As a premise, it underlines the difficulties in understanding 'terrorism' if one remains captive in a language trap. It will argue that the concepts of 'terrorism' and 'terrorist' mask rather than unveil what they try to describe, 'provide an alias for what remains hidden', to borrow de Certeau's expression, and thus should be avoided in any discussion of armed movements. The 'New Global Terrorism', for instance, is no more than a discursive mode used by governments, the media, and the UN to fight what is perceived as an assault on the civilized world. Locked in this language, there is no understanding possible. Governments and the media in South Asia, imbibing these frameworks with much willingness, have been instrumental in spreading these notions from Nepal to Sri Lanka. The limits of their language are the limits of their world, would comment a Wittgenstein! The second section will question the framing of 'terrorism' as the effect or reflection of an 'era of globalization', before turning more specifically to South Asian countries to suggest an alternative framing in terms of networks and interconnectedness. The third section will complicate the picture further by pointing to structures that have remained very similar to what is sometimes described as 'old terrorism' in present armed struggles in South Asia. The final section is the conclusion.

I

VOCABULARIES OR THE LIMITS OF LANGUAGE

It has been suggested that violence is a total phenomenon which comes to us as a total fragment.[2] The same observation can be made about the acts that are generally described as acts of 'terrorism'. When an act of terrible violence happens, at first there seems to be no plot, no narrative, only traces which lead nowhere. Rather than attempt to piece the puzzle it is easier and more reassuring to speak of terrorism to qualify particular violent acts. To go beyond the surface and attempt to comprehend these acts fully, the first step would be to acknowledge that 'terrorism' is not a tangible object, but rather the result of a particular type of analysis and its postulates. The second step is to ponder on what is comprehensible and what are the conditions of understanding.

The issue of terrorism has always been addressed, whether in academic work, in popular media or policy documents, within a given frame that commands a certain type of reflection. The very use of the term is, in a sense, a closure of any alternative frame. The urgency of a refoundation and a conceptual mutation at once semantic, lexical and rhetorical when addressing the issue of terrorism has been stressed in the wake of 9/11.[3] More generally, the Althusserian concept of the problematic underpins the point that it is always the system of questions that commands the answers given. The problematic indeed determines which problems, questions, and answers are part of the game—and which should be blacklisted and never so as much as mentioned. It is a structure of theory (ideology), a framework, and the repertoire of discourses which, ultimately, yield a text or a practice. Language creates the limits of what can be thought. As the twentieth century witnessed the transformation of the philosophy of consciousness into the philosophy of language, especially since the philosophy of the later Wittgenstein, it has been realized that consciousness is linguistically organized and is only accessible in and through language.

It is then important to unthink the process of naming and defining by asking first, who names and defines and for what purpose? Derrida has made the point that 'the more confused the concept the more it lends itself to appropriation'.[4] Self-appointed representatives of Western rationality attempt to establish a coherence in the concept of terrorism by circumscribing it, establishing boundaries that are as much about identification as they are about exclusion. The partition into dimensions does not, however, have a universal and constant validity. For example, saying terrorism is violence for political aims is not relevant in Islamic movements if one accepts that the dissociation of the 'political' from the 'sacral' or the aesthetic is a historical production which results from the advent of a modern type of civilization that has not always existed. Furthermore, if one accepts with Habermas that objectively terrorism can be granted political content only if it has politically realistic goals, since only the future can judge whether the goals of terrorism have been accomplished, terrorism can only be a retrospective designation.[5]

Terrorism as a modern concept acquired a paradigmatic status in the late 1980s. The moment is important. Baudrillard has suggested that it is our very modernity or hypermodernity that has produced a specific type of violence the special effects of which—terrorism—is an integral part.[6] Terrorism entered the discourse of states, infiltrated constitutions, spawned special regulations and imposed itself as a dominant prism through which the people were invited to read their world. There was, of course, no universalized conception of terrorism. While states in South Asia gleefully adopted variations of the hegemonic US State Department discourse, non-state organizations and actors displayed scepticism if not downright opposition to the very framing of resistance movements in terms of terrorism. There is no doubt, however, that it is the western world that invented the word, the techniques, and the politics of terrorism.

There were in fact different and contradictory understandings of terrorism by global discourses. It is often assumed by Southern thinkers critical of a Western blanket understanding of terrorism that the dominant discourse on 'terrorism' stems from the corridors of power in Washington DC. There are, in fact, at least two competing globalizing interpretations and definitions of terrorism. The most commonly accepted one by states and defence institutions is indeed that of the US Department of Defense, namely; 'the unlawful use of, or threatened use of force or violence against individuals or property to coerce and intimidate governments or societies, often to achieve political, religious or ideological objectives'.[7]

This definition tends to refuse the complexities that exist in strategies and objectives of the groups that claim to be armed resistance movements rather than terrorist groups. It dismisses the issue of the right to rebel against tyranny or injustice and the possibility of the law of the state being itself detrimental to certain groups in society. In a sense, after 9/11, the US has succeeded in imposing and legitimating, or indeed legalizing, on a national or world stage, the terminology and the interpretation that best suits it in a given situation. This chapter is concerned first with the way in which different South Asian states define and conceive terrorism, and second whether they draw a line between different types of armed resistance.

Reading against the grain certain texts produced by states can prove to be a fascinating exercise. Most South Asian states found it necessary from the 1980s to 1990s to promulgate anti-terrorism Acts, many of them modelled, just as the recent American Acts, on similar Acts in force in the State of Israel. The Government of Sri Lanka was the first to follow this course with the Prevention of Terrorism (Temporary Provisions) Act No. 48 of 1979, modelled on the British PTA of 1974. This Act was designed by the state to address the security risks presented by an insurrection in the north and east of the major ethnic minority in the country, the Tamils, who constitute approximately 12.6 per cent of the population. The grievances of the Tamils were the following: the Sinhala majority had tried to impose its language, culture, and religion through a monopoly of the political power; the system of selection to institutions of higher education and the procedures of recruitment to the administrative service put in place in the 1970s made access more difficult to young Tamils; there was also a perception that Tamil regions did not benefit from the large-scale agricultural projects and setting of industrial zones of the 1970s. The 1972 Constitution which gave Sinhala and Buddhism a privileged place consolidated the disaffection of Tamils towards the state. The same year Velupillai Prabhakaran and thirty young men formed the Tamil New Tigers. In 1976 the separatist party, the Tamil United Liberation Front or TULF, asked for an independent and secular state of Eelam while the Tamil New Tigers became the LTTE (Liberation Tigers of Tamil Eelam) and began to use violence to reach this same aim. The elections of 1977 saw the TULF winning all its seats in the Tamil areas. The second Republican Constitution which was introduced in 1978 was in no way an answer to the demands of self-determination on the part of Tamil parties and groups. Tamil insurrectionary activity intensified.

In May 1978 the LTTE and 'any similar organizations' were proscribed by Act of Parliament.[8] In 1979, a State of Emergency was declared in Jaffna and massive army counter-insurgency operations were started, thus alienating even further the people of Jaffna. This Act, unlike the more recent anti-terrorism Acts of Pakistan or Nepal, did not provide for a discrete definition of 'terrorism' but described in its preamble in more general terms the purview of the Act:

> And whereas public order in Śri Lanka continues to be endangered by elements or groups of persons or associations that advocate the use of force or the commission of crime as a means of, or as an aid in, accomplishing governmental change within Sri Lanka, and who have resorted to acts of murder and threats of murder of members of Parliament and of local authorities, police officers, and witnesses to such acts and other law abiding and innocent citizens, as well as the commission of other acts of terrorism such as armed robbery, damage to State property and other acts involving actual or threatened coercion, intimidation and violence.[9]

Interestingly 'terrorism' encompassed not only the commission of violent anti-state Acts for political aims but also the advocacy of such methods. Thus terrorism was also a state of mind which had to be erased if the rule of law and public order was to be maintained.

More than ten years later, Bangladesh promulgated the Suppression of Terrorist Offences Act 1992—Act No. 44 of 1992. This act defined terrorism and provided for institutional mechanisms to deal with it. Unlike its Sri Lankan counterpart, the definition of terrorism was detailed and very specific to Bangladeshi culture and politics:

'Terrorist offence' means—

(a) by holding out any kind of threat or applying any kind of illegal force—

(i) to collect or acquire from any person or institution money or property as contributions, assistance or by whatever other name it may be called;

(ii) to obstruct or impede the traffic by land, on railroads, by water or on air routes, or to alter the course of any vehicle against the wishes of the conductor of the vehicle;

(b) to intentionally damage any vehicle;

(c) to intentionally destroy or damage any property, whether movable or immovable, belonging to the government or any institution under the control of the government, or to any institute, authority or institution founded, established or created under the law, or to any company, firm or private non-governmental organization, any embassy or foreign institute or institution, or any person;

(d) to steal or seize by force from any person any money, jewellery, valuable article or any other article or vehicle;

(e) to outrage the modesty of, or to molest, any minor or adult woman, including any female child, adolescent and young woman on the streets or *ghats*, in vehicles, in educational institutions or in the vicinity thereof or in public places;

(f) to create, alone or in a group, with or without premeditation, fear, terror, confusion or anarchy by ostentatiously displaying force or power at any place, in any building, shop, market and *bazar*, on any street or *ghat*, in any vehicle or in any institution;

(g) to obstruct or impede by use of force the buying, accepting or entering of bills of sale by any institution or to illegally compel anybody to accept bills of sale.[10]

This definition was all at once very general since it covered any act that involved intentional destruction of state property, and very culturally specific since attempts to outrage the modesty of women or to molest women were covered under this act. Most interestingly, terrorism was not defined as a violent act motivated by a particular political aim. Even intentionally damaging a vehicle constituted a terrorist act. It differed from the Sri Lankan act, too, insofar as it involved only committed acts and not intentions.

The Terrorist and Destructive Activities (Control and Punishment) Ordinance was promulgated by the King of Nepal on the advice of the Cabinet on 26 November 2001. The government resorted to this measure on 26 November 2001 after the Maoist insurgents brought to an end the ceasefire that was being observed between them and the government since 23 July 2001, with a series of attacks across the country on 23 November. The terrorist and destructive activities include:

Any act or plan of using any kinds of arms, grenades, or explosives, or any other equipment or goods with the objective of affecting or hurting sovereignty or the security and law and order of the Kingdom of Nepal or any part thereof or the property of the Nepalese diplomatic missions abroad thereby causing damage to property at any place or any act causing loss of life or dismemberment or injury or setting fire or hurting physically and mentally or any act of poisoning goods of daily consumption causing loss of life or injury, or any other aforesaid acts thereby causing panic among the people in motion or assembled; acts of intimidation or terrorizing individuals at any place or in any vehicle or abducting them or creating terror among them by threatening to abduct them from vehicles and places or abduction of people traveling on such vehicles as well as activities like taking the life of others, causing physical mutilation, injury and harm or causing other types of damage by using substances mentioned in the relevant section in that connection or by threatening to use such substances or any other substances other than those mentioned in that section or threatening to use them, or,

Acts like the production, distribution, accumulation, peddling, import and export, marketing or possession or installation of any kind of arms and ammunition or bombs or explosive substances or poisonous substances or any assistance in this connection, and;

Acts of gathering people or giving training for this purpose;

Any other acts aimed at creating and spreading fear and terror in public life;

Act such as extortion of cash or kind or looting of property for this purpose, forcibly raising cash or kind or looting property in pursuit of the said purpose.

Any attempt or conspiracy to engage in terrorist or disruptive activity, or to encourage or force anyone to take up such activity, gathering more than one individual for such purpose, constituting any group to the same end, or assigning anyone to such activity or participating in such activity with or without pay or engaging in publicity for such activity, causing obstruction to government communications systems, or giving refuje to any individual engaged in terrorist or disruptive activity, or hiding any person doing any of this things.[11]

This act constitutes an example of a modern state response to an armed movement that is using an array of methods to further it aims. As in the Sri Lanka case, terrorism is defined in terms of its purpose and objective 'affecting the sovereignty or the security and law and order of the kingdom'.

These three examples from South Asia show clearly that each state defines terrorism differently in a manner suitable to address the particular threat of the moment to the stability of the country concerned. In the SAARC Regional Convention on Suppression of Terrorism, signed at Kathmandu on 4 November 1987, the seven

South Asian countries nevertheless agreed to include in the meaning of terrorism 'offences' that were defined in conventions signed by the SAARC members such as the Convention for the Suppression of Unlawful Seizure of Aircraft and also a series of other offences such as murder, manslaughter, assault causing bodily harm, kidnapping, etc. Interestingly a political motivation is not included in the meaning as in most international definitions.[12]

State actors are not always bound by the definitions contained in acts and treaties. Events and circumstances command the use or non-use of the term 'terror' or 'terrorism'. In 2000, for instance, when the Sri Lanka state was still waging war against the Tamil separatists, the Sri Lanka ambassador made the following statement at the UN Human Rights Commission:

> We have an extensive programme to provide humanitarian assistance including provision of free food supplies to the affected areas despite the fact the terror group, the LTTE continues to siphon off a substantial part of these supplies for its own use. A large number of international and national organizations and NGOs are operating in the areas assisting and complimenting [*sic*] the efforts of the Government.[13]

But three years later, although the Peace Talks had been suspended a few months earlier, former Prime Minister Ranil Wickremasinghe's speech at the Tokyo donor conference on 9 June 2003, where 4.5 billion dollars were pledged made no mention of the word 'terrorism'. The use by state actors of certain words in place of others is not innocent as is evidenced in other contexts too. In France the Algerian rebellion became a 'war' retrospectively in the 1990s, a quality conferred by the French parliament so as to enable pensions to the veterans.[14]

Apart from the state discourse, another global discourse on terrorism has emerged from within what is sometimes called global civil society. While the emergence of a civil society in South Asia has been discussed in numerous works of scholars and practitioners its incorporation into a global network has rarely been investigated or its approach to 'terrorism' seriously addressed. There is much evidence that in the South, the rise of an 'international', 'global' or 'world civil society' including NGOs as well as networks of scholars, religious and other voluntary organizations, research institutes and media collectives is leading to a redefinition of the compass between state and society. This 'world civil society' supports and harnesses values such as human rights in a form that tends to challenge the primacy of the state and contest the state formulations on anti-state actors. World civil society—in the form of UN organizations, human rights organizations, international NGOs, etc.—focuses its interest primarily on state terror perpetrated against its citizens, and only recently has widened its mandate to critique the human rights violations of non-state actors such as guerrilla or armed resistance movements.

A study of the 'orderly field of statements' produced by global civil society on South Asia is a possible entry point to understand in what ways terrorism as a concept has been appropriated or ignored.

The United Nations for a long time resisted using the term terrorism, although from the 1960s it has deliberated on terror acts and adopted twelve conventions on such acts between 1963 and 1999.[15] While violent acts were condemned in a number of conventions deposited with the Secretary-General of the United Nations, it was only in 1997 that the term 'terrorist' appeared in a convention, the International Convention for the Suppression of Terrorist Bombings, adopted by the General Assembly of the United Nations on 15 December 1997. It was followed in 1999 by the UN Convention for the Suppression of the Financing of Terrorism. Among international actors an organization such as Amnesty International (AI) plays a guiding role and its political position *vis-à-vis* 'terrorism' influences the position of smaller human rights organizations. The AI Report of 2003 is as critical of the government of Sri Lanka for 'torture in police custody', 'lack of accountability of perpetrators of human rights violations including disappearances and tort' as it is of the 'members of the LTTE' for 'hostage taking and widespread recruitment of child soldiers'.[16] The words 'terrorist' and 'terrorism' do not enter the text, the LTTE being referred to only by its name, rather than by any attribute describing its nature. The AI Report for 2001, although still concerned with avoiding value judgements, is less neutral and refers to the LTTE, which was responsible in 2000 for a number of civilian deaths in Colombo through suicide bombers, as 'the main armed opposition group':

> The continuing armed conflict and a general rise in violence dominated Sri Lanka in 2000. April and May saw particularly ferocious fighting between

the security forces and the Liberation Tigers of Tamil Eelam (LTTE), the main armed opposition group fighting for an independent state, Eelam, in the north and east of Sri Lanka.[17]

Interestingly, the AI Reports describe the violence perpetrated by the LTTE against civilians in 1999 under the heading 'Human Rights abuses by the LTTE', thus analysing the actions of non-state groups within the same framework as the state, also castigated for human rights abuses. The following excerpts describe in a scientific and non-partisan manner the violent acts committed by the LTTE against civilians:

There were ominous signs that the LTTE might be returning to large-scale deliberate attacks on civilians in Colombo and areas bordering the north and east, a practice from which it had largely refrained over the last three years. More than 50 Sinhalese civilians were killed in a pre-dawn raid on three villages in Amparai district. The deliberate targeting of members of parliament and local councillors belonging to Tamil political parties represented in parliament also became more pronounced.

- On 29 July, a prominent member of parliament and member of the Tamil United Liberation Front, Dr Neelan Thiruchelvam, was killed on his way to work by a suicide bomber. In Jaffna, the total number of local councilors killed for not complying with orders by the LTTE to resign from their post rose to 11. Among those killed was 50-year-old Bandari Kandasamy, of the Eelam People's Democratic Party, who was shot dead on his way home from church in February.
- In two attacks on election rallies in and near Colombo on 18 December, at least 25 civilians were killed. Numerous others, including President Chandrika Bandaranaike Kumaratunga and four ministers, were injured.[18]

The vocabulary used to describe the political violence perpetrated by both the Maoists and the state in Nepal is different, couched not in human rights terms but in terms of extra-legal acts: 'Against a background of mounting political crisis, there was a sharp rise in the incidence of *unlawful killings*, "disappearances", torture and arbitrary arrest and detention by the security forces, and of deliberate killings, hostage-taking and torture by the Maoists.'[19] The concept of unlawful killing leads one to wonder what, for Amnesty International, constitutes 'lawful killings'!

The question we can ask is: which of the two understandings of terrorism, statist or non-statist, prevails in South Asian societies?

The spread of the public sphere largely determines the people's perception of anti-state activities as terrorism or as something else. The public sphere generally refers to institutions such as publishing houses, newspapers, or journals that could nurture public discussions on issues of common concern that would ideally have an effect on public policy.[20] In most South Asian states, however, the majority of people listen to and watch state-run media, radio or television, where the terms 'terrorism' and 'terrorist' are used ad nauseam. The public sphere is in that sense still very much informed by the ideas of the state on a variety of issues. Even the more globalized sections of the population who listen to international networks such as CNN and the BBC would hear the same rhetoric, albeit relating to international events such as the 'war against terror' or 'global terror'.

Quite clearly the global discourse that denies 'terrorism' as a tool of analysis is only touching an intelligentsia that constitutes a minute proportion of the public in South Asia. For the rest, terrorism and terrorists exist as a tangible reality, the reality of charred bodies and destroyed homes. The point is not to deny or condone acts of violence perpetrated against civilians by armed groups, but to understand that no intellectual ground can be covered by inquiries that foreground that the sign 'terrorism' has no origin, no historical, cultural or linguistic limit. Furthermore, as Derrida has quite provocatively suggested, 'letting die' from hunger, AIDS, lack of medical treatment, is also terrorism. What, then, is the option for local social scientists in search of a language to think with? One possibility is to abandon the notion of terrorism and terrorists but keep the adjective 'terrorist' to qualify acts that lead to the willful killing of civilian targets. Thus an armed group could commit, at some point in its life, a terrorist act. In the same way the acts of states during wars where civilians are intimidated or slain by regular armies can also be described as terrorist acts. The essence of the armed group or movement or state escapes being condensed into being terrorist by its very nature. For the purpose of this chapter, the term 'terrorist' will be used as a descriptive term and the term 'terrorism' only insofar as it is understood as part of a dominant/authoritative discourse of states.

II

IS THE CONCEPT OF 'GLOBALIZATION' USEFUL TO UNDERSTAND SOUTH ASIAN ARMED RESISTANCE?

It has been advanced that the central place of terrorism in state and international narratives can only be understood in the context of the process known as globalization, which describes the intensification of global interconnectedness—political, economic, military and cultural in the 1980s-90s. Have armed struggles in South Asia changed to a significant extent in the last decades, and is globalization as a concept helpful to understand the directions on these changes?

The term globalization itself merits some scrutiny. Indeed, although it has been subject to much criticism for its lack of substance and fuzziness, it remains in use in a number of contexts. In Fred Cooper's subtle rendering, 'there are two problems with the concepts of globalization, first the "global", and second the "ization". The implication of the first is that a single system of connection—notably through capital and commodities markets, information flows, and imagined landscapes—has penetrated the entire globe; and the implication of the second is that it is doing so now, that this is the "global age".' 'What is not evoked,' continues Cooper, 'are the limits of interconnection, the areas where capital cannot go, and the specificity of the structures necessary to make connections work.'[21]

That the world is today interconnected in so many ways is obvious to any observer. The different forces and processes that induce this connectedness are, however, best looked at separately rather than encompassed in the framework of a shibboleth-like term such as globalization. The contradictions and inequalities inherent to globalization belie in fact the meaning of the term. Curiously both friends and foes of globalization are engaged in an assessment of its effects: diffusion of the benefits of growth versus increasing concentration of wealth, homogenization of culture versus diversification.[22] In arguments that see a clear relation between the emergence in the last twenty years of a 'new/global terrorism' and 'globalisation' there is an underlying assumption of the reality of such a process. Gunaratne speaks unhesitatingly of the 'era of globalisation', while Kaldor develops an alternative concept which she calls 'regressive globalization' to describe the terrain where the new terrorism blossoms. Both their works have some value, Gunaratne for the intricacy of detail with which he describes 'terrorist organizations'—although his claims are often unsubstantiated—and Kaldor for her empathic stance on the ill-effects of capitalism on less developed societies. But both analyses are flawed owing to their totalizing pretensions.

Critiques of 'globalization', such as by Kaldor, nevertheless accept the category as reflecting a tangible reality, and advocate that it has accelerated the defensive reaction that accompanies the fear of the 'violent uprooting of traditional ways of life' of which modernization is generally accused. It has divided the world into winners, beneficiaries and losers. The speed of 'modernization'—yet another overused and meaningless term—is seen as responsible for a defensive reaction elicited on the part of so-called 'traditional' ways of life. Terrorism in turn constitutes the effect of the trauma of modernization which has spread around the world at a pathological speed.[23] Derrida too points to the fact that in the so-called age of globalization the disparities between human societies and the social and economic inequalities have probably never been greater and more spectacular. Technological inequalities are particularly striking: 5 per cent of humanity has the access to Internet. Half of US households have the facility. Ninety per cent of servers are in English.[24] Although television is more evenly distributed, it serves to display the 'offensive prosperity of others'. His description of globalization conveys the double-edged character of the process:

> it is a simulacrum, a rhetorical artifice or weapon that dissimulates a growing imbalance, a new opacity, a garrulous and hypermediatised non communication, a tremendous accumulation of wealth, means of production, teletechnologies and sophisticated military weapons and the appropriation of all these powers by a small number of states or international corporations.[25]

One can also read the 'new terrorism', following Habermas, as a communicative pathology that feeds its own destructive input. Globalization injects fuel into the spiralling movement of communicative violence and puts on stage distributive injustice. The cause of the communicative ailment is not cultural but economic. It is the consumerist blast that accompanies globalization which elicits the spiritual reaction of terror.[26]

It seems, however, more useful to relate each occurrence of armed violence to a specific conjuncture informed by a variety of variables ranging from imbalances or inequalities in the world economy, in the distribution of technological advances, to national politics, cultural deprivation and many other issues. The use of one single term, such as 'globalization', as an explicative factor only serves to constrict the political imagination. It is of course easier to generalize than to engage in empirical analysis, and the last years have spawned a plethora of works on 'global terrorism'. Kaldor, who is especially representative of this tendency, has repeatedly argued that a new type of organized violence developed in the 1980s and 1990s formed one aspect of the current globalized era. In most of the social science literature the new wars are described as internal or civil wars, or else framed as 'low-intensity conflicts' in studies that belong to the International Relations tradition. The term 'low intensity conflict' was in fact coined during the Cold War period by the US military to describe guerrilla warfare.[27] Although localized the conflicts involve a myriad of transnational connections so that the distinction between internal and external, between aggression (attacks from abroad) and repression (attacks from inside the country) or even local and global are difficult to sustain. Marc Duffield uses the term postmodern war to distinguish these wars that take the shape of virtual wars and wars in cyberspace from the wars of classical modernity.[28]

These new wars emerged, according to Kaldor, as a consequence of the end of the Cold War, which led to four intertwined processes, namely, the availability of surplus arms, the discrediting of socialist ideologies, the disintegration of totalitarian empires, and the withdrawal of superpower support to client regimes. These new wars can be contrasted with the old wars in terms of their goals, the methods of warfare, and how they are financed. Their goals can, broadly speaking, be encompassed in the idea of identity politics at a local, global, national as well as transnational level. The mode of warfare is also strikingly different: in conventional warfare the goal is the capture of territory; the strategies of the new warfare, in contrast, draw on the experience of both guerrilla warfare and counter-insurgency but are yet quite distinctive. While guerrilla warfare in the tradition of Che Guevara aims at capturing hearts and minds, the strategic goal here is to sow fear and hatred, expulsion through mass killing or forcible resettlement. Violence is directed against non-combatants. Finally the new war is part of a new globalized war economy where crime, drugs, etc., form a major component. The acts of violence perpetrated against civilian targets by such organizations as Al Qaida have led to the coining of the term 'new terrorism' to describe what some analysts see as a totally new phenomenon, encapsulated in the term 'global terrorism'. Building on the theory of new wars, in a recent article, Kaldor analysed the four main features of the 'new forms of terrorism' of today, namely:[29]

1. They seek political power—generally control of the state;
2. They see themselves as opposed to modernity;
3. Emphasis is placed on the need to regenerate and unify a corrupt society; and
4. They believe they are part of a Great War against an 'other'.

She uses the term 'regressive globalization' to describe what she sees as the character of new groups which make use of and even promote globalization, when it is in the interests of a particular religious or nationalist group.

Two questions must be asked. First, is there a better way—outside the framings of terrorism and globalization—to describe and discuss the way armed groups' function and chart the changes that are taking place within armed movements and between them? Second, is Kaldor's 'regressive globalization' model applicable to South Asian armed groups (Kaldor specifically mentions the LTTE, and the Sikh movement for Khalistan)?

Most scholars—Kaldor is no exception—who see a relation between 'new terrorism' and 'globalisation' explicitly or implicitly accept the terms set by the US State Department in naming 'terrorist groups'. The US State Department currently reports that more than sixty active terrorist groups exist (with some 1,00,000 members) and over one-third of them have the capacity for global reach.[30] The State Department's list of foreign terrorist organizations is interesting, as it includes only organizations, which, according to Legal Criteria for Designation (Reflecting Amendments to Section 219 of the INA in the USA PATRIOT Act of 2001), 'threaten the security of US nationals or the national security (national defense, foreign relation, or the economic interests) of the USA.' It provides an initial understanding of which South Asian organizations have a global reach in so far as global is equated with the US. Among the thirty-six organizations cited, the South Asian based organizations are: Lashkar-e-Jhangvi (Pakistan); Lashkar-e Toiba (LT) (Army of the Righteous), Harakat ul-Mujahidin (HUM) (active in Kashmir); Jaish-e-Muhammad (JEM) (Army of Muhammad); Liberation Tigers of Tamil Eelam (LTTE).

Thus, in US terms, South Asian organizations that practise terrorist acts which affect the global order are few. There are, however, South Asian organizations that have a reach outside their own country of origin but whose activities do not appear to disturb the US. This is the case of the Nepali Maoists who have established links with the Maoist Communist Centre which operates in the state of Bihar and the People's War Group which is active in five Indian states. Since 1980 clashes between police and Naxalite Maoist revolutionaries of the PWG have taken place in north-western Andhra Pradesh. The PWG champions the cause of the landless and targets landlords, law enforcement personnel and other symbols of authority in the north-east, east central, and southern states of Andhra Pradesh, Bihar, Madhya Pradesh, Maharashtra and Orissa. There is also some speculation that they have or at least had some contacts with the LTTE of Sri Lanka. These links have taken place oblivious to the process of globalization, in fact in a manner totally unrelated to it. Analysts find it more convenient to leave exceptions outside their purview or try to fit them in even though they do not have all the necessary features. The norm or model of the 'new terrorist group' being Al Qaida, other groups are read as slight variations if not regional extrapolations of the master global terror organization. As will be shown later, the LTTE hardly fits the template.

One must then acknowledge two important factors. There is no norm: in today's world other forms of armed violence too exist that may be older or newer than the terrorist acts of the recent years. Since 9/11, the international media and the Western States have, however, focused most of their attention on a particular type of violence because more than ever before, the West or Western interests have become the victims or potential targets. This has given the impression of a uniform 'global terror created by a single cause: 'globalization'. This is not to deny that these acts are outrageous in their targeting of civilians and scale of destruction. It is the intangibility of these acts that lends violence a terrifying quality. But in parts of the world, other forms of violence exist, some that have been falsely put in the same category as Al Qaida, others that are completely ignored and under analysed by 'terrorism specialists'.

Gunaratne's body of work, although it frames issues in the given categories of 'global terrorism' and 'globalization', has the merit—unlike the works of Kaldor—of being based on a more precise study of armed movements. He refers to nodes, blockages, and networks as the main feature of these new movements, which suggests the possibility of a new vocabulary to think about these armed movements outside the vague and ineffectual terms that derive from the 'global'.

Transnational Organizations or Networks?

One of the important features of armed struggles in South Asia today is the porous aspect of national boundaries. Fighters easily cross over to adjoining countries where they fight causes that are of a more global nature. In recent years it is Islam that has provided the most potent gel and reason. But is this feature so new? The Jehad of the twentieth century has no national boundaries but neither did the medieval Crusades led by Christian kings. Furthermore, the Abbasid and Fatimid empires aimed at propagating the faith as far as possible in Europe and Africa. Today's armed struggles resemble other circuits common to most world religions such as age-old religious pilgrimages, regional systems of shrines, scholarly networks where national attributes are easily shed by those who enter a wider circle of belonging. Most studies fail to highlight the perennial feature of these networks and tend to read them as singularly new forms of mobilization that have come to be with modern communication technologies. What has changed, nevertheless, is that these armed groups have turned against the most powerful power in the world and its allies.

Armed violent acts by Pakistani groups are related to the presence of Al Qaida in Pakistan after 9/11. Indeed Pakistan became, after Afghanistan, the main refuge for Al Qaida members. Al Qaida trained and financed several Islamist, anti-Shia groups in Pakistan such as the Sipah-e-Sahaba of Pakistan (SSP: Army of the Prophet's Companion) and its underground splinter Lashkar-e-Jhangvi. These groups were transnational in their location. Lashkar's leadership was, for instance, based in Kabul until the American intervention. The SSP leaders who were not gunned down by the Pakistani State took refuge on the Afghan–Pakistan border.[31] Furthermore, Al Qaida's guerrilla organization, the 055 Brigade was composed of Arabs, Central Asians, and South and South-East Asians such as Pakistanis, Bangladeshis, Filipinos, and Malaysians. These fighters were transnational too in their fighting mode. Mujahidins from Afghanistan were diverted to the Kashmir theatre from late 1989, where they fought alongside Kashmiri and Pakistani groups. Al Qaida is believed to have penetrated several Pakistani groups, in particular Harkat-ul-Mujahidin), Jaish-e-Muhammad and Lashkar-e-Toiba. Furthermore, recent reports point towards the existence of Al Qaida special training camps in Pakistan and Kashmir for 'sleeper cells' in the US.[32]

South Asia as the Theatre and Target of Global Wars

Thus South Asia has become a theatre of terror perpetrated by groups often tied to more global networks. India has been cast as a prime target with the escalation of the Islamist threat to it in the last decade. Al Qaida has played an overt and covert role in its fight against India. After 9/11, India was often condemned in pronouncements released by Al Qaida for being a country that was receiving help from the US in their fight against the Muslims in Kashmir. Even more explicitly, in 2001 Mullah Muhammad Omar appears to have denounced as the true terrorists the enemies of Islam, the United States, India, Russia, and Israel. Both India and Pakistan have become targets for Al Qaida operatives. After Pakistan's head of state, General Pervez Musharraf strategically sided with the USA in the 'war against terror', Al Qaida has called upon the Pakistani people to rebel against his corrupt regime. Some of the failed attacks included a plan to attack the US embassy in New Delhi, a plan to hijack an Indian Airlines, Pakistan Airlines or Sri Lankan Airlines airliner and crash it on a US warship in the Indian Ocean in February 2002. Among the successful attacks was the attack on the US Information Service Centre (USIS) in Calcutta which was linked to the Harkat-ul-Jehad-al-Islami.[33]

These global networks are indeed made possible by the financial support given to them by diasporic communities sometimes involved in operations such as trade in drugs, armaments, etc. Rather than speak of globalization or 'regressive globalization', it is preferable to be more precise and refer to transcontinental, or transnational mobilization of capital and people. The growth of these networks of crime and arms dealers can be traced to the collapse of the Soviet Union and the sudden arrival on the market of cheap armament. Another factor is the sudden increase in the speed of communication that linked the diasporas of the world to their people. The information age permitted armed groups to access fast and easily the dispersed communities of refugees and migrants for fund-raising purposes as well as propaganda or image building and transform their movement into a network. The Lashkar-e-Toiba, a Mujahidin group fighting the Indian army in Kashmir has become the envy of other groups on account of its ability to attract donors through its extensive website with its versions in Urdu, English and Arabic.

Most of these armed groups rely on donations from outside benefactors. The Lashkar-e-Toiba for instance, collects donations from the Pakistani community in the Persian Gulf and United Kingdom, Islamic NGOs, and Pakistani and Kashmiri businessmen. The Harakat-ul-Mujahidin collects donations from Saudi Arabia and other Gulf and Islamic states and from Pakistanis and Kashmiris.[34] According to reports from India, the Jehad in Jammu & Kashmir is being internationally funded by expatriate Kashmiris and Muslims around the world who sympathize with the Kashmiri people. The Pakistani share in this funding appears to be minuscule, only 10 to 25 per cent. Indian intelligence sources estimate the total amount that comes in from international charities and support groups to be around four to five billion Indian rupees while India spends about hundred times that amount on the Kashmir war.[35] The advantage for the insurgents is that they do not have to lean on the Kashmiri people for their sustenance, unlike, for instance, the Sikh militant organizations which were forced to plunder the population to keep themselves going a decade before. The capacity to raise money and draw on the resources of the diaspora can thus be related to an explosion of communication which, according to friends and foes of the concept, characterizes the 'era of globalization'.

It has been argued that the rise of the LTTE would not have been possible without the enabling situation provided by the acceleration of globalization.[36] Capital flows from the Tamil diaspora permitted the LTTE to build a near business empire, which includes broadcasting stations, newspapers, restaurants, stores, and a shipping fleet in the late 1980s and early 1990s. It has also been advanced that the LTTE was engaged in narcotics trading and gunrunning.[37] Those years were evoked by Michael Ondaatje in *Anil's Ghost*: 'It was Hundred Years War with Modern weaponry, and backers on the sidelines in safe countries, a war sponsored by gun and drug-runners.'[38]

The links between diasporas, economic integration, and the consolidation of armed groups in South Asia need to be empirically studied. This paper can only make a few hypotheses. For the Tamil diaspora from Sri Lanka a case can be made that it was from the late 1980s that the armed struggle rose to another level of intensity. Following the surge in ethnic violence, over one and a half million Tamils left their homes to seek refuge in other countries. The less affluent crossed the Palk Straits and settled in India. The more adventurous emigrated to Australia, the USA, and European countries.

In 1995, three quarters of the non-Indian Tamil population of Sri Lanka, locked in a cultural condition of liminality, was either internally displaced or had sought asylum overseas. Seven hundred thousand were classified as displaced and were receiving Sri Lanka government assistance; 200,000 are in Colombo and its suburbs; and a further 320,000 people have sought political asylum in Europe and North America.[39] Diasporas have existed since time immemorial; what makes scholars like Kaldor argue that 'a new global terrorism' blossomed in this 'era of globalization' is the facility with which members of these diasporas communicate, and link up politically motivated often armed groups in their own country. Sri Lankan

Tamils across the globe form today a cultural and political community linked through Computer Mediated Communication (CMC) by a common language, culture, and, for some, a dream of returning to a land called Eelam. Comprised of different systems such as electronic mail, bulletin-board systems, and real-time chat services, CMC is both an interpersonal, one-to-one medium of communication and a one-to-many or even many-to-many form of mass communication. It is playing a central role in the formation of a transnational Tamil community.[40] Today over one-fourth of the Sri Lanka Tamil population lives overseas. Although 90 per cent of the population originates from peninsular Jaffna, there are significant divisions within the exiled population. In Switzerland, for instance, Tamils who arrived between 1983 and 1989, largely comprising lower-middle class Vellalas (the dominant caste in the Jaffna peninsula), feel the presence of a growing non-Vellala, lower-class Tamil population and the threat that this poses to their long-term security.[41]

Kaldor has argued that 'new global terror groups', among which she includes the LTTE, see themselves as opposed to modernity. The LTTE clearly differs from this template. Indeed at its inception it strove to reform a caste-ridden Tamil society, gave women a leading role in the struggle, and very rarely appealed to Hindu religious symbolism. In fashioning Tamilness in the diaspora, history and collective memory do, however, play a crucial role but this does not suffice to categorize the movement as anti-modern. New rituals linked to the LTTE movement have been incorporated into the festivals of the diaspora Tamils: the Black Tigers Day or Black July, and the birthday of LTTE leader Velupillai Prabhakaran, are celebrated the world over. Toronto, which has a population of 200,000 Sri Lankan Tamils, has been a privileged venue for the celebration of Great Warriors' Day, which lasts a week from 21 to 27 November. 'The venue for the ceremonies is designed as a cemetery complete with artificial tombstones. These tombstones are inscribed with names and dates of birth and heroic deaths of Tigers whose kith and kin live in Toronto.'[42] The LTTE has in this sense succeeded in its objective of radicalizing the Sri Lanka Tamils overseas through ritual links to an imagined nation of Eelam.

The question that must be posed is whether the transnational character of the LTTE is so very special to our 'era' as many scholars seem to stress. It is beyond doubt that the LTTE has established a wide network of offices and cells practically all across the globe. They have secured a considerable degree of visibility in the United Kingdom—the headquarters of its 'International Secretariat'—as well as in Canada, France, Germany, Holland, Switzerland, Italy, Sweden, Denmark, Norway, Australia, and, more recently, South Africa. These networks of offices and cells carry out propaganda, organize the procurement and movement of weapons, and raise funds from the Tamil diaspora. Gunaratne estimates that 40,000 Tamil families residing in Germany alone contributed an estimated DM 1,000 per family, annually. After 1997, for instance, the LTTE solicited one day's pay per working person per month. Businessmen were often approached for donations.[43] While it is preferable not to state numbers that cannot be verified what is important is the level of expectation of the LTTE. 'We regard all those who live outside Tamil Eelam and make their contribution as friends of the liberation of the Tamil land,' said Velupillai Prabhakaran in 1997.[44] It can be argued that the network type of structure of the LTTE is not a new feature of the 'era of globalization': the socialist international movement from the late nineteenth century or more recently the Palestinian diaspora were networked in a very similar manner. What is new today is the efficiency of the networking, the scale of the fund-raising and the use of electronic media to obtain contributions to the cause. The fundamental structure of networked armed groups is not unique to our era . . . it is new only in so far as it—somewhat like Columbus's America—has been 'discovered' by states that until recently were insulated from violent acts.

NEW AGE WARFARE: CYBER-WAR

Armed groups such as the LTTE whose origins are in South Asia have used the Internet to spread propaganda and reach out to their potential supporters all over the world. Governments are helpless to force them off the web as they can set up their sites in countries with free-speech laws. A fitting example is the government of Sri Lanka's inability to take down the LTTE's London-based website at a time they banned this organization.[45] With the spectacular changes in connectivity and the spread of the information system a new type of warfare has emerged which strikes the nerve centre and information structures of states and organizations. In 1998, nearly half of the thirty organizations designated as Foreign Terrorist Organizations under the Anti-Terrorism and Effective Death Penalty Act of 1996 maintained websites. By the end of 1999 nearly all groups had established their presence on the net. Cyber-war has turned the balance of information and knowledge in favour of the underdogs. The term 'cyber terrorism', a component of cyber-war, is sometimes used to describe a premeditated, politically motivated attack against information computer systems, computer programmes and data which result in violence against non-combatant targets by sub-national groups or clandestine agents.

The LTTE was the first organization on the US terrorist organization list to use cyber attacks when it swamped Sri Lankan embassies with thousands of electronic mail messages saying 'We are the Internet Black Tigers and we are doing this to disrupt your communications.'[46] This type of practice is however exceptional. In the final analysis, cyberspace appears to have become a significant theatre in the battle but has not succeeded in any way in ousting the physical battle theatre from the equation. Guns and conventional weapons have so far remained the weapons of choice for most armed movements in South Asia. These weapons remain easy to acquire, use, and cause many casualties. Neither the LTTE nor any anti-Indian group in Pakistan has shown interest in acquiring chemical, biological, radiological, or nuclear (CBRN) capability. The LTTE is believed to have used chlorine gas against a military camp in 1990 but has never used it again.

Thus in the past twenty years, some armed struggles in South Asia have undergone substantial changes. New and faster modes of communicating have proved to be the crucial instigator of transnational forms of organizing, recruiting, and raising funds. South Asian Islamist groups appear to be the less territorialized and most geographically spread of South Asian movements, understandably with the growth of pan-Islamist movements such as Al Qaida allegedly creating training camps in Pakistan and Bangladesh. In countries such as Nepal and Sri Lanka there is evidence that integration of economies and the spread of information technology has changed some aspects of armed movements. But what proponents of causal relations between globalization and global terror selectively ignore is what has remained unchanged and lasting in this so-called 'era of globalization'.

III

THE UNCHANGING NATURE OF ARMED RESISTANCE: THE LIMITS OF GLOBALIZATION

Two important features of South Asian armed movements are not of recent origin: first, the aim of most groups remains either to create a sovereign state, carving it from an existing nation-state or to capture state power from a regime they perceive as illegitimate; and second, the methods of combat, which can be a mix of guerrilla warfare, conventional warfare, and on exceptional occasions, suicide bombings involving high civilian casualties. In South Asia, one is reminded more of the revolutionary movements of the Cold War period than of Al Qaida-style groups. Blanket explanatory devices such as globalization and naming/denouncing modes practised in the singling out of 'global terrorists' fail both to appreciate differences and to historicize the emergence of these movements.

In this era, where the nation-state is believed to be falling apart, many armed groups in South Asia are demanding the right to exercise powers traditionally reserved for the sovereign state. Their quest is for social power within the boundaries of a territory. The war over Kashmir, which involves a number of armed groups is one such war over territory. For the majority of the armed groups fighting the Indian army in Kashmir and the Indian state by attacking symbols of Indian rule such as the Indian Parliament, the long-term aim is to annex Jammu & Kashmir to the existing Pakistani state. Groups that aimed at creating a sovereign Kashmir independent of either Pakistan or India have disappeared after the beginning of the insurrection in 1988.[47] For the LTTE the aim has been, until the recent move towards accepting a confederal type of solution, a sovereign Tamil Eelam constituted by their imagined 'Tamil homelands' in the north and east. Indeed in both cases sovereignty is understood as the ultimate aspiration of a nation, its fundamental completion. The Maoists in Nepal, according to their leader

Prachanda, want to replace the current constitutional monarchy with an internationally recognized 'People's Republic',[48] while the Islamists in Pakistan aim at destabilizing the military regime that has lent its support to the USA as a 'frontline state against terrorism' in order to create a 'genuine' Islamic state. Thus the state remains as the referent in all instances and the aim is anti-regime rather than an anti-system, anti-state or anti-global world order. Their aspiration remains in consonance with the age-old quest for sovereignty over a demarcated territory, an aspiration that resonates more with the twentieth century wars that were waged by minority groups, oppressed majorities or revolutionaries than with the twenty-first century dissolution of national references. These wars are, however, marred by a number of complicating factors that belie the neat pattern and clear-cut aims of the leaders of the movements. In Nepal, for instance, the Kham Magars' country has become the stronghold of the People's War. Interestingly, the Kham Magar are a Tibeto–Burman population of west Nepal whose support for the Maoists is couched in ethnic terms. Their battle against the Nepali state is for ethnic autonomy of their own region. Clearly the needs of the Maoists and those of the villagers coincide even though their projects are not the same.[49]

Mao said that the revolutionary had to be like a fish in the water. While there are many cases where armed groups in South Asia have grown with contributions from the diaspora, in other cases armed groups have survived the last decades of confrontation with the state without drawing from transnational networks. The case of the insurgency in the north-east of India belies the assumption that globalization was the sine qua non of success. In the north-east of India rebels appear to have raised taxes in a systematic fashion from the common people, and extorted ransoms from business groups and government organizations. In Tripura, the spate of kidnappings to secure ransoms gained momentum in the mid-1990s. Rebel group even have formal tax legislations as it were, replicas of state Legislation aimed at streamlining fund-raising activities. This is the case of rebel groups such as the United Liberation Front of Asom (ULFA), the Bodo Security Force (BdSF), the Peoples Liberation Army of Manipur, and the National Socialist Council of Nagaland (NSCN), which have raised large sums of money.[50] Weapons were first obtained from Pakistan and China where the rebels went for training in the 1960s and 1970s. In more recent years rebel groups of north-east India have turned to the black markets of South-East Asia for arms purchase. Thailand is the main arms purchase centre where Chinese made weapons from the Khmer Rouge era are sold at very small costs. Smuggling is thriving, especially in the field of narcotics. Manipur, Mizoram, Nagaland, Assam, and Tripura are figuring on the route that takes heroin from the Golden Triangle to other parts of the world. This trade must, however, be read not so much as a reflection of the spread of 'globalization' but more as an exacerbation of relations that predated the boundaries of the nation-state.

Analyses that relate armed violence to 'globalization' rarely highlight the examples that contradict the trend. South Asia offers many such examples. The People's War in Nepal casts doubts on any links between revolution (or terror as defined by the Nepali state) and the globalized world.[51] The Maoist rebels in Nepal constitute, in many ways, a 'significant anachronism in the post-Cold War world'.[52] Their emergence in 1996 is closely related to the People's Movement led by the Movement for the Restoration of Democracy (MRD), which brought together liberal parties and communists, both of which were banned under the Panchayat regime. This led to the promulgation of a new constitution in 1990 which established parliamentary democracy and the growth of mass politics. In a sense, the revolution was prepared by the gradual development of political awareness in the country. The Communist Party of Nepal (Mashal) grew out of a radical faction of the Communist Party of Nepal founded in 1949, which found inspiration in the Indian Naxalite movement of the 1960s. In the late 1970s and 1980s, the CPN (Mashal) was one of the many world revolutionary international movements against imperialism and revisionism. In 1984, at a conference of Maoists parties in London, nineteen revolutionary movements including the Peruvian Shining Path signed a declaration that saw the birth of the Revolutionary International Movement or RIM. This was the other side of globalization, the un-liberal, people-oriented, anti-capitalist network braving the overarching paradigm. One of the young leaders of the CPN (Mashal), Baburam Bhattarai, organized an alliance of extreme leftist groups under the name of the United People's Front

(Samyukta Jan Morcha) or SJM, to keep pressurizing the movement for the Restoration of Democracy to extract more concessions from the king.[53]

On 13 February 1996, when the government failed to respond to the list of forty demands submitted by the SJM, the People's War began with simultaneous raids against police stations in Haleri and Athbiskot. The Kham Magar country became the Maoist stronghold partly because of the woods and forests and the primitive state of the communication network that keeps the hills in isolation. The Maoists in Nepal make full use of the terrain, a large and complex mountain scape designed for guerrilla action, and thrive on the lack of communication in this age of connectivity. The insurgents move freely in the villages where through coercion and persuasion they obtain protection from the villagers. Their methods of fighting remained archaic for a long time, a few guns and homemade grenades. But this has changed. On 20-21 March 2004, when the insurgents ransacked Beni Bazaar headquarters of the Myagdi district they were reported to have made use of a range of modern weapons including 81 mm mortars, rocket launchers, M16 and AK 47 rifles, machine guns and hand grenades. These arms were mainly looted from the army in earlier operations and allegedly from the Indian weapons black markets in Uttar Pradesh.[54] Could this indicate that so-called forces of 'globalization' are touching the Nepali insurgents and transforming them into a new type of formation? One could also argue to the contrary. Indeed the loot of the enemies' weapons was a common practice in the guerrilla warfare of the 1960s or even of revolutionary movements in Europe that sprang up throughout the nineteenth century to oust the ancient regimes.

The People's Army is organized in such a way that the fighters in any one district always come from outside it. They are mostly young peasants (all castes mixed up) some of whom have suffered setbacks when attempting to migrate to the town or abroad. Their leaders are believed to have received special training, sometimes in India. In order to rise up in the hierarchy of the revolutionary army and to achieve the status of *chhapamar*, it is necessary to kill a 'class enemy'.[55] Maoists benefit from a meager level of foreign support and from some cooperation with Maoists in neighbouring India. They function as a total anomaly in the post-Cold War era, where the ascendancy of global capitalism has led to a general downfall of revolutionary spirits. In this case the Maoists commenced their action after the fall of communism in Europe and they fight their war in a manner completely disconnected to the world around them. Nowhere has the local and the global seemed more separate.

The LTTE has been able to combine guerrilla war tactics, conventional warfare and suicide bombing as their methods of combat from the early years. Although there has been a clear evolution of the LTTE from an insurgent movement to something of a completely different scale, this has not meant a move from purely guerrilla-type fighting to terror attacks which would legitimate the appellation of 'terrorist group' by the state and the US State Department. Indeed from the very outset the LTTE practised both methods of combat. Only later, after it had built a secure financial base, did it include the more conventional fighting methods of a fully fledged army. Only recently did the Sri Lanka state come to understand the transformation of a diaspora-supported insurgent group into an organization with transnational networks, investments, lawyers, ships, and armies, and has begun to lobby Western powers to help destroy LTTE interests in their own countries.[56]

Guerrilla war was the main method of combat used by the LTTE, although the organization started with violent acts against figures of authority. The SLFP organizer in Jaffna, one-time MP for Jaffna and former mayor Alfred Durayappah, was assassinated by a group of Tamil youths led by Velupillai Prabhakaran in 1975. From then on insurrectionary acts escalated. Parliamentarism and civilian politicians were abandoned by the disenchanted youth of Jaffna. They rebelled against traditional norms of Tamil society and became known as 'the boys', a term that was first used in a patronizing fashion by Tamil parliamentarians. In the following thirty years the Tamil insurrection underwent many changes, not least in the number of militant youth groups—approximately thirty—that emerged. Some of these had very fleeting existences while others survive till today.

The origins of militancy among Tamil youth is generally traced to the founding in 1970 of the Tamil Students' Federation (TSF) to which a young public servant, Sivakumaran, who killed himself by swallowing a cyanide capsule to avoid capture by the police, belonged. The TSF adopted the name Tamil New Tigers in 1972 and finally in 1975 became the Liberation Tigers of Tamil Eelam. The LTTE declared itself the heir to Chelvanayakam, the leader of the Federal Party, referred to as 'Thantai Selva'—Father Selva—who by 1976 had abandoned federalism and was arguing for the creation of an independent Tamil Eelam. Unlike Chelvanayakam, the LTTE did not hesitate to resort to murder in the pursuit of its goal, a practice begun by it with the murder of the mayor of Jaffna in 1975. The Tiger name was taken from the Chola kings whose emblem it was. Under the Cholas, the kingdom of Jaffna flourished and this ancient glory furnished the LTTE with a powerful nationalist ideology. There was little Marxism in the LTTE ideology even when reference was made to a society where caste and other traditional hierarchies would be eradicated.[57] Its leader, Velupillai Prabhakaran, born in the coastal town of Valvettiturai a well-known smuggling centre, of Karayar caste, listed in a 1986 interview as his role models men such as Subhas Chandra Bose, Tiruppur Kumaran, a Tamil revolutionary, *Mahabharata* heroes such as Karna and Bhima, and Napoleon.

There were lulls and periods of intense militancy: the years 1981-3, for instance, saw a gradual escalation of the Tamil insurrection. Tamil policemen, informants, and supporters of the government were targeted. The establishment of District Development Councils (DDC), which incorporated the principle of autonomy without any financial or administrative teeth, was rejected by Tamil secessionist groups. The army was again deployed to Jaffna where the insurrection was turning into a small-scale war. The Tamil insurrection entered a heightened phase in 1983. The outbreak of violence against Tamils in July 1983 was an immediate reaction to an ambush by the LTTE in which thirteen Sinhalese soldiers died. Riots broke out on the night following the killings. During ten days of widespread violence, the lives and property of innocent Tamil civilians were destroyed in a systematic way. Government sources estimated the number of deaths as between 300 and 400 while unofficial sources give figures of 3,000 deaths. Refugees numbered up to 200,000. When the need of the hour was to appease the Tamil people the Parliament enacted the Sixth Amendment to the Constitution—that asked all parliamentarians to disavow separatism—after a single day's debate.

Sixteen TULF Members of Parliament vacated their seats.

It was 1983 that made 'terrorists'. For the insurrectionist groups it was a bonanza in that their ranks suddenly multiplied. New organizations emerged but their members were soon absorbed into the five main guerrilla groups. Media coverage of the riots created a wave of sympathy towards the cause of Tamil self-determination among Tamil expatriates as well as foreign governments. The riot of 1983 had a homogenizing influence. With social dislocation the normal boundaries governing interaction between the rich and the poor changed.[58] Being Tamil acquired a virtually emblematic significance.

After 1983, the attacks on policemen, police stations, and armed forces personnel in the north and east reached renewed heights. Resources were coming in for the insurrection from expatriates and new recruits were being trained in south India. While the Jaffna peninsula was effectively under guerrilla control except for the military camps sprinkled here and there, the eastern province, which had more population diversity, was still under government control. Tamil insurgents operated from bases in the jungle.[59] During the years following the 1983 riots, insurgent groups gained control over civil society in Jaffna through propaganda and collection of 'taxes' or extortion. The message was put across to the people through journals such as *Viravankai* (Brave Tiger), magazines such as *Tamil Ilam*, pamphlets, books, songs, poems, plays and even video tapes on the progress of the struggle. The insurgents took over the responsibility of imparting justice, punishing criminal elements and 'anti-social elements'. 'Lamp post killings', in which bodies of criminals were tied to lamp posts, were a common feature.[60]

Thus naming the LTTE a terrorist organization is tantamount to denying its history as an insurgent group that fought its rivals and the Sri Lanka state through guerrilla warfare, suicide killings, assassinations, and conventional warfare. The greatest strength of Prabhakaran is that he created his organization as a guerrilla force. In the late 1980s, the LTTE had defeated the Indian army sent to Sri Lanka as a peace-keeping force—one of the largest armies in the world—by using hit-and-run ambushes, booby traps and minefields. It was in fact in 1990 that for the first time the LTTE was involved in a conventional battle with the Sri Lankan army at Elephant Pass, the garrison located at the base of the Jaffna Peninsula. As it did not have tanks, it was reported to have converted bulldozers and tractors into armoured vehicles and dug trenches up to the camp. More than 3,000 Tigers were involved in the fighting. After they had pounded the base relentlessly for three weeks and fired at the helicopters with their anti-aircraft guns, mortars, and home-made rocket systems, they were eventually defeated when 8,000 Sri Lanka army troops were sent to rescue the camp.

The LTTE's withdrawal into the Vanni jungles was a carefully planned move. It took along looted valuables, its materials, and a good fraction of the civilian population. In July it attacked the isolated Mullaitivu camp on the east coast, once again a completely conventional attack. Most of the officers and soldiers numbering around 1,200 were killed.[61]

In April 2000, the LTTE launched a massive attack on Elephant Pass and the withdrawal from the Pass was ordered by the army commander in late April. A week later, Palai was attacked and the army was forced to pull back to a new defence line. The government badly lacked the ships and aircraft to pull the 34,000 or so troops from Jaffna and President Chandrika Kumaratunga appealed to India, Pakistan, and other countries for help. Relations with Israel were quickly restored.[62] By mid-May 2000, civilian sources from Jaffna reported that the army morale had improved and they were fighting back.[63] Jaffna did not fall.

The term 'terrorist' is cast upon the LTTE on account of its use of suicide bombings as a method of warfare where civilian casualties have taken their toll. It must be remembered, however, that such attacks were always only one element of the LTTE war strategy. This is often forgotten because the LTTE is unequivocally the most effective and brutal organization ever to utilize suicide attacks. Between July 1987 and February 2000, it had carried out 168 suicide terror attacks in Sri Lanka and India leaving thousands of innocent bystanders dead or wounded. In the 1990s, suicide killings of politicians perceived as enemies of Eelam multiplied. Among them were the former Indian Prime Minister Rajiv Gandhi, in Tamil Nadu in May 1991, the then Sri Lankan Foreign Minister and Deputy Minister of Defence Ranjan Wijeratne; Admiral Clancy Fernando who headed the Sri Lanka navy; and in 1993, President Premadasa in Colombo. The LTTE was also the prime suspect in the assassination of Minister Lalith Athulathmudali.

The LTTE with its considerable resources showed no signs of weakness in the late 1990s and continued using suicide bombers in the south. A van with explosives detonated in October 1997 in the business centre of Colombo leading to a considerable decline in foreign investment. The celebration of the fifty years of independence of Sri Lanka was hampered by an attack against the Temple of the Tooth in Kandy, symbol of power and a Buddhist sacred centre. In 1999, the LTTE was interdicted following a suicide bombing attempt during the campaign for presidential elections, which caused the deaths of 38 persons and wounded 129 including the President herself.

More than any other armed group, except perhaps Hamas, the LTTE has struck at targets in a way that civilian casualties have been high. Death is incidental for the suicide bomber and for his or her victims. This factor has led some scholars to see the LTTE as an anti-modern formation although there is much to point towards LTTE members breaking with the past rather than reinforcing it. The ideology of the LTTE contains a glorification of death and members who die for the cause, both men and women, are valorized. Its women do not symbolize the role of mother, nurturer and caregiver but that of the purveyor of death. Neloufer de Mel quotes from the war poetry of the LTTE, especially that of Captain Vanathi, a member of the LTTE's women's wing who died in the battle of Elephant Pass at the age of twenty-seven.[64] These extracts from the poem entitled 'She, The Woman of Tamililam' reflect the break with tradition that comes with joining a militant group combined with the cult of martyrdom:

> Her forehead shall be adorned not with
> *kunkumam* (but) with red blood.
> All that is seen in her eyes is not the sweetness
> of youth (but) firm declarations of those
> who have fallen down.
> On her neck will lay no *tali* (but) a
> Cyanide flask!

From men, too, Prabhakaran demands total loyalty. Traitors have been, on occasion, condemned without mercy: the headmaster of St John's College who organized a cricket match between his pupils and the armed forces was shot dead.[65] Loyalty is nurtured through propaganda of various sorts from the repeated screening of the blockbuster film *Omar Mukthar: the Lion of the Desert* to instil nationalist feelings among the youth, to the recounting of tales of the violence and discrimination perpetrated by the government in the south against the Tamil people.[66] Insubordination is not tolerated. The ultimate sacrifice to Prabhakaran's will is martyrdom. All fighters carry a cyanide capsule in case of capture. The landscape of the Jaffna Peninsula in the years of LTTE control was marked with memorials to martyrs: lanes, pictures, even children's playgrounds were reminders. Violence had created a community of common substance based upon an idiom of sacrifice. Traitors were erased from the landscape of Jaffna. Attempts to discover historically enduring mindsets, static characteristics, ancient dispositions (for example, towards militarism and suicide) common to the quintessential Tamil both in India and Sri Lanka are questionable.[67] Discerning enduring martial traditions or some inherent penchant for self-immolation and suicide going back centuries among Tamils leads to a denial of any sense of politics as an open-ended process. This picture must contend with that of the LTTE as a quintessentially modern formation that evolves in a disenchanted secular frame where age-old traditions of Hindu society are razed to the ground and replaced by new ethics and values.

In the Nepali Maoist movement too there is a cult of 'martyrs', a term which refers both to the communist victims of repression under the Panchayat regime and to the present-day Maoists killed by the police. Although the Maoists rarely figure in any listings on 'new terror groups', they seem to have at least one of the features that the LTTE lacks which is a reliance on age-old traditions to legitimate violent acts of sacrifice. According to Ramirez, this cult can be traced back to traditional conceptions in which 'the martyr who dies a violent death can only escape from eternal wandering by recognition of his status, which is the equivalent of reintegrating him into society'.[68] Gardens, wayside stopping places with stone platforms are built in their honour as traditionally resting platforms and paths were once built to honour the dead who then become ancestors.

In these two cases, locked in 'combat mode' within a present of permanent or sporadic violence, will the combatants ever consent to disarm and return to a life without arms? Can they build a new society based on justice and equal rights on the ruins of the old one without the memories of decades of ruthless violence corroding its very foundation? Analyses that link two questionable concepts—'terrorism' and 'globalization'—cannot help us answer these fundamental questions. What is clear is that armed movements such as the LTTE have adapted to the changes of their time, the movement of people to faraway lands, the increasing facilities to reach out to them and their remittances, the rapidity of capital flows. But other structures remained untouched, the vertical line of command, the army fatigues, the jungle ambushes against security forces, and overall, the powerful dream of creating a state.

IV

CONCLUSION

If the scholar has a role to play in the forging of a better world for all, she or he must begin by critically examining the way issues are framed in the public discourse, why certain issues are prioritized while others are ignored, which concepts are more obstacles to our understanding than tools of knowledge. This paper has tried to show that the two concepts of 'terrorism' and 'globalization', taken together or separately slide over the most interesting and problematic issues of our time, for the following reasons. Through the artifice of naming/denouncing certain groups as 'terrorist', state and international discourses cast an essentializing and ahistorical gaze on movements that have other characteristics than committing hideous but on the whole occasional attacks on civilians for political purposes. Many scholars—generalists and terrorism experts who have suddenly blossomed with ready-made knowledge and solutions—have completely internalized these procedures without questioning their consequences. Once a group has been cast as a terrorist group there is no possible understanding except in terms of how to find the antidote for a venom. By acquiring the terminology of the US State Department, scholars have tended to indulge in faulty generalizations: South Asian armed groups are uneasily fitted in a mould designed for Islamist movements. The old and the new cohabit in the armed movements of South Asia. A fundamental difference is visible between the Islamist movements that look well beyond the region for inspiration and have ties with transnational movements with a global agenda, and movements in South Asia that are still seduced by the sovereign state form or born out of a desire for regime change. Some scholars have spoken of network forms of organization to describe the pattern according to which the members of these Islamist 'global terror' groups coalesce. The hub or star network is the most common in these groups where a set of actors are tied to a central node or actor and must go through that node to communicate and coordinate with each other. Networks, it is often assumed, are the result of the computerized information revolution. But in most South Asian contexts, older technologies together with cellular telephones, fax machines, electronic mail, web sites, and computer conferencing are used to reach constituents and continue to be used in armed struggles. An organization such as the LTTE combines a network formed in its relation with the world with a hierarchical structure in Sri Lanka where the leader Velupillai Prabhakaran plays a crucial role and dispenses orders to individual members. The Maoists in Nepal on the other hand appear to be quite clearly a hierarchical organization more than a network. Thus South Asian movements present many different faces, a reflection that 'globalization' has not spread to every corner of the globe, has not superseded modernity's creations—state, sovereignty, self-determination—but has invaded and shaped the core of movements such as Islamist movements that were already intrinsically global—or the modus operandi of armed movements such as the LTTE permitting it to sustain its war against the state for nearly thirty years. The landscape of South Asian armed movements is full of contrasts and defies generalizations. Scholars must be mindful to use concepts that are less sweeping and more precise to emphasize the nature of spatial linkages and their limits. This chapter can be read as an attempt to write about large-scale, long-term processes without overlooking specificity and contestation. Unthinking the terrorism-globalization nexus means most importantly accepting the significance of language in framing practice and history.

NOTES

1. Rohan Gunaratne, 'Transnational Terrorism Support Networks and Trends', www.satp.org/satporgtp/publication/faultline/Fault7-Gunaratnaf.htm; Mary Kaldor, 'Terrorism as Regressive Globalisation', www.opendemocracy.net/debates/articles-3-77-1501.jsp, 25/9/2003.
2. Gyanendra Pandey, *Remembering partition: Violence, Nationalism and History in India* (New York: Cambridge University Press, 2001).
3. Giovanna Borradori, *Philosophy in a Time of Terror: Dialogues with Jürgen Habermas and Jacques Derrida* (Chicago: University of Chicago Press, 2003), p. 105.
4. Ibid., p. 103.
5. Ibid., p. 56.
6. Cited in Michel Wievorka (ed.), *Un Nouveau Paradigme de la Violence* (Paris: l'Harmattan, 1998).
7. Walter Lacqueur, *The New Terrorism: Fanaticism and the Arms of Mass Destruction* (New York: Oxford University Press, 1999), p. 4.
8. On the Tamil insurrection see, for instance the works of S.J. Tambiah, *Leveling Crowds: Collective Violence and Ethnonationalist Conflict in South Asia* (New Delhi: Vistaar Publications, 1997); A.J. Wilson, *Sri Lankan Tamil Nationalism: Its Origins and Development in the Nineteenth Century* (London: C. Hurst, 2000); R. Cheran, *The Sixth Genre: Memory, History and the Tamil Diaspora Imagination* (Colombo: Marga Institute 2001); Dagmar Hellman-Rajanayagam, *The Tamil Tigers' Armed Struggle for Identity* (Stuttgart: Franz Steiner, 1994).
9. Documents in South Asia Terrorism Portal: http://www.satp.org
10. Ibid.
11. Ibid.
12. http://www.un.org, UN Treaty collection.
13. South Asia Terrorism Portal.
14. Borradori, *Philosophy in a Time of Terror*, p. 104.
15. Samuel M. Makinda, 'Global Terrorism versus Norms and Institutions in Africa and Asia', *Identity, Culture and Politics*, vol. 3, no. 1, July 2002 (pp. 37-58), p. 45.
16. http://www.amnesty.org/ailib/aireport/index.html
17. Ibid.
18. Ibid.
19. Ibid.
20. Jurgen Habermas, *The Structural Transformation of the Public Sphere*, (Cambridge: MIT Press, 1989).
21. Fred Cooper, 'What is the Concept of Globalization Good For? An African Historian's Perspective', *African Affairs*, vol. 100, 2001 (pp. 189-213) p. 189.

22. See as an example of the denunciatory mode of globalization literature, Richard Falk, *Predatory Globalization: A Critique* (Cambridge: Polity Press, 1999), and for a recent whitewash of globalization, Jagdish Bhagwati, *In Defence of Globalization* (New Delhi: Oxford University Press, 2004).
23. Borradori, *Philosophy in a Time of Terror*, p. 19.
24. Ibid., p. 121
25. Ibid., p. 123.
26. Ibid., p. 64.
27. Mary Kaldor, *New and Old Wars: Organized Violence in a Global Era* (Stanford: Stanford University Press, 2001).
28. Marc Duffield and Chris Hables Gray, *Post-Modern War: the New Politics of Conflicts* (London and NY: Routledge 1997).
29. Kaldor, 'Terrorism as Regressing Globalisation'.
30. LTC Antulio J. Echevarria II, *Globalization and the Nature of War, Strategic Studies Institute* (Carlisle PA: US Army War College, 2003), p. 3.
31. Rohan Gunaratne, *Inside al Qaeda: Global Network of Terror* (Columbia University Press, 2002), p. 206.
32. South Asia Terrorism Portal, South Asia Intelligence Review 2.31.
33. Gunaratne, *Inside Al Qaeda*, op. cit., p. 218.
34. John Prados, *America Confronts Terrorism: Understanding the Danger and How to think about it* (Chicago: Ivan R, Dee Inc., 2002), pp. 118-119.
35. *Daily Times*, 19 February 2003.
36. Darini Rajasingham Senanayake, work in progress.
37. Gunaratne, 'Transnational Terrorism Support Networks'.
38. Michael Ondaatje, *Anil's Ghost* (New York: Alfred A. Knopf, 2000), p. 43.
39. Christopher McDowell, *A Tamil Asylum Diaspora. Sri Lankan Migration, Settlement and Politics in Switzerland* (Oxford: Berghahn Books Providence, 1996), pp. 5-6
40. Harinda Vidanage, work in progress on Tamil diaspora.
41. McDowell, *A Tamil Asylum Diaspora.*, p. 229.
42. R. Cheran, *The Sixth Genre*, p. 17.
43. Gunaratne, 'Impact of the Mobilised Tamil Diaspora on the protracted conflict in Sri Lanka', in Kumar Rupesinghe, *Negotiating Peace in Sri Lanka: Efforts, Failures and Lessons* (International Alert of London, 1998), pp. 301-28.
44. Cited in Gunaratne, ibid., p. 301.
45. Dorothy Denning, 'Activism, Hacktivism and Cyberterrorism', in *Networks and Netwars: The Future of Terror, Crime and Militancy*, ed. Arquila and David Rofeldt (California: Rand, 2001), p. 252.
46. Ibid., p. 269.
47. See Sumantra Bose, *Kashmir: Roots of Conflict, Paths to Peace* (Boston: Harvard University Press), 2003.

48. 'Inside the Revolution in Nepal. An Interview with Comrade Prachanda', in Arjun Karki and David Seldon (eds.), *The People's War in Nepal: Left Perspectives* (New Delhi, Adroit Publishers, 2003), pp. 75-116.
49. Anne de Sales, 'The Kham Magar Country, Nepal: Between Ethnic Claims and Maoism', *European Bulletin of Himalayan Research*, vol. 19, Autumn 2000, p. 65.
50. Subhir Bhaumik, 'North-East India: The Evolution of a Post-Colonial Region', in Partha Chatterjee, *Wages of Freedom: Fifty Years of the Indian Nation State* (New Delhi: Oxford University Press, 1998), p. 323.
51. For an exhaustive bibliography on the Maoists see Ramesh Parajuli, *Maoist Movement of Nepal: A Selected Bibliography* (Kathmandu, 2004); for different perspectives on the rise and nature of the People's War see, Karki, *The People's War in Nepal*; Deepak Thapa, *Understanding the Maoist Movement of Nepal* (Kathmandu: Martin Chautari Centre for Social Research and Development, 2003).
52. Peter Santina, 'The People's War'. *Harvard International Review*, Cambridge, Spring 2001, vol. 23, no. 1, p. 1.
53. de Sales, 'The Kham Magar Country', p. 54.
54. P.G. Rayamohan, Asia Intelligence Review (South Asia Intelligence Portal) Weekly Assessment and Briefings, vol. 2, no. 37, 29 March 2004.
55. de Sales, 'The Kham Magar Country', p. 63.
56. Gunaratne, 'Internationalization of the Tamil Conflict and its implications', in Siri Gamage and I.B Watson (eds.), *Conflict and Community in Contemporary Sri Lanka: Pearl of the East or the Island of Tears?*, pp. 109-37.
57. Dagmar Hellman-Rajanayagam, 'The Groups' and the Rise of Militant Secessionism', in C. Manogaran and B. Pfaffenberger (eds.), *The Sri Lankan Tamils: Ethnicity and Identity* (Boulder: Westview Press, 1994), pp. 170-3.
58. Pradeep Jeganathan, 'All the Lord's Men? Ethnicity and Inequality in the Space of a Riot', in Michael Roberts (ed.), *Collective Identities Revisited* vol. 2 (Colombo: Marga Research Institute, 1998), pp. 221-45.
59. Jagath Senaratne, *Political Violence in Sri Lanka 1977-1990: Riots, Insurrections, Counterinsurgencies, Foreign Intervention* (Amsterdam: VU University Press, 1997), pp. 68-74.
60. Ibid., pp. 74-87.
61. Rajan Hoole, *The Arrogance of Power: Myths, Decadence and Murder* (UTHR, 2001), p. 391.
62. Ibid., pp. 392-3.
63. Ibid., p. 399.
64. Neloufer de Mel, 'Agent or Victim? The Sri Lankan Woman Militant in the Interregnum', in Michael Roberts (ed.), *Collective Identities Revisited*, vol. 2, pp. 199-200.
65. Hellman-Rajanayagam, 'Rise of Militant Secessionism', p. 67.

66. S.I. Keethaponcalam, 'Underage Soldiers and Intervention: The Global Challenge of Violence Reduction and Conflict Resolution', Nova Southeastern University, Ph.D. thesis, 2001, p. 35.
67. This type of interpretation is present in recent essays by D.P. Sivaram, 'Tamil Militarism: The Code of Suicide', *Lanka Guardian*, May-Aug. 1992, and Michael Roberts, 'Filial devotion in Tamil Culture and the Tiger Cult of Martyrdom', *Contributions to Indian Sociology*, vol. 30, 1996, pp. 245-72.
68. Philippe Ramirez, cited in de Sales, 'The Kham Magar Country', p. 65.

Contributors

NIRA WICKRAMSINGHE is Professor of History and International Relations, University of Colombo, Sri Lanka. She studied in Paris and at Oxford, where she obtained a D.Phil. in History. She was recently Fulbright-Hays Senior Scholar at New York University. Her recent publications include *Dressing the Colonised Body* (2003), *Civil Society in Sri Lanka: New Circles of Power* (2001), and *Sri Lanka: A Modern History* (forthcoming). She is presently working on rebellions in Sri Lanka under the East India Company rule in the late eighteenth century.

RANABIR SAMADDAR is the Director of the Calcutta Research Group, and has pioneered along with others peace studies' programmes in South Asia. He has worked extensively on issues of justice and rights in the context of conflicts in South Asia. The recently published *Politics of Dialogue* (2004) is the culmination of his work on justice, rights, and peace. His particular researches have been on migration and refugee studies, the theory and practices of dialogue, nationalism and post-colonial statehood in South Asia, and technological restructuring and new labour regimes. He has recently completed a three-volume study of Indian nationalism, the third one titled as, *A Biography of the Indian Nation, 1947–1997* (2001). These political writings which include other noted works such as *Paradoxes of the Nationalist Time* (2002), and *The Marginal Nation* (1999) have challenged the prevailing cultural accounts of the birth of nationalism and the nation state, popularized by the western academia in the form of cultural studies, and have brought to the fore a new turn in the inquiry into the current history of post-colonial politics in South Asia.

RUBINA SAIGOL is Country Director, ActionAid, Pakistan. She was trained in psychology and education and has written several books and papers on the issues of education, gender, human rights, the state, nationalism, militarization, and conflict. Saigol also conducted teacher training programme in all provinces of Pakistan on gender and human rights in education. Among her several publications are *Education: Critical Perspectives* (1993); *Symbolic Violence: Curriculum, Pedagogy and Society* (1994); *Knowledge and Identity* (1995); *Aspects of Women and Development* (co-edited) (1995); *Engendering the Nation-State* (co-edited) (1997); *The Human Rights Movement: A Critical Overview* (in Urdu) (1997); *Nationalism, Education and Identity* (in Urdu) (1999); and *Woman and Resistance* (in Urdu) (2000).

JEHAN PERERA is Director, Media and Research at the National Peace Council of Sri Lanka where he is responsible for analysis and policy recommendations relating to the peace process, liaison with the media and other agencies, advocacy, fund-raising, providing conflict resolution training for the media and grass-roots politicians, and developing project proposals. He has conducted several evaluations on the capacity of civil society organizations and the role for civil society in the peace process. He is also an award-winning political columnist for the *Daily Mirror* newspaper and *Lanka Monthly Digest* magazine. He has also contributed to several international publications on the Sri Lankan ethnic conflict and peace process.

DHRUBA KUMAR is Professor of Political Science at the Centre for Nepal and Asian Studies, Tribhuvan Universitry, Kirtipur, Kathmandu, Nepal. He is a member of the BIISS-FORD Foundation Collaborative Study on Human Security in South Asia under which he has recently completed a study, *Nepali State, Society and Human Security: An Infinite Discourse* (2005). The latest among his numerous academic contributions, is 'Proximate Cause of Conflict in Nepal' published in contributions to *Nepalese Studies*, January 2005.

SHAHEDUL ANAM KHAN is a retired officer of the Bangladesh Army having served in it for thirty-two years. He was the Director-General, Bangladesh Institute of International and Strategic Studies, Dhaka, and is currently editor, 'Defence and Strategic Affairs', *The Daily Star*, the leading English daily of Bangladesh. Among his various publications are a co-edited volume, *Chandabaji versus Entrepreneurship: Youth Force in Bangladesh* (1999).

SANJOY HAZARIKA is a journalist, author, documentary film-maker, policy adviser and analyst who works in and on the north-east of India, one of the world's most complex regions. He is currently Managing Trustee of the Centre for North East Studies and Policy Research and Consulting Editor of *The Statesman*. He is also Visiting Research Professor at the Centre for Policy Research in New Delhi. A former reporter for *The New York Times*, Hazarika is an award-winning journalist whose celebrated books include *Bhopal: The Lessons of a Tragedy* (1987) (listed by *The Observer* in 1988 as one of the top ten science books); *Strangers of the Mist: Tales of War and Peace from India's North East* (1995); and *Rites of Passage: Imagined Homelands, Border Crossings, India's East and Bangladesh* (2000). He has been a member of the National Security Advisory Board, a part of the National Commission to Review the Working of the Constitution and currently is a member of the Review Committee on the Armed Forces Special Powers Act (1958).

FARID AHMED BHUIYAN is a retired officer of the Bangladesh Army and is currently a Ph.D. student in the Department of International Relations, University of Dhaka. He has also served as a researcher and analyst in an armed forces organization. Major Farid participated in UN peacekeeping operations in UNIKOM. His forthcoming publication is *Sun Tzu and Modern Strategic Thinking: Technology, Morality and War*.

IMTIAZ AHMED is Professor of International Relations, University of Dhaka and is also the Executive Director of the Centre for Alternatives. He is the editor of *Theoretical Perspectives: A Journal of Social Sciences and Arts* and co-editor of *Identity, Culture and Politics: An Afro-Asian Dialogue* (Colombo and Dakar) and *South Asian Refugee Watch* (Colombo and Dhaka). Aside from numerous articles in national and international journals and several edited volumes, his other publications include *State and Foreign Policy: India's Role in South Asia* (1993); *The Efficacy of the Nation State in South Asia: A Post-nationalist Critique* (1998); *The Construction of Diaspora: South Asians Living in Japan* (2000). His most recent publications are two edited volumes, *Women, Bangladesh and International Security: Methods, Discourses and Policies* (2004), and *State, Society and*

Displacement: Displaced People in South Asia (with Abhijit Dasgupta and Kathinka Sinha-Kerkhoff) (2004). His forthcoming publication is *Beyond Nationalism*, a special issue of *Futures: The Journal of Policy, Planning and Futures Studies*, Elsevier Science, UK, vol. 37, no. 9, November 2005 (as guest editor).

Index